Violent Conjunctures in Democratic India

This is a pioneering study of when and why Hindu nationalists have engaged in discrimination and violence against minorities in contemporary India. Amrita Basu asks why the incidence and severity of violence differ significantly across Indian states, within states, and through time. Contrary to many predictions, the Hindu nationalist Bharatiya Janata Party has neither consistently engaged in anti-minority violence nor become a centrist party but has alternated between moderation and militancy. Hindu nationalist violence has been conjunctural, determined by relations among its own party, social movement organization, and state governments, and by opposition states, parties, and movements. This study accords particular importance to the role of social movements in precipitating anti-minority violence. It calls for a broader understanding of social movements and a greater appreciation of party-movement relations.

Amrita Basu is the author of *Two Faces of Protest: Contrasting Modes of Women's Activism in India*. She is the editor or coeditor of *Appropriating Gender: Women's Activism and Politicized Religion in South Asia*, *Beyond Exceptionalism: Violence and Democracy in India*, *The Challenge of Local Feminisms: Women's Movements in Global Perspective*, *Community Conflicts and the State in India*, *Localizing Knowledge in a Globalizing World*, and *Women's Movements in a Global Era: The Power of Local Feminisms*. She has received research awards from the National Endowment for the Humanities, Social Science Research Council, John D. and Catherine T. MacArthur Foundation, and American Institute of Indian Studies. She is a member of the American Political Science Association Council and vice president of the American Institute of Indian Studies. She serves on the editorial boards of the *American Political Science Review; Critical Asian Studies; International Feminist Journal of Politics; International Political Science Review; Meridians: Feminism, Race, Transnationalism;* and *Politics and Gender,* and she was the South Asia editor for *The Journal of Asian Studies.*

Cambridge Studies in Contentious Politics

Editors

Mark Beissinger   *Princeton University*
Jack A. Goldstone   *George Mason University*
Michael Hanagan   *Vassar College*
Doug McAdam   *Stanford University and Center for Advanced Study in the Behavioral Sciences*
Sarah Soule   *Stanford University*
Suzanne Staggenborg   *University of Pittsburgh*
Sidney Tarrow   *Cornell University*
Charles Tilly (d. 2008)   *Columbia University*
Elisabeth J. Wood   *Yale University*
Deborah Yashar   *Princeton University*

Ronald Aminzade, *Race, Nation, and Citizenship in Post-Colonial Africa: The Case of Tanzania*
Ronald Aminzade et al., *Silence and Voice in the Study of Contentious Politics*
Javier Auyero, *Routine Politics and Violence in Argentina: The Gray Zone of State Power*
W. Lance Bennett and Alexandra Segerberg, *The Logic of Connective Action: Digital Media and the Personalization of Contentious Politics*
Amrita Basu, *Violent Conjunctures in Democratic India*
Clifford Bob, *The Marketing of Rebellion: Insurgents, Media, and International Activism*
Charles Brockett, *Political Movements and Violence in Central America*
Valerie Bunce and Sharon Wolchik, *Defeating Authoritarian Leaders in Postcommunist Countries*
Lars-Erik Cederman, Kristian Skrede Gleditsch, and Halvard Buhaug, *Inequality, Grievances, and Civil War*
Christian Davenport, *How Social Movements Die: Repression and Demobilization of the Republic of New Africa*
Christian Davenport, *Media Bias, Perspective, and State Repression*
Gerald F. Davis, Doug McAdam, W. Richard Scott, and Mayer N. Zald, *Social Movements and Organization Theory*
Donatella della Porta, *Clandestine Political Violence*
Mario Diani, *The Cement of Civil Society: Studying Networks in Localities*
Todd A. Eisenstadt, *Politics, Identity, and Mexico's Indigenous Rights Movements*
Daniel Q. Gillion, *The Political Power of Protest: Minority Activism and Shifts in Public Policy*

(continued after index)

Violent Conjunctures in Democratic India

AMRITA BASU
Amherst College

CAMBRIDGE
UNIVERSITY PRESS

CAMBRIDGE
UNIVERSITY PRESS

32 Avenue of the Americas, New York, NY 10013-2473, USA

Cambridge University Press is part of the University of Cambridge.

It furthers the University's mission by disseminating knowledge in the pursuit of education, learning, and research at the highest international levels of excellence.

www.cambridge.org
Information on this title: www.cambridge.org/9781107461321

© Amrita Basu 2015

First published 2015

Printed in Great Britain by Clays Ltd, St Ives plc

A catalog record for this publication is available from the British Library.

Library of Congress Cataloging in Publication Data
Basu, Amrita, 1953–
Violent Conjunctures in democratic India / Amrita Basu.
    pages cm. – (Cambridge studies in contentious politics)
Includes bibliographical references and index.
ISBN 978-1-107-08963-1 (hardback) – ISBN 978-1-107-46132-1 (paperback)
    1. India – Politics and government – 1977– 2. India – Social conditions – 1947– 3. Political violence – India. 4. Minorities – Violence against – India. 5. Bharatiya Janata Party.
6. Hindus – India – Politics and government. 7. Democracy – Social aspects – India.
8. Nationalism – Social aspects – India. 9. Social movements – Political aspects – India.
10. Social conflict – India. I. Title.
DS480.853.B378 2015
303.6'20954–dc23   2014044903

ISBN 978-1-107-08963-1 Hardback
ISBN 978-1-107-46132-1 Paperback

For Mark

Contents

Figures and Tables

Figures

Tables

Acknowledgments

I have received generous support from many institutions and individuals during the many years I've spent researching and writing this book, including senior fellowships from the American Institute of Indian Studies and the Social Science Research Council, and a Research and Writing Award from the John D. & Catherine T. MacArthur Foundation. I also received a grant from the Amherst College Faculty Research Award Program, funded by the H. Axel Schupf '57 Fund for Intellectual Life.

I presented my work in the United States at Harvard, Tufts, the University of Pennsylvania, the University of Chicago, Princeton, Yale, Cornell, Columbia, and the University of Wisconsin at Madison; in New Delhi at the Jawaharlal Nehru University and the India International Center; in London at the School of Oriental and African Studies; in Vaduz, Liechtenstein, at a conference on Democratization and Decentralization in India; and in Göttingen, Germany, at the Center for Modern Indian Studies. I am grateful to Ashutosh Varshney, Sugata Bose, Ayesha Jalal, David Ludden, Martha Nussbaum, Lloyd and Susanne Rudolph, Atul Kohli, Steven Wilkinson, Mary Katzenstein, Myra Marx Ferree, Aili Mari Tripp, Pralay Kanungo, Zoya Hasan, Srirupa Roy, and the late Julia Leslie, for these invitations.

I am truly grateful to Amherst College for its generosity, flexibility, and openness; for many wonderful colleagues; and for exceptional students. Among the students who have provided research assistance, special thanks to Khushy Agarwal, Andrew Halterman, Christophe Hebe, Kyra Ellis-Moore, and especially Sairam Nagulapalli. Andy Anderson created the maps, Katherine Duke formatted the manuscript, and Maryanne Alos worked on the index and spent many late nights getting the final manuscript in shape.

At Cambridge University Press, Lewis Bateman, senior editor for political science and history, offered wise and helpful counsel. Shaun T. Vigil, Kanimozhi Ramamurthy, and Ami Naramor shepherded the book to completion.

In India, Ajay Kant, who accompanied me in the early stages of my field-work, was energetic, enthusiastic, and knowledgeable. Nagraj Adve provided able research assistance. I had helpful conversations with Javeed Alam, Yogesh Chandrani, Pralay Kanungo, Ghazala Khan, the late Rajni Kothari, Rita Kothari, Harsh Mander, Ritu Menon, the late Ashok Priyadarshi, Tanika Sarkar, Ghanshyam Shah, the late Mukul Sinha, Nirjari Sinha, and Achyut Yagnik.

Several friends and colleagues made helpful suggestions on selected chapters of the book. They include Javier Corrales, Kanchan Chandra, Joan Cocks, Margaret Hunt, Atul Kohli, Lloyd and Susanne Rudolph, Martha Saxton, Ghanshyam Shah, Kamala Visveshwaran, and Laura Vogel. Lakshmi Iyer, at the Harvard Business School, generously provided updated figures on Hindu-Muslim violence. I presented what I thought was the final version of my manuscript at a workshop in New York. Thanks to excellent suggestions I received from Karen Barkey, Tariq Thachil, Paula Chakravartty, Raka Ray, Sudipto Kaviraj, Mary Katzenstein, and David Ludden, I realized that I wasn't done. This book is far better as a result of their comments.

I would not have completed this book without the advice, involvement, and encouragement of several friends. Karen Barkey has helped me think methodically and historically. Praful Bidwai spent many hours talking with me about Hindu nationalism and made helpful comments on the entire manuscript. Zoya Hasan shared with me her vast understanding of Indian politics and challenged me to think through my argument. Uday Mehta has provided the most trenchant and loving criticism and contributed immeasurably to my intellectual growth. I have learned so much by collaborating with Srirupa Roy in planning a conference, editing a book, and coauthoring a paper on Hindu nationalism. Sayres Rudy introduced me to relevant scholarship and encouraged me to be both more subtle and more audacious. Elisabeth Wood provided detailed comments on the manuscript and brought her capacious knowledge of comparative politics and her analytical rigor to bear on this project. And then there is Mary Katzenstein, who organized the workshop on my manuscript, provided feedback on several drafts, and helped me sharpen my analysis. My mentor since I was an undergraduate, Mary has taught me not only about feminism, social movements, and Indian politics, but also, by the example she sets, about rigor, compassion, and integrity.

My family – Elijah Basu-Kesselman, Kanval Dhillon, Rebecca Dreyfus, Annette Hansen, Jonathan and Judy Kesselman, Sandy Spadavechia, Patwant Singh, and Meher Wilshaw – have helped me balance work and play. My parents, Rasil and Romen Basu, are responsible for this book and for everything else. I have been inspired by their worldliness, political passion, love of books and writing, and aversion to social injustice. My late father published several poetry books during the time I was working on this project and encouraged me to let go of it sooner. I wish he had lived to see this book in print. I cannot adequately thank my sister Rekha for her care, encouragement, and companionship, and for my two extraordinary nephews, Raj and Romen. My sons, Javed and Ishan, have grown up alongside this book into wonderful young men. I have learned more with and through them than I could have imagined. Mark has lived with this book for more years than he had bargained for. He has read endless drafts of the manuscript with as much care and attention to detail as if it was his own. This book is for him, with boundless love and gratitude for his good humor, love of life, and years of morning bed tea.

Glossary of Indian Words and Terms

Adarsh Hindu Ghar	Ideal Hindu house
Adivasi	Aboriginal resident, refers to India's tribal population. Officially known as Scheduled Tribes
Akhand Bharat	"Undivided India," encompasses Pakistan and Bangladesh (pre-Partition India)
Antyodaya	An Indian government scheme that provides subsidized rice and wheat for the poorest families
Apadharma	Literally "heresy," derived from dharma (religious guidance)
Asthi Kalash Yatra	A VHP-organized procession carrying the ashes of kar sevaks
Ayodhya	A city in Uttar Pradesh, believed by Hindu nationalists to have been the birthplace of Ram, one of the avatars of Vishnu; Ayodhya was the home to the Babri Masjid that Hindu nationalists demolished in 1992
Ayurveda	Traditional Indian medicine made from natural herbs
Babri Masjid	Literally "Babur's Mosque." Hindu nationalists believe that Babur, the first Mughal emperor, constructed the mosque over a Hindu temple dedicated to Ram
Bandhs	Literally "closed," refers to general strikes where commercial activity is brought to a halt

Basti	Literally "habitation," refers to a slum or a ghetto
Bharat Bandh	A bandh across India
Bharat Mata	Mother India. Bharat Mata is the personified Indian nation, often portrayed as a Hindu goddess
Bhojan Mantras	Hindu prayers recited before meals. Some BJP governments have attempted to enforce mandatory recitation of these prayers in state-run hospitals
Brahminical Hinduism	Interpretation of Hinduism based on the authority of the Vedas (Sanskrit scriptures) and Brahmin priests
Crore	An Indian unit of measurement that equals 10 million
Dalits	Literally "suppressed" or "crushed." Officially termed Scheduled Castes, formerly called untouchables or outcastes, dalits constitute almost a quarter of the Indian population
Dargah	A Sufi Islamic shrine frequented by both Muslims and Hindus
Devas/Devis	Devas are Hindu deities. Devis are the female equivalents
Dhancha	Structure
Dharamsala	Literally "religious sanctuary" or guesthouse for the poor
Dharma	A set of religious principles. In Hinduism, dharma refers to duties, laws, virtues, and the right course of action
Dharma Sansad	A religious parliament or conclave, organized by the VHP
Dharmacharya	Someone who is committed to upholding dharma, often a religious leader
Dharna	A nonviolent civil disobedience protest involving sit-ins
Gata	A subdivision of an RSS shakha or branch, which consists of about 100 members, further divided into groups based on age and interest

Ghar Vapsi	Return home. Ceremonies conducted by the VHP to "reconvert" Christians, Buddhists, and Muslims into Hindus
Gherao	A civil disobedience tactic where protesters encircle the offices of targeted groups
Goonda	Hired thug
Harijans	"Children of God." A term coined by Mahatma Gandhi to refer to dalits
Hartal	Mass protest involving the complete shutdown of offices, shops, and courts
Hindutva	A term Hindu Mahasabha leader Vinayak Damodar Savarkar coined for Hindu nationalism
Imam	Muslim religious leader
Jagirdari	A feudal land tenancy system. The Indian government eliminated this system through land reforms
Jagti Puch	An open court to consult with local deities
Jai Shri Ram/Jai Sita Ram	"Victory to Lord Ram/Victory to Sita Ram"
Jail Bharao	A civil disobedience tactic where people fill the jails to break what they consider unjust laws
Jan Jagran	A mass contact campaign
Kabristan	Graveyard
Kar Sevaks	Religious volunteers. The term was initially used by Sikhs but adopted by Hindu nationalists
Khalistan	A separatist movement organized by a group of Sikhs who demanded a separate homeland called "Khalistan." The suffix "stan" means region/place
Khap Panchayats	Unelected village councils created by members of the same gotra or clan, dominated by upper-caste leaders
Kulp	A scheme for the moral development of children Hindu nationalists devised that mandated the celebration of Hindu holidays in state-run schools
Lakh	An Indian unit of measurement that equals 100,000

Lathi	A stick or a cane used by the Indian police
Lokayukta	An independent ombudsman organization that monitors government corruption
Madrasa	Muslim religious school
Mahant	A Hindu religious official, often the chief priest of a large temple
Mahila Morcha	The women's organization of the BJP
Mandal-Mandir	Phrase used to describe Hindu nationalists' strategy for gaining support for building a *mandir* (Hindu temple) in Ayodhya by mobilizing opposition to reservations for OBCs
Matri Shakti	Literally "Power of Motherhood," a VHP-affiliated organization that provides aid to women in hospitals, slums, and schools
Mohalla	An area of a town or village
Moharam	The first month of the Islamic calendar; the Moharam festival is celebrated during this time
Naitik Shiksha	"Moral Education," organized by the RSS to propagate Hindu values in government schools
Namaz	Muslim prayer
Nari Siksha	*Women's Education*, an RSS publication that opposes Western feminism for destroying "Hindu values"
Om	Mantra and mystical Sanskrit sound of Hindu origin
Other Backward Classes (OBCs)	Socially and economically disadvantaged castes whose status is higher than dalits and tribals but lower than upper-caste Hindus
Paan stalls	Small roadside kiosks that sell *paan* (betel leaf), cigarettes, and snacks
Panchayats	A branch of local government that is officially recognized by the Indian government
Panchjanya	A weekly RSS newspaper

Pracharak	RSS volunteer
Rajniti	Politics. JP Narayan interpreted Rajniti as rule by the state (as opposed to Lokniti, direct rule by the people)
Rakhi	A bracelet that sisters tie to their brothers' wrists during the Hindu holiday of Raksha Bandhan
Ram Bhajans	Community prayers that sing the praises of Lord Ram
Ram Bhakt Sammelan	"Meeting of Hindu Devotees," organized by the VHP to generate support for the BJP
Ram bhakts	Ram devotees
Ram Janmasthan	Birthplace of Lord Ram
Ram Jyoti	A torch relay lighting ceremony organized by Hindu activists to generate support for the Ayodhya movement
Ram Mandir	Temple dedicated to Ram
Ram Rajya	"Rule of Ram." According to Hindu scriptures, this was an ideal period in Indian history
Ram Setu	"Ram's Bridge," a bridge that the Ramayana claims was built by the monkey army of Ram from the southern tip of India to Sri Lanka
Ram Shila Pujas	Ceremonies to sacralize the bricks that would be used to build a Hindu temple in Ayodhya
Rashtra	State
Rasta Rokos	A civil disobedience tactic that entails blocking roads and railways
Rath Yatra	Traditionally a procession of Hindu deities on chariots during Hindu festivals; the BJP has organized such processions to achieve political goals
Ration cards	Documents that guarantee subsidized food and fuel to poor segments of the population
Ravana	The primary antagonist of the Hindu epic, the Ramayana. Ravana kidnaps Sita, the

	wife of Ram, but Ram defeats him in a battle. The Hindu holiday of Dussehra commemorates Ram's victory over Ravana by burning Ravana's effigies
Roti and Beti Rishta	Inter-dining and intermarrying relations
Sadhu	Male ascetic
Sadhvi	Female ascetic
Saffronisation	Hindu nationalist interpretation of history and politics. Saffron is an auspicious color in Hinduism and the color the BJP uses in its flag and election campaigns
Sannyasin	A person in the Sannyasi phase of Hinduism
Sanskritize	A process whereby lower castes improve their social standing by adopting upper-caste practices
Sant	Saint
Sanyasi	Last of four life stages within Hinduism that entails the renunciation of worldly pleasures
Saraswati Vandana	A prayer to Saraswati, the Hindu goddess of education. Hindu nationalists have sought to make recitation of this prayer compulsory in many states
Sarsangchalak	Supreme leader of the RSS
Sarvadaliya Goraksha Maha-Abhiyan Samiti	Committee for the Great All-Party Campaign for Cow Protection
Sati	An ancient practice in India of immolating widows on the funeral pyres of their husbands. This practice was outlawed by the British government
Satyagraha	Literally "truth force" or "soul force." Gandhi coined the term and developed the practice of nonviolent civil disobedience with which it is associated
Shaivite	A branch of Hinduism whose adherents worship Shiva (as opposed to Vaishnavite Hinduism, which worships Vishnu)
Shakhas	Daily gatherings of RSS members in which men participate in physical exercises, recite prayers, sing devotional songs,

	and develop a commitment to RSS ideas and goals
Shakti pith	Temple dedicated to worship of Shakti, a Hindu goddess
Shankaracharya of Kanchi	The head of a Hindu monastic institution who has a high social standing as a Hindu leader
Shehri	An urban, modern woman
Shilanyas	Ceremony to lay the foundation for a temple in Ayodhya
Sindhoor	A red cosmetic powder that married Hindu women wear in the parting of their hair
Swadeshi	Self-sufficiency. The anticolonial nationalists opposed the British by demanding swadeshi. The RSS has called for swadeshi to oppose globalization
Tala Kholo	"Open the locks," a campaign that Hindu nationalists organized demanding that the locks of the babri masjid should be unlocked so that Hindus could worship there
Taluqdars	Large landowners who were responsible for collecting taxes on behalf of the Mughals and later the British
Tilak	A red mark on the forehead, which both Hindu men and women use either daily or on special religious occasions
Trishul Diksha	A VHP gathering where *trishuls* (tridents) are distributed to members
Upanishads	Religious texts that provide a philosophical commentary on the Vedas
Vande Mataram	Hail the motherland
Vanvasi	Forest dwellers
Vedas	Ancient Hindu scriptures that contain hymns and rituals
Yajna	A Hindu ritual where prayers are chanted over a pit of fire
Zamindars	Large landlords who were responsible for collecting taxes

Indian Organizations, Institutions, and Political Parties

All India Muslim Personal Law Board	An NGO that advocates the protection and maintenance of Muslim personal law
Arya Samaj	A Hindu reformist organization that was established in the nineteenth century
Bajrang Dal	Literally "Hanuman's Army," the militant youth wing of the Vishva Hindu Parishad. Hanuman, a major Hindu god, is associated with devotion and bachelorhood
Balidhan Jatha	Literally "Sacrifice Brigade," trained in guerilla warfare to destroy the Babri Masjid
Bharatiya Janata Party	Right wing Hindu nationalist party; one of the major parties in India
Bhartiya Shikshan Mandal	"Indian Education Division," a network of RSS-affiliated teachers that propagates Hindu nationalist ideas in schools
Biju Janata Dal	Regional party that split from the Janata Dal; active in Odisha (previously Orissa)
Congress I	Faction of Congress that was loyal to Indira Gandhi during the 1960s and 1970s
Congress O	Also called "Old Congress" or the "Syndicate," which split with Indira Gandhi's Congress Party. Its most famous leader was Morarji Desai

Durga Vahini	Literally "Durga's Army," the women's wing of the Vishva Hindu Parishad. Durga is a major Hindu goddess
Ekal Nari Shakti Sangathan	Organization of Empowered Single Women, an NGO in Rajasthan
Ekal Vidyalayas	Single-teacher schools run by the VHP, mainly in rural areas
Hindu Dharma Raksha Samiti	"Committee for the Defense of the Hindu Religion," formed by Hindu nationalists
Hindu Mahasabha	A Hindu nationalist party founded in the early twentieth century. No longer active
Hindu Rashtra Sena	A militant Hindu nationalist organization
Jan Morcha	A network of social movements that VP Singh created
Jan Sangh	Political party, predecessor of the BJP
Janata Dal	A political party, created by factions of the Janata Party and other organizations
Janata Party	Formed by the Janata Morcha, the Janata Party was a coalition of non-Congress parties; it came to power in 1977
JP Movement	Named after its leader, JP Narayan, the JP Movement advocated a peaceful, total revolution against the Congress Party
Kanya Suraksha Samiti	"Organization to Protect Hindu Daughters," created by Hindu nationalists to oppose interfaith marriages
Lashkar-e-Taiba	"Army of the Pure." A "terrorist" organization based in Pakistan
Lok Sabha	"House of People," the lower house of the Indian parliament, analogous to the House of Commons in England
Narmada Bachao Andolan	A social movement that opposes building the Sardar Sarovar Dam on the Narmada River
Nav Nirman Movement	A student movement in Gujarat that protested corruption and unemployment in the mid-1970s
Naxalites	Maoists who are waging a violent struggle against the Indian government; named after the Naxalbari village in West Bengal where the movement originated

Praja Mandal Movements	Nationalist movements in princely states during the colonial era
Provincial Armed Constabulary	Armed reserve of the Uttar Pradesh state government, often called in to quell "riots" and other social unrest
Rajya Sabha	"Council of States," the upper house of the Indian parliament, analogous to the House of Lords in England
Rashtriya Sevika Samiti	"National Women's Volunteer Committee," affiliated with the RSS
Rashtriya Swayamsevak Sangh	Right wing Hindu Nationalist nongovernmental organization
Sachar Committee	A committee headed by former chief justice of Delhi High Court Rajinder Sachar that the Indian government formed to investigate the conditions of Muslims
Sadhvi Shakti Parishad	"Organization of Sadhvi Strength," a VHP-affiliated organization comprised of female ascetics
Sangh Parivar	Literally "Family of the Sangh," refers to the RSS and its affiliates, including the BJP and VHP
Shiv Sena	"Shiva's Army," an extremist, often violent political party in Maharashtra that demands preferential treatment of native Maharashtrians over migrants from other states and advocates Hindu nationalism
Shri Ram Sena	"Lord Ram's Army." An extremist group that has gained notoriety for violent attacks on those perceived to be engaging in Western or anti-Hindu activities. The RSS has distanced itself from the Shri Ram Sena
Students' Islamic Movement of India	A banned extremist Islamic organization with numerous links to "terrorist" groups
Trinamool Congress	A regional party in West Bengal
Vidya Bharati Akhil Bharatiya Shiksha Sansthan	Educational wing of the RSS that runs a large network of schools
Vishva Hindu Parishad	World Hindu Council, a Hindu nationalist social movement organization that has close ties to the RSS

Abbreviations of Political Parties and Organizations

ABVP	Akhil Bharatiya Vidya Parishad, RSS student wing
AIADMK	All India Anna Dravida Munnetra Khazagam, regional political party that split from the DMK, active in Tamil Nadu
BAMCEF	Backward and Minority Communities Employees Federation, an NGO formed by dalit activist Kanshi Ram
BJP	Bharatiya Janata Party
BKS	Bharatiya Kisan Sangh, a farmers' organization, affiliated with the RSS
BMS	Bharatiya Mazdoor Sangh, Indian Workers' Union, RSS-affiliated
BSP	Bahujan Samaj Party
CPI	Communist Party of India
CPI-(M-L)	Communist Party of India-Marxist-Leninist, a radical offshoot of the CPM
CPM	Communist Party Marxist, active in West Bengal and Kerala
DMK	Dravida Munnetra Khazagam, a regional party in Tamil Nadu
IM	Indian Mujahideen
NDA	National Democratic Alliance led by the BJP; the NDA government occupied office from 1998 to 2004 and from 2014 to the present
RSS	Rashtriya Swayamsevak Sangh

SIMI	Students' Islamic Movement of India
SJM	Swadeshi Jagran Manch, Platform to Promote Swadeshi, affiliated with the Sangh Parivar
SP	Samajwadi Party, split from the Janata Dal; active in Uttar Pradesh
TDP	Telugu Desam Party, a regional party in Andhra Pradesh
UPA	United Progressive Alliance, a center-left alliance of parties led by the Congress Party; the UPA government was in power from 2004 to 2014
VHP	Vishva Hindu Parishad

Introduction

India's christening, like that of many nation-states, was violent: 1 million people killed, 13 million uprooted, and property worth millions of rupees destroyed during Partition. India's subsequent relative stability seemed to disprove Alexis de Tocqueville's foreboding that nations seldom outgrow the conditions of their birth. However in the late 1960s and early 1970s, Hindu groups engaged in violent attacks on Muslims in Jabalpur, Bhiwandi, and Ahmedabad. The late 1980s witnessed violent ethnic struggles in Punjab, Kashmir, and several northeastern states. Following Indira Gandhi's assassination in 1984, Congress Party members instigated the massacre of more than 2,000 Sikhs. Hindu nationalists organized attacks on Muslims and Christians in several Indian states in the late 1980s, early 1990s, and intermittently, thereafter.[1]

What explains Hindu nationalists' intermittent anti-minority violence?[2] When Hindu nationalists destroyed a sixteenth-century mosque in Ayodhya in 1992, many observers anticipated the simultaneous growth of Hindu nationalism and anti-minority violence. Instead, the Bharatiya Janata Party (BJP) adopted a relatively moderate electoral stance to achieve national office (1999–2004), only to be implicated in extensive anti-Muslim violence in Gujarat in 2002. The BJP-led National Democratic Alliance (NDA) government did not stop the violence. Understanding the conjunctural nature of Hindu nationalism acquires unprecedented significance with the BJP's resounding electoral victory and Narendra Modi's ascent to power in 2014.

---

[1] Major incidents of organized Hindu violence against Muslims include Meerut (1987), Ahmedabad (1969, 1985), Moradabad (1980), Bhagalpur (1989), Jaipur, Kota, Bhopal, Indore, Khargone, and Delhi (1990–2), Bombay (1992–3), and Gujarat (2002).

[2] I do not analyze in-depth anti-Hindu violence by Muslim organizations. The most serious have been in Jammu and Kashmir. "Terrorist" attacks by Muslims, of which the most notable was in Mumbai in 2008, have also increased in recent years.

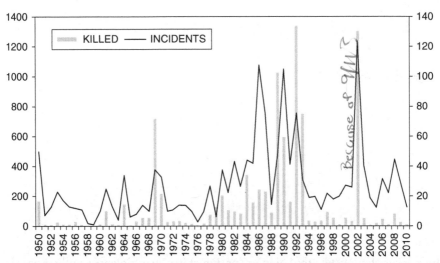

FIGURE I.I. Trends in Hindu-Muslim Violence in India, 1950–2010.
Source: Data from Kaysser, Nina, Sonia Bhalotra, Irma Clots-Figueras and Lakshmi
Iyer (2014). Hindu-Muslim violence in India, 1950–2010: An update of the
Varshney-Wilkinson Dataset on Hindu-Muslim violence in India (unpublished).

Hindu-Muslim Violence across Time and Place

Numerous investigations have held Hindu nationalists responsible for extensive anti-Muslim violence in postindependence India.[3] A high point was
from the late 1980s to the early 1990s, when Hindu nationalists organized
a campaign to build a temple in Ayodhya that they claimed sixteenth-century
Muslim rulers had destroyed and replaced with a mosque (the *babri masjid*).
They orchestrated campaigns that claimed 1,000 lives in Meerut (April–May
1987) and, following other campaigns, another 1,000 lives in Bhagalpur, Bihar
(1989). As Figure I.1 shows, violence escalated from 1986 to 1992 as a result
of the Ayodhya campaign. From 1980 to 2008, the largest number of "riots"
occurred in 1986, 1990, 1992, and 2002, and the most Muslims were killed in
1990–2 and in 2002.[4]

---

[3] Accounts of Hindu nationalists' responsibility for anti-minority violence include Paul R. Brass,
The Production of Hindu-Muslim Violence in Contemporary India (Seattle, WA: University of
Washington Press, 2003); Christophe Jaffrelot, *Religion, Caste, and Politics in India* (Delhi: Primus
Books, 2010); Martha Nussbaum, *The Clash Within: Democracy, Religious Violence, and India's
Future* (Cambridge, MA: Harvard University Press, 2007); and numerous investigative reports
by the People's Union for Civil Liberties, Human Rights Watch, and Amnesty International.

[4] Both the incidence of "riots" and numbers of lives lost dramatically declined in 1993; the death
toll spiked although there were fewer "riots" in 2002. I put "riots" in quotes because the term
implies that two or more parties engaged in violence and does not accurately depict one-sided
attacks by one community against another.

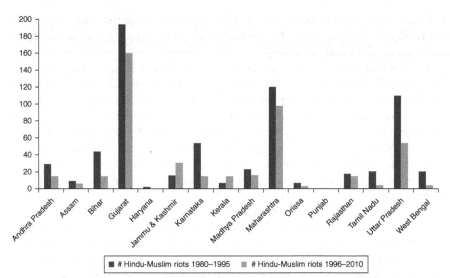

FIGURE I.2. Hindu-Muslim Violence by State; Varshney and Wilkinson data set, extended to 2010 by Bhalotra, Clots-Figueras and Iyer.
Source: Sonia Bhalotra, Irma Clots-Figueras, and Lakshmi Iyer, "Politician Identity and Religious Conflict in India," (unpublished work in progress, July 2012). Reproduced with authors' permission.

However, where and when Hindu nationalists have precipitated violence against minorities remains unexplained. The incidence of anti-Muslim violence was highly uneven across Indian states from 1980 to 2008 (see Figure I.2). For example, it was limited in Himachal Pradesh (HP) and extensive in Gujarat. Further, the timing of the violence differed across states. Uttar Pradesh (UP) experienced more violence in the early 1990s than in 2002; the reverse was true of Gujarat.

I argue that Hindu nationalist anti-minority violence is likely to be most extensive when an ideologically-driven, well-organized Hindu nationalist political party, the BJP, with close ties to a social movement organization, the Vishva Hindu Parishad (VHP, World Hindu Council), and parent body, the Rashtriya Swayamsevak Sangh (RSS), has achieved power in federal states and when the national government (which need not be headed by the BJP) has condoned their actions. The alignment of these forces is uncommon. Relations between the party and movement, party and state, and movement and state are often strained.

The likelihood of violence is also determined by the extent and character of opposition Hindu nationalists encounter from the lower castes and classes. Hindu nationalist forces are apt to be most aligned and most militant in regions where the upper castes and classes are strong and fully support the BJP and lower-caste parties and movements are weak. Conversely, Hindu

Relates to Santino's concept of Symbolism [handwritten margin note]

nationalism is likely to be weaker and less militant where the upper castes are politically divided, lower castes are unified and organized, and class identities are stronger than caste identities.

Scholars have attributed mass violence to parties, states, mobs, gangs, and institutionalized riot systems. However they have accorded little attention to the roles of social movements and their affiliated civil society organizations in promoting and curtailing violence. If India was considered a textbook case of strong political institutions, it furnishes an equally compelling illustration of vibrant social movements. Indian newspapers are filled with accounts of protests on the streets and in the corridors of power. Social movements include a range of activists – rich and poor, men and women, young and old, devout and secular, conservative and liberal – who are committed to every conceivable cause. Indian social movements are performative. They appropriate public spaces by mounting *dharnas* (sit-ins), *gheraos* (encirclement of officials or their offices), *bandhs* (literally stoppages – of shops and businesses), *hartals* (shut down of shops and offices), jail *bharaos* (filling the jails – or courting voluntary arrest), and *rasta rokos* (blockages of traffic). They communicate colorful visual symbols through banners, flags, arm bands, caps, and clothes. Their festive, theatrical modes of protest frequently invite media attention and popular support.

Social movement scholarship largely concerns urban middle-class movements in Europe and North America. It devotes little attention to ethnic (including linguistic and religious) movements in the postcolonial world.[5] There is no theoretical rationale for this neglect. Ethnic struggles in the postcolonial world are neither defined nor delimited by primordial identities. Like other social movements, they deploy repertoires of contention that are both innovative and familiar. They select, interpret, and frame particular facets of ethnic identities in order to create solidarities and organize collective action. They confront and negotiate with the state and other authoritative institutions.

Another selective bias in the scholarship on social movements is its focus on progressive, nonviolent struggles of oppressed groups for rights, justice, and equality.[6] However, groups with divergent ideological orientations and class backgrounds have organized social movements to demand rights, resources, power, and territory. What defines them as social movements are their protest tactics, collective organizing, and targeting of authorities. Conservative social movements – sometimes called countermovements – often seek to

---

[5] Doug McAdam, Sidney Tarrow, and Charles Tilly, "To Map Contentious Politics," *Mobilization: An International Quarterly* 1, no. 1 (1996): 17–34.

[6] The relatively small literature on conservative social movements includes Donatella della Porta, *Social Movements and Violence: Participation in Underground Organizations* (Greenwich, CT: JAI Press, 1992); Charles Tilly, *The Politics of Collective Violence*, (New York: Cambridge University Press, 2003); and Jens Rydgren, ed., *Movements of Exclusion: Radical Right Wing Populism in Western Europe* (New York: Nova Science Publishers, 2005).

reverse the gains that underprivileged groups have achieved by claiming that dominant majorities are victimized. Because social movements in India are not simply organized by the dispossessed but by class-stratified caste, ethnic, and religious groups that have ties to parties and the state, they include countermovements.

The design of social movements is equally diverse and scholars have not adequately explored their organizational diversity. Social movements can be either loosely or highly structured at different points in their life cycles. Institutionalization need not be antithetical to their strength and success. Contrary to the claim that social movements necessarily become de-radicalized once they become institutionalized, activists may continue to pursue radical goals through institutions.[7]

Nor have scholars sufficiently studied relations between social movements and political parties. The social movement literature primarily focuses on autonomous social movements in North America and Western Europe. In Latin America and many regions of the postcolonial world, the relationship between social movements and political parties is synergistic: parties often emerge from social movements and retain ties to them. Such movement-parties are often less institutionalized, more ideological, and more linked to civil society groups than European and North American parties. Conversely, many social movements morph into or have strong ties to nongovernmental organizations (NGOs).

Parties and movements have different and potentially complementary strengths. Movements are more radical and more cyclical than parties. Movements are strongest in localities and parties, in federal and national states. Temporally, movement activity is episodic whereas party work is more sustained. Social movements can help parties win elections by strengthening collective identities, creating a sense of urgency, and identifying them with seemingly selfless causes. Ties to radical movements can influence factional divisions within parties. Ruling parties can prevent social movements from "burning out" by institutionalizing their gains and placing their activists in state institutions.

Once parties attain power, they face contending pressures – from the movement to sustain their radicalism and from the electorate and coalition partners to demonstrate their moderation. Some parties and movements are sufficiently well-integrated and uncontested by adversaries to sustain their militancy in office. Some retreat from their radical goals because the ruling

(margin note: Advantages e disad.)

7 The literature on the institutionalization of social movements includes Mary Fainsod Katzenstein, *Faithful and Fearless: Moving Feminist Protest Inside the Church and Military* (Princeton, NJ: Princeton University Press, 1998); David S. Meyer and Sidney Tarrow, eds., *The Social Movement Society: Contentious Politics for a New Century* (Lanham, MD: Rowman & Littlefield, 1998); and Dieter Rucht and Friedhelm Neidhardt, "Towards a Movement Society? On the Possibility of Institutionalizing Social Movements," *Social Movement Studies* 1, no. 1 (2002): 7–30.

party is factionalized, the movement ceases to enjoy societal support, and other social movements and parties challenge their beliefs and capture their constituencies.

As scholars have recognized, social movements are deeply influenced by state structures, policies and actions. The state defines, promotes, and undermines group identities and plays a key role in determining the extent and character of violence. Some movements and opposition parties have grown by challenging and contesting state policies and state-endorsed identities. Ironically, in doing so, they have highlighted the state's power. Movements and parties are especially likely to contest the state when its policies are inconsistent and when the electoral interests of ruling parties determine state policies.

Why Study the Causes of Violence?

Some scholars claim that examining the causes of Hindu-Muslim violence risks obscuring its human costs and local underpinnings. From this perspective, causal accounts often make inaccurate assumptions about which identities are most salient. Assuming that the axis of conflict involves Hindu and Muslim religious identities ignores the multiple sources of complex lived identities. People's perceptions of what transpired are often refracted through the lenses of outside observers, including journalists, state officials, and scholars.[8] In *Theft of an Idol*, Paul Brass describes the difficulties of establishing the precise causes of a "riot" because of the temporal distance between initial precipitating events and interpretations of these events by local politicians and state authorities.[9] "Riots," in his view, are narratives that the courts, police, witnesses, and scholars construct.

In writing about violence, there is a risk of discursively reproducing the very problems that we seek to explain.[10] The 2006 government-appointed

---

[8] In an insightful account of a "riot" in Panipur village in Bangladesh in the early 1990s, Beth Roy describes the conflict that ensued when one man's cow strayed onto another man's field and grazed his crops. The conflict was not initially a product of Hindu-Muslim enmity but became seen through a national lens as a full-scale "communal riot." Beth Roy, *Some Trouble with Cows: Making Sense of Social Conflict* (Berkeley, CA: University of California Press, 1994).

[9] Paul Brass, *Theft of an Idol: Text and Context in the Representation of Collective Violence* (Princeton, NJ: Princeton University Press, 1997). Stanley Tambiah also shows how the depiction of "riots" suits the political interests of the actors involved. Stanley Tambiah, *Leveling Crowds: Ethnonationalist Conflicts and Collective Violence in South Asia* (Berkeley, CA: University of California Press, 1996).

[10] I avoid employing such politically loaded words as appeasement, pseudo-secularism, and terrorism or use them in quotation marks. I prefer to use the more secular term the "Ayodhya movement" and the term "activists" rather than the Hindu nationalist term *kar sevaks* (religious volunteers) to refer to the movement's followers. We also lack a term to describe frequent instances of the state's indirect responsibility for violence. A pogrom, an officially organized persecution of a minority community, provides an apt description of the state's direct role in orchestrating anti-minority violence but does not capture the complicity of people on the ground.

Sachar Committee Report comments that Muslims "carry a double burden of being labeled anti-national and appeased." It states that alleged appeasement has failed to improve Muslims' socioeconomic standing while forcing them to continually disprove that they are anti-national and "terrorists." The report challenges the common perception that Muslims are averse to banking and secular schools on religious grounds; only 4 percent of Muslim children attend *madrasas* (religious schools).[11]

Excessive attention to context and precipitating events implicitly denigrates both victims' suffering and resilience. Gyanendra Pandey suggests that compared to social science accounts, testimonies of survivors better illuminate the meaning, significance, and causes of violence.[12] He contrasts the view from below with the view from the center, that is informed by the logic of the state and official archives. The role of the state is best understood, Veena Das argues, from the margins.[13] Reflecting on her experiences working in relief camps for Sikh survivors in 1984, she suggests that national dramas which implicated the state and community were staged in local places.

Ethnographic studies have explored the meaning and significance of inter-community violence in localities, rather than simply viewing violence as the product of political ideologies, party strategies, and state actions. Using violence can empower groups that otherwise feel powerless. Violence that denigrates and humiliates members of another community can forge subjectivities among its perpetrators. Describing mass violence, Terrence Des Pres' words are haunting:

Killing was ad hoc, inventive, and in its dependence on imagination, peculiarly expressive. ... This was murder uncanny in its anonymous intimacy, a hostility so personally focused on human flesh that the abstract fact of death was not enough.[14]

---

[11] The report documents the underrepresentation of Muslims in professional, managerial, and administrative positions. Muslims constitute 14 percent of India's population but only 3 percent of the Indian Administrative Service, 1.8 percent of the Indian Foreign Service, and 4 percent of the Indian Police Service. Muslim literacy rates (59 percent) are significantly lower than the national average (65 percent). Villages with large Muslim populations are underserved with respect to educational infrastructure, medical, post, and telegraph facilities, paved roads, and bus stops. Poverty levels are higher in urban areas and slightly lower nationwide among Muslims than among Scheduled Castes and Scheduled Tribes. Although Scheduled Castes and Scheduled Tribes had lower literacy levels than Muslims from 1953 to 2001, the trend reversed thereafter because Scheduled Castes and Scheduled Tribes have been greater beneficiaries than Muslims of government programs to ameliorate inequalities. Rajinder Sachar et al., *Sachar Committee Report on Social, Economic and Educational Status of the Muslim Community of India* (New Delhi: Prime Minister's High Level Committee, Cabinet Secretariat – Government of India, 2006).

[12] Gyanendra Pandey, *Routine Violence, Nations, Fragments, Histories* (Stanford, CA: Stanford University Press, 2006).

[13] Veena Das, *Life and Words: Violence and the Descent into the Ordinary* (Berkeley, CA: University of California Press, 2007).

[14] Terrence Des Pres, "The Struggle of Memory," *The Nation*, April 10, 1982, 433.

Those who enact violence may increasingly fear being marginalized by the state and international forces as a result of the hopes and fears that globalization generates.[15]

These powerful analyses of lived, local violence sound an important cautionary note about social scientific approaches.[16] The identification of broad causes of violence can displace responsibility onto external actors. Depicting the state as a monolithic entity ignores the complex webs that link state and civil society actors. Studies of extreme, organized violence can also ignore extensive quotidian violence.

I seek to identify, for both normative and analytical reasons, some broad probable explanations for violence. Asking "Why did it happen?" and "Was it inevitable?" implies that people are capable of both causing and preventing violence. Without suggesting that violence is ever completely absent, I try to understand when and why it is more or less pervasive and its effects are more or less lasting. Why, for example, does it leave greater scars years after its occurrence in some places than in others? I also give due to the quotidian violence that precedes and follows large-scale violence. While most narrative accounts of violence focus on localities, I explore the forces that bind localities to the nation. A close-up photo brings into sharp relief images that are blurry from a distance while the panoramic view reveals what close-ups cannot. I provide both sets of images and establish connections between the violence itself and precipitating events.

I also hope to demonstrate that both local and national forces are often responsible for local violence. Hindu nationalists have at times been notably successful at bridging the local-national divide by harnessing local grievances to their national campaigns. Many activists harbor resentments toward large national forces, such as the Congress government's "appeasement" policies and the Congress Party's vote bank politics. Through local violence, Hindu nationalists can seek to symbolically right the wrongs they believe they have suffered, demonstrate their strength, and redeem their honor. Similarly, the notion that the state has discriminated against Hindus and favored Muslims underlines Hindu nationalists' sense that Hindus are victims and Muslims are pampered minorities. Far from being an external entity, the state has influenced people's understandings of their own identities.[17]

[15] See, for example, Allen Feldman, *Formations of Violence: The Narrative of the Body and Political Terror in Northern Ireland* (Chicago, IL: University of Chicago Press, 1991); Thomas Blom Hansen, *Wages of Violence: Naming and Identity in Postcolonial Bombay* (Princeton, NJ: Princeton University Press, 2001); and Oskar Verkaaik, *Migrants and Militants: Fun and Urban Violence in Pakistan* (Princeton, NJ: Princeton University Press, 2004).

[16] On local violence, see Veena Das, "Introduction: Communities, Riots, Survivors – the South Asian Experience," in Veena Das, ed., *Mirrors of Violence: Communities, Riots and Survivors in South Asia* (New Delhi: Oxford University Press, 1990), 12–13; and "Privileging the Local: The 1984 Riots," in Steven Wilkinson, ed., *Religious Politics and Communal Violence* (New Delhi: Oxford University Press, 2005).

[17] Arjun Appadurai brilliantly describes the psychology of majority violence amid globalization in *Fear of Small Numbers: An Essay on the Geography of Anger* (Durham, NC: Duke University Press, 2006).

In the end, some questions about violence can never be answered, particularly the deepest, most existential questions about why certain groups engage in violence against others. While seeking answers, I recognize the impossibility of definitive explanations. I linger on stories of violence to give due to its horrors while highlighting the opportunities it creates for refashioning institutions and identities.

Why Violence?

Political scientists have extensively explored relations between ethnic violence and core political institutions. A number of studies examine the implications of different institutional arrangements – parties, electoral systems, and federalism – for ethnic violence. Some studies compare the salience of a single institutional factor in places where violence occurs and is absent. In studies of this kind, variations in the timing and location of violence are essential to determining its causes. Three bodies of political science scholarship are especially germane to explaining ethnic violence in India.

The first approach accords political parties a central role in shaping political life and precipitating violence. Steven Wilkinson's *Votes and Violence* argues that the more numerous parties are in an Indian state, the more valuable minority voters become and the more political parties will compete with one another for their votes and, consequently, attempt to prevent the spread of Hindu-Muslim violence.[18] He suggests that most Indian state governments can but do not prevent ethnic violence. Wilkinson believes that with increasing party competition, northern states will come to resemble southern states, and ethnic violence will diminish.

Pradeep Chhibber's *Democracy without Associations* argues that parties responded strategically to the weakness of associational life by creating a cleavage-based party system that magnifies social cleavages.[19] He attributes the growth in collective violence – or the increased incidence of "riots" in the fifteen largest states from 1967 to 1993 – to closer alignment between social cleavages and the party system. He argues:

Political parties are the key link between society and the state. As the party system comes to be rooted in social cleavages, political conflict between parties translates into conflict among groups and vice versa. Second, political parties are central to governance in India, especially with the politicization of the bureaucracy and the judiciary. In times of cabinet instability and elections, it is not clear, then, who carries the authority of the state. This enables the mobilization of "gangs" by political parties and local political aspirants, and violent conflict ensues.[20]

---

[18] Steven Wilkinson, *Votes and Violence: Electoral Competition and Ethnic Riots in India* (New York: Cambridge University Press, 2004).

[19] Pradeep K. Chhibber, *Democracy without Associations: Transformation of the Party System and Social Cleavages in India* (Ann Arbor, MI: University of Michigan Press, 1999).

[20] Ibid., 192.

A second approach attributes variations in the extent of Hindu-Muslim violence to the character of civil society organizations. Ashutosh Varshney argues that cities and towns are more likely to resist severe ethnic conflict when they possess local, preferably mass-based interethnic institutions of civic engagement, such as clubs, political parties, festival groups, business associations, trade unions, professional organizations, and NGOs.[21] Where such networks exist and engage both Hindus and Muslims, they defuse tensions and conflicts; where they are absent, violence is endemic and serious.

③ A third approach explores state-society interactions and particularly the state's role in preventing or controlling violence. Atul Kohli's "Can Democracies Accommodate Ethnic Nationalism?" argues that state policies determine the rise and decline of self-determination movements and their proclivity to engage in violence.[22] Kohli's *Democracy and Discontent* seeks to explain "the crisis of governability and its correlate, the growth of political violence, in India."[23] Kohli attributes what he describes as the growing crisis of governability to the changing role of the political elite, weak and ineffective political organizations, the mobilization of previously passive groups into electoral politics, and growing conflict between contending social groups.

These scholars differ in the significance they accord to different political domains. Wilkinson and Chhibber suggest that local governments play subordinate and secondary roles to state governments. Wilkinson states:

[W]hile local precipitants are important, state level politics does much more than simply provide the context for local mechanisms to work. Because states control the police and the local deployment of force, state-level politics in fact largely determines whether violence will break out, even in the most riot-prone towns.[24]

By contrast, Varshney argues "local (or regional) variations can best be explained with local (or regional) variables, not with national or global factors which are, by definition, constant across local settings."[25] In *Democracy and Discontent*, Kohli explores the sources of violence in districts, states, and nationally.

My project builds on these important contributions and shares their interest in analyzing both places where large-scale violence occurs and is absent. But my focus is distinctive in several ways. First, I seek not only to ①

[21] Ashutosh Varshney, *Ethnic Conflict and Civic Life: Hindus and Muslims in India* (New Haven, CT: Yale University Press, 2002).
[22] Atul Kohli, "Can Democracies Accommodate Ethnic Nationalism? The Rise and Decline of Ethnic Self-Determination Movements in India," in Amrita Basu and Atul Kohli, eds., *Community Conflicts and the State in India* (New Delhi: Oxford University Press, 1995).
[23] Atul Kohli, *Democracy and Discontent: India's Growing Crisis of Governability* (New York: Cambridge University Press, 1990), 10.
[24] Wilkinson, *Votes and Violence*, 58.
[25] Varshney, *Ethnic Conflict and Civic Life*, 28.

understand the negative conditions associated with violence and instability – that is, the absence of strong states, interethnic civil society associations, and multiparty systems – but also to highlight the purposeful actions of institutions, organizations, and movements in precipitating violence. This in turn necessitates attention to ideology and the interrelationships among institutions.

(2) Second, I argue that the strength and cohesion of certain political parties can actually promote rather than inhibit their use of violence. The BJP has been more apt to precipitate violence at those times and places in which the party has been more unified than where and when it has been factionalized; the reverse is true of the Congress Party. During the Ayodhya movement in the early 1990s, the BJP had a unified chain of command that extended from Delhi to UP, to small towns within the state. Conversely, factional divisions based on personality, caste, and ideology, have inhibited the BJP from pursuing an ideologically-driven agenda.

(3) Third, I explore reciprocal influences among parties, states, and social movements. In contrast to Chhibber, I argue that social movements, along with political parties, promote linkages between state and society. Parties have not only responded to social cleavages but also to social movements among *dalits* (Scheduled Castes), OBCs, farmers, and Hindus. However, tensions in party-movement relations have often emerged when parties seek and attain national office.

(4) Fourth, I compare the incidence of violence across spatial domains and ask why, although violence generally remains confined to localities, it sometimes spans larger territories.[26] My particular interest is in how ties between parties, movements, and states have helped Hindu nationalists mediate relationships between local, state, and national politics. I suggest that parties and movements are strongest within different spatial settings: movements tend to be strongest locally and parties, federally and nationally. Collaboration among these institutions enables them to become stronger in their respective domains.

National parties are more autonomous than their subsidiary branches from movements and states. They demonstrate their worthiness for national office by accentuating their moderation. Members of governing coalitions may pressure parties to maintain a distance from sectarian movements. Conversely, boundaries between parties, movements, and the state are relatively porous

---

[26] Scholarship that examines networks that caste elites, the state, and political parties have employed to navigate the different scales of political life includes, Ward Berenschot, *Riot Politics: Hindu-Muslim Violence and the Indian State* (New Delhi: Rupa Publications, 2013); Tariq Thachil, "Embedded Mobilization: Nonstate Service Provision as Electoral Strategy in India," *World Politics* 63, no. 3 (2011): 434–69; and Jeffrey Witsoe, *Democracy against Development: Lower-Caste Politics and Political Modernity in Postcolonial India* (Chicago, IL: University of Chicago Press, 2013).

in localities. At the local level, parties often have close ties to a variety of civil society groups; they may share offices and jointly plan events. Local party members engage in militant protest that national parties at least in principle oppose. Spatial proximity to an issue and intensity of engagement around it are often closely related.

The state's complicity in violence is much greater in localities than at the national level. As a general rule, the national state's legitimacy rests on its demonstrating autonomy from societal groups, particularly religious associations. Various political institutions check the growth of violence more effectively nationally than at lower levels of government. The international system places pressure on national states to maintain law and order.

In India, the national state has sometimes directly engaged in extensive, violence against activists (such as the Naxalites and Punjabi and Kashmiri separatists). More often, however, the national state's responsibility for violence has been indirect. For example, it has created the conditions for potentially violent activism by sharpening religious identities – regulating religious personal law, making Hindu prayers mandatory in schools, and allowing Hindus to worship at contested mosques.

State governments are more directly accountable than the national government for inter-community violence. The maintenance of law and order and control over the police force are state government responsibilities. Judicial commissions of inquiry, fact-finding reports, and national commissions have extensively documented state governments' abdication of responsibilities, biases, and even active complicity in anti-minority violence, as well as their failure to compensate victims in the aftermath of violence. State governments are more likely than national governments to have close links with the ruling party, because multiparty governing coalitions have become common at the national level whereas single parties more often govern federal states. Local state agencies are especially permeable to societal influences, including the demands of social movements. Local bureaucrats are much less able than their national counterparts to insulate themselves from political pressures. When Hindu-Muslim violence breaks out, civil servants often violate Weberian bureaucratic norms and openly side with the majority community.

Hindu Nationalists

This study examines relations among the RSS, the VHP, and the BJP through the prism of party-movement relations.[27]

---

[27] The most important study of the BJP remains Christophe Jaffrelot's richly researched account, *The Hindu Nationalist Movement and Indian Politics* (New York: Columbia University Press, 2003). Other important studies on the Jan Sangh and the BJP include: Bruce D. Graham, *Hindu Nationalism and Indian Politics: The Origins and Development of the Bharatiya Jana*

I characterize the VHP as a social movement organization and the BJP as a political party. The RSS has participated in protests and election campaigns, but is neither a political party nor a social movement organization. It is India's largest and oldest NGO. It is far more insulated from society than political parties and social movements. It is more restrictive about criteria for membership, more financially self-sufficient, and less dependent on public validation. Thus, while it has adapted to changing social conditions, it has insisted since its founding that the state and religious minorities should accept the economic and social dominance of Hindus. The RSS appreciates the different contributions of electoral participation and political mobilization. It has embraced both strategies, sometimes providing greater support for the VHP, and at other times for the BJP.

The RSS endorsed the formation of an affiliated political party – the Jan Sangh in 1951 – because the national government had curtailed its political activities. It played a crucial role in determining the policies, leadership, and strategies of the Jan Sangh and its successor, the BJP, which was formed in 1980. However, the BJP was electorally weak until the late 1980s, when it joined the VHP's campaign to construct a temple in Ayodhya.

The BJP and VHP both achieved unprecedented strength as a result of their alliance. As a result of its ties to the VHP and the temple movement in the 1980s and 1990s, the BJP claimed to be more ethical and religious than other political parties. Support for the campaign from women, the low castes, and poor helped transform the BJP's elitist image. The BJP also benefited materially and organizationally from the VHP's vast networks of ancillary organizations in India and transnationally. The Ayodhya movement enabled the BJP to harness and channel popular fear and anger. For example, it tapped into the rage of upper-caste youth over the government's decision to provide reservations for the OBCs amid high unemployment rates and limited prospects for upward mobility. The movement captured antipathy toward the state, interlaced with anti-Muslim sentiment.

Sangh (Cambridge, UK: Cambridge University Press, 1990); Thomas Blom Hansen, *The Saffron Wave: Democracy and Hindu Nationalism in Modern India* (Princeton, NJ: Princeton University Press, 1999); Partha Ghosh, *BJP and the Evolution of Hindu Nationalism: From Periphery to Centre* (New Delhi: Manohar Publishers & Distributors, 1999); and Yogendra K. Malik and VB Singh, *Hindu Nationalists in India: The Rise of the Bharatiya Janata Party* (New Delhi: Vistaar Publications, 1995). On the RSS and VHP, see Walter K. Andersen and Shridhar D. Damle, *The Brotherhood in Saffron: The Rashtriya Swayamsevak Sangh and Hindu Revivalism* (Boulder, CO: Westview Press, 1987); Manjari Katju, *Vishva Hindu Parishad and Indian Politics* (Hyderbad: Orient Longman Private Limited, 2003); Pralay Kanungo, *RSS's Tryst with Politics: From Hedgewar to Sudarshan* (Delhi: Manohar Publishers & Distributors, 2004); and AG Noorani, *The RSS and BJP: A Division of Labour* (New Delhi: LeftWord Books, 2000).

The BJP was electorally successful in several federal states in the early 1990s as a result of the Ayodhya movement, but only retained national power in 1999, after aborted attempts in 1996 and 1998, by dropping its most contentious demands and assuming more centrist positions. The BJP-led NDA government refused to concede to all the VHP's demands concerning temple construction in Ayodhya. The VHP, with RSS backing, publicly decried the BJP for its ideological retreat.

Tensions between the VHP and the BJP reflect some of the core differences between movements and parties. While the BJP was committed to attaining and retaining power, the VHP's goals were more radical and far-reaching. In this respect the alliance between the VHP and BJP resembles many other party-movement alliances that are of limited duration and typically culminate in the dominance of the party over the movement, especially if the party achieves electoral success.

However, it would be inaccurate to describe the BJP as having become a centrist party. The BJP challenges the assumed binary between parties and movements and exemplifies the features of a movement-party because it has independent ideological, activist commitments that are further fortified by its ties to the VHP and RSS. Unlike most political parties, the BJP's ideology has not been diluted by the centrist pressures of democracy.[28] The BJP's top-ranking leaders are RSS members and its most influential leaders are the most ideologically committed. The BJP has maintained strong ties to the RSS even when it is electorally strong enough to relinquish them.

Although both the RSS and BJP are devoted to Hindu nationalist ideals, they are willing to make strategic compromises to achieve their long-term goals. For example, the RSS conceded to federal principles and the creation of linguistic states despite its support for a unitary state. It agreed to the BJP's participating in coalition governments on pragmatic grounds in the hopes that "the period of one-party rule will come."[29] In supporting Narendra Modi's candidacy, the RSS compromised its long-standing opposition to economic liberalization and support for *swadeshi* (self-sufficiency) and its historic opposition to the cult of strong leadership.

Like other single-issue movements, the movement around temple construction has waned. In recent years, there has been greater popular support for movements opposing corruption and violence against women than for religious movements. However, the decline of the Ayodhya movement and of Hindu nationalist militancy are not synonymous. First, some VHP leaders,

[28] On the centripetal forces in Indian democracy, see, Susanne Hoeber Rudolph and Lloyd I. Rudolph, "New Dimensions in Indian Democracy," *Journal of Democracy* 13, no. 1 January (2002): 52–66 and Baldev Raj Nayar, "The Limits of Economic Nationalism in India: Economic Reforms under the BJP-led Government, 1998–1999," *Asian Survey* 40, no. 5 (2000): 792–815.
[29] "All Alliances Are Temporary: RSS," *The Telegraph* [Calcutta], February 19, 1998.

including Uma Bharati, Mahant Avaidyanath, and Vinay Katiyar, have continued to espouse militant views as BJP parliamentarians and legislators.

Second, a raft of violent Hindu nationalist organizations have joined the VHP and its youth organization, the Bajrang Dal. They include the Abhinav Bharat (Pride of India), Rashtriya Jagran Manch (National Revival Forum), Sri Ram Sena (Army of God Ram), Hindu Dharam Sena (Army for Hindu Religion), and Sanatan Sanstha (Eternal Organization). They have engaged in "terrorist" bombings modeled on those of the Indian Mujahideen (IM) and the Students' Islamic Movement of India (SIMI). They have policed civil society by destroying or seeking to ban publications they deem offensive to Hindu sensibilities and have sought to control women's sexuality and Hindu-Muslim relations.[30] They have accused Muslim men of engaging in "love jihad," by supposedly coercing Hindu women into sexual relations and then converting them to Islam. They have launched Web sites, produced audiotapes, and distributed pamphlets warning that "love jihad" is the work of international "terrorist" organizations. Hindu nationalist expressions of cultural nationalism have become more aggressive at the very time that their commitment to economic nationalism has diminished.

The dynamic relationships among RSS, VHP, and BJP and their variable propensities to engage in violence are best appreciated by exploring changes over time and in different federal states. On the one hand, BJP state governments have collaborated more with the VHP at the state than at the national level. They have pursued some of the VHP's long-standing demands to curtail religious conversion, prohibit beef consumption, and reform educational institutions, through both activism and policy initiatives. On the other hand, the relative strength of the RSS, VHP, and BJP differs across states and within states through time. In some states, the movement has grown at the expense of the party while the reverse is true elsewhere.

The States

In the chapters that follow, I explain why the extent of anti-minority violence has differed in four BJP-ruled states – Rajasthan, HP, UP, and Gujarat – by exploring the variable relationships among the party, movement, and state and national governments. My key claim is that variations in these relationships

---

[30] See, for example, Sonia Faleiro, "An Attack on Love," *New York Times*, October 31, 2014. Accessed November 17, 2014. http://www.nytimes.com/2014/11/02/opinion/sunday/its-not-jihad-its-just-love.html?ref=opinion&_r=o; Tanika Sarkar, "Love, Control and Punishment," *The Indian Express*, October 16, 2014, Accessed November 17, 2014. http://indianexpress.com/article/opinion/columns/love-control-and-punishment/ and Aditi Raja, "VHP Steps Up Campaign against 'Love Jihad,'" *The Indian Express*, September 20, 2014. Accessed November 17, 2014. http://indianexpress.com/article/india/india-others/vhp-steps-up-campaign-against-love-jihad/#sthash.JpLPzo4G.dpuf.

influence the magnitude, spatial dimensions, timing, and long-term consequences of violence: the closer the ties between party, movement, and state,
the greater the extent of violence. I also explore the influence of caste and class
alignments in these regions on the likelihood of violence. Regions in which
the dominant classes and castes are more politically powerful than the lower
castes and classes are more susceptible to Hindu nationalist militancy and
violence.[31]

I chose states in which the extent of Hindu nationalist militancy and violence had varied but where the BJP was electorally strong. In all four, the BJP
came to power in the 1990 Legislative Assembly elections and has since occupied office at least twice and in one case, Gujarat, four times (see Figure I.3).
Of these states, two (UP and Gujarat) experienced extensive violence and two
(Rajasthan and HP) did not. But there are also differences in the extent of
Hindu nationalist militancy and violence within these states over time: UP
experienced more extensive violence than Rajasthan from 1990 to 1992; after
2002, the VHP fomented more violence in Rajasthan than in UP. HP never
experienced much violence and Gujarat experienced significant violence in the
early 1990s and (especially) in 2002.

Tables I.1 and I.2 identify the different implications of party, movement, and
state relations for the extent of violence. By party strength and cohesion I refer
either to the absence of factional divisions or to the BJP's ability to prevent
factional disputes from weakening the party. Movement strength refers to the
VHP's ability to mobilize mass support, from youth and upper-caste Hindus as
well as *dalits* and/or tribals.

A comparison between Tables I.1 and I.2 demonstrates the dynamic character of institutions and organizations and the implications of their varied
relationships for the extent of violence. For example, when UP experienced
extensive violence in the early 1990s, the BJP and the VHP were strong
and closely allied with each other and with the BJP state government. The
Congress-led national government permitted Hindu activists to organize in
Ayodhya. By contrast, in the early 2000s, the BJP was factionalized, the VHP
was weak, and relations between them were conflictual. Lacking the support of the state and national governments, Hindu nationalist violence was
minimal.

Among the four states, I devote the most attention to UP, which is often
seen as a microcosm of India because of its large size, population, demographic
diversity, and lack of distinctive regional identity. Many towns in UP experienced violence in the early 1990s as a result of the interplay of national,

---

[31] There are clearly other significant differences between these states, such as their levels of capitalist development, with Gujarat at one end of the continuum and UP at the other end. The BJP
may well be stronger in Gujarat than in UP because Gujarat has a larger, more influential middle
class. However, these economic differences cannot explain the timing of violence within UP and
other states.

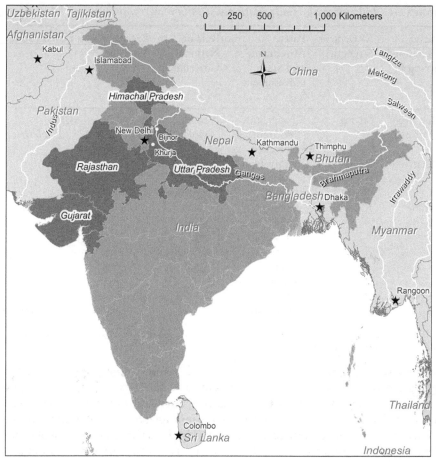

FIGURE I.3. Map of India Indicating Areas of Research.
Source: Map prepared by Andy Anderson, Amherst College, using data in the ESRI Data and Maps 2012 collection from the ArcWorld Supplement and DCW.

federal, and local forces. It was home to the major social movement that Hindu nationalists organized in Ayodhya. But nowhere did the BJP experience as precipitous a decline because of the growth of countervailing parties and movements as in UP.

Research Strategy and Methods

I studied Hindu nationalism over the course of a year (1990–1) and during shorter visits (1991–3) when the campaign around Ayodhya was under way and the BJP had attained power in several states. I pursued a two-pronged approach: one entailed studying the BJP's electoral appeals, performance,

TABLE I.I. *Influences on Hindu Nationalist Militancy, 1990–1992*

Party Cohesion/ Strength	Movement Strength	Party, Movement, and State Government Ties	Role of National Government	Extent of Violence	Federal States
Relatively strong	Strong	Strong. State encourages violence.	Permits violence	Extensive	*Uttar Pradesh*
Relatively strong	Relatively strong	Relatively strong	Permits some violence	Moderately extensive	*Gujarat*
Strong	Moderate	Strong party-state ties. State permits some violence.	Permits some and prevents some	Moderate	*Rajasthan*
Strong	Weak	Strong party-state ties.	NA	Slight	*Himachal Pradesh*

Source: Compiled by author.

strategies, and governance in four federal states.[32] The other entailed a fine-grained focus on the causes, character, and outcomes of violence in two towns, Bijnor and Khurja in UP. The relatively small size of these towns enabled me to undertake an in-depth analysis of the multiple, overlapping causes of the violence. I was able to appreciate the ways Hindu activists could provoke violence against Muslims because of prior patterns of residential segregation and class and caste inequalities. Religious exhortations exacerbated class animosities and political rivalries.[33]

The large majority of victims in all cases were Muslims and they seldom retaliated in kind. The Muslim victims described the events that preceded

[32] I interviewed BJP government officials and examined their actions around temple construction, religious conversion, and economic policies in New Delhi, the national capital, and Jaipur, Ahmedabad, Shimla, and Lucknow, the capitals of the four states I studied. I assessed relations among the BJP, RSS, and VHP by interviewing their leaders and rank-and-file members, attending their meetings and demonstrations, and observing interactions in their offices. I interviewed government officials, members of the Provincial Armed Constabulary, and police force.

[33] For other historical examples of this phenomenon, see Suranjan Das, "The 1992 Calcutta Riot in Historical Continuum: A Relapse into 'Communal Fury?'" *Modern Asian Studies*, 2000, Vol. 34, no. 2, 291–306, and Pramod Kumar, "Communal Riots in Mau Nath Bhanjan," in Wilkinson, ed., *Religious Politics and Communal Violence*.

TABLE I.2. *Influences on Hindu Nationalist Militancy, 2000–2002*

Party Cohesion/ Strength	Movement Strength	Party, Movement, and State Government Ties	Role of National Government	Extent of Violence	Federal States
Moderate	Moderate	Weak party-state ties. State deters violence.	Prohibits violence	Minimal	*Uttar Pradesh*
Strong	Strong	Strong. State organizes violence.	Permits large-scale violence	Extensive	*Gujarat*
Strong	Moderate	Weak party-movement ties	Prohibits violence	Moderate	*Rajasthan*
Strong	Weak	Weak party-movement ties	NA	Slight	*Himachal Pradesh*

Source: Compiled by author.

the violence and whether, when the violence occurred, their neighbors had protected or attacked them and the local administration had ignored or responded to their pleas for help. In subsequent interviews I asked for details about the roles of Hindu nationalist organizations and elected officials, prior relations between Hindus and Muslims, and other social movements in the region.

I extended my research on two occasions. The first was after the BJP-led NDA government assumed office in 1999. I wanted to learn how the BJP's strategy of attaining and maintaining power had altered its ideological commitments and relations with the RSS and VHP. I returned to the states that I had studied earlier, and interviewed party and state officials and movement activists to assess relations among members of Hindu nationalist organizations and the policies of federal and national governments. The second occasion was in response to the Gujarat violence in 2002. No place that I had studied in the early 1990s had experienced violence of this magnitude. In contrast to Khurja, at one end of the spectrum, where ninety-six people died in the violence that occurred in 1990–1, approximately 2,000 people were killed in Gujarat in 2002. My trips to Gujarat allowed me to study the BJP's role in precipitating violence when it secured control over the state government and powerful social movement organizations.

The Chapters that Follow

In Part I, Chapters 1–3 develop the central themes of this book. Chapter 1 examines the rise and partial decline of Hindu nationalism in relation to state policies and analyzes changing relations among Hindu nationalist organizations when the BJP has been in power nationally and in federal states.

Chapter 2 explores the character of party politics and the symbiosis and synergies between parties and movements. It seeks to explain the BJP's unusual success in creating a movement-party in which the party is organizationally strong
and activist in orientation and has strong ties to a social movement organization. Chapter 3 examines Hindu nationalist social movements and assesses the
varying success of two important campaigns, demanding temple construction
in Ayodhya and opposing globalization.

Part II explores Hindu nationalist militancy and violence. Chapter 4 provides a detailed account of violence in two towns in UP, Bijnor and Khurja,
in the early 1990s. Hindu nationalism emerged in part as a countermovement against a powerful farmers' movement and lower-caste movements
that enjoyed state support. The BJP was ideologically and organizationally cohesive and closely tied to the VHP. The movement that the BJP and
VHP jointly organized undermined the state and national governments and
brought the BJP to power in UP in 1991. Thus, when the movement was at
its height in the early 1990s, all the vectors converged: the VHP and BJP
were both independently strong, their relationship was mutually beneficial,
and a BJP government was in power in UP. The national Congress government, headed by Pamulaparti Venkata (PV) Narasimha Rao, allowed the
movement to grow and become violent.

My account of Bijnor and Khurja explores the ways a national campaign
ignited local violence. In both towns, Hindutva activists mobilized against
prominent Muslim political figures. Before actually precipitating violence, they
spread rumors and fears that made the violence they unleashed appear defensive
and retaliatory. Local officials ignored mounting tensions and delayed intervening to stop the violence. Neither of these "riots" was simply local. Activists'
propaganda replicated the VHP's national discourses about Muslim extremism and antinationalism. In these cases and countless others, their provocations coincided with significant events in the Ayodhya campaign. Conversely,
a decade later, the movements in Bijnor and Khurja were overtaken by new
forms of mobilization by minorities and the lower castes which had national
reverberations.

Chapter 5 examines Gujarat, where serious anti-minority violence occurred in 1968, 1992, and above all 2002. The magnitude and severity of
the violence in Gujarat was greater than in other states: larger numbers
of Muslims were killed, and they were killed in a more brutal fashion,
more Muslim women were raped and more Muslim property was looted
and destroyed. Human rights investigations have documented the roles of
state government officials, party members, and movement activists in precipitating the violence.[34] Gujarat in 2002 represented "the perfect storm,"

---

[34] See, for example, Kamal Mitra Chenoy et al., *Gujarat Carnage 2002: A Report to the Nation by
an Independent Fact Finding Mission* (Ahmedabad: Centre for the Study of Culture and Society,
2002); Smita Narula, *We Have No Orders to Save You: State Participation and Complicity in*

the convergence of the state, party, and movement. The BJP was in power nationally and in the state, under the leadership of the powerful Narendra Modi. The VHP and its affiliates were strong and closely allied with both the BJP and the state government. The national government did nothing to stop the violence.

Strong party-movement ties were in part the result of the RSS's painstaking work. The RSS intervened frequently in the BJP's affairs and selected its leaders because the Gujarat BJP was deeply factionalized. The RSS installed Narendra Modi at the helm of the state over more moderate leaders. Even prior to Modi's rise, the RSS had established strong ties to officials from small towns and villages up to the state capital. The VHP and its affiliates had engaged in religious conversions and social service activity with poor rural communities. The BJP state government was especially strong because it had governed Gujarat almost continuously since 1990, save for 1996–7, when Congress was in office. It has occupied power on its own, without coalition partners, since 1995. In contrast to UP, where the BJP's tenure in office was patchy, the BJP government in Gujarat steadily cultivated the support of bureaucrats. In contrast to UP, the upper castes defeated lower-caste movements demanding caste reservations. Of the four states, transnational influences were greatest in Gujarat.[35]

Part III examines intermittent violence in UP after 1993 (Chapter 6), HP (Chapter 7), and Rajasthan (Chapter 8). In UP, the strength of Hindu nationalist organizations and the violence they precipitated dramatically declined after the destruction of the mosque in Ayodhya. Hindu nationalists temporarily halted the growth of lower-caste parties and movements but were unable to compete with them in the long run. The BJP could only govern by forming temporary alliances with the Bahujan Samaj Party (BSP), which primarily represents *dalits*, and the Samajwadi Party (SP), which primarily represents OBCs. The growth of a multiparty system in UP facilitated Muslims' emergence as a political force. The politicization of caste identities generated tensions within the BJP between upper and lower caste leaders. The BJP was divided over its choice of strategy and periodically revived militancy and violence to expand its social base and placate militant movement activists. However, the BJP was unable to return to power.

Hindu nationalist violence has not been significant either in HP or in Rajasthan. The movement is relatively weak in HP and strong in Rajasthan, although in Rajasthan it has not received consistent support from the BJP state

Communal Violence in Gujarat (Asia Division: Human Rights Watch, April 2002); Concerned Citizens' Tribunal, "*Crime against Humanity: An Inquiry into the Carnage in Gujarat,*" (Gujarat: Concerned Citizens' Tribunal, Citizens for Justice and Peace, 2002).

[35] Hindu nationalists claimed that transnational "terrorists" had ignited a fire in a train returning from Ayodhya, killing fifty-nine mostly Hindu passengers. In the post-9/11 world, in which there was a great deal of suspicion of transnational Muslim "terrorism," this unsubstantiated allegation needed little justification.

government. Neither the Jan Sangh nor the BJP in HP relied on movement strategies to achieve power. Although the VHP organized activists to travel to Ayodhya in 1990 and again in 1992, HP did not figure prominently on the Ayodhya circuit as either an exporter or importer of Hindutva activists. The VHP has not targeted the Muslim population although it has periodically harassed and attacked Sikh and Christian groups for being antinational. Both the BJP and the RSS have adapted to political conditions in the state and promoted development. They differ from Congress mainly with respect to the caste and class groups they favor and support.

Hindu-Muslim violence has been greater in Rajasthan than in HP but less than in UP and Gujarat, judged by the number of people killed, the duration of the violence, and its geographic spread within the state. Hindu nationalism was far less militant from 1990 to 1998 than from 1998 to 2008. During the earlier phase, the party rose to power by disavowing ties to the movement, forming alliances with other political parties, and incorporating their dissidents. Although the BJP benefited from the Ayodhya campaign, the BJP state government curtailed movement influence over the party and the state. However, after 1998, the movement became the driving force behind the BJP's electoral success. Chief Minister Vasundhara Raje faced more pressure and made more concessions than her predecessor, Bhairon Singh Shekhawat, to the RSS and the VHP. Hindutva activists engaged in attacks on Muslims and Christians and disruptive activism within institutions. The party's concessions to the movement did not pay off. The BJP lost the 2008 elections because the party was factionalized; some of its high-ranking members, with RSS support, opposed the chief minister and her allies. The BJP government also faced opposition from movements organized by lower castes demanding reservations as well as from civil liberties groups opposing state policies.

A comparative analysis of four states reveals that the central explanation for differences in the extent and timing of Hindu nationalist violence and militancy centers on relationships among ideologically-driven parties, movements, and the state. The closer the relationship between the BJP, the social movement organized by the VHP, and the state government, the greater the violence, if a sympathetic government is in power at the national level. What enables Hindu nationalist organizations to achieve such coherence and force is their ability to capture the support of the upper castes without forfeiting that of the lower castes.

Caste divisions deterred large-scale violence in three of the four states. In UP, lower castes opposed upper-caste domination both within the party and within society at large. In HP, the lower castes were not organized and the upper castes supported both Congress and the BJP. In Rajasthan, the BJP confronted opposition from Jats, Gujjars, and Meenas. It was only in Gujarat that the upper and middle castes were strong and united behind the BJP and lower-caste movements were weak. Hindu nationalists have engaged in extensive anti-minority violence amid attempts to gain upper-caste support and subdue lower-caste activism. In both UP and Gujarat, the BJP grew by mobilizing the upper castes and segments of other castes into movements opposing state-mandated reservations. However in UP, the BJP could not withstand the growing political influence of the lower castes whereas in Gujarat it maintained power because lower-caste movements were suppressed in the 1980s.[36]

The Conclusion discusses the conditions associated with anti-minority violence in India's multiethnic, federal democracy. It analyzes the forces that have inhibited such violence at the national level and explores the sources of democratic stability. It reflects on the sources and significance of the BJP's election to power in 2014. It explores the comparative implications of this study for understanding the interconnections among movements and among parties, movements, and states in other settings.

My study calls for greater scholarly attention to conjunctural violence in federal, multiethnic democracies. While it is important to differentiate between stable democracies and chronically unstable violence-prone nations, it is equally important to recognize the extent of anti-minority violence in well-established democracies. Doing so necessitates re-theorizing political institutions, associations, and organizations. The multilevel nature of state power in federal polities can create partisan convergence across levels of government and thereby possibilities for violence at lower levels of the state without jeopardizing national stability. Anti-minority violence is often a combination of "top down" and "bottom up" because it results from the synergies between parties, movements, and states.

We should also re-theorize the character of political parties, social movements, and civil society, and devote more attention to party structure and ideology as well as to parties' capacities to shape identities, especially when they ally with social movements. Movements and parties in multiethnic federal democracies have given voice to minorities and the dispossessed as well as to dominant groups. They have both precipitated and curtailed violence. Their combined actions tell us less about the direction of change than about the power associated with their coalescence.

---

[36] The ideological orientation of the BJP in different states is influenced by the proclivities of its leadership. The most striking difference is between the relatively moderate Bhairon Singh Shekhawat, former chief minister of Rajasthan, and the ideologically committed Narendra Modi, former chief minister of Gujarat. However, many chief ministers cannot be so easily categorized. Former UP Chief Minister Kalyan Singh combined appeals to Hindutva and to OBCs. Rajasthan Chief Minister Vasundhara Raje made far-reaching concessions to Hindutva militants and thereby encouraged their growing influence, despite her personal predilections. Former HP Chief Minister Shanta Kumar supported the Ayodhya movement while he was in office but later criticized the BJP's actions in Gujarat. Thus leaders' proclivities do not systematically explain the extent of Hindu nationalist militancy and violence. However, factional tensions – both ideological and caste related – have at times undermined the party's strength and the relations between BJP chief ministers and the national RSS and BJP leadership.

PART I

THE PILLARS OF HINDU NATIONALISM

I

The State

Dialectics of States, Parties, and Movements

Social movements' appeals, demands, and objectives reveal the state's authoritative power. Even when movements oppose, reject, or claim indifference to the state, they seek access to state resources and allies in the courts and bureaucracy. Craig Jenkins and Bert Klandermans aptly suggest:

As the institutionalized center for the legitimate monopoly on the means of violence, the state is the ultimate arbiter for the allocation of socially valued goods. ... The state is simultaneously target, sponsor and antagonist for social movements as well as the organizer of the political system and the arbiter of victory.[1]

"Collective identities are not simply given but must be validated and recognized," argue Doug McAdam, Sidney Tarrow, and Charles Tilly, and "states are the most symbolically powerful agencies for conferring recognition."[2] The Indian Constitution defines identities and prescribes how they should be treated. Its affirmation of federal principles and cultural pluralism has inspired ethnic minority struggles for the devolution of power and the creation of linguistic states. Its provision of reserved quotas, a form of compensatory discrimination, has encouraged the emergence of low-caste movements and parties.[3] By identifying Muslims as a religious rather than a socioeconomic community, the Constitution has encouraged Muslims to organize around cultural and religious issues rather than for economic and political advancement.[4]

[1] J. Craig Jenkins and Bert Klandermans, eds., *The Politics of Social Protest, Comparative Perspectives on States and Social Movements* (Minneapolis, MN: Taylor and Francis, 1995), 3.
[2] Doug McAdam, Sidney Tarrow, and Charles Tilly, *Dynamics of Contention* (Cambridge, UK: Cambridge University Press, 2001), 27.
[3] *Dalit* political parties were directly inspired by constitutionally mandated reservations. Bhimarao Ambedkar founded the Independent Labor Party (1936), which was succeeded by the All India Scheduled Castes Federation (1947) and the Bharatiya Republican Party, which Ambedkar's grandson Prakash Ambedkar founded.
[4] Zoya Hasan, *Politics of Inclusion: Castes, Minorities and Affirmative Action* (New Delhi: Oxford University Press, 2011).

The state sets an agenda to which opposition parties and movements respond. Accordingly, changes in the structure and policies of the postindependence Indian state are associated with changing modes of protest. Raka Ray and Mary Katzenstein argue that state policies during three distinct periods – the social democratic (1947–66), populist (1967–88), and religious nationalist and market-oriented (1989 to the present) – influenced the character of political opposition.[5] During the last period, religious nationalist movements were much stronger under the NDA than under United Progressive Alliance (UPA) governments.

This chapter explores the reciprocal influences of social movements and political parties on the state and of state policies on movements and parties. Its focus is on a few significant dimensions of state influence. The first is the (1.) extent to which the state shapes, heightens, and mobilizes identities. The more the state acknowledges and appeals to identity groups, the more it strengthens identity-based movements and parties. Second, state factionalism encourages (2.) the emergence of social movements. During the era of single-party dominance, social movements were most likely to emerge when the ruling party and the ✕ state were factionalized.

(3.)   Third, movements contesting state policies emerge when there are tensions and contradictions between the state's promises and its actions: between secular tenets and concessions to religious groups, socialist ideals and concessions to market forces, and commitments to transparency amid official corruption. Religious nationalist, anticapitalist, and anticorruption movements have followed. The state has provoked feminist and lower-caste struggles when it has been indecisive about whether to implement reservations for women and Other Backward Classes (OBCs). Women's movements, which were historically ambivalent about legislative reservations for women, have increasingly supported them. The government appointed commissions to explore reservations for OBCs and then stalled on implementing their recommendations and determining which groups to designate as OBCs. As a result, movements and parties have demanded that certain groups should be classified or declassified as OBCs and have mobilized potentially eligible groups to demand caste quotas.

Once parties and movements present the state with identity-based demands, there is considerable variation in whether and how the state has responded. State governments are more likely than the national government to make concessions. Most national governments have either ignored or only partially conceded to social movements' demands. When they have engaged in repression, social movements have grown and sometimes become more militant and violent.

Social movements also differ with respect to how they respond to state concessions. Movements that have demanded the creation of new federal states and greater lower-caste political representation have generally subsided in

5 Raka Ray and Mary Fainsod Katzenstein, eds., *Social Movements in India: Poverty, Power and Politics* (Lanham, MD: Rowman and Littlefield Publishers, 2005), 3.

response to state concessions. By contrast, when both Congress and BJP-led governments made some concessions to the VHP around the Ayodhya dispute, its demands escalated. The VHP was arguably less committed to constructing a temple in Ayodhya than to destabilizing the government and mobilizing potential supporters.[6] Thus the impact of state concessions on Hindu nationalist and other social movements has differed.

The first part of this chapter explores the impact of state policies on the strength and character of the BJP and its predecessor, the Jan Sangh, during five different phases. I argue that Hindu nationalism grew historically during periods when the state directly appealed to community identities. During these times, the Jan Sangh and BJP were most successful when they pursued a dual strategy of forging alliances with ideologically dissimilar parties while sustaining a commitment to Hindu nationalist goals.

The BJP's strategy changed when it attained national power. It partially curtailed its radical Hindu nationalist stance in response to pressures from the electorate and coalition partners. Its de-radicalization provoked opposition from ideologically committed RSS and VHP members, who contributed to the BJP's electoral defeat in 2004. As part of the opposition, from 2004 to 2014, the BJP shifted its attention away from Ayodhya to join anti-Congress movements against corruption. It also engaged in noisy, boisterous, sometimes violent protest on the floor of Parliament.

The second part of the chapter examines the policies that BJP state governments have pursued. As a general matter, BJP state governments, especially when they govern independently, have demonstrated much greater commitment than BJP-led national governments to Hindutva.[7] The state is less autonomous from civil society groups, such as the VHP, nationally than at the state level. Conversely, the VHP and its affiliates, like most other social movement organizations, is stronger federally than nationally. Although BJP state governments have generally not engaged in anti-minority violence directly, they have made violence likely by harassing and discriminating against minorities. They have also demonstrated partisanship in dealing with the culprits and victims of violence.

Parties, Movements, and the State through Time

When the national state has maintained autonomy from civil society groups and prioritized economic issues, identity movements have been relatively weak. The more explicitly the state makes identities (based on religion, caste, and ethnicity) the basis of privilege or privation, the more it encourages the growth of identity

---

[6] Amrita Basu, "Reflections on Community Conflicts and the State in India," *Journal of Asian Studies,* 56 no. 2, (May 1997): 391–7.

[7] VD Sarvarkar, *Hindutva, Who is a Hindu?* Accessed November 24, 2014. https://archive.org /details/hindutva-vinayak-damodar-savarkar-pdf.

movements and parties. Jawaharlal Nehru emphasized economic inequalities and refrained from mobilizing civil society groups. When Indira Gandhi first came to office, she too highlighted economic inequalities but, unlike her father, directly mobilized the poor. Later, the Congress government under Indira Gandhi, and to some extent Rajiv Gandhi, encouraged the growth of Hindu nationalism by mobilizing Hindu electoral support. The National Front government, under VP Singh's leadership, prompted counter-mobilization by the BJP when it introduced reservations for OBCs. In all of these cases but the first, the state provoked or strengthened social movements by sharpening group identities and mobilizing groups in defense of entitlements.

Phase I: The Nehruvian Era (1947–1967)
In the aftermath of independence, social movements were weak (with one exception explored later in this chapter), in part because the state was relatively autonomous from civil society, the Congress Party was unified, and relations between the ruling party and state were strong. The Nehruvian state upheld social democratic principles, and groups that challenged this consensus were ineffectual and unpopular. Dissidents could hope to achieve greater change by influencing the Congress Party from within rather than by organizing against it from without.

There was little resistance in the 1950s to the kinds of state policies that social movements opposed two decades later. The government constructed several big dams, including the Bhakra Nangal in Punjab, Tungabhadra on the Andhra Pradesh-Karnataka border, and Rihand in UP. It promoted large-scale, capital-intensive industries that favored urban over rural areas and fostered uneven regional development.[8] However, federal states did not allege that the central government was discriminating against them. Nor did protest movements emerge among the thousands of people whom big dams displaced, fishing communities whose fish stocks and jobs mechanized trawlers destroyed, and forest dwellers whose work and subsistence deforestation threatened. Although peasants demanded higher prices for their crops, they did not organize movements challenging the preferential terms of trade for urban over rural areas. The limited success of Congress land reforms did not provoke struggles for land among tenant farmers and landless agricultural laborers. Even the Communist Party simply questioned the pace of Congress land redistribution but did not propose a more radical land reform program. The government's decision to forego passage of a uniform civil code as a concession to conservative religious groups did not generate feminist activism in support of secular laws. Although the Congress government, especially in UP, made some concessions to Hindu nationalists, the strength, autonomy, and broad secular commitments of the postindependence state deterred popular protest.

[8] Madhav Gadgil and Ramachandra Guha, *Ecology and Equity: The Use and Abuse of Nature in Contemporary India* (Abingdon, UK: Oxford University Press, 1995), 71.

The one important exception to this pattern was violent protest demanding the reorganization of states along linguistic lines. In 1952, Telugu speakers in Madras Presidency demanded the creation of Andhra Pradesh. Four years later, the Samyukta Maharashtra Samiti (United Maharashtra Committee) organized massive agitations for the creation of a Marathi-speaking state. These movements challenged the contradictions between the Congress government's proclaimed commitment to pluralism, minority rights, and federal principles, and its construction of a centralized, unitary state. Furthermore, although Congress had promised to create states on a linguistic basis in the 1920s, Nehru retracted this promise after independence for fear of precipitating a second partition of the country, distrust of what he considered parochial identities, and a belief that a centralized state could best pursue public-sector-led industrialization.[9] Nehru ultimately acceded to pressures to reorganize state boundaries on linguistic lines and linguistic movements in south India declined.[10]

The postindependence national Congress government was unyielding, however, with respect to Hindu nationalism. It sponsored an act that forbade parties from using religious symbols in elections. In 1952, the Nehruvian government circulated a memo instructing Congress members to disassociate themselves from RSS campaigns demanding a national ban on cow slaughter and blocked a constitutional national ban. The Jan Sangh was unsuccessful in obtaining such a ban in 1952, 1954, and 1964. It performed poorly in the first three general elections: its share of the vote was 3.1 percent in 1952, 5.9 percent in 1957, and 6.4 percent in 1962, partly because it opposed Nehruvian ideals.[11]

The Jan Sangh's few attempts at mass mobilization in the 1950s failed. It demanded full integration of Kashmir into India (1953), protested the division of Punjab along linguistic lines (1955–7), and opposed the official recognition of Urdu in UP (1954–61). The Jan Sangh also organized violent protests against Portugal's continued colonization of Goa. The Indian government ignored the Jan Sangh's demand for police action against the Portuguese and sealed the Goa border.

[9] Paul Brass, *Language, Religion, and Politics in North India* (New York: Cambridge University Press, 1974).

[10] Atul Kohli, "Can Democracies Accommodate Ethnic Nationalism? The Rise and Decline of Ethnic Self Determination Movements," in Amrita Basu and Atul Kohli, eds., *Community Conflicts and the State in India* (New Delhi: Oxford University Press, 1998).

[11] Election data for 1952, 1957, 1962 is from Motilal A. Jhangiani, *Jana Sangh and Swatantra: A Profile of the Rightist Parties in India* (Bombay: Manaktalas, 1967), 136. The Jan Sangh supported Hindi as the national language and took a strong stand against the special constitutional status the Congress government granted to Kashmir. Its 1954 manifesto declared that "for maintaining the unity and integrity of the country, Jan Sangh considers a Unitary form of government more appropriate than the Federal one." It argued that federalism would undermine the concept of the nation as "One Country, One People and One Culture." Bharatiya Jana Sangh, Party Documents, 1951–72, Vol. 1, *Principles and Policies, Manifestos and Constitution* (New Delhi: Navchetan Press, 1973), 9.

Phase II: The Decline of the Nehruvian Consensus (1966–1989)
The second phase, which began after Nehru's daughter, Indira Gandhi, became prime minister in 1966, witnessed dramatic changes in the character of the state, parties, and movements. Divisions within the Congress Party grew and dissidents formed alliances with opposition parties and movements to defeat Congress in several federal states. They organized *bandhs, gheraos,* and demonstrations, among other places in Bihar and UP, to protest government corruption and food shortages.

The Jan Sangh came to appreciate the potential power of social movements. Its president, Deendayal Upadhyaya, stated in 1967: "In the changing situation at present, public agitations are natural and even essential. In fact, they are the medium of expression of social awakening."[12] Amid the weakening of state authority as a result of factionalization of the Congress Party and subaltern social movements, Hindu nationalists organized their first major social movement around banning cow slaughter. In 1966, the RSS created a social movement organization, the Sarvadaliya Goraksha Maha-Abhiyan Samiti, or the All Party Cow Protection Campaign Committee, which organized numerous agitations around the country, including an attack on Parliament on November 7, 1966, followed by a hunger strike, which resulted in eight deaths. Prime Minister Indira Gandhi ordered arrests of 1,400 RSS members and fired officials, including Home Minister Gulzarilal Nanda, whom she suspected were implicated.[13]

The Jan Sangh denied that it had supported the agitation, although its senior leaders Atal Bihari Vajpayee and Balraj Madhok attended the procession and Kedar Nath Sahini, the Delhi general secretary, organized the demonstration. Jan Sangh members undertook fasts to protest the arrests, and Vajpayee defended Swami Rameshwaran, one of the principal organizers. The Jan Sangh then engaged in negotiations with the government. Party-movement collaboration, the party's denial of its links to the movement, and the party's attempt to influence the state, all anticipated the Ayodhya movement scenario. The Jan Sangh's social movement activity contributed to its improved performance in the 1967 parliamentary elections. It received 9.3 percent of the vote and 35 of 520 seats.[14]

A reorientation of the Jan Sangh followed the state's adopting a pro-poor orientation. Prime Minister Indira Gandhi promised to nationalize banks and

[12] Deendayal Upadhyaya, "Presidential Speech at Calicut" (speech, Kerala, December 1967). A Complete Deen Dayal Reader. Accessed July 14, 2015. http://deendayalupadhyay.org /leacture8.html.

[13] Christophe Jaffrelot, *The Hindu Nationalist Movement and Indian Politics: 1925 to the 1990s* (London: Hurst & Co., 1996), 206–9.

[14] See Election Commission of India. *Statistical Report on General Elections 1967 to the Fourth Lok Sabha.* ECI-GE67-LS (Vol. I). New Delhi: Election Commission of India, 1968. Accessed July 7, 2014. http://eci.nic.in/eci_main/StatisticalReports/LS_1967/Vol_I_LS_67.pdf.

Election Commission of India. *Statistical Report on General Elections 1962 to the Third Lok Sabha.* ECI-ECI-GE62-LS (Vol. I). New Delhi: Elections Commission of India, 1962. Accessed July 7, 2014. http://eci.nic.in/eci_main/StatisticalReports/LS_1962/Vol_I_LS_62.pdf.

insurance companies, abolish princely privileges, limit urban property hold-ings, redistribute land, and create jobs. She threatened to ban the RSS and proscribe *shakhas* (daily gatherings of RSS members) in Delhi. Echoing the state's leftist appeals, the Jan Sangh vowed to win the war on poverty, imple-ment land reform laws, secure tenure for tenant farmers, and reduce credit costs for cultivators. Its 1971 manifesto stated:

The development of the Indian economy is a vast enterprise which only the reawakened mass of the Indian people can execute with success. It is a task beyond a handful of moneybags, or petty ministers doling out a license here or a permit there. Indian econ-omy is not a baby of big business or of bad government; it is the job of the Indian peo-ple. It can come into its own only with the tremendous release of national energies.[15]

However, the Jan Sangh could not compete with the state's appeals to the poor and won only twenty-two seats and 7.4 percent of the vote in the 1971 elec-tions. It lost its majority in the Delhi municipal council elections and experi-enced setbacks in state assembly elections in Punjab, Rajasthan, and Madhya Pradesh.[16] The Jan Sangh intensified its attempt to dispel its pro-rich image by advocating a land ceiling policy and building new bases among landless laborers, lower castes, industrial workers, and students. Vajpayee encouraged people to violate laws that kept basic commodities scarce and supported those who looted government fair price shops to feed their families.[17] He shelved the demand for cow protection, a key plank in 1967. Lal Krishna (LK) Advani pursued the same orientation after becoming Jan Sangh president in 1974.

Indira Gandhi's leftist rhetoric also encouraged social movements among disadvantaged groups. Urban feminist organizations addressed domestic vio-lence, "dowry deaths," and the rape of women by the police and security forces. Environmental movements opposed the displacement of people and ecologi-cal destruction associated with the commercialization of agriculture. *Dalits* challenged caste exploitation. The urban poor organized movements to defend the rights of pavement dwellers, vendors, and rickshaw pullers. Peasants par-ticipated in movements around inequitable terms of trade between urban and rural areas. Gandhian leader Sunderlal Bahuguna led the Chipko movement against deforestation and a movement opposing the construction of the Tehri Dam in northern UP. Ambersingh Suratvanti, a former Sarvodaya member, formed the Shramik Sangathana (Workers' Organization) to mobilize Bhil tribals in Dhule district of Maharashtra against landlessness, low wages, and landlord exploitation. The Kerala Sasthra Sahitya Parishad, or Kerala Science

See Election Commission of India. *Statistical Report on General Elections 1957 to the Second Lok Sabha.* ECI-GE57-LS (Vol. I). New Delhi: Election Commission of India, 1957. Accessed July 7, 2014. http://eci.nic.in/eci_main/StatisticalReports/LS_1967/Vol_I_LS_67.pdf.

[15] Bharatiya Jan Sangh, *Party Documents 1951–1972*, Vol. 1 (New Delhi: Bharatiya Jan Sangh, 1973), 175.

[16] Bruce Graham, "The Jana Sangh and Bloc Politics, 1967–80," *Journal of Commonwealth and Comparative Politics*, 25, no. 3 (November 1987), 253.

[17] Ibid., 186.

Literature Movement, mobilized against the Silent Valley hydroelectric project in Kerala. Medha Patkar led the largest and most sustained of these movements, the Narmada Bachao Andolan (Save the Narmada Movement), opposing the construction of the Sardar Sarovar dam.

Indira Gandhi's increasing centralization of power and decision to declare a state of emergency (1975–7), which entailed banning political parties and abrogating civil rights and liberties, ushered in a new phase in party-movement relations. Gandhian socialist leader Jayaprakash (JP) Narayan organized the first national social movement in the postindependence period, for "peaceful, total revolution." He founded an ideologically heterogeneous national coalition of social movements, the Janata Morcha (People's Front), to oppose the Congress government.

The "JP movement" brought the Jan Sangh into the political mainstream. The RSS-affiliated student organization, the Akhil Bharatiya Vidyarthi Parishad (ABVP), or All India Student Council, participated in agitations against rising prices and food scarcity in Gujarat and Bihar. JP Narayan publicly praised the RSS and its "family" for opposing economic inequality and corruption. LK Advani claimed that JP Narayan did more than any other person to strengthen the Jan Sangh.[18]

Congress returned to power and unwittingly encouraged the growth of three very different social movements in the 1980s. Its repressive response to the growth of ethnic self-determination movements gave rise to political extremism and separatism in Punjab, Assam, and Kashmir. Its increased commitment to economic liberalization and its emphasis on urban, industrial growth threatened agrarian groups while its support for the green revolution emboldened rural cultivators; both policies resulted in a farmers' movement. Its appeals to the Hindu majority encouraged the growth of Hindu nationalist social movements.

Congress emerged as the champion of the majority community in the early 1980s. Indira Gandhi began appealing to Hindus as her support among the poor and lower castes declined during her second term as prime minister (1980–4). She developed close ties to the RSS and participated in some VHP campaigns. Congress soundly defeated the BJP in the 1983 Legislative Assembly elections in Jammu and Kashmir.[19] In the 1984 general election, Congress captured the Hindu vote and the BJP won only two seats in Parliament and 7.7 percent of the national vote.

After becoming prime minister in 1984, Rajiv Gandhi continued to heighten and politicize Muslim and Hindu identities. To gain support among conservative Muslim groups, he opposed a Supreme Court decision in the Shah Bano

---

[18] LK Advani, *The People Betrayed* (New Delhi: Vision Books, 1979), 75–6.
[19] Partha Sarathy Ghosh, *BJP and the Evolution of Hindu Nationalism: From Periphery to Centre* (New Delhi: Manohar Publishers & Distributors, 1999), 87.

case in 1986. He pushed through the misleadingly titled Muslim Women's (Protection of Rights in) Divorce Act, which denied Muslim women the right to maintenance from their husbands beyond a three-month period. To regain Hindu support, Congress allowed the VHP to organize the *shilanyas,* a ceremony to lay the foundation for a temple in Ayodhya. Rajiv Gandhi subsequently launched his 1989 election campaign from the town of Faizabad, adjacent to Ayodhya, and promised to create Ram Rajya (Rule of the Lord Ram). Congress used Ram as a symbol throughout its election campaign and many local Congress activists supported the VHP's demand for a temple at Ayodhya.[20]

To summarize, whereas the Nehruvian state's strength, focus on poverty, and autonomy from civil society groups deterred political opposition, Indira Gandhi's insecure control over the state, political partisanship, and recourse to identity issues provoked extensive protest. As she feared losing control over the state, she sought support within civil society, first among the poor, and later among Hindus. The changing ideological and policy orientations of the state, rifts within the ruling party, state repression to quell dissent, and the state's direct mobilization of identity groups all brought about the growth of varied and diverse social movements, some with strong ties to parties.

Whereas most social movements in the 1970s were locally based and thus ill-equipped to work with state parties, the farmers' organizations that emerged a decade later, including the Shetkari Sanghathana (Farmers' Organization) in Maharashtra, Karnataka Rajya Rayot Sangha (State Farmers' Association), Bharatiya Kisan (Indian Farmers') Union in UP, and Khedut Samaj (Farmers' Association) in Gujarat, all organized on a statewide basis. The VHP also became increasingly active in larger areas of several north Indian states.

Phase III: Coalition Governments (1989–1999)

The BJP's national ascent began with the 1989 parliamentary elections. It won eighty-five seats and 11.4 percent of the vote, compared to only two seats and 7.7 percent of the vote in 1984. The BJP was determined to maintain its movement connections and commitments and first the National Front and then the Congress governments allowed it to do so. Because the Janata Dal needed the BJP's backing to form the National Front government, it retracted its demand that the BJP renounce contentious positions and unconditionally accepted its support.

The BJP decided at its national executive committee meeting at Palampur (June 9–11, 1989) to maintain ties to the VHP-led movement in Ayodhya. Its formal resolution stated: "The sentiments of the people must be respected and

[20] Ibid., 93.

the *Ram Janmasthan* (birth place of Ram) handed over to the Hindus."[21] It also took a hard line on Kashmir, pushing the government to crack down on militants and reject Kashmiri demands for greater autonomy.

The VHP and BJP organized the Ayodhya campaign immediately after VP Singh announced that he would implement the Mandal Commission recommendations and reserve 27 percent of posts in the central government for OBCs. On September 5, 1990, Giriraj Kishore, senior vice president of the VHP, warned that the BJP would withdraw support from the government if it opposed temple construction.[22] A week later, Advani announced his decision to take a *rath yatra* (chariot procession) to Ayodhya. VP Singh did not stop him for fear of precipitating the government's downfall. The Bihar state government arrested Advani on October 23; the BJP called for a no-confidence motion that led to the government's collapse.

Both Hindu nationalists' destruction of the mosque in Ayodhya, the high point of the campaign, and its subsequent decline and retreat from militancy, are linked to changing policies of the ruling Congress Party. The BJP's performance significantly improved in the 1991 general elections as a result of the campaign.[23] Hindu nationalists were able to destroy the *babri masjid* in December 1992 because the national Congress government allowed a Hindu nationalist procession to reach Ayodhya. Thereafter, Prime Minister PV Narasimha Rao ordered the arrest of Hindu nationalist leaders, dismissed BJP state governments, and banned the VHP for two years. This reassertion of the national government's authority broke the movement's momentum.

The BJP took heed. At its national council meeting in Bangalore in June 1993, it depicted itself as a responsible political party, affirmed its support for secularism, downplayed building a temple in Ayodhya, and pledged to end corruption and pursue economic liberalization. Two years later, at the Goa conclave, the BJP sought to dispel its anti-Muslim image. Party president LK Advani asked party members to rid Muslims of their "misapprehensions of the BJP." When asked why the BJP had ceased to campaign around the temple, LK Advani responded, "There is less intensity of feeling around the issue now that the structure has been removed."[24] Along the same lines, Uma Bharati commented that the campaign had achieved its desired impact.[25]

[21] The Bharatiya Janata Party, "National Executive Meeting, June 9–11, Palampur, Himachal Pradesh," 14.

[22] "Why BJP Withdrew Support from Shri VP Singh Government, Speech Delivered by Shri LK Advani MP in Parliament on November 7, 1990" (published by the BJP Central Office, New Delhi, 1990).

[23] Compared to the previous elections, the BJP's share of the vote increased from 11 percent to 21 percent and its parliamentary seats from 85 to 119. The BJP was especially successful in UP, where its share of the vote increased from 7.6 percent (eight seats) in 1989 to 35.3 percent (fifty seats) and Gujarat, where its votes and seats climbed from 30 percent (twelve seats) to 52 percent (twenty seats).

[24] Interview with LK Advani, New Delhi, June 27, 1995.

[25] Interview with Uma Bharati, New Delhi, December 17, 1991.

The November 1993 state assembly election results were a public referendum on the BJP's militant social movement activities. Significantly, the BJP's electoral losses were greatest in Madhya Pradesh, followed by UP, where its posture was most militant and violence was extensive. By contrast, the BJP retained power in Rajasthan, where it benefited from the moderate leadership of Chief Minister Bhairon Singh Shekawat. In the 1994 and 1995 assembly elections, the BJP was only elected in two states, as a result of popular discontent with incumbent Janata Dal governments.

From 1996 to 1998, the BJP tried and failed to create stable national governments.[26] Over the next two years, it sought to project itself both as a movement and as a governing party.[27] For example, in an essay entitled "The Sangh is my Soul," that the BJP posted on a Web site created for the 1998 election campaign, Vajpayee lauded the regeneration of Hindu India as a result of the demolition of the mosque and argued that "this was the prime test of the RSS. Earlier Hindus used to bend before an invasion. Not now, this change in Hindu society is worthy of welcome."[28] Its 1998 election manifesto promised to build temples in Ayodhya, Kashi, and Mathura; abrogate Article 370, which provided special status to Kashmir; introduce a uniform civil code; abolish the Minority Commission; ban cow slaughter and beef export; and prevent what it described as the infiltration of foreign nationals. However, it distanced itself from movement politics by claiming that it would seek "consensual, legal, constitutional means to facilitate the construction of the Ram Mandir." It sought to attract Muslim voters by promising to address their socioeconomic conditions. Just prior to its electoral victory in March 1998, the NDA published a national agenda that dropped the issues of the temple, the uniform civil code, and Article 370, and focused instead on nuclear policy, foreign investments, and a review of the Constitution. The BJP captured 182 seats (25.6 percent of the vote) in the 1998 general elections, stitched together alliances with regional parties, and formed a government that lasted a year but narrowly

---

[26] It gained a plurality of parliamentary seats (29.6 percent) but won only 20.3 percent of the popular vote in the 1996 general elections. Exit polls showed that although it succeeded in fracturing the OBC vote, only 11 percent of Scheduled Castes voted for the BJP compared to 31 percent for Congress, 21 percent for the National Front, and 16 percent for the Bahujan Samaj Party (BSP). The remaining 14 percent supported state parties and 7 percent supported other parties. "How India Voted," *India Today*, May 11, 1996, 50.

[27] As the BJP sought to demonstrate its secular commitments, its *yatras* (processions or pilgrimages) failed to generate the passions and antagonisms they had in the past. For example, Advani led a *suraj yatra* (justice pilgrimage) that began in Kerala on March 9, 1996, and ended in UP thirty-five days later, and a *swarna jayanti yath ratra* (celebration of Indian independence procession) that covered 15,000 kilometers and twenty-two states from May 18 to July 15, 1997. The procession foundered on its lack of clear objectives. While Uma Bharati participated in the *rath yatra* and shouted slogans like "Garv Seh Kaho Hum Hindu Hen" ("Say with pride, I am a Hindu"), Advani sought unsuccessfully to link the dangers of corruption, zero development, and political instability with the need for Hindu unity.

[28] "The Sangh Is My Soul" was first published in *Organiser* in 1995.

lost a confidence vote after the All India Anna Dravida Munnetra Kazhagam (AIADMK) withdrew support.[29]

By the 1999 general elections, the BJP was increasingly committed to depicting itself as a moderate, centrist party. The BJP-led NDA briefly took office (March–April 1999) followed by a full term (October 1999–January 2004) with a stable majority and thirteen coalition members.[30] Vajpayee placed a moratorium on the contentious issues that the BJP had supported earlier.[31]

Phase IV: The NDA Government (1999–2004)

Once the BJP attained power, it was caught between placating its coalition partners, who urged moderation, and the RSS and VHP, who favored militancy. The BJP was haunted by opposition parties' claim that the RSS had run its previous short-lived government by "remote control."[32] It had experienced electoral reversals and the removal of its state governments following the destruction of the mosque in 1992 and did not want to risk reprisals around temple construction. It sought to placate the VHP by appointing its leaders to political office and revising income tax laws to regularize the VHP's status as a charitable organization so that it could receive overseas contributions. However, it did not concede to the VHP's building a temple in Ayodhya. The VHP, with tacit RSS support, increasingly challenged the NDA government.

With respect to foreign and domestic policies, the BJP rejected the RSS' opposition to economic liberalization and support for the *swadeshi* paradigm. In the sphere of foreign policy, the RSS pressured the NDA government to assume a more belligerent posture toward Pakistan. The BJP sought to find a middle ground between an ideologically-driven and a pragmatic approach. Vajpayee

[29] It received 31 percent of the vote and seventy-two seats in eastern and southern states in 1998 in comparison to 9 percent and seven seats in 1996, almost matching Congress' percentage in these regions. Although the BJP still relied heavily on upper-caste votes, its support among OBCs increased dramatically. Forty-two percent of OBCs voted for the BJP, making the BJP the largest recipient of OBC votes of any political party. "Post Poll: Who Voted for Whom?" *India Today*, March 16, 1998, 33–4.

[30] In 1998, BJP partners in the NDA, included the Shiv Sena, Akali Dal, Haryana Vikas Party, Samata Party, BSP, NTR Telugu Desam Party (TDP), Lok Shakti, AIADMK, Biju Janata Dal, and Trinamool Congress. In 1999, NDA partners included the TDP, Dravida Munnetra Kazhagam (DMK), Janata Dal United, Rashtriya Lok Dal, National Conference, Lok Jan Shakti, Samata Party, Akali Dal, and Trinamool Congress.

[31] The BJP tried to capture *dalit* support by opposing the 1992 Supreme Court ruling that limited reservations for Scheduled Castes and Tribes to recruitment but not promotion. In September 1995, the BJP organized a *dalit* convention in Kanpur and promised low cost tenements for slum dwellers, one-rupee meals, and 10 percent reservations for economically backward sections in education and employment.

[32] "Vajpayee Denies Being Remote Controlled by RSS," *Rediff News*, May 4, 1998. Accessed June 24, 2014. http://m.rediff.com/news/1998/may/04vaj1.htm.

appealed to Hindu nationalist sentiment around nuclear testing, relations with Pakistan, and disputes over Kashmir. With strong support from the RSS and some opposition from NDA members, the BJP government tested five nuclear bombs on May 11 and 13, 1998. However, the NDA then bowed to international pressures and sanctions by declaring a moratorium on further nuclear testing and stringent controls on the export of nuclear and missile technology. It also sought to improve relations with Pakistan through a series of diplomatic negotiations in 1998, 1999, and 2001.

The BJP-led government yielded more to RSS pressures on social and cultural than on economic policies. It proposed a constitutional amendment, which coalition members blocked, banning the export of cows and sale of beef and making killing or injuring cows a cognizable, non-bailable offense. It introduced federal legislation that would prevent people from converting out of Hinduism.

The BJP followed the movement's lead on Muslim immigrants. It identified Bangladeshi Hindu migrants as "refugees" who deserved Indian citizenship because they were fleeing religious persecution and Muslim migrants as "infiltrators" who constituted a security risk. VHP international president Praveen Togadia claimed: "The infiltrators have damaged the economy of the nation and it is time that they should be beaten and chased out of the country."[33] The VHP and the ABVP organized campaigns in Assam, Bihar, West Bengal, and Delhi, demanding that Muslim immigrants who arrived after 1951 should be removed from voter registration lists and deported to Bangladesh. The Home Ministry released a plan to issue identity cards, with priority to areas bordering Bangladesh. It ordered the construction of a fence on the border between Bangladesh and India.[34] Thirteen states agreed to implement the plan but Bihar refused to do so.[35]

In compliance with the RSS, despite criticisms from three NDA coalition members, (the Dravida Munnetra Kazhagam (DMK), TDP, and Trinamool Congress), the BJP overhauled educational policies and institutions. Minister of Human Resource Development Murli Manohar (MM) Joshi sought to "Indianize, nationalize and spiritualize Indian education." He recommended incorporating Vedas and Upanishads into the curriculum, requiring Sanskrit for third through tenth grade, and making Saraswati Vandana (hymn to the

similar to Rwanda

[33] "Act Tough against Bangladeshis: Togadia to Govt," *Times of India*, Jan. 26, 2003. Accessed June 24, 2014. http://timesofindia.indiatimes.com/india/Act-tough-against-Bangladeshis-Togadia-to -govt/articleshow/35594765.cms?referral=PM.

[34] "Advani Cracks Whip on Illegal Immigrants," *The Economic Times*, Jan. 8, 2003. Accessed July 9 2014. http://articles.economictimes.indiatimes.com/2003-01-08/news/27537234_1_proxy- war-multi-purpose-national-identity-cards-lk-advani.

[35] "Bihar Government Refuses to Implement ID-Card Plan," *Times of India*, Feb. 13, 2003. Accessed July 9, 2014. http://timesofindia.indiatimes.com/city/patna/Bihar-govt-refuses-to- implement-ID-card-plan/articleshow/37306745.cms.

goddess Saraswati) compulsory at government functions.³⁶ Joshi appointed BJP and RSS members to head major institutions of higher education.³⁷ The UGC provided funding for university-level courses in Vedic astrology. In 2001 NCERT issued the National Curriculum Framework for school education, which rewrote school textbooks and removed essays by prominent left-leaning Indian historians Romila Thapar, Bipan Chandra, and Harbans Mukhia. The revised books depicted Indian history as the valiant and glorious struggle of Hindus to resist Muslim domination. They portrayed Muslim emperors as ruthless invaders and later generations of Muslims as nationalist enemies.³⁸ The NDA government increased budgetary allocations for military and nuclear research to the detriment of research in agriculture, health, medicine, and general science.

Phase V: Congress Party–Led UPA Governments (2004–2009, 2009–2014)
Hindu nationalist movement activity declined in the aftermath of the 2004 elections in which the Congress-led UPA defeated the BJP-led NDA alliance by a wide margin.³⁹ A VHP demonstration pledging to build a temple in Ayodhya, on December 6, 2004, the twelfth anniversary of the mosque's demolition, was small and uneventful. RSS spokesman Ram Madhav called an armed attack on the mosque-temple complex in Ayodhya on July 5, 2005 "unfortunate" and asked people to shun violence and protest peacefully.⁴⁰ The VHP organized a lackluster *bandh*, without the BJP's support. BJP *yatras* (religious processions)

---

³⁶ Sukumar Muralidharan and SK Pande, "Taking Hindutva to School," *Frontline*, Nov. 7–20, 1998, Vol. 15, no. 23. http://www.frontline.in/static/html/fl1523/15230040.htm. Harinder Baweja, "M.M Joshi's Hindutva Agenda on Education Backfires on the Government," *India Today*, Nov. 2, 1998. http://indiatoday.intoday.in/story/m.m-joshis-hindutva-agenda-on-education-backfires-on-the-government/1/266225.html.

³⁷ They included the Indian Council of Social Science Research (ICSSR), Indian Council of Historical Research (ICHR), University Grants Commission (UGC), Institute of Advanced Studies, Nehru Museum and Memorial Library, Indian Institute of Mass Communication, All India Council for Technical Education, and National Council for Research Education and Training (NCERT).

³⁸ See "Redefining NCERT: The Saffronising of Academia," *Education for All in India*, April 11, 2001. Accessed June 24, 2014. http://www.educationforallinindia.com/page135.html. Amrik Singh, "Saffronisation and Textbooks," *The Hindu*, Aug. 25, 2001, Accessed June 24, 2014. http://www.hindu.com/2001/08/25/stories/05252524.htm.

³⁹ The UPA won 219 seats and 40 percent of the vote compared to the BJP-NDA's 185 seats and 34 percent of the vote. Congress captured 145 seats and 27 percent of the vote, while the BJP won 138 seats and 25 percent of the vote. The BJP's performance was highly uneven across states. It performed well in Madhya Pradesh, where it won twenty-five out of the twenty-nine seats it contested and 48.1 percent of the valid votes; Rajasthan, where it won twenty-one out of twenty-five seats and 49 percent of the vote; and Chhattisgarh where it won ten out of eleven seats and 47.8 percent of the vote. It suffered setbacks in UP where it won only 22 percent of the valid votes and ten seats compared to its peak in 1998 with 36.5 percent of the vote and fifty-two seats.

⁴⁰ "RSS Conclave Expresses Concern," *Tribune India*, July 5, 2005. Accessed June 24, 2014. http://www.tribuneindia.com/2005/20050706/nation.htm#3.

opposing the UPA government (the Suraksha *yatra* in April 2006 and the Vijay Sankalp *yatra* in March 2008) were poorly attended. Rifts between party and movement and unsympathetic state and national governments contributed to the Ayodhya movement's decline.

The Sangh Parivar sought unsuccessfully to organize a mass campaign around the "Ram Setu" (Ram's bridge) issue. It opposed the UPA government's decision in June 2005 to dredge a canal to enable the passage of large commercial ships between Sri Lanka and India. It contended that the dredging would destroy Ram Setu – an underwater causeway that features in the Hindu epic the *Ramayana*. The government signed an affidavit denying that matters of religious faith were at stake and turned the issue over to the courts. The RSS created the Rameshwaran Ram Setu Raksha, which organized protests against the project in various parts of the country in 2007, including a rally in Rameshwaran on August 27, a road blockade in several cities on September 12, and a rally in Delhi on December 30.

These agitations had the makings of a mass movement. VHP activists drew on earlier repertoires of protest, like organizing *Ram bhakts* (devotees) to participate in *rath yatras*. They invoked the existence of a sacred geography, in which Hanuman constructed a bridge to Lanka to wage war against Ravana and rescue Sita. As in Ayodhya, they buttressed their demands through a combination of historical and archaeological arguments but also contended that matters of faith required no substantiation. Activists framed this as a transnational issue by identifying an ancient bridge connecting Hindus in India, Indonesia, Thailand, and Cambodia. Hindutva activists Sadhvi Rithambara and Uma Bharati claimed that dredging the canal would hurt the poor, damage the environment, and allow international "terrorists" to enter India from Sri Lanka.[41] Several spokespersons contrasted the commitments of Muslims, Christians, and Jews to protecting their religious sites with the failures of Hindus to do so.

However, the Ram Setu movement foundered on a lack of party and state support. The NDA government, under pressure from its coalition partner, the DMK, had initially authorized the project. Although some BJP leaders supported the Ram Setu campaign and attended a few rallies, the BJP as a whole and BJP state governments did not wholeheartedly support it. The Ayodhya movement mobilized mass support by generating hostility toward Muslims and the state. Although some Ram Setu activists targeted Sonia Gandhi and described the call for scientific evidence of the historic existence of Ram Setu "an Islamo-Christian conspiracy," anti-minority themes did not figure prominently in the Ram Setu campaign. Moreover, both the state and central governments opposed the movement. The BJP was not in power in Tamil Nadu and the DMK government questioned whether Ram and Ram Setu were founded

---

[41] Uma Bharati, "Sri Ram and History of Ram Sethu," and Sadhvi Rithambara, "An Assault on the Soul of India," *Organiser*, Deepavali Special, November 11, 2007.

in historical reality or mythology. The VHP's denunciations of the DMK for openly questioning the historical veracity of Ram's life antagonized Tamils. As a result, the Ram Setu campaign did not take root either nationally or in Tamil Nadu.

The BJP suffered consecutive defeats in two general elections, despite its attempt to capitalize on Hindu nationalist appeals in 2009. Its election manifesto that year promised to explore all possible means of building a temple in Ayodhya and vowed to "protect and promote the cow and its progeny." It took a strong stand on national security, promising within 100 days of coming to office to revive the "antiterrorism" mechanisms that the UPA government had dismantled and reinstate an improved version of the Prevention of Terrorism Act (POTA). It also vowed to launch a massive campaign to detect and deport illegal immigrants, introduce national identity cards, and develop nuclear technology. The BJP projected Advani as prime minister and made Narendra Modi its star campaigner. It refused to concede to the Election Commission's suggestion that it drop Varun Gandhi from its list of candidates following his vitriolic anti-Muslim statements for which he was briefly imprisoned.[42]

Hindutva proved to be electorally unpopular. The BJP suffered an even more significant defeat in 2009 than in the previous elections. It won 116 seats (17.9 percent of the vote) in contrast to Congress, which won 206 seats (27.3 percent of the vote). The BJP's 2009 defeat confirmed its weaknesses in key federal states including Kerala, West Bengal, Tamil Nadu, and, to a lesser extent, Andhra Pradesh. It was unable to compensate for the loss of important coalition partners, who feared that they would lose minority votes by remaining part of the NDA in the aftermath of the Gujarat violence. It failed to devise effective antipoverty and employment-generating schemes. The BJP's image of a cohesive and disciplined party was tarnished by conflicts among its leaders. The RSS and the BJP reverted to the strategy they had pursued during the Emergency, of joining other political parties in an anticorruption movement directed against the Congress government.

The UPA displaced identity demands by prioritizing economic issues around both growth and social welfare. Its victory in the 2009 elections revealed the popularity of its agrarian debt forgiveness scheme and its efforts to provide employment through the National Rural Employment Guarantee Act. The UPA government counteracted the "saffronisation" of education by launching a program to "detoxify" textbooks after a three-member committee of historians reviewed them and withdrew the most controversial textbooks. In 2005, it unveiled a new curriculum designed to promote secular values; it issued revised textbooks the following year. The government

---

[42] Gandhi, who was already a member of the BJP's national executive committee, was elected to parliament from Philbit district in UP. The BJP made him its national secretary in March 2010 and national vice president in 2014.

stopped funding for *ekal vidyalayas* (single teacher schools) because an inquiry commission found that government funds were being used to generate hatred toward minorities. It took an important step in promoting free basic education to all children between the ages of six and fourteen by adopting "The Right of Children to Free and Compulsory Education Bill, 2009."

The UPA government established the Ministry of Minority Affairs, National Commission for Religious and Linguistic Minorities, and National Commission for Minority Educational Institutions.[43] It sought to enhance educational opportunities for Muslims by improving the quality of *madrasas*, providing scholarships to minority students, creating more facilities for teaching Urdu, and establishing Muslim universities. Prime Minister Manmohan Singh adopted a Fifteen Point Program for the Welfare of Minorities, which called for bettering minorities' living conditions, employment opportunities, and access to resources. The Eleventh Plan endorsed these objectives.

The UPA government appointed the Sachar Committee, which issued a damning report on Muslims' economic and social disadvantages.[44] The Sachar Committee Report galvanized public attention in a similar fashion to the Mandal Commission Report on OBCs.[45] Congress focused its energies on regaining Muslim support as did the SP, which promised to nominate Muslim candidates and create reserved seats for Muslims. All of this discredited the BJP.

BJP Governments in Federal States

Hindu nationalists have introduced their most significant policy initiatives within federal states. As regional political parties and governments have become stronger, the BJP and RSS have become greater proponents of federalism. In 2000, the NDA government recognized Uttarkhand, Jharkhand, and Chhattisgarh, where the BJP had performed well in the 1998 elections, as new federal states. The RSS has supported the creation of new states and called for the division of other states like Maharashtra, Andhra Pradesh, Karnataka, Gujarat, Rajasthan, West Bengal, Assam, and Jammu and Kashmir.[46]

---

[43] Hasan, *Politics of Inclusion*, 57.

[44] In 2007, the National Commission for Religious and Linguistic Minorities (Misra Commission) arrived at many of the same conclusions as the Sachar Committee. It recommended that 15 percent of seats in educational institutions should be reserved for minorities and reservations for non-Hindu Scheduled Castes and non-Hindu OBCs.

[45] The BJP was the only political party that objected to the UPA government's decision in December 2011 to create a sub-quota of 4.5 percent for "backward Muslims" within the existing 27 percent reservation for OBCs.

[46] *Asian Age*, September 25, 2000. "Now, RSS Supports Smaller States," *Express News Service*, New Delhi, Jan. 5, 2010. Accessed June 24, 2014. http://archive.indianexpress.com/news/now-rss-supports-smaller-states/563529/.

BJP governments, in close collaboration with the VHP and RSS, have dog-
gedly pursued three Hindu nationalist commitments – educational reform,
cow protection, and religious conversion. All three issues promote discrimination and violence against minorities. Cow protection and religious conversion
legislation empower the state to engage in surveillance and repression. They
reveal the importance of party-movement-state government collaboration
in pursuing an ideologically-driven agenda through legislation and popular
mobilization.

Educational Reform

The RSS has long been committed to creating a network of schools that
propagate its beliefs. In 1969, it formed the Bhartiya Shikshan Mandal, an
organization of RSS-affiliated teachers, and, in 1978, the Vidya Bharati Akhil
Bharatiya Shiksha Sansthan, to coordinate its educational initiatives. Its Vidya
Bharati schools employ 80,000 teachers who instruct over 1.8 million students.
The NDA government provided extensive financial support to 14,000 Vidya
Bharati nursery, primary, and secondary schools in every state but Mizoram.
The Central Board of Secondary Education recognized 5,000 of these schools,
primarily in BJP-ruled states.[47]

Ekal vidyalayas perform a crucial role in disseminating Hindu nationalist
beliefs. Praveen Togadia described them as educating youth about the dangers
of forced conversion and the subversive activities of Pakistani intelligence.[48]
The *ekal* Web site describes it as a movement, in fact, "one of the greatest
non-governmental movements in the country."[49] There is some truth to this
depiction. The schools provide teachers with special training in Hindutva
ideals. They typically have prayer halls with idols of Hindu deities. The birth-
days of Hindu *sants* (saints) and RSS leaders are school holidays. Students
are required to recite "Saraswati Vandana" and "Vande Mataram" (Hail the
Motherland). The prescribed textbooks equate Indian culture with Hindu
culture and represent minorities as foreigners who are disloyal to India. The
Sangh Parivar has been especially active in promoting its schools in the states
of Chhattisgarh and Karnataka.

Cow Protection

Although most states had passed legislation fully or partially banning cow
slaughter and the sale of beef, BJP state governments introduced more stringent legislation. During the brief period that the BJP was in office in UP
in 1991–2, it ordered a complete ban on cow slaughter, stopped the sale

[47] Venkitesh Ramakrishnan, "A Spreading Network," *Frontline*, Nov. 7–20, 1998. Accessed July 7,
2014. http://www.frontline.in/static/html/fl1523/15230100.htm.
[48] "VHP Schools on Border to Counter Anti-Nationalists," *Gomantak Times*, May 9, 2001.
Accessed June 24, 2014. http://www.hindunet.org/hvk/articles/0501/35.html.
[49] http://www.ekal.org/.

of tinned beef, and prohibited killing sick cows for medical and scientific research.[50] The Delhi state government took the lead in introducing a bill banning cow slaughter in 1994. Rajasthan followed by placing a ban on the slaughter of all bovine species the following year. The BJP-BSP coalition government in UP repealed the Cow Slaughter Prevention Act of 1955 and imposed a total ban on cow slaughter in 2003. That same year, the Madhya Pradesh government, led by Chief Minister Uma Bharati, imposed a total ban on cow slaughter. The Modi government in Gujarat re-imposed a ban on cow slaughter (that the High Court had deemed unconstitutional) with the Supreme Court's backing. The Jharkhand Assembly passed the Cow Protection Commission Bill in 2005, which criminalized killing, cruelty to, and smuggling of cows.[51]

The BJP claimed that the new legislation would make more milk available, promote humane treatment of cattle, and signify the sanctity of cows to Hindus. However, the 1960s legislation already achieved all these objectives. What the new legislation created was increased state surveillance and punishment.[52] It also denied poor Muslims and *dalits* income from a variety of leather-related trades as well as affordable meat (given the higher prices of mutton and chicken than beef). The legislation creates suspicions that Muslims are engaging in anti-Hindu, criminal activities. It has emboldened the VHP and Bajrang Dal to engage in violence against Muslims whom they suspect of slaughtering cows. For example, on January 11, 2003, the VHP and Bajrang Dal attacked the home of a Muslim man whom they claimed was slaughtering cows and selling beef in the small town of Ganj Basoda in Madhya Pradesh. Within hours, VHP and Bajrang Dal activists burned down 132 of 144 Muslim shops in the town. At a press conference that day, Praveen Togadia vowed to "paint Madhya Pradesh in saffron colors" in the

---

[50] "Holy Cow," *The Indian Express*, March 30, 2010. Accessed July 7, 2014. http://archive .indianexpress.com/news/holy-cow/597403/.

[51] The Uttarkhand State Assembly passed the Uttarkhand Protection of Cow Progeny Bill, 2007. The new law imposed rigorous penalties for cow slaughter (3–10 years imprisonment and fines ranging from approximately $119 to $238) and required a veterinarian to certify that only diseased or injured cows had been slaughtered. The BJP government in Karnataka replaced the Prevention of Cow Slaughter and Cattle Preservation Act, 1964 with the punitive Prevention of Slaughter and Preservation of Cattle Bill, 2010. Among other measures, this bill made slaughter of all cattle of any age – including male and female buffaloes – a punishable crime. It also criminalized the "possession or usage of beef."

[52] The Karnataka government provides any competent authority the power to enter and inspect premises that he or she believes are violating the law. The Delhi government allows competent authorities to enter, search, and seize property, including cattle, from people's homes, businesses, and vehicles. It places the burden on the accused to prove that confiscated meat is not beef. In 1994, the Delhi government's penalties of up to $319 and jail terms of up to five years seemed high. But in 2010, the Karnataka government instituted fines of up to $1,111 and jail sentences of up to seven years for a first offense and doubled the fine for repeated offenses.

forthcoming assembly elections.[53] Uma Bharati made the passage of more punitive legislation a major plank of her election campaign. The incident culminated in mounting pressure on the national government to introduce a national ban on cow slaughter.

In 2006, BJP president Rajnath Singh instructed BJP state governments to stop cow slaughter and religious conversions and deport illegal Bangladeshi migrants. While the political climate was not propitious for the BJP to launch a national political offensive, it could engage in activism at the local level.

Religious Conversions

BJP governments strengthened existing legislation or passed new legislation against religious conversions in Gujarat, Rajasthan, Madhya Pradesh, and Chhattisgarh.[54] The legislation that BJP governments introduced after 2003 was more punitive and restrictive than the legislation the Jan Sangh had introduced in the 1960s. The laws passed in Gujarat in 2003 and in Chhattisgarh, Himachal Pradesh, and Madhya Pradesh in 2006 made conversions that were deemed to have entailed force or allurement non-bailable and cognizable. They required individuals to inform the local administration about their intention to convert and allowed district magistrates to determine whether these conversions entailed force or coercion. They introduced harsh penalties for those who violated the law. Fines for conversions by force or allurement in Gujarat and Rajasthan were up to $1,087, in Chhattisgarh $435, and in HP, $544. The jail sentences in these states were between two and five years.

On the face of it, as the term freedom of religion acts implies, the legislation sought to prohibit coercion and ensure individuals' rights to freely choose their faith. In fact, its intent and effects were just the opposite. It increased the state's authority to engage in surveillance and punishment while undermining religious freedom. In some instances, the state questioned individuals who said they had converted voluntarily.[55] By heightening scrutiny around conversions, Hindutva activists popularized the notion that Christians and Muslims are ruthless foreigners who take advantage of gullible, passive victims. The laws in HP, Tamil Nadu, Gujarat, and Rajasthan impose the stiffest penalties for the conversion of *dalits*, women, and tribals.[56]

---

[53] The Bhopal Group on Communalism, "The Riot Economy: The Ganj Basoda Case," South Asia Citizen's Web Special, Oct. 4, 2003. http://www.sacw.net/new/CommunalMPOct2003.html.

[54] Himachal Pradesh was the only state where a Congress rather than BJP government introduced such legislation.

[55] Laura Dudley Jenkins, "Legal Limits on Religious Conversion in India," *Law and Contemporary Problems* 71, no. 2 (2008), 116.

[56] The enhanced penalties for conversions by women, minors, Scheduled Castes, and Scheduled Tribes entailed fines up to $2,174 and four years imprisonment in Gujarat and fines of $1,087 and up to three years imprisonment in HP.

The legislation inaccurately implied that all poor Hindus who had converted to Islam and Christianity wanted to convert back to Hinduism. However, many of those whose ancestors had been forcibly converted centuries earlier no longer considered themselves or wanted to become Hindu. Many *dalits* freely converted from Hinduism to Buddhism, Christianity, and Islam to escape rigid caste stratification.

The assumption that conversion out of Hinduism is coercive whereas conversion to Hinduism is voluntary underlies the VHP's mass reconversion ceremonies, tellingly named *ghar vapsi* (homecoming or return to the flock) in BJP-ruled states.[57] The VHP claimed to have "reconverted" 12,857 people in 2004, 3,727 of whom were Muslim and 9,130 Christian.[58] This included 3,925 people in Rajasthan, 1,055 in Odisha, 250 in Jharkhand, and 6,548 (more than 50 percent of "reconversions" in the country) in Gujarat. The VHP organized several ceremonies that converted Maharashtrian tribals in Gujarat because the Maharashtrian government prohibited these ceremonies. The proposed laws discouraged conversion out of Hinduism while encouraging conversion into it by deeming it "reconversion." The bills in Rajasthan and HP stipulated that returning to one's forefathers' original religion or to one's own original religion would not be deemed conversion.[59] In Gujarat, the BJP government even introduced an amendment to the law in 2006 that identified Jains and Buddhists as Hindus.

Ultimately, the central government blocked passage of several of the proposed amendments – in Gujarat, Madhya Pradesh, and Rajasthan.[60] However, in the years that elapsed between the introduction of the bills in Rajasthan and Madhya Pradesh and the president tabling them, Hindu nationalists engaged in extensive conversions to Hinduism. Nor is it clear that many prosecutions would have occurred had the laws been passed. Prosecutions have been rare in Odisha and Madhya Pradesh where anti-conversion laws have existed for more than forty years. The UN Special Rapporteur's Report on the Freedom of Religion or Belief of January 2009 stated that she had not received any complaints about coerced conversions in Odisha.[61]

---

[57] The RSS describes tribals as *vanvasis* (forest dwellers) rather than *adivasis* (original inhabitants) to highlight their distinctive occupations and to assert their Hindu origins.

[58] U.S. Department of State, *U.S. Department of State Annual Report on International Religious Freedom for 2005 – India*, November 8, 2005. Accessed June 29, 2014. http://www.refworld.org/docid/437c9cf111.html.

[59] Himachal Pradesh Freedom of Religion Bill, Number 31 of 2006. Accessed July 9, 2014. http://indianchristians.in/news/images/resources/pdf/Himachal_Pradesh_Freedom_of_Religion_Act.pdf.

[60] Tamil Nadu passed the bill in 2002 when the AIADMK needed the BJP's support to form the government but repealed it two years later after the BJP lost the national elections.

[61] Asma Jahangir, *Report of the Special Rapporteur on Freedom of Religion or Belief*, United Nations Human Rights Council, 2007. Accessed July 7, 2014. http://daccess-dds-ny.un.org/doc/UNDOC/GEN/G09/101/04/PDF/G0910104.pdf?OpenElement.

The Sangh Parivar's concerns about conversions are part of its larger preoc-
cupation with the size and growth of minority populations. UP Chief Minister
Ram Prakash Gupta stated, "There are groups and communities which feel
that if they go on increasing their number, they will capture power one day.
Such a way of thinking has to be disincentivised." One disincentive, he added,
would be to prevent those communities with high population growth rates
and couples with more than two children from contesting the *panchayat* elections.[62] RSS joint secretary Dattatreya Hosabale claimed at a large public gathering that neither Muslims nor Christians used birth control but that Hindus
were victims of family planning policies.[63] In his words, "teen se kam nahi,
aap jitna jyada kar sakein utna achcha" ("produce at least three children each.
Not less than three; the more you produce the better"). Madhya Pradesh Chief
Minister Babulal Gaur decided to do away with the eligibility norm that bars
people with more than two children from contesting elections to *panchayats*,
civic bodies, and cooperative societies.[64] The VHP's Ashok Singhal appealed to
Hindus to have at least five children.[65]

Hindutva activists have made conversions a pretext for anti-minority violence. National Commission for Minorities member Harcharan Singh Josh,
who investigated allegations of harassment of Christians in Madhya Pradesh
and Chhattisgarh, two BJP-ruled states, stated:

> Bajrang Dal, VHP and Dharam Dal activists freely raid Christian homes, carry out
> searches and humiliate women there on the pretext of curbing proselytism. There is
> a total failure of administration to protect human and religious rights of Christian
> minorities in Madhya Pradesh and Chhattisgarh.[66]

In the aftermath of Odisha's passage of the Freedom of Religion Act, Hindu
nationalist organizations engaged in large-scale conversions of *dalits* and tribals
to Hinduism and molested Christians who refused to "reconvert," particularly
after the BJP-Biju Janata Dal coalition government came to power in 2000.[67]

[62] Purnima S. Tripathi, "New UP Population Policy Targets Minorities." *The Asian Age*, Monday,
March 6, 2000, Vol. 3, no. 65, 1.

[63] T. Ramavarman, "Hindu Families Should Have at Least Three Kids: RSS," *The Times of
India*, Oct. 27, 2013. Accessed June 24, 2014. http://timesofindia.indiatimes.com/india
/Hindu-families-should-have-at-least-three-kids-RSS/articleshow/24764051.cms.

[64] Department of Public Relations, Madhya Pradesh Government, Nov. 2005. Accessed June 30,
2014. http://mpinfo.org/MPinfoStatic/English/cd/221105.asp.

[65] *Asian Age*, Dec. 11, 2005. Milind Ghatwai, "Hindus Should 'Produce' at Least 5 Children Says
VHP Leader Ashok Singhal," *The Indian Express*, Feb. 2014. Accessed June 24, 2014. http://
indianexpress.com/article/india/politics/singhal-hindus-should-have-at-least-5-children/.

[66] "Christians not Safe in MP, Chhattisgarh," *The Indian Express*, June 19, 2006. Accessed June
24, 2014. http://www.indianexpress.com/news/christians-not-safe-in-mp-chhattisgarh/6828/.

[67] By late September 2008, more than forty people had been killed, more than 4,000 Christian
homes destroyed, and fifty churches demolished. Around 20,000 people were living in relief
camps and more than 40,000 people were hiding in forests and other places. Jahangir, *Report of
the Special Rapporteur on Freedom of Religion or Belief*.

Hindutva organizations in Karnataka have organized attacks on Protestant organizations since 2003–4, with increasing ferocity since the BJP assumed power there in 2008.[68] The National Commission for Minorities issued a report to the prime minister's office "strongly criticizing the BJP government in Karnataka for its failure to control communal violence." It denied that forced conversions led to the clashes and claimed that the government did not provide evidence of a single such complaint the previous year.

Conclusion

State policies and actions have been crucial determinants of the strength and character of Hindu nationalism. During the era of coalition governments, Hindu nationalists made significant gains, when the ruling party was factionalized and governments were relatively weak and needed Jan Sangh or BJP support. The Jan Sangh's success in 1967 resulted from the Congress Party split leading to the creation of the Congress O and Indira Gandhi's Congress I. Congress O included the Jan Sangh in governing coalitions in several states. In 1977, Congress was destabilized by opposition to its declaration of a state of emergency, which was itself an indication of its weakness. First the JP movement and later the Janata Party allied with the Jan Sangh and then included it in the governing coalition that occupied office from 1977 to 1980. Congress was weakened again by factionalism and charges of corruption in 1989. The BJP provided outside support to the National Front government but then called for a no-confidence vote that brought it down. The BJP made important gains in the 1991 elections.

In the mid-1980s, the period of the BJP's greatest growth until 2013–14, state leaders inadvertently encouraged Hindu nationalist mobilization by appealing to identity groups. Indira Gandhi and subsequently Rajiv Gandhi courted the Hindu vote. Furthermore, state leaders have been inconsistent. The same Indira Gandhi who threatened to ban the RSS and proscribe *shakhas* in 1971 was courting the Hindu vote and forging closer ties to the RSS in the early 1980s. The same Rajiv Gandhi who was making concessions to conservative Muslim elites around the Shah Bano case was appealing to Hindu voters in the 1989 elections. The same VP Singh, who in principle opposed divisive religious politics, sought the BJP's support to form the national government in 1989.

Hindu nationalist movements declined under two successive UPA governments. The BJP's revival of Hindutva appeals prior to the 2009 elections was

[68] Bajrang Dal and Shiv Sena activists in Karnataka vandalized thirty churches, resulting in the injuries of seventy-one people, including forty-five policemen from August through September 2008. DP Satish, "'New Life' under Fire from Hindus, Catholics," *IBN News*, September 18, 2008. Accessed June 24, 2014. http://ibnlive.in.com/news/new-life-under-fire-from-hindus -catholics/73816-3.html.

electorally unpopular. Certain features of the UPA government help explain this. UPA governments did not mobilize civil society groups around populist demands and generally did not engage in identity appeals and programs. The first UPA government emphasized social welfare and the second UPA government emphasized economic growth. The one identity issue that UPA governments addressed concerns the inequalities and injustices that Muslims face. Although the government did not implement the Sachar Committee's most potentially useful but controversial recommendation – reservations for Muslims in education and employment – it supported reservations for Muslim OBCs and took steps to improve Muslims' conditions. The UPA government's actions persuaded most parties and several state governments to support some form of reservations for Muslims; the BJP was isolated in opposing such quotas. For example, when Maharashtra Chief Minister Prithviraj Chavan approved 4.5 percent reservation for Muslims in government, jobs, and education, Congress and other parties supported the decision, while the BJP termed it "unconstitutional" and politically motivated.[69]

Several features of Hindu nationalist movements are striking when viewed comparatively and historically. First, compared to most other social movements, they have endured and sometimes become stronger when the state has made concessions. Hindu nationalists continuously escalated their demands, in 1985, when Congress ordered the *babri masjid* to be unlocked so that Hindus could worship there, in 1989, when it allowed the VHP to organize the *shilanyas*, and in 1992, when PV Narasimha Rao allowed the VHP to organize a procession to Ayodhya and perform religious rituals there. By contrast, ethnic self-determination movements have subsided when the state has conceded to demands for the devolution of power. Parties that have championed the cause of lower castes have distanced themselves from lower-caste movements after assuming power.

Second, in contrast to most parties, the BJP has retained close ties to the social movement organization with which it was previously affiliated after achieving power. The BJP was far too interconnected with the RSS to ban *shakhas* and imprison *pracharaks* (RSS volunteers) when it occupied national office, as Nehru and Indira Gandhi did on different occasions. To the contrary, the NDA government made concessions to the RSS and the VHP. Allowing the VHP to hold a prayer ceremony in Ayodhya in March 2002 provided the spark that ignited the Gujarat violence. That the party did not wholly control the movement became evident when the NDA sought but failed to quell VHP mobilization around Ayodhya. By contrast, Prime Minister VP Singh weakened ties to the social movements that helped the National Front government achieve power in 1989.

[69] "Maharashtra Government Okays 16 Per Cent Quotas for Marathas, 5 Per Cent for Muslims," *The Indian Express*, June 25, 2014. Accessed July 9, 2014. http://indianexpress.com/article/india/india-others/maharashtra-govt-okays-16-per-cent-quotas-for-marathas-5-per-cent-for-muslims/.

③ Third, Hindu nationalist governments have engaged in greater discrimination against minorities in federal states than nationally. Even when the Jan Sangh participated in coalition governments in 1967, it pursued a number of RSS goals. These included championing acts that restricted religious conversions, attacks on missionary institutions, and the creation of RSS schools. After coming to power in several states in 1990, the BJP increased and broadened these activities. In states like Gujarat and Karnataka where it has been especially strong, it has failed to curtail the VHP's violence against Christians and Muslims.

State governments have been more apt than national governments to pursue anti-minority policies and allow anti-minority violence for a variety of reasons. The Constitution permits state governments to determine their own policies on questions like religious conversion and cow protection. State governments are less constrained than national governments by international opinion and institutional regulations. State leaders are closer to civil society groups and more susceptible to electoral pressures. At the same time, national governments can support or constrain their activities. While the NDA was in office, it funded RSS schools, proposed stringent restrictions on Muslim immigration, and sought to pass a constitutional amendment on cow protection. It did not block the amendments that several BJP state governments proposed to so-called freedom of religion bills.

A paradox underlying these developments concerns the simultaneous growth of militant Hindu nationalism amid the growth of democracy. It is striking that the Jan Sangh and the BJP grew at the very time that new political parties emerged. The BJP has especially flourished during the decline of the one-party system and the emergence of coalition governments. The movements in which Hindu nationalists have participated have achieved mass support. The creation of new federal states and the growth of state parties and their participation in national governance have all increased the power and autonomy of state governments and freed them to pursue anti-minority policies with less fear of national government sanction. Alliances of parties, movements, and states have both advanced and undermined democracy and minority rights.

2

Party Politics

Disrupting Party-Movement Boundaries

This chapter explores party-movement relations and asks why some parties
engage in political activism and forge alliances with social movement organizations. I argue that the prevailing assumption that political parties tend to
become increasingly centrist and institutionalized has confounded our understanding of movement-parties in India. After discussing the relevant comparative and theoretical literature on political parties, I explore the embeddedness
of many Indian parties in social movements. I then suggest that the BJP has
been especially activist because of its ideology, organizational structure, and
linkages to the RSS and VHP.

Comparative Perspectives on Parties and Movements

Students of political parties in democratic regimes believe that parties' most
significant attributes derive from their relationship to electoral processes: nominating and supporting candidates for political office, securing resources, staff-
ing bureaucracies, organizing election campaigns, and framing issues and
policies. A party, as classically understood, is "any political group identified
by an official label that presents at elections, and is capable of placing through
elections, candidates for public office."[1] Mature political parties, according to
the political development literature, construct and maintain boundaries against
societal pressures.[2] In this understanding, parties are the polar opposite of
social movements. Movement work – forging collective identities, confronting
authorities, and engaging in protest – is not designed for competition in the
political marketplace.

---

[1] Giovanni Sartori, *Parties and Party Systems: A Framework for Analysis*, Vol. 1 (New York:
Cambridge University Press, 1976), 64.
[2] Gabriel Almond, "Introduction," in Gabriel Almond and James Coleman, eds., *The Politics of
Developing Areas* (Princeton, NJ: Princeton University Press, 1960).

There are indeed some important differences between social movements and political parties.[3] Most parties address questions of identity, meaning and belonging only for pragmatic electoral purposes. By contrast, social movements are the conveyers of social and cultural beliefs and historical memories concerning identity, meaning, and belonging. Compared to parties, movements tend to be more radical, expressive, and skilled in forging collective identities.[4] Their location within civil society enables them to act as translators, amplifiers, and transmitters of cultural norms and values.

Movements tend to employ evocative, symbolically rich appeals that encourage intense engagement. They do not simply transmit culture but also produce and reshape it.[5] Movements are neither compelled nor constrained by the logic of electoral competition to make ideological compromises.[6] Indeed, they often polarize identities and interests. Movements are more apt than parties to adopt extreme positions and engage in violence because they are not bound by the rules that govern parties.

The temporal and spatial logics of parties and movements often differ. The work of parties tends to be structured around elections and increasingly so in India, given the short time between elections. By contrast, movement work is both episodic and quotidian. Movements are driven by questions that emerge and recede in keeping with the state's response, public receptiveness, and activists' energies. Movements often also labor among marginalized communities whom the state has neglected.

The very differences between parties and movements may draw them together. Parties are attracted to movements because movements understand and influence what's happening on the ground. Movements help parties aggregate, select and transmit demands originating in civil society to the political sphere.[7] As EE Schattschneider suggests, parties profit from recognizing and channeling societal conflicts.[8] Parties can become divorced from popular grievances and demands

---

[3] Herbert Kitschelt provides a succinct summation of the differences between parties and movements. He defines parties as actors that participate in institutions of territorial democratic representation through competitive multicandidate elections to legislatures and movements as actors that resort to street protest and disruption of institutions outside or against institutionalized channels of political communication. Herbert Kitschelt, "Movement Parties," in Richard S. Katz and William Crotty, eds., *Handbook of Party Politics* (London: Sage Publications, 2006), 278–9.

[4] Goldstone, "Introduction: Bridging Institutionalized and Non-Institutionalized Politics," in Goldstone, ed., *States, Parties and Social Movements*, 8.

[5] I do not distinguish between social and political movements because all the social movements I discuss have political ambitions. In this respect, they belong to what Partha Chatterjee describes as civil rather than political society. Partha Chatterjee, *The Politics of the Governed: Popular Politics in Most of the World* (New York: Columbia University Press, 2004).

[6] Leon D. Epstein, *Political Parties in Western Democracies* (New York: Frederick A. Praeger, 1967), 13.

[7] Norberto Bobbio and Peter Kennealy, trans., *Democracy and Dictatorship: The Nature and Limits of State Power* (Cambridge: Polity Press, 1989), 25.

[8] Eric Elmer Schattschneider, *The Semisovereign People: A Realist's View of Democracy in America* (New York: Holt, Rinehart and Winston, 1960).

TABLE 2.1. *Ideal Type Differences Between Parties and Movements*

	Political Parties	Social Movements
Accountable to	The electorate	Their supporters
Objectives	Electoral success	Social change
Modes of organizing	Negotiation, compromise	Confrontation, direct action
Organizational Structure	Vertical	Horizontal
Use of Violence	Rare	Sometimes
Periods of greatest activity	Around elections	Episodic and quotidian

Source: Compiled by author.

as a result of over-institutionalization.[9] Movements can help parties gain mass support and communicate popular grievances to the state.[10] They can broaden party programs and constituencies and promote citizen involvement in decision-making.[11] When movements and parties ally, they can potentially combine ideological and pragmatic appeals. Through linkages to movements, parties have appealed to new groups and revitalized older constituencies. Conversely, parties have extended the life cycle of movements and enabled movement activists to achieve political office.

And yet the distinction is not airtight: party and movement activities are sometimes indistinguishable. Movement activists frequently campaign in elections, seek political office, and interact with the state. Their expressive activities are both identity- and interest-based.[12] Social movements both protest and negotiate to attain their goals. Conversely, many parties use confrontational tactics and violence to achieve far-reaching social change. Parties do not simply respond to social cleavages but forge, strengthen, and transform political identities.[13] They organize strikes that immobilize government and

[9] Scott Mainwaring and Mariano Torcal, "Party System Institutionalization and Party System Theory after the Third Wave of Democratization," in Richard A. Katz and William J. Crotty, eds., *Handbook of Party Politics* (London: Sage Publications, 2006), 204–27.

[10] Peter Mair and Stefano Bartolini, "Challenges to Contemporary Political Parties," in Larry Diamond and Richard Gunther, eds., *Political Parties and Democracy* (Baltimore, MD: Johns Hopkins University Press, 2001), 339.

[11] Herbert Kitschelt, "Social Movements, Political Parties, and Democratic Theory," *The Annals of the American Academy of Political and Social Science, 1993*, Vol. 528, 13–29 and Mildred A. Schwartz, "Interactions between Social Movements and US Political Parties," *Party Politics*, Vol. 16, no. 5, 587–607.

[12] Doug McAdam, Sidney Tarrow, and Charles Tilly, "To Map Contentious Politics," *Mobilization: An International Quarterly* 1, no. 1 (1996): 17–34.

[13] See, for example, Manali Desai, "From Movement to Party to Government: Why Social Policies in Kerala and West Bengal Are so Different," in Goldstone, ed., *States, Parties and Social Movements*, 170; and Oliver Heath and Yogendra Yadav, "The Rise of Caste Politics: Party System Change and Voter Realignment, 1962–2004," in Anthony Heath and Roger Jeffery, eds.,

TABLE 2.2. *Blurred Boundaries Between Parties and Movements*

	Political Parties	Social Movements
Accountable to	The electorate and other party members, social movements, their own ideological convictions	Their supporters
Objectives	Electoral success and social change	Social change and access to power
Modes of organizing	Negotiation, compromise and protest, violence	Confrontation, direct action, and negotiation and compromise

Source: Compiled by author.

business.[14] Inordinate attention to elections has truncated our understanding of both parties and democracy. There are enough exceptions to the neat distinctions between parties and movements to call ideal types into question. A more accurate representation of party-movement relations appears in Table 2.2.

To appreciate the synergy between parties and movements, it is fruitful to situate them historically and comparatively. There were close links between parties and movements in early stages of European development. Social movements, the state, and political parties all emerged and assumed a national form in Western Europe in the mid-nineteenth century. The development of national electoral politics expanded vehicles for collective action and promoted the rise of national social movements.[15] Parties often used disruptive movement tactics to get candidates elected.[16] The late nineteenth-century European mass party had strong links to civil society organizations that mobilized youth and veterans.[17] They included

Diversity and Change in Modern India: Economic, Social and Political Approaches (New York: Oxford University Press, 2010), 216.

[14] E. Sridharan and Peter Ronald DeSouza, "Introduction," in E. Sridharan and Peter Ronald DeSouza, eds., *India's Political Parties* (New Delhi: Sage Publications, 2006), 16–17.

[15] Charles Tilly, "Social Movements and National Politics," in Charles Bright and Susan Friend Harding, eds., *Statemaking and Social Movements: Essays in History and Theory* (Ann Arbor, MI: University of Michigan Press, 1984).

[16] Ronald Aminzade, "Between Movement and Party: The Transformation of Mid-Nineteenth Century French Republicanism," in J. Craig Jenkins and Bert Klandermans, eds., *The Politics of Social Protest: Comparative Perspectives on States and Social Movements*, Vol. 3, Social Movements, Protest and Contention, (Minneapolis, MN: University of Minnesota Press, 1995), 39–40.

[17] See, for example, Maurice Duverger, *Political Parties: Their Organization and Activity in the Modern State* (London: Methuen and Co., 1954); Anthony Downs, *An Economic Theory of Democracy* (New York: Harper & Row, 1957); Joseph A. Schlesinger, "On the Theory of Party

both ideologically-oriented center-left (Social Democratic) and center-right (Christian Democratic) parties.[18]

The aftermath of World War II witnessed the evolution of parties of mass representation into catch-all parties whose primary goal was attaining political office by gaining cross-class electoral support. As a result, party pragmatists trumped party ideologues.[19] This development was not free of costs, Otto Kirchheimer contends.[20] Bowing to the laws of the political marketplace, catch-all parties abandoned their distinctive ideological commitments and appealed to the broadest possible constituency. As a result, catch-all parties ceased to provide channels for protest, sources of protection, and visions of the future.

However, parties that appealed to the median voter did not entirely displace radical parties and movements.[21] Fringe parties remained active in the heyday of catch-all parties, and Europe and the United States have recently witnessed the growth of religious and anti-immigrant parties and movements. Radical parties and activists have influenced the orientation of mainstream political parties.[22]

Scholars have exaggerated parties' autonomy from civil society and social movements' apolitical, anti-institutional character. Indeed, many studies only recognized as movements collective action outside and against institutions. In part this reflects the importance and appeal of the New Left in the sixties and seventies. Scholarship on student activism, civil rights struggles, and feminism often regarded their decentralized, democratic, nonhierarchical forms as

Organization," *The Journal of Politics*, 1984, Vol. 46, no. 2, 369–400; and Otto Kirchheimer, "The Transformation of the Western European Party System," in Joseph LaPalombara and Myron Weiner, eds., *Political Parties and Political Development* (Princeton, NJ: Princeton University Press, 1966).

[18] Stathis N. Kalyvas, *The Rise of Christian Democracy in Europe* (Ithaca, NY: Cornell University Press, 1996).

[19] Anthony Downs, "An Economic Theory of Political Action in a Democracy," *Journal of Political Economy*, April 1957, Vol. 65, no. 2, 137.

[20] Otto Kirchheimer, "The Transformation of the Western European Party System," in LaPalombara and Weiner, eds., *Political Parties and Political Development*, 177–200.

[21] See, for example, MA Berger and MN Zald, "Social Movements in Organizations: Coup d'état, Insurgency, and Mass Movements," *American Journal of Sociology*, 1978, Vol. 83, 823–61 and Donatella della Porta and Sidney Tarrow, "Unwanted Children: Political Violence and the Cycle of Protest in Italy, 1966–1973," *European Journal of Political Research*, November 1986, Vol. 14, no. 5–6, 607–32.

[22] Norman Schofield and Itai Sened, *Multiparty Democracy: Elections and Legislative Politics* (Cambridge, UK: Cambridge University Press, 2006) demonstrate that political elites see party activists as valuable resources in Israel, the Netherlands, Britain, and the United States. Bonnie M. Merguid explores the important strategic considerations that mainstream political parties devote to niche parties like the radical right, the green party, and ethnic parties in Western Europe. Bonnie M. Meguid, *Party Competition between Unequals: Strategies and Electoral Fortunes in Western Europe* (Cambridge, UK: Cambridge University Press, 2010).

constitutive of movements.[23] However, social movements do not necessarily dissipate once they enter institutions.[24] Movements that seek to influence and enter state institutions are especially likely to work closely with political parties. Furthermore, many social movements in the postcolonial world address the state's failures to serve disadvantaged communities by providing these groups with vital social services.

The complementarities between parties and movements are most evident when they engage in violence. Movements may employ violence strategically to refashion identities. Parties sometimes strategically employ violence to polarize and mobilize the electorate and thereby achieve electoral gain. They also employ violence to resolve factional disputes and forge party unity.

Parties and Movements in India

Neither parties nor movements have evolved in a linear fashion in India. Many parties have emerged from movements to which they have retained close ties. The only Indian party that has functioned as a catch-all party and that too, inconsistently, is the Congress Party.[25] However, Congress ceased to function as a centrist, catch-all party after Nehru's death in 1967. It responded to growing challenges to its authority by rejecting centrism, heightening social cleavages, and directly appealing to identity groups. It is possible, as Pradeep Chhibber argues, that India's party system has changed since 1989 into a cleavage-based system in which political parties articulate and mobilize social identities.[26] It is also possible that Congress secured broad support less from being a catch-all party than from dispensing patronage to local elites.[27] Even within the contemporary neoliberal context, Kanchan Chandra argues, the concentration of jobs and services in the public sector leads to the formation of patronage parties when ethnic elites gain the electoral support of large

[23] See, for example, Alberto Melucci, "The New Social Movement: A Theoretical Approach," *Social Science Information*, 1980, Vol. 19, no. 2, 199–226; Claus Offe, "New Social Movements: Challenging the Boundaries of Institutional Politics," *Social Research*, 1965, Vol. 52, 817–68; and Russell J. Dalton, "Strategies of Partisan Influence: West European Environmental Groups," in Jenkins and Klandermans, eds., *The Politics of Social Protest*.

[24] See, for example, Mary Fainsod Katzenstein, *Faithful and Fearless: Moving Feminist Protest inside the Church and Military* (Princeton, NJ: Princeton University Press, 1998); David S. Meyer and Sidney Tarrow, eds., *The Social Movement Society* (Lanham, MD: Rowman & Littlefield, 1998), 20–4; Lee Ann Banaszak, *The Women's Movement Inside and Outside the State* (New York: Cambridge University Press, 2010); and Amy G. Mazur and Dorothy McBride Stetson, eds., *Comparative State Feminism* (London: Sage Publications, 1995).

[25] Rajni Kothari, "The Congress System in India," *Asian Survey*, 1964, Vol. 4, no. 12, 1161–73.

[26] Pradeep K. Chhibber, *Democracy without Associations: Transformation of the Party System and Social Cleavages in India* (Ann Arbor, MI: University of Michigan Press, 1999). The classic work on cleavage-based parties is Seymour Martin Lipset and Stein Rokkan, *Party Systems and Voter Alignments: Cross-National Perspectives* (New York: Free Press, 1967).

[27] Heath and Yadav, "The Rise of Caste Politics," 13.

ethnic constituencies.[28] She fruitfully draws attention to parties' roles in selectively filtering identities and forging powerful ties between their constituencies and the state.

Indian political parties have a long history of collaborating with social movements, in opposing colonialism, creating new federal states, challenging corruption, and destabilizing, removing, and replacing national and state governments. Social movements preceded the emergence of the Congress Party and laid the foundations for the nationalist struggle.[29] Peasant and tribal movements emerged in the late nineteenth century and persisted well into the early twentieth century. Awadh in UP witnessed intermittent agitations from 1867 to 1913. During the Deccan riots in Maharashtra, one of many nineteenth-century anti-moneylender campaigns, peasants burned records of their money-lending transactions. In the 1920s and 1930s, peasants mobilized against paying land revenue and defended their right to forest produce. Similarly, peasant movements in Champaran, Bihar and Kheda, Gujarat laid the foundations for Congress-led noncooperation movements.[30]

Congress was formed as a party in 1885 but its electoral and legislative functions were limited and it achieved decolonization by combining party and movement roles. Mohandas Karamchand Gandhi led the movement, and Nehru, and others led the party. The movement dominated the party until Congress contested the 1936 elections and won majorities in six of eleven provinces of British India.[31] The election results prompted competitive mobilization between Congress and the Muslim League. Nehru led a Congress-Muslim "mass contacts" program that addressed bread-and-butter economic issues.[32] In response, the Muslim League increasingly transformed itself into a party of mass appeal.[33]

With what Partha Chatterjee terms the "moment of arrival," relations between the ruling party and the state became stronger while party-movement ties attenuated.[34] Social movements outside and against Congress were weak. Congress co-opted potential opponents through a nationwide patronage system. Many medium and large landowners became part of the Congress

[28] Kanchan Chandra, *Why Ethnic Parties Succeed: Patronage and Ethnic Head Counts in India* (New York: Cambridge University Press, 2004), 13–14.

[29] Gyanendra Pandey, "Congress and the Nation, 1917–1947," in Richard Sisson and Stanley Wolpert, eds., *Congress and Indian Nationalism: The Pre-Independence Phase* (Berkeley, CA: University of California Press, 1998), 122.

[30] Sumit Sarkar, *Modern India* (New Delhi: MacMillan, 1992), 183–7.

[31] Bimal Prasad, "Congress versus the Muslim League, 1935–1937," in Sisson and Wolpert, eds., *Congress and Indian Nationalism*, 311.

[32] Mushirul Hasan, "The Muslim Mass Contacts Campaign: Analysis of a Strategy of Political Mobilization," in Sisson and Wolpert, eds., *Congress and Indian Nationalism*, 209.

[33] Stanley Wolpert, "The Indian National Congress in Nationalist Perspective," in Sisson and Wolpert, eds., *Congress and Indian Nationalism*, 36–7.

[34] Partha Chatterjee, *Nationalist Thought and the Colonial World: A Derivative Discourse* (London: Zed Books, 1986), 132.

political machine. Progressive movements could not compete with Congress in establishing patronage relations and in claiming to represent minorities and the poor.

The Communist Party was at its strongest in the 1940s when it engaged in radical social movements, in Tebhaga, Bengal (1946–7) and in Telengana, the former Hyderabad state (1946–50). The Tebhaga movement took up share-croppers' demand to retain from landlords two-thirds rather than half of their harvested crops. Poor peasants organized the Telengana movement against evictions, forced labor, illegal exaction, and low wages. The Communist Party Marxist (CPM) in Kerala and the Communist Party of India-Marxist-Leninist (CPI-ML) in West Bengal, Andhra Pradesh, and elsewhere, grew as a result of these peasant struggles.

India's multiparty system came into existence largely as a result of social movement activity. Ironically, social movements, which in principle opposed political parties, were partially responsible for their creation. Four of the most important social movements in postindependence India, the movement for total democracy, led by JP Narayan, VP Singh's Jan Morcha (People's Front), the Naxalites, and Hindu Nationalists, strongly criticized political parties. But three of the four movements backed anti-Congress political parties that subsequently defeated Congress and achieved national power.

The "JP movement," as it was known, called for "total revolution" and "partyless democracy" to oppose the national Congress Party and the corrupt practices of several Congress-led state governments. JP Narayan, MK Gandhi's disciple, placed *lokniti* (rule of the people) above *rajniti* (rule of the state). He criticized political parties for their excessive concern for power and failure to engage in constructive activities. For Narayan, India could not regain its ethical moorings through political parties but only through citizens' direct, active involvement in politics.[35] However, Narayan did not reject parties entirely. He argued: "I believe that it is possible to develop a party-less democracy. But I am not asking you to abolish the party system immediately. It would be foolish because there is nothing to take its place."[36] JP Narayan supported the morphing of the movement into a political party, the Janata Party, which embodied many social movement features.

VP Singh participated in a broad-based struggle against the Congress government and supported the farmers' movement. His speeches condemned the exploitation of workers and the lower castes and decried imperialism, corruption, and "communalism." He created the Jan Morcha, with a *dalit* convener, as a professedly apolitical, struggle-oriented body.[37] The Jan Morcha gave rise to

[35] Jayaprakash Narayan, *Towards Total Revolution: Search for an Ideology* (Bombay: Popular Prakashan, 1978).

[36] Ibid., 178–9.

[37] "VP Singh, Raja Babbar Launch New Jan Morcha," *The Hindu*, April 24, 2006. Accessed July 4, 2014.http://www.thehindu.com/todays-paper/vp-singh-raj-babbar-launch-new-jan-morcha/article3151718.ece.

the National Front, a loose coalition of regional parties and social movements. Although VP Singh insisted that he was not politically ambitious and that the Jan Morcha would not participate in elections, he became a party leader and prime minister (1989–90) of a Janata Dal government.[38]

The point of this historical summary is not to claim that all parties have roots in movements, or that parties and movements always make good allies. Some movements – among feminists, environmentalists, and civil liberties groups – have resisted ties to parties because they are disinterested in achieving power and unwilling to sacrifice their autonomy. Conversely, some parties have seen autonomous movements as rivals and dismissed them as incapable of bringing about large-scale social change.

However, more often than not, parties have emerged from movements, allied with them, and been influenced by (and influenced in turn) movement discourses, demands, and constituencies. Among India's right-wing parties, the closer links between party and movement explain the greater strength of the Jan Sangh than the Swatantra (Freedom) Party. Formed in 1959 to oppose the ruling Congress Party's land reform policies and constraints on private enterprise, the Swatantra Party lost ground to the Jan Sangh partly because it failed to mobilize mass support around emotive social and cultural issues.[39] Close links between the OBC and farmers' movement and the Janata, Janata Dal, and Samajwadi parties, as well as between the VHP and the BJP, have shaped and defined Indian politics over the past two decades.

Alliances between movements and parties are cyclical. Parties tend to form the strongest alliances with movements before elections but marginalize or co-opt movement allies if they achieve power. Tensions arise on both sides of the divide: while movements may organize more militant agitations than parties find acceptable, parties may compromise on matters that movements consider nonnegotiable.

However, fissures between parties and movements need not be permanent. Parties that distance themselves from movements when they first attain power frequently seek out movements when they experience reversals and defeats. Parties may then provide movements programmatic incentives to regain their support. Furthermore, even when parties and movements do not re-establish formal ties, movement influences on parties are often subtle and enduring.[40]

The simultaneous growth of a multiparty system and of regional politics has given rise to new party-movement combinations. Contrary to Maurice Duverger's expectations, the first-past-the-post system of legislative

---

[38] Gail Omvedt, *Reinventing Revolution: New Social Movements and the Socialist Tradition in India* (Armonk, NY: M. E. Sharpe, 1993), 259.

[39] Motilal A. Jhangiani, *Jana Sangh and Swatantra: A Profile of the Rightist Parties in India* (Bombay: Manaktalas, 1967), 23.

[40] Doug McAdam and Sidney Tarrow, "Ballots and Barricades: On the Reciprocal Relationship between Elections and Social Movements," *Perspectives on Politics*, June 2010, Vol. 8, no. 2, 533.

representation has not resulted in a two-party system nor led parties to eschew ideology in favor of pragmatism in India. Multiparty systems are more likely than two-party systems to include far-right and far-left anti-system parties that thrive on accentuating conflict.[41] Furthermore, the growth of a multiparty system in India, as in many regions of the world, is associated with the rise of identity movements. India's thirty-four officially recognized state parties comprise two broad types.[42] The first is ethnic movements that have turned into parties. Most ethnic movements and the parties they have spawned have fought for linguistic and territorial rights.[43] A few have been nativist.[44] The second group is parties that have grown out of movements of farmers and OBCs.[45]

Leaders have multiple incentives to form new, ideologically cohesive parties before elections. They can thereby reduce the likelihood of conflict between individual legislators and the party leadership.[46] The 1985

[41] Sartori, *Parties and Party Systems.*

[42] State parties are more numerous than national parties in part because they can more easily achieve recognition by the election commissioner. A "national party" achieves that designation if it is active in four or more states for at least five years and elects at least 4 percent of the state's quota to Parliament or at least 3.3 percent to the state assembly.

[43] The Dravida Munnetra Kazhagam (DMK), formed in 1949, has its roots in the anti-Brahmin movement that opposed the national government's proposal to make Hindi a national language. This movement first brought the DMK to power in Tamil Nadu in 1967. In Punjab, the Shiromani Akali Dal, a collection of political parties, led the movement to create a Sikh majority state that resulted in the bifurcation of Punjab into the three states of Haryana, Punjab, and Himachal Pradesh in 1966. The Mizo National Front (MNF), formed in 1958, organized a mass movement that protested the government's inadequate response to famine in the region. The insurgency led to the formation of Mizoram in 1987 and brought the MNF to power in the state in 1998 and 2003. The Telengana Rashtra Samiti was formed in 2001 to organize a movement for the creation of a separate state of Telengana. The Jharkhand Mukti Morcha's prolonged struggle to create a separate state of Jharkhand achieved success in 2000. For an account of how political parties' demand for the creation of three new states, of Jharkhand, Uttarkhand, and Chattisgarh, grew out of community-based social movements, see Louise Till, "Questioning Borders: Social Movements, Political Parties and the Creation of New States in India," *Pacific Affairs*, June 2012, Vol. 85, no. 2, 261.

[44] The Shiv Sena in Maharashtra was formed in 1966 to mobilize Marathi speakers against migrants from other parts of India. It later evolved into an anti-Muslim party that maintained all the attributes of a movement. The All Assam Student Union organized a prolonged struggle to detect, detain, and deport illegal Bangladeshi immigrants. It gave rise to the Asom Gana Parishad of Assam party, which first contested and won the 1985 Legislative Assembly elections in Assam.

[45] They include the Janata Party – later the Janata Dal and its offshoots: the Samajwadi Party, Rashtriya Janata Dal, Rashtriya Lok Dal, Biju Janata Dal, Janata Dal (Secular), Janata Dal (United), and Lok Janshakti. The Rashtriya Lok Dal, led by Ajit Singh, claims fidelity to the legacy of the Lok Dal farmers' movement led by Charan Singh. Mulayam Singh Yadav, the leader of the Samajwadi Party, claims a commitment to socialist principles and the OBC movement. Ram Vilas Paswan, who formed the Lok Janshakti Party in 2000, established the Dalit Sena and was active in the Jan Morcha, a coalition of social movements led by VP Singh.

[46] Csaba Nikolenyi, "Recognition Rules, Party Labels and the Number of Parties in India: A Research Note," *Party Politics*, 2008, Vol. 14, 211–22.

Constitutional Amendment Bill, which restricts party defections and switching by members of the state and national legislatures, has inadvertently contributed to the growth of parties in India.

Challenges to the one-party dominant system emerged first in federal states, mainly from parties that grew out of movements.[47] National parties have become dependent on state parties to form and sustain governing coalitions. State parties largely determined the outcome of general elections and participated in every coalition government from 1989 to 2009.[48] Even in the 2014 elections, which the BJP won by a large margin, other political parties, mostly state parties, won 50 percent of the vote.

Of the six parties that were designated national parties in 2014 – the National Congress Party, BJP, Communist Party of India (CPI), CPM, and BSP – Congress alone can be considered a centrist, catch-all party, at certain points in its history (until 1966 and possibly since 2004). The BJP is a rightist Hindu nationalist cadre party. The CPI and the CPM are both leftist cadre parties with large front organizations. The BSP is linked to the *dalit* movement. However, the very distinction between national and state parties is tenuous because national parties can become state parties at the turn of an election.

To some extent, pressures on parties to become centrist come from members of multiparty coalitions. The dominant party may modify its electoral platform or insist that minority parties do so to attract the median voter. However, governing coalitions in India have sometimes excluded centrist parties and included parties of the right, like the BJP, and of the left, like the communists. Most parties in India that participate in coalitions seek short-term electoral gains or the removal of the incumbent party from power rather than long-term programmatic change. The dominant party has often formed alliances with ideologically divergent minority parties. Conversely, minority parties have often been ineffective in challenging dominant parties, either because they choose not to out of expediency or because they are too small and weak to do so.

---

[47] See Pradeep Chhibber and Ken Kollman, "Party Aggregation and the Number of Parties in India and the United States," *American Political Science Review*, 1998, Vol. 92, 2, 329–42, and Pradeep Chhibber and Ken Kollman, *The Formation of National Party Systems: Federalism and Party Competition in Canada, Great Britain, India and the United States* (Princeton, NJ: Princeton University Press, 2004), 201–4.

[48] According to the Election Commission, in the five national elections between 1991 and 2004, the vote share of national parties (those with a base in several states) dropped from 81 percent in 1991 to 68 percent in 1998 and the proportion of seats they controlled went from 86 percent in 1991 to 72 percent in 1998. By contrast, parties based in single states increased their share of the vote from 17 percent to 27 percent and their seats from 16 percent to 29 percent. A party that has a small presence in four states or wins eleven parliamentary seats from any three states is designated a national party.

The BJP's Distinctive Attributes

The BJP represents an alternative to the centrist catch-all party. The Jan Sangh and the BJP have accentuated and refashioned social cleavages to promote Hindu political identities. Although since the late 1990s the national BJP has adopted more centrist positions, it has never compromised its core values and has continued to mine religious and caste differences for political gain.

In some respects the BJP resembles other Indian parties that have resisted centrism and forged strong and durable ties to social movement organizations. However, the BJP stands out for the extent of its activist orientation, ideological commitments, and organizational cohesion. Although the Janata Party and the National Front achieved power in 1977 and 1989 respectively, as a result of extensive movement support, they severed movement ties after taking office. By contrast, the Jan Sangh and the BJP maintained allegiances to their beliefs and movement allies while participating in coalition governments during both these periods. The BJP challenges the assumed binary between parties and movements because the party pursues activism both independently and through a social movement organization. The BJP exemplifies the features of a movement-party.[49]

The BJP, and before that the Jan Sangh, have long engaged in Hindu nationalist activism. The Jan Sangh mobilized protests around banning cow slaughter in the late 1960s; the BJP and its affiliates continue to do so. Indeed, until 1993 the Jan Sangh and later the BJP achieved their most significant electoral gains by participating in movements (1967, 1977, 1989, and 1991). Following the Jan Sangh's prolonged agitation demanding that the state ban cow slaughter, its share of the vote increased from 4 percent in 1957, to 6 percent in 1962, to 9 percent in the 1967 parliamentary elections. It paid for relinquishing movement activities in 1971, when it received only 7 percent of the vote, and in 1984, when it received just 6 percent of the vote. By 1989, at the start of the Ayodhya campaign, the BJP's share of the national vote increased to 11 percent and by the 1991 elections, when the campaign was in full flower, 20 percent.

Many rank-and-file members pressed the BJP to assume a more activist role after its electoral setback in the 1984 general elections. BJP leaders concurred and called for frequent agitations on national issues. They recommended that any party unit that did not participate regularly in agitations should be considered defunct.[50] In March 1985, the party's national executive created a working committee that advised the BJP to reconstitute itself as a "cadre based mass party." The committee argued that to reconcile the differences between cadre and mass parties, the BJP should remain tightly organized while forming *morchas* (organized gatherings) to mobilize peasants, workers, tribals, and other

[49] Richard Gunther and Larry Jay Diamond, "Species of Political Parties: A New Typology," *Party Politics*, 2003, vol. 9, no. 2, 167.

[50] *Bharatiya Janata Party Policy Documents*, 1980–2005, Vol. 2 (New Delhi: Bharatiya Janata Party, 2005), 200.

groups. The BJP thus redefined itself as part of a broader national movement, as the following statement by its national executive suggests:

The BJP is not an ordinary political party in pursuit of power for the sake of power alone. Rather it is part of a wider movement. ... We should not be defensive or apologetic about our distinctive ideological identity. ... We should, in particular, mount a powerful and sustained counter-offensive against all those ideologies and political forces, especially the Congress and the Communists, who reject Hindutva as the basic identity of the Indian Nation.[51]

The BJP changed its programmatic goals following the reorganization of its party structure. At a plenary meeting in Bombay (May 9–11, 1986), it supported abrogating Article 370 of the Constitution, which provided autonomy to Kashmir, and passing a uniform civil code. RSS veteran LK Advani became BJP president and three RSS men became general secretaries. Advani denounced the Congress Party and identified with Hindutva goals. He called for close ties to the RSS and emphasized party discipline and ideological consensus. In April 1987, the national executive prohibited participating in national fronts and vowed to contest future elections independently. The BJP made far-reaching electoral gains by accentuating its Hindu nationalist commitments.

The BJP has encouraged and rewarded activism by creating a two-tiered membership system. Anyone over age eighteen can become an ordinary member by paying party dues, belonging exclusively to the BJP, and respecting constitutional principles. After three years, an ordinary member can become an active member by paying additional fees and participating in agitational activities and mass organizations. The BJP's constitution specifies that only active members are eligible to contest elections for *mandal* (administrative subdivision) committees or become members of any higher-level committee or council. BJP affiliated organizations, including the Mazdoor (Workers), Kisan (Farmers), Mahila (Women), Yuva (Youth), Scheduled Tribe, and Scheduled Caste *morchas*, also organize protest activities among their respective constituencies.[52]

The BJP's organizational structure combines democratic elections to local party posts alongside centralized leadership control at the national level, as the term cadre party suggests. Since its formation in 1980, the BJP has held elections for its district, *mandal*, and local committees, each headed by an elected president. However, the rules for intraparty advancement are less democratic

---

[51] Ibid., 2–3.
[52] Soon after the BJP was formed, as Mahila Morcha leader Mohini Garg related, Vijayraje Scindia formed an affiliated women's organization that Garg, Scindia, and Mridula Sinha co-convened. The BJP supported the creation of a women's organization to bolster support for the party. The Mahila Morcha's governing body consists of a president, three vice presidents, one general secretary, three secretaries, and a treasurer. According to its own estimates, the Mahila Morcha has offices in Delhi, all state capitals, 220 out of 440 districts, and 70 percent of all wards. By 2002, according to Surama Padhi, its national secretary, the Mahila Morcha had 30,000 active members who each paid Rs 100 in annual fees. Interview with Surama Padhi, Delhi, March 11, 2002.

above the district level. State and national presidents can nominate at least 25 percent of state and national executive committee members. The BJP gives its president great power by enabling him or her to nominate and fire all office bearers at will.

The BJP Parliamentary Board consists of twelve members, including the party president, who serves as leader of the party in Parliament.[53] Board decisions do not have to await regular meetings and do not require the national executive's authorization. Board members serve on the BJP's central election committee and play a vital role in determining the party's electoral strategy, candidates, and coalition partners. The Board has unilateral power to discipline even high-ranking members, as it did when it expelled former NDA cabinet minister Jaswant Singh in April 2009. By according extensive powers to the Parliamentary Board, the BJP ensures that its officeholders will remain ideologically committed to the party and that its leaders who serve in office will remain closely tied to the organizational wing[54] (see Figure 2.1).

[53] Parliamentary Board members as of 2014 were Ram Lal, Amit Shah, Narendra Modi, M. Venkaiah Naidu, Rajnath Singh, Nitin Gadkari, Arun Jaitley, Sushma Swaraj, Ananth Kumar, Thawarchand Gehlot, Sivraj Singh Chouhan, and Jagat Prakash Nadda.

[54] Composition of the state councils:

"(a) Members elected by the District Units as laid down in sub-clause two.
  (b) Ten percent of Party legislators to be elected by all the members of the legislative party, but not less than 10; if the total number of legislators is below ten, then all of them.
  (c) Ten percent of Party Parliament members from the state, but not less than 3. If the number of Parliament members from the state is below three, then all of them.
  (d) All members of National Council from the State.
  (e) All former State Presidents.
  (f) All members of the State Executive.
  (g) All office-bearers of a Regional Committee.
  (h) Leaders of the Party in State Assembly and State Council.
  (i) Presidents and General Secretaries of the District Committees in the State.
  (j) Party Presidents/Chairmen of Corporations, Municipalities, Zila Parishads and Blocks.
  (k) Nominated members (not more than twenty-five) by the State President.
  (l) State Presidents of allied Morchas and Cells."

Composition of National Council:

"(a) Members elected by the State Council as laid down in sub-clause 2;
  (b) Ten percent of the Party members of Parliament to be elected by all the Party members of Parliament, but not less than ten; if the total number of Party members is less than ten, then all of them.
  (c) All former National Presidents;
  (d) All State Presidents;
  (e) Leaders of the Party in Lok Sabha and Rajya Sabha;
  (f) Leaders of the Party in State Assemblies and Councils;
  (g) Nominated members (not more than forty) by the National President;
  (h) All members of the National Executive; and
  (i) All India Presidents of Allied Morchas and Cells."

This information is from the BJP constitution, available at http://www.bjp.org/content /view/745/480/.

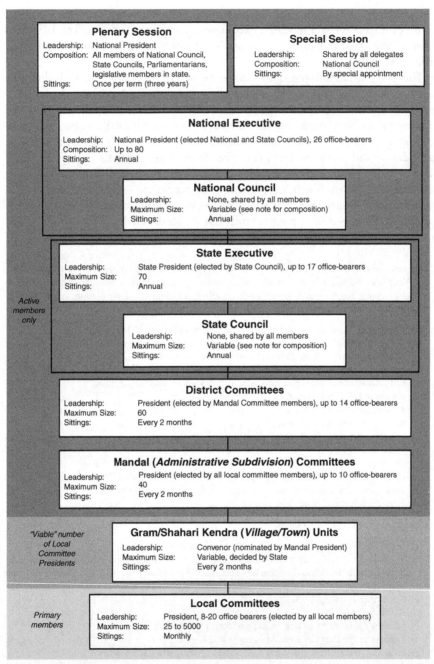

FIGURE 2.1. BJP's Organizational Structure.
Source: Compiled by author, permissions not necessary.

Many powerful, high-ranking BJP leaders have been party members for decades and began their apprenticeships in other Sangh Parivar organizations. Atal Bihari Vajpayee, LK Advani, Bangaru Laxman, Kushabhau Thakre, Jana Krishnamurthi, Rajnath Singh, and MM Joshi were all active in the Jan Sangh and joined the BJP when it was formed in 1980. Other party leaders, including Nitin Gadkari, Narendra Modi, and Venkaiah Naidu, were student activists in the ABVP.

There is a dramatic contrast between the BJP's cohesiveness and the Socialist Party's dependence on particular leaders, loose organizational structure, and amorphous ideology, which have complemented and reinforced each other, resulting in a dizzying history of splits and mergers.[55] The parties that emerged from the old Socialist Party remained as factionalized as their predecessor. The Janata Dal, that emerged out of the Socialist Party, failed to unify its disparate constituents, split, and gave rise to the SP. Lacking a well-developed organizational structure, the SP relied on Mulayam Singh Yadav's charisma and the Yadav caste association, the All India Yadav Mahasabha. The Socialist Party and its successors have participated in movements to remove the ruling party from office but have been hindered by their weak organizational structures from advancing positive political agendas.

The BSP is poorly organized and informally structured. Until 1997, the party leadership nominated all office bearers and even after that only held elections for heads of state units and continued to appoint members of the state executive committee and district bodies. The BSP in UP, unlike in other states in which it is active, has state and district-level committees but their responsibilities are not clearly delineated.[56] BSP founder Kanshi Ram and, since his death in 2006, Mayawati, have been the ultimate sources of the party's authority on ideological and organizational matters. The BSP's dependence on powerful leaders has undermined its receptiveness to grassroots activism. Some *dalit* activists feel that the BSP's focus on political power has displaced its commitments to cultural change and economic redistribution.[57]

The BJP bears some resemblance organizationally to the CPM. Both are cadre parties with hierarchical structures that extend from the national to

---

[55] The Congress Socialist Party (CSP) was formed within Congress in 1934. Some of its major leaders, including Acharya Narendra Dev, Rafi Ahmed Kidwai, and Triloki Singh, left the CSP to form new parties that merged in 1952 into the Praja Socialist Party. In 1955, the Lohia faction split and formed the Socialist Party (Lohia). The Praja Socialist Party (PSP) and the Socialist Party merged in UP in 1962 and at the all-India level in 1964 to form the Samyukta (United) Socialist Party. That same month, several PSP legislators joined Congress. After the 1974 elections, the Samyukta (United) Socialist Party merged with the Bharatiya Kranti Dal to form the Bharatiya Lok Dal, which folded into the Janata Party.

[56] Sudha Pai, *Dalit Assertion and the Unfinished Democratic Revolution* (New Delhi: Sage Publications, 2002), 101.

[57] Ibid., 2.

the local level. Their disciplined, cohesive party organizations complement and support their ideological commitments. However, the BJP has been more successful than the CPM in forging strong ties with civil society organizations. Except in Kerala, the CPM has expressed hostility and distrust toward social movements and NGOs. Whereas the BJP engages in social movement activities through its own front organizations as well as through the RSS and its affiliates, the CPM generally organizes movements exclusively through ancillary front organizations that experience the same victories and defeats as their parent body. Unlike the BJP and the VHP, neither the communist parties nor the peasant movements they have assisted have attained a national following.

The BJP challenges the notion that the centrism and cohesion of political parties are correlated. It has been most militant during periods and in states like Gujarat in which it has been most unified. In other states, including Rajasthan and UP, factionalism has prevented the BJP from mobilizing mass support for Hindu nationalist campaigns. However, unlike every other major party in India, the BJP has never split at the national level; its leaders who have formed their own parties in federal states have had limited success and have often later rejoined the BJP. After Uma Bharati was expelled from the BJP, she formed the Bharatiya Janashakti Party (Indian People's Power Party) in 2006 but rejoined the BJP in 2011. After being expelled from the BJP in 1999, Kalyan Singh rejoined in 2004, before leaving again in 2009 and rejoining in 2014. A number of BJP dissidents, led by Fakir Chauhan and Gordhan Zadaphia in Gujarat, resigned from the party and formed the Mahagujarat Janata Party. It lost all five of the seats it contested in the 2009 elections and merged with the BJP in 2014.

The Jan Sangh and the BJP have maintained their distinctive ideologies both when they have been minority and majority parties in coalition governments. The Jan Sangh pursued Hindu nationalist goals in 1967 when it formed coalition governments with the Samyukta Socialist Party and Swatantra Party in Bihar, Rajasthan, Haryana, Madhya Pradesh, Punjab, and UP, and acquired important roles in several state governments. In Odisha and Madhya Pradesh, it proposed freedom of religion acts that made conversions punishable by imprisonment and fines.[58] The Jan Sangh campaigned to suspend government aid to Christian missionary schools in several states. In UP it promoted

[58] The Madhya Pradesh Freedom of Religion Act (1967) prohibited conversion by "force," "fraud," and "inducement." The punishment was imprisonment for up to one year and/or a fine of up to $667, and in the case of conversion of minors under the age of eighteen, women and members of the Scheduled Castes and Scheduled Tribes, a maximum penalty of two years imprisonment and a fine of $1,334. The offenses were cognizable, inviting arrest, and were to be prosecuted with the sanction of the district magistrate. The BJP government introduced a similar act in Madhya Pradesh in 1968 but added the term "allurement" (including gifts) to the list of proscribed conversion methods.

Saraswati Shishu Mandir (Saraswati – the goddess of knowledge– Children Temple) schools that popularized Hindu nationalist ideals. The Jan Sangh forced Charan Singh to resign from his post of chief minister when he tried to prevent its ministers from nominating party members to powerful government positions.

When the Jan Sangh joined the Janata Front and subsequently the Janata government in 1977, it retained its ideological commitments and ties to the RSS.[59] It sought to introduce major educational reforms and to persuade Prime Minister Morarji Desai to support several Hindu nationalist measures including a national Freedom of Religion Bill. It gained his support for a constitutional amendment to ban cow slaughter; however, the government fell before it could pass the amendment.[60]

The BJP dictated the terms of the NDA government (1999–2004). Most parties joined the NDA on the basis of short-term, pragmatic considerations and did not actively challenge BJP policies or were ineffective in doing so.[61] Although the DMK, TDP, and Trinamool Congress protested the BJP's "saffronisation" of educational institutions and textbooks, they did not have much influence over government policy. Nor could they stop the BJP from making concessions to the VHP's demands around temple construction. The only party that resigned from the NDA in opposition to the BJP's actions in Gujarat was the small Lok Janshakti.

The RSS

The RSS converted necessity – the restrictions that the government placed on its direct involvement in politics in 1949 – into opportunity. It claimed an apolitical identity while actively engaging in politics, both indirectly, through its immersion in quotidian life, and directly, through the Jan Sangh and then the

---

[59] The Jan Sangh's central working committee developed the group's electoral strategy. It instructed its units in UP, Madhya Pradesh, Rajasthan, Punjab, Haryana, and Delhi to organize mass agitations and authorized Atal Bihari Vajpayee to form a united bloc in parliament. Nanaji Deshmukh, Jan Sangh general secretary, drafted the opposition front program. P. Dutt, "The Emergency in India: Background and Rationale," *Asian Survey*, December 1976, Vol. 16, no. 12, 1130–1.

[60] Atal Bihari Vajpayee became minister of foreign relations, LK Advani minister of information and broadcasting, and Brij Lal Varma minister of industry. Jan Sangh chief ministers included Kailash Chandra Joshi in Madhya Pradesh, Bhairon Singh Shekhawat in Rajasthan, and Shanta Kumar in HP.

[61] The DMK, Samata Party, Akali Dal, and Trinamool Congress had all fared poorly in the Legislative Assembly elections preceding the Gujarat violence and needed BJP support. The BJP formed coalition governments with the Ajanta Dal (U) in Karnataka and the Telugu Desam Party in Andhra Pradesh in 1999. The BSP and the BJP formed a coalition government in UP in 2002 and BSP leader Mayawati (who employs a single name) campaigned for Modi's reelection in Gujarat that year. Although Mayawati rose to prominence as an opponent of the BJP, she played a major role in enabling it to weather the political crisis in 2002.

BJP. The RSS often described the BJP as "a party with a difference" because it was less corrupted than other political parties by the blandishments of power. The RSS has straddled the divides between state and civil society, and party and movement, by forming a range of social organizations, creating Hindu nationalist subjects through daily *shakhas*, and influencing the membership and orientation of the BJP and its governments.

RSS-affiliated organizations are active in diverse spheres – education, science, technology, medicine, industry, commerce, governance, development, health, law, media, intellectual property rights, human rights, the environment, and the diaspora – and engage diverse communities – tribals, *dalits*, women, produc-ers, consumers, workers, students, teachers, lawyers, doctors, the handicapped, and retired soldiers. India's largest trade union, the Bharatiya Mazdoor Sangh (BMS), numbering more than 10 million members, its largest student union, the ABVP, and one of its largest NGOs, the Sewa Bharati, are all affiliated with the RSS (see Figure 2.2).

Shakhas
Since 1927, the RSS has groomed BJP leaders physically, intellectually, and ideologically, through *shakhas* – community gatherings that do not require membership in the RSS but strictly subscribe to its principles. Madhav Sadashiv Golwalkar (1906–73), the second RSS *sarsangchalak* (supreme leader), claimed, "If the top men are morally upright, then morality will trickle down to the low-est stratum of society and general good character will be the result."[62] *Shakhas* forge powerful bonds between small groups of men and the larger Hindu nationalist project.

One Sunday morning at 6 A.M. in South Extension, an upscale neighbor-hood in Delhi, I joined fifteen middle-aged men who had assembled in a public park with authorization from the municipal authorities. The men formed a *gata*, a subdivision of a *shakha* that consisted of about 100 members who were subdivided into groups based on age and interest. The gathering included advocates, businessmen, and real estate developers who had been meeting daily since they settled in this colony after Partition. They were members of the VHP, BJP, and other affiliated organizations but owed their principal loyalties to the RSS.

Shakha rituals sought to cultivate strength, faith, and masculinity. The first half hour was devoted to physical exercises and games. The next half hour consisted of singing patriotic songs, saluting the saffron flag, and hearing the convener describe the fundamental differences between Islam and Hinduism. He argued that, because Hinduism was at its core characterized by tolerance and Islam by intolerance, secularism could flourish only among Hindus, not among Muslims. During our conversation over breakfast, *shakha* members spoke of their plight as refugees in Delhi in the aftermath of Partition. One man described arriving in

[62] Madhav Sadashiv Golwalkar, *Bunch of Thoughts* (Bangalore: Vikrama Prakashan, 1966), 306.

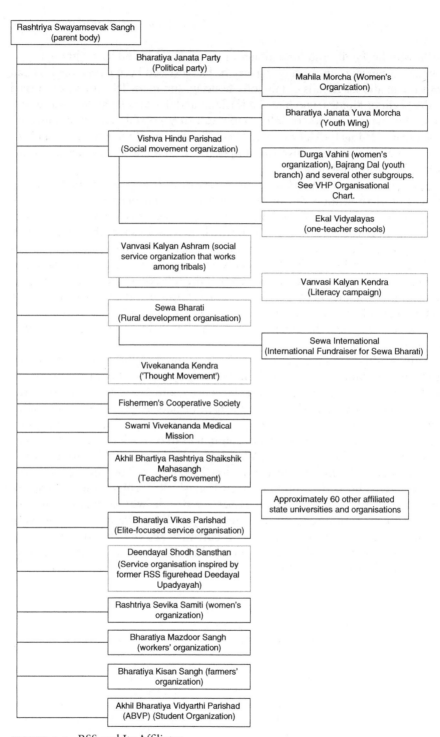

FIGURE 2.2. RSS and Its Affiliates.
Source: Compiled by author, permissions not necessary.

Delhi with his family and little money in his pocket. He said that, although government compensation for the property he had lost had been paltry, the RSS had helped him and his friends obtain jobs, housing, and food. The discussion turned to the plight of Hindus who had fled Kashmir and the dangers of Muslim aggression. One man asked rhetorically, "How can they possibly face discrimination when they ruled us for eight hundred years?" Another, alluding to the Gulf War, said, "It's good if the US pulverizes Iraq or it will continue to be a menace to the world. Better to finish it off."

Several features of this *shakha* are noteworthy. It kept alive Hindus' experiences of victimization during the Partition era and warned Hindus of the dangers they still faced. It combined service, political education, and solidarity building. It provided a social space in which men could share their experiences of daily life. The conversations resembled discussions that take place in tea stalls throughout India. The RSS' genius was to tether these everyday practices to a larger cause. Ram Madhav argued that the RSS recognized the vital importance of establishing direct personal contacts with recruits. [63] He claimed that a million people participated in *shakhas* and that they had grown from 30,000 to 50,000 from 1991 to 2008. In 2014, the RSS held about 45,000 *shakhas* across the country.

Ram Madhav noted that *shakhas* have adapted to the times by targeting students and young professionals and taking up issues of contemporary relevance like nuclear weapons, national security, and "terrorism." In 2013, the RSS created software *shakhas*, known as information technology (IT) *milans* (meetings), in Mumbai, Pune, Hyderabad, Kolkata, Delhi, and Bangalore. Their members are professionals in companies like Hewlett Packard, Philips, General Electric, Textron, IBM, Wipro Ltd, Mindtree, and Deutsche Bank. Participants in IT *milans* need not don khaki shorts or engage in physical exercises and can communicate in English. RSS chief Mohan Bhagwat described them as "weekend" *shakhas* for people whose nine-to-five jobs prevent them from attending daily meetings.[64] Many housewives and nonresident Indians (NRIs) participate in software *shakhas* because they cannot attend traditional *shakhas*.[65] One middle-class woman I interviewed in Delhi said that she had always envied her husband for being active in a

---

[63] Interview with Ram Madhav, Delhi, November 17, 2009.

[64] Anil Lulla, "Sangh's e-Sevaks," *Open Magazine*, February 27, 2010. Accessed June 30, 2014. http://www.openthemagazine.com/article/nation/sangh-s-e-sevaks.

[65] Gaut Siddharth, "'Software Shakhas' Draw Pros to RSS," *The Times of India*, January 28, 2008. Accessed June 23, 2014. http://timesofindia.indiatimes.com/india /Software-shakhas-draw-IT-pros-to-RSS/pmredirectshow/2736140.cms. TA Johnson, "Sangh in Cyber City Connects through Software Shakhas," *The Indian Express*, June 3, 2007. Accessed June 23, 2014. http://archive.indianexpress.com/news/sangh-in-cyber-city -connects-through-software-shakhas--------/32611/.Satyajit Joshi, "Cyber-Savvy Sangh Plans to Set Up E-shakhas," *Hindustan Times*, June 11, 2010. Accessed June 23, 2014.

shakha. Thanks to the Internet, she had found a community of like-minded Hindu women.

The RSS has expanded its national and transnational following through the use of social media. Its volunteers edit Wikipedia and saturate e-mail lists, blogs, and Twitter accounts.[66] The RSS has 72,826 subscribers on the social networking site Orkut. In 2009, it started a channel on YouTube that has 14,660 regular subscribers; its videos have been viewed 5,780,751 times.[67] The VHP started a Web TV program that provides up-to-date information on its activities in India and abroad.

The RSS and the BJP

The RSS participates in BJP decision-making by consulting with the BJP's central election committee on candidates and campaigns. Circumventing the BJP's procedure for election to party posts, the RSS appoints BJP district, state, and national organizational secretaries. Lower-level party bodies do not elect organizational secretaries. Although they need not be members of the BJP's executive committee, they have as much, if not more, authority than party presidents at comparable levels (district, state, and national). Given the power of senior BJP and RSS members, posts for national and state president are rarely contested. The BJP's national executive, the party's principal decision-making body, is composed of senior RSS-affiliated BJP leaders. This structure is replicated at the state level, with a president, executive, appointed by the president, and council. The RSS has ensured that the BJP's party organization has maintained autonomy and supremacy over its government or legislative wing.

The RSS sought to maintain control over the Jan Sangh. It undermined the Jan Sangh's second president, Mauli Chandra Sharma, who wanted to make the Jan Sangh organizationally and financially independent.[68] When the RSS forced Sharma to resign from the party in 1954, it became clear, as former Jan Sangh president Balraj Madhok stated, that the Jan Sangh would "henceforth function as a front organization of the RSS and not as an independent political organization."[69] By the late 1950s, the Jan Sangh was wholly dependent on the

---

http://www.hindustantimes.com/india-news/cyber-savvy-sangh-plans-to-set-up-e-shakhas /article1-496087.aspx http://timesofindia.indiatimes.com/india/Software-shakhas-draw-IT -pros-to-RSS/pmredirectshow/2736140.cms.

[66] Gyan Varma, "RSS Uses Social Media to Recruit Cadre in Cities," *Live Mint* and *The Wall Street Journal*, September 11, 2013. Accessed June 23, 2014. http://www.livemint.com/Politics /XKmDvhzTCG5RkbZ5I4AJPL/RSS-uses-social-media-to-recruit-cadre-in-cities.html.

[67] http://www.youtube.com/RSSOwner. "'Patriotic Warriors' YouTube Profile." YouTube, April 6, 2009. Accessed June 25, 2014. http://www.youtube.com/user/RSSOwner/videos?sort=p&flow =grid&view=0.

[68] Bruce D. Graham, *Hindu Nationalism and Indian Politics: The Origins and Development of the Bharatiya Jana Sangh* (Cambridge, UK: Cambridge University Press, 1990), 59–68.

[69] Balraj Madhok, *RSS and Politics* (New Delhi: Hindu World Publications, 1986), 57.

RSS. Party general secretary Deendayal Upadhyaya, who succeeded Sharma, strengthened ties between the RSS and the Jan Sangh. Under his leadership, 90 percent of Jan Sangh officeholders in Delhi, Maharashtra, and UP had RSS backgrounds.[70] When Balraj Madhok, who became party president in 1966, sought to free the party from the RSS, it marginalized him in favor of Atal Bihari Vajpayee, who won the presidency in 1968.

The RSS allowed Jan Sangh members to participate in the Janata government as long as they remained active in the RSS. When the Janata Party prohibited its members from participating in the RSS in March 1980, 3,500 people, including fifteen of the twenty-eight Janata Members of Parliament (MPs), split and formed the BJP. In its early years, the BJP's relations with the RSS were strained because of the BJP's commitment to integral humanism and Gandhian socialism instead of Hindu nationalism. In fact, the RSS considered supporting Congress rather than the BJP when Indira Gandhi began courting the Hindu vote. The BJP regained RSS support and became a stronger electoral force after committing itself to Hindutva in the late 1980s.

The RSS became openly critical of the BJP after its defeat in the 2004 general elections. It expressed "serious concern over the ideological erosion, behavioral misdemeanor and violation of organizational discipline" in the BJP.[71] RSS head Kuppalli Sitaramayya (KS) Sudarshan urged Vajpayee and Advani to step aside and make way for a new generation of BJP leaders.[72] The RSS expressed displeasure that the BJP made Advani party president after he visited Pakistan and described Muhammed Ali Jinnah as a secularist. When Advani challenged RSS interference in the BJP's affairs in 2005, RSS spokesperson Ram Madhav stated that "the RSS naturally wanted its ideological commitments to be reflected in all Sangh Parivar organizations."[73] Rajnath Singh, who succeeded Advani as party president, affirmed the BJP's commitment to core Hindu nationalist goals, including constructing a temple in Ayodhya. He amended the BJP's constitution to increase RSS representation within the party. The RSS also played a key role in choosing Nitin Gadkari as Rajnath Singh's successor.

RSS influence over the BJP's organizational structure, leadership, and objectives grew after Mohan Bhagwat became its *sarsangchalak* in 2009. Under Bhagwat's leadership, the RSS ensured that the BJP enlisted a large number of *pracharaks* and promoted party members with RSS backgrounds. It supported

---

[70] Walter K. Andersen and Shridhar D. Damle, *The Brotherhood in Saffron: The Rashtriya Swayamsevak Sangh and Hindu Revivalism* (Boulder, CO: Westview Press, 1987), 189.

[71] The RSS expressed these views at a two-day RSS "chintan baithak" (brainstorming session) that concluded that the BJP's distancing itself from Hindutva ideology had contributed to its defeat in the 2004 elections. Neena Vyas, "Advani in a Dilemma," *The Hindu*, October 25, 2004. Accessed July 4, 2014. http://www.hindu.com/2004/10/25/stories/2004102504491200.htm.

[72] "Vajpayee, Advani Should Make Way for New Leaders: Sudarshan," *Rediff News*, April 10, 2005. Accessed June 29, 2014. http://www.rediff.com/news/2005/apr/10rss.htm.

[73] Interview with Ram Madhav, Delhi, November 17, 2009.

the appointment of two hardliners to key positions: Narendra Modi, to the BJP's Parliamentary Board, and Vinay Katiyar, VHP leader in the Ayodhya movement, as BJP general secretary. It supported the expulsion of Vasundhara Raje as leader of the opposition in the Rajasthan Assembly, and Jaswant Singh, who served as NDA minister of external affairs and finance, for publishing a book praising Jinnah. Bhagwat overruled the objections of senior BJP leaders, particularly LK Advani, by promoting Narendra Modi as the BJP's candidate for prime minister.

RSS influence was apparent in the appointments that the BJP government made shortly after coming to power in 2014. Five of the party's eight general secretaries, two of eleven vice presidents, and all four joint secretaries have RSS backgrounds. (The number of joint secretaries has doubled, from two to four.) Three chief ministers who were elected in 2014, Laxmikant Parsekar in Goa, Mohan Lal Khattar in Haryana, and Devendra Fadnavis in Maharashtra, have RSS affiliations. The BJP appointed five RSS-affiliated governors. One of the government's most controversial decisions was to appoint Professor Yellapragada Sudershan Rao to chair the Indian Council of Historical Research. Rao's academic credentials are thin and his views echo those of the RSS. He has claimed that the *Ramayana* and *Mahabharata* are historically accurate, Ayodhya was clearly the birthplace of Ram, and the caste system worked well until Mughal rule.[74]

The VHP

The VHP can afford to take greater risks than the Jan Sangh or the BJP because it is not a political party and its success does not hinge on electoral outcomes. Unlike the BJP, its membership does not subscribe to democratic rules of governance. Like the RSS, it is a nonelected body that disdains procedural democracy. It has explicitly challenged electoral motivations, the rule of law, and parliamentary principles and claimed that democracy should reflect the interests of the Hindu majority. Giriraj Kishore stated in an interview that while politicians manipulated people to achieve short-term advantages, VHP *sants* sought to educate future generations. He described the VHP's religious advisory bodies as being guided by popular faith. "Politicians engage in poli-tricks," he said, whereas *dharmacharyas* [religious leaders] are guided by philosophical principles.[75] Former VHP president Vishnu Hari Dalmia concurred. He believed the VHP could claim a much higher moral

---

[74] "'Ramayana, Mahabharata Are True Accounts of the Period ... Not Myths,' Outlook Interviews Yellapragada Sudershan." Accessed December 1, 2015. http://www.outlookindia.com/article /Ramayana-Mahabharata-Are-True-Accounts-Of-The-PeriodNot-Myths/291363 and Romila Thapar, "History Repeats Itself," *India Today*, July 11, 2014: Accessed December 1, 2015. http:// indiatoday.intoday.in/story/romila-thapar-smriti-irani-old-history-baiters-of-bjp/1/370799 .html.

[75] Interview with Giriraj Kishore, New Delhi, April 17, 1991.

standing and engage in more extensive grassroots organizing by rejecting a political identity.[76]

The VHP's organizational structure differs from that of political parties. Its major advisory board, the Dharma Sansad, (Religious Parliament) an assembly of VHP-appointed religious leaders, is guided by its interpretation of Hindu faith. Furthermore, the VHP's organizational structure reflects its geographic conception of the Hindu nation. Rather than organizing units in federal states, the VHP identifies five major cultural zones (north, west, central, east and south India), which are further divided by region, province, block, district, and *prakhand* – units inhabited by about 100,000 people. The *prakhand* forms the epicenter for political organizing. The VHP has also created a vast network of organizations among different segments of the population (see Figure 2.3).

The VHP is committed to protecting and defending Hindus transnationally and to identifying the foreign sources of Hindu oppression in India. One of its earliest campaigns, against the reported conversion of *dalits* to Islam in Meenakshipuram, Tamil Nadu, in 1981, identified proselytization by transnational Islamic and Christian forces as a major threat to national security and urged the government to stop it. The Ayodhya movement achieved extensive support from the Hindu diasporic community. The VHP has created strong transnational networks in five zones of the world, each headed by a zonal coordinator: the United States and neighboring countries; the United Kingdom and Europe; Africa and West Asia; Southeast Asia, Australia, New Zealand, Pacific Islands; and "Bharat Khand," comprising India, Nepal, Bhutan, Sri Lanka, Bangladesh, Pakistan, and neighboring islands.

The VHP has been extremely successful in fundraising, both in India and abroad. The most infamous of the many transnational organizations that fund the VHP is the India Development and Relief Fund (IDRF), which was founded in 1989. According to a 2002 report, which examined the tax returns that the IDRF filed with the Internal Revenue Service, from 1995 to 2002, the IDRF distributed $5 million to 184 associations, 82 percent of which were affiliated with the RSS and its affiliates.[77] All these associations worked exclusively with Hindus and more than half engaged in religious conversion of poor tribals. My own examination of tax returns from 2001 to 2008 shows that the IDRF's funding grew steadily, with donations totaling $14.7 million from 1999 to 2008.

The VHP has engaged in two sets of activities. The first is to provide social services, such as primary health care, education, vocational training, and relief services in the aftermath of crises.[78] It runs orphanages and homes for

[76] Interview with Vishnu Hari Dalmia, New Delhi, April 10, 1991.

[77] *The Foreign Exchange of Hatred* (Mumbai: Sabrang Communications and Publishing, Mumbai, and the South Asian Citizens' Web, 2002).

[78] For a fine account of Hindu nationalists' social service work among the poor, see Tariq Thachil, "Embedded Mobilization: Nonstate Service Provision as Electoral Strategy in India," *World Politics*, July 2011, Vol. 63, no. 3, 434–69.

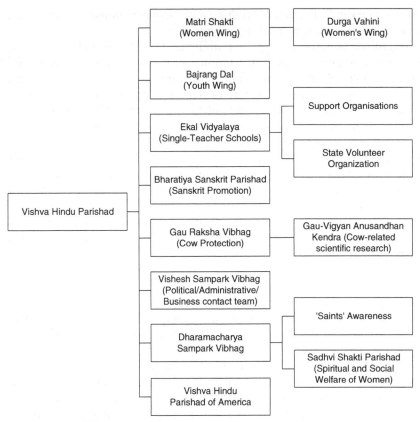

FIGURE 2.3. VHP and Its Affiliates.
Source: Compiled by author; permissions not necessary.

widows, the infirm, and physically disabled groups. Some of the most marginalized groups – *dalits*, tribals, and women – are beneficiaries. The VHP's women's organizations, the Durga Vahini (hereafter Vahini), and Matri Shakti, run vocational training centers that foster women's self-reliance and provide free legal aid and social services for women in hospitals, schools, and slums. Asha Sharma, a Vahini activist, observed that it appealed to low-caste women because it treated them as equals and helped families in times of need. For example, the Vahini would help families who could not afford marriage expenses.[79]

The Vahini ties service to national sacrifice. Its Web site states that women can find "fresh ways of rendering service to humanity," among other ways by creating blood donation camps. BL (known as Premji) Sharma, former VHP

[79] Interview with Asha Sharma, New Delhi, March 11, 2002.

general secretary in Delhi, described this coupling of consciousness raising and
social service as constituting a silent revolution.[80]

A second set of activities entails mobilizing Hindus around claims that
their identities are endangered by religious conversions, cow slaughter, and
the destruction of Hindu temples. The most important of these movements,
around the construction of a temple in Ayodhya, enabled the BJP to gain
the support of the lower castes and to identify with the VHP's emotive cultural appeals. Its ties to the VHP enabled the BJP to contend that it spoke
from moral conviction rather than from electoral self-interest. In certain
times and places, as in UP in the early 1990s, the BJP could short-circuit
the long, slow, hard work of party building by hitching its fortunes to the
VHP. Govindacharya commented that people often assumed that the BJP
was stronger than the VHP and failed to appreciate the VHP's influence
over the BJP.[81] Not surprisingly, the VHP, which shared Govindacharya's
view, deeply resented the BJP's centrist reorientation once it assumed
national power.

Party-Movement Tensions
The VHP made its support for the NDA government conditional on the government sanctioning the construction of a temple in Ayodhya. Its leaders
were unequivocal. Giriraj Kishore said: "We wholly support the BJP because
we want a Hindu government in power. But if the BJP does not abide by its
promises, we would cease to support it."[82] Surya Krishna, VHP general secretary, similarly remarked that if the BJP abandoned the Ram Janmabhoomi
issue, the VHP would "drop" the BJP.[83] Vahini leader Sadhvi Rithambara
declared that she was ready to oppose Kalyan Singh (then BJP chief minister
of UP) in favor of Mulayam Yadav if he opposed the VHP's campaign in
Ayodhya.[84]

Ashok Singhal, international president of the VHP, argued that the BJP
would have no political future if it followed the path of so-called secular parties. Vishnu Hari Dalmia, stated:

Though we are not a political organization ... being representatives of Hindus we will
now voice our concern on political issues which have plunged the nation into uncertainty. The petty games of our politicians have made the country an object of ridicule
in the eyes of the world.[85]

The BJP initially refused to concede to the VHP's demands, but then partially
caved. Vajpayee stated in December 2000 that support for temple construction

[80] Interview with BL Sharma, Delhi, February 20, 1991.
[81] Interview with Govindacharya, Delhi, February 20, 1991.
[82] Interview with Giriraj Kishore, Delhi, March 19, 1991.
[83] Interview with Surya Krishna, Delhi, April 15, 1991.
[84] Interview with Sadhvi Rithambara, Khurja, May 12, 1991.
[85] "VHP Set to Unfurl Hindutva Flag Again," *The Times of India*, May 2, 1999.

was "an expression of national sentiment" and that this task "remained unfinished." In early February 2002, BJP president Jana Krishnamurthi claimed there was some basis for the VHP's demand.[86] He defended his position some weeks later:

> The VHP has been emphasizing that a beautiful temple should come up in the place called *Ramjanmasthal*. ... They have collected historical and archeological data in support of their claims. Hindu sentiment demands a temple there. The VHP as a representative body of the Hindus has been putting forth this demand. And hence I said it is logical.[87]

The VHP increased pressure on the BJP. It attributed the BJP's poor performance in several Legislative Assembly elections in 2001 and 2002 to its backtracking on Ayodhya. It gave the government a year to clear the legal obstacles to building the Ram temple.[88] The VHP stated boldly, "The BJP must do some soul-searching if it is to prevent domino effect of recent reverses. Let the party give a thought to the consequences of not including the party's commitment to building a temple at Ayodhya in its election manifesto."[89] Ashok Singhal claimed that the prime minister had weakened the BJP and warned BJP president Venkaiah Naidu that the BJP would suffer if it opposed the VHP.[90] After the NDA government refused to pass legislation authorizing temple construction, the VHP engaged in far-reaching activism around Ayodhya from 2001 to 2003.[91]

The NDA government's concessions to the VHP merely strengthened the movement. Prime Minister Vajpayee legitimated the VHP's authority by meeting with its leaders in Delhi on January 27, 2002 and agreeing to resolve the issue, as the VHP demanded, by March 12.[92] Although the government refused to transfer land to the VHP for temple construction, it ordered Arun Jaitley, the

---

[86] V. Venkatesan, "We Cannot Control the VHP," *Frontline*, March 1, 2002. Accessed June 24, 2014. http://www.frontline.in/static/html/fl1904/19040060.htm.

[87] Ibid.

[88] Sarath Kumara, "Indian Government Reeling after Website Exposes High-level Arms Procurement Corruption," *World Socialist Website*, March 24, 2001. Accessed June 24, 2014. http://www.wsws.org/en/articles/2001/03/ind-m24.html.

[89] Shyam Khosla, "Mandate not against Ideology but Its Dilution," *Organiser*, March 10, 2002. Accessed June 24, 2014. http://www.hindunet.org/hvk/articles/0502/24.html.

[90] Pradeep Kaushal, "BJP Chief Sends VHP a Stinker," *Indian Express*, October 1, 2012. Accessed June 24, 2014. http://archive.indianexpress.com/oldStory/10471/.

[91] They included a *chetavani yatra* (warning procession) in January 2002 and a *sankalp yatra* (procession to make a pledge) in October 2003. It planned a number of *yagnas* (sacrificial rituals), including a 100-day-long *purnahuti yagna* (the final offering), followed by a *Ram naam japa yagna* in February 2002. It distributed *Ramraksha Sankalp Sutras* (sanctified threads) at a *yagna* from July to October 2003 and asked its followers to keep them tied to their wrists until the Ram temple was constructed.

[92] AG Noorani, "Land and Legality," *Frontline*, March 1, 2002. Accessed June 24, 2014. http://www.frontline.in/navigation/?type=static&page=archive.

law minister, to expedite the Ayodhya hearings before a Special Bench of the Allahabad High Court.[93]

The VHP was not placated. It participated in a first round of violence against Muslims in Gujarat on February 27–8, 2002 and another on March 15, the day of a VHP prayer ceremony. Prime Minister Vajpayee bowed to RSS pressure and retracted his initial statement of regret at the 2002 Gujarat violence. But thanks to pressure from coalition members and fears about its own culpability, the NDA government prohibited VHP activists from entering Ayodhya and prevented the VHP from organizing an *asthi kalash yatra*, with ashes of the victims of the Godhra train fire in February 2002. Venkaiah Naidu stated that the government could not ensure passage of legislation to construct a temple and instead supported negotiations between leading Hindu and Muslim religious institutions to settle the Ayodhya dispute. The BJP rejected the VHP's claims on the mosques adjoining temples in Kashi and Mathura.

The VHP was outraged. In June 2002, it announced that it would cease to abide by the Supreme Court's verdict that prohibited religious activity in Ayodhya. It directed its state units to mobilize Hindus to demand temple construction.[94] Giriraj Kishore claimed that Vajpayee had never helped the Ram temple agitation and warned that the VHP would campaign against his reelection to Parliament from Lucknow.[95] Praveen Togadia expressed contempt for the prime minister by calling him "Gandhi-II, for sidelining the VHP" and negotiating with the All India Muslim Personal Law Board, which he characterized as "a body of Muslim fundamentalists."[96] He threatened to launch a mass agitation against the government.

The VHP organized a much-publicized procession to Ayodhya on October 17, 2003. However, the SP decisively curtailed the movement and the NDA government did not protest Mulayam Singh Yadav's decision to arrest VHP activists. The combination of the national BJP's diminished commitment to temple construction and the state government's actions forced the VHP to suspend its campaign.

The movement that had promoted the party's rise thus became its formidable critic. The VHP refused to back the NDA in the 2004 elections and sought unsuccessfully to gain the support of other political parties for its eleven-point agenda, which included temple construction, banning cow slaughter, and

---

[93] Sheela Bhatt, "The Election Interview with Arun Jaitley," *Rediff News*, February 21, 2002. Accessed June 24, 2014. http://www.rediff.com/election/2002/feb/21_upr_shee_int_1.htm.

[94] V. Venkatesan, "Ayodhya: Promises to Break," *Frontline*, July 19, 2002. Accessed July 7, 2014. http://www.frontline.in/static/html/fl1914/19140230.htm.

[95] V. Venkatesan, "The Schism in the Sangh Parivar," *Frontline*, August 12, 2003. Accessed July 7, 2014. http://www.frontline.in/static/html/fl2014/stories/20030718003902600.htm.

[96] Ibid.

passing a uniform civil code. The VHP was furious that the NDA election manifesto proposed finding a resolution to the Ayodhya dispute through negotiation or the judiciary rather than legislation. The VHP did not campaign for the BJP or express disappointment at its electoral defeat. Ashok Singhal said, "The NDA government's policies disappointed us so we did not encourage our cadre to campaign for the BJP. You can see for yourself what happened."[97] At the BJP's national executive meeting in July 2004, LK Advani stated that there had been "a sense of alienation in our *Parivar* and a weakening of the emotional bond with our core constituency."[98]

The RSS supported the VHP's opposition to the NDA government. It condemned the BJP for putting Hindutva on the back burner and for increasingly resembling the Congress Party.[99] The RSS issued directives to the BJP on how it should function, called for its leaders to meet regularly with the RSS, and demanded the right to veto government policy decisions. Govindacharya, a committed RSS member who served as BJP general secretary, argued in an interview that the BJP's decision to withdraw support from the National Front government in 1990 reflected its placing ideology over political expediency.[100] Seventeen years later, Govindacharya said that the BJP's priorities had changed since it had assumed office in the NDA. "At best the BJP is Congress with a saffron stripe."[101] Despite BJP pleas, the RSS did not restrain the VHP from embarrassing BJP leaders and denouncing Prime Minister Vajpayee. The RSS delayed announcing its support for the BJP's candidacy in the 2004 elections.

The VHP's relations with the BJP also became estranged in Gujarat. Many VHP leaders turned against Narendra Modi because they felt that he wanted to undermine their power and demonstrate moderation at the expense of Hindu nationalist commitments. VHP leader Praveen Togadia, once Modi's ally, became his adversary and critic. Tensions flared up again in April 2014, when Togadia delivered a speech in Bhavnagar calling on Hindus to evict Muslims from their neighborhoods. Modi issued a statement on Twitter that criticized Togadia's remarks.

Relations between the VHP and RSS have also deteriorated. The RSS strongly supported the VHP in its early years. It encouraged the VHP to criticize the BJP-led NDA government. However, after Mohan Bhagwat became RSS *sarsangchalak* and began exerting increasing control over the BJP, the RSS no longer needed the VHP to serve as its proxy.

[97] "Temple Issue: VHP Targets Vajpayee," *The Hindu*, June 28, 2003. http://www.hindu.com/2003/06/28/stories/2003062805130100.htm.

[98] "We Lost Touch with Ideological Parivar: Advani," *The Economic Times*, June 24, 2004. Accessed June 24, 2014. http://articles.economictimes.indiatimes.com/2004-06-24/news/27411603_1_parivar-hindutva-bjp-leader-lk-advani.

[99] Kumara, "Indian Government Reeling."

[100] Interview with Govindacharya, New Delhi, February 20, 1991.

[101] Interview with Govindacharya, New Delhi, July 24, 2007.

Conclusion

Analyzing the character of party-movement relations and the trajectory of Indian parties dispels some misconceptions about political parties in democratic settings. India has become a multiparty system amid what scholars describe as a democratic resurgence over the past two decades.[102] Many new parties have grown out of social movements and have themselves participated in protest activities that are sometimes violent.

Movements and parties have both undermined and strengthened democratic processes in India.[103] Several ethnic groups that constitute majorities within federal states have organized exclusionary, chauvinistic movements and parties. More often, however, ethnic, territorially-based movements and parties have fought for cultural and linguistic pluralism and the devolution of power to federal states. Lower-caste movements and parties have expanded political participation and representation and sometimes sought a more egalitarian distribution of power and resources. Although the BJP has promoted the growth of federal parties by including them in coalitions, it has embraced less democratic goals when it has allied with the VHP.

Alliances between parties and movements in India as elsewhere tend to be unstable. Parties that attain power often seek to coopt movements, and movements that fear losing autonomy may seek to discredit parties with which they were formerly allied. Parties and movements may compete with one another in framing issues and gaining adherents.

However, in the case of Hindu nationalism, divisions between moderate and militant party members have never endangered party stability because they tend to be tactical rather than philosophical. The BJP cannot purge radical activists when they include its highest-ranking and most influential members. The VHP has resisted cooptation because the RSS has supported its autonomy from the BJP and its participation in disruptive protest. Indeed, it is hard to fully differentiate the RSS from the BJP because so many BJP leaders have RSS backgrounds. The RSS may sometimes publicly challenge the BJP but it also influences the BJP's structure, goals, and leadership.

---

[102] Yogendra Yadav, "Understanding the Second Democratic Upsurge: Trends of Bahujan Participation in Electoral Politics in the 1990s," in Francine R. Frankel et al., eds., *Transforming India: Social and Political Dynamics of Democracy* (New Delhi: Oxford University Press, 2000), 120–45.

[103] Important works on the quality of democracy include Larry Diamond and Leonardo Morlino, eds., *Assessing the Quality of Democracy* (Baltimore, MD: Johns Hopkins University Press, 2005) and Guillermo A. O'Donnell, Jorge Vargas Cullell, and Osvaldo M. Iazzetta, *The Quality of Democracy: Theory and Applications* (Notre Dame, IN: University of Notre Dame Press, 2004).

3

Movement Politics

Globalized Markets and Sacred Spaces

Understandings of social movements have changed dramatically from purportedly scientific but in fact heavily normative accounts that depicted mass action as anomic and irrational. Reification reached its peak in North American social science during the 1950s and 1960s when scholars made a sharp disciplinary and conceptual distinction between conventional and unconventional politics.[1] William Gamson aptly notes, "Political science claimed 'normal' prescribed politics as its bailiwick, leaving social movements to the social psychologist whose intellectual tools prepare him to better understand the irrational."[2]

Since the 1970s, social movement scholarship has taken several turns. First, the resource mobilization approach challenged assumptions about the irrational character of social movements by demonstrating the significance of their organizations, networks, and resources.[3] Next, scholars argued that social movements emerge when political opportunities exist and sought to link the emergence and growth of social movements to changes in the political environment.[4] Scholars

[1] David S. Meyer, "Opportunities and Identities: Bridge Building in the Study of Social Movements," in David S. Meyer, Nancy Whittier, and Belinda Robnett, eds., *Social Movements: Identity, Culture and the State* (Oxford, UK: Oxford University Press, 2002), 5.

[2] William Gamson, *The Strategy of Social Protest* (Homewood, IL: Dorsey Press, 1975), 133.

[3] Doug McAdam, John D. McCarthy, and Mayer N. Zald, eds., *Comparative Perspectives on Social Movements: Political Opportunities, Mobilizing Structures, and Cultural Framings* (Cambridge, UK: Cambridge University Press, 1996); Mayer N. Zald and John D. McCarthy, eds., *The Dynamics of Social Movements: Resource Mobilization, Social Control, and Tactics* (Cambridge, MA: Winthrop Publishers, 1979); and J. Craig Jenkins and Bert Klandermans, eds., *The Politics of Social Protest: Comparative Perspectives on States and Social Movements* (Minneapolis, MN: University of Minnesota Press, 1995).

[4] Hanspeter Kriesi, "The Political Opportunity Structure of New Social Movements: Its Impact on Their Mobilization," in Jenkins and Klandermans, eds., *The Politics of Social Protest*; David S. Meyer and Suzanne Staggenborg, "Movements, Counter Movements, and the Structure of Political Opportunity," *American Journal of Sociology*, 1996, Vol. 101, no. 6, 1628–60; Herbert

then emphasized the cultural dimensions of protest by exploring how social movements framed their demands and drew upon earlier repertoires of contention.[5]

Social movements are collective actions that challenge authorities to effect change.[6] Although their goals differ, many of their cultural repertoires are similar. They combine ideological appeals with symbolic acts and discourses to identify and interpret what they deem social injustice. Movements call on people to take personal risks even when the odds are against them. They crystallize deeply held identities and beliefs and simultaneously express popular anger, frustration, pride, and fear. They rouse people to action by providing them with a sense of efficacy, common purpose, and the possibility of a better, if idealized, world. They appeal to moral values to purify what is commonly seen as the dirty world of politics. Social movements are less constrained than parties in the ideologies they promote, the constituencies they represent, the demands they make, and the tactics and strategies they deploy. Social movements are simultaneously expressive and instrumental, and voluntaristic and organized. Their emotionally charged activity entails purposeful interactions with the state.[7] David Meyer comments, "Unlike pigeons in Skinner's boxes, people who make movements are moral and instrumental actors, if not always narrowly 'rational calculators.'"[8] Movements often affirm established moral codes even as they question and subvert them.

P. Kitschelt, "Political Opportunity Structures and Political Protest: Anti-Nuclear Movements in Four Democracies," British Journal of Political Science, January 1986, Vol. 16, no. 1, 57–85.

[5] D. A. Snow, "Framing Processes, Ideology, and Discursive Fields," in H. Kriesi, D. A. Snow, and S. A. Soule, eds., The Blackwell Companion to Social Movements (Oxford, UK: Blackwell Publishing Ltd., 2007); Robert D. Bedford, E. Burke Richford, David A. Snow Jr., and Steven K. Worden, "Frame Alignment Processes, Micro-mobilization, and Movement Participation," American Sociological Review, August 1986, Vol. 51, no. 4, 51:4 (Aug. 1986): 464–81; H. Johnston, "A Methodology for Frame Analysis: From Discourse to Cognitive Schemata," in H. Johnston and B. Klandermans, eds., Social Movements and Culture (Minneapolis, MN: University of Minnesota Press, 1995). On social movements' meaning-making work, see Mary Fainsod Katzenstein, Faithful and Fearless: Moving Feminist Protest inside the Church and Military (Princeton, NJ: Princeton University Press, 1998); and Robert L. Wood, Faith in Action: Religion, Race, and Democratic Organizing in America (Chicago, IL: University of Chicago Press, 2002). By the 1980s, debates about the relative merits of each of these approaches gave way to synthetic studies. Some social movement scholars took a further step in elaborating more dynamic and interactive frameworks for understanding what they termed "contentious politics." Doug McAdam, Sidney Tarrow, and Charles Tilly, Dynamics of Contention: Power in Movement (Cambridge, UK: Cambridge University Press, 2001).

[6] Smitu Kothari, Uday Mehta, and Mary Katzenstein, "Social Movement Politics in India: Institutions, Interests and Identities," in Atul Kohli, ed., The Success of India's Democracy (New York: Cambridge University Press, 2001), 246.

[7] Claus Offe, "The Two Logics of Collective Action." Political Power and Social Theory, 1980, Vol. 1, 67–115 and Nancy Whittier, "Meaning and Structure in Social Movement," in Meyer, Whittier, and Robnett, eds., Social Movements, 292.

[8] Meyer, "Opportunities and Identities," 12–13.

The stories they tell draw on established values and practices and prevailing standards of rights and justice, even as they direct these resources toward seeking to promote change.[9]

The question of violence deserves special mention. Violence can be productive to social movements in forging solidarities, empowering people, and fostering egalitarianism among stratified groups. Donatella della Porta identifies several processes that are associated with social movements' use of violence.[10] Activists justify what they characterize as defensive violence by claiming that it is legitimated by powerful, often religious institutions. They engage in a narrative construction of the past in which they make heroic attempts to defeat absolute enemies and disregard or repudiate alternative understandings of both the past and present. Groups that engage in violence have strong affective links to other activists and are prepared to make great sacrifices for them.

Activists' violence purportedly redeems the honor of groups that they claim have been victimized. Within and through violence, people may find opportunities to both circumvent and assume the powers of the state. "Nothing so inspires group violence against outsiders or perceived transgressors as the sense that the group is carrying out a legal, law-making or law-preserving mission," argues Robert Weisberg. "Armed with the belief that it is acting in the name of law, a group of rioters feels like a state itself, a body politic."[11]

It is appropriate, if controversial, to speak of Hindu nationalist social movements. By defining a social movement analytically rather than normatively, we can best appreciate Hindu nationalists' success in generating and harnessing political discontent. The strength of the RSS and VHP lies in their commitment to some of the values, practices, and beliefs that constitute the grammar of political dissidence and thereby connects social movements to "politics as usual" in India.

Most social movements, including many Hindu nationalist movements, have been peaceful. However, some, including the most successful, have employed violence to highlight the harm that activists claim Hindus have experienced as a result of purportedly unjust state policies and Muslim (and sometimes Christian) aggression. Provoking violence against minorities has enabled Hindu nationalists to truncate the long, slow, hard work of forging collective identities in order to rapidly build solidarities among Hindus across caste, class, and gender lines.

[9] Charles Tilly, *The Contentious French* (Cambridge, MA: Belknap Press, 1986), 4.
[10] Donatella della Porta, *Clandestine Political Violence* (New York: Cambridge University Press, 2013).
[11] Robert Weisberg, "Private Violence as Moral Action: The Law as Inspiration and Example," in Austin Sarat and Thomas Kearns, eds., *Law's Violence* (Ann Arbor, Michigan: University of Michigan Press, 1995), 185.

Hindutva activists have generally depicted, and perhaps sometimes genuinely considered, their use of violence defensive and retaliatory. Fights in which Hindus are injured, regardless of whether religious affiliations caused those injuries, are often catalysts for anti-minority violence. Hindu nationalists place such incidents within what they see as a history of Muslim dominance, a state that protects minority interests, and the growth of transnational Islamic movements. Engaging in violence that provokes retaliation by either Muslims or the state enables Hindu nationalists to depict Hindus as victims rather than aggressors. Retaliation also constitutes an attempt to "teach Muslims a lesson" so that they cease to constitute a threat to Hindus.

The first section of this chapter explores the elements of the most successful Hindu nationalist social movements, beginning with their politicization of religion. Hindu nationalist movements that employ religious appeals have often been violent. Mobilizing religious sentiment and engaging in violence have refashioned community and gender identities. Women are key actors in most social movements, including Hindu nationalist movements. Gendered appeals have featured prominently in Hindu nationalist campaigns, particularly when they have been violent.

The second section compares two movements, around Ayodhya and globalization. Ayodhya was the more successful and violent of the two because of its religious appeals, ability to organize across scales of political life, and refashioning of identities. Furthermore, the Ayodhya movement at its height, unlike the anti-globalization movement throughout, had the full support of the BJP and BJP-led state governments.

Religious Activism

Some of the most influential social movements have issued religious appeals and gained access to resources and networks through religious institutions.[12] Historically, religious processions provided the only opportunities for cross-class gatherings and protest in elite-dominated colonial public spheres.[13] Religious discourses lend themselves to grassroots organizing because they are

---

[12] On the resources social movements gain through religious institutions, see Peter B. Clarke, ed., *Encyclopedia of New Religious Movements* (London, UK: Routledge, 2006); John D. McCarthy and Mayer N. Zald, "Resource Mobilization and Social Movements," in Kriesi, Snow, and Sarah Soule, eds., *The Blackwell Companion to Social Movements* and Mayer N. Zald and John D. McCarthy, "Religious Groups as Crucibles of Social Movements," in John D. McCarthy and Mayer N. Zald, eds., *Social Movements in an Organizational Society: Collected Essays* (New Brunswick, NJ: Transaction Books, 1987).

[13] Sandria Freitag, *Collective Action and Community: Public Arenas and the Emergence of Communalism in North India* (Berkeley, CA: University of California Press, 1989), 26.

familiar to ordinary people.[14] Hindu nationalists have organized *yatras* (pilgrimages) that provide public voice and visibility to groups that are excluded from Brahmanical rites and confer a common Hindu identity on people from different regions and religious sects.[15] The religious character of these activities masks their political intent and can encourage people to break laws, take risks, and engage in violence that would otherwise be morally unacceptable.[16]

RSS-affiliated organizations provide religious justification for Hindu nationalist activism. For example, the Rashtriya Sevika Samiti (National Women Volunteers' Committee, hereafter the Samiti) justifies violence to uphold *dharma* (duty) and establish India as a Hindu state.[17] It derives inspiration from the Bhagvad Gita, which privileges action over knowledge in attaining freedom.[18] Novelist Bankim Chandra Chattopadhya invented the major deity that the Samiti worships, *Bharat Mata* (Mother India), in 1882. Samiti founder Lakshmibai Kelkar created Ashtabhuja (an eight-armed goddess), who combines the attributes of three goddesses, including the fierce Kali, whom it also worships.[19]

Among the most militant Hindu nationalists in the Ayodhya movement were *sadhvis* (female ascetics), who enjoined Hindu men to engage in anti-minority violence. Their privileged religious status enabled them to challenge the unethical nature of political life based on Hindu conceptions of the inferiority of the worldly political domain compared to the other-worldly religious domain. These women claimed that Muslims, with the support of some Hindu traitors, threatened to shatter the private spheres of religion and family by violating both Hindus' sacred places and their women. Their anger enabled them to demean the seemingly powerful, thereby inspiring confidence in those who were angry but disempowered.

---

[14] Rhys H. Williams, "From the 'Beloved Community' to 'Family Values': Religious Language, Symbolic Repertoires, and Democratic Culture," in Meyer, Robnett, and Whittier, eds., *Social Movements: Identity, Culture and the State*, 251.

[15] Diana Eck, *Darśan: Seeing the Divine Image in India* (New York: Columbia University Press, 1998), 338.

[16] Mark Juergensmeyer, *Terror in the Mind of God: The Global Rise of Religious Violence* (Berkeley, CA: University of California Press, 2003), 162.

[17] The RSS created the Samiti in 1936 because it opposed women's membership in the RSS. Today, the Samiti consists of a highly dedicated cadre of women who educate girls and women in its philosophy through weekly *shakhas*. A *pramuk sanchalika*, the all-India general secretary, presides over twenty-four officeholders at the Samiti headquarters in Nagpur, where the RSS is also based. According to its own estimates, in 2007 the Samiti had 4,392 branches in India and offices in twenty-two countries.

[18] Kalyani Devaki Menon, *Everyday Nationalism: Women of the Hindu Right in India* (Philadelphia: University of Pennsylvania Press, 2010), 87.

[19] Paola Bacchetta, "Hindu Nationalist Women Imagine Spatialities/Imagine Themselves: Reflections on Gender-Supplemental Agency," in Paola Bacchetta and Margaret Power, eds., *Right-Wing Women: From Conservatives to Extremists around the World* (New York: Routledge, 2002), 50.

The VHP has organized religious bodies, gatherings, and ceremonies to promote Hindu nationalist causes by inventively reinterpreting Hinduism. For example, it has elevated the significance of certain religious festivals by observing them with more fanfare than in the past. It has incorporated symbols of other faiths into its own observances and sought to semitize Hinduism.[20] It has imbued political events with religious significance. When the BJP government that briefly attained power in May 1998 exploded a nuclear device, the VHP announced that it would build a *Shakti pith* (Shakti temple) near Pokhran to honor the site where it was detonated. In keeping with its other national campaigns, Ashok Singhal, proposed distributing radioactive sands throughout India.[21]

The VHP has tried to erode the distinctive regional characteristics of religious ceremonies by homogenizing and nationalizing them. The *yatras* that it has organized since the 1980s traverse larger stretches of territory, last longer, occupy public spaces more aggressively, and identify more strongly with particular causes than other *yatras*. The VHP acquired national prominence by organizing a month-long *ektamata yatra* (unity procession) from November to December 1983 that culminated in a rally in Delhi. This paved the way for the *rath yatra, shilanyas, Ram shila pujas* (ceremony to sacralize bricks), and *Ram jyotis* (torch lighting ceremony) that began or ended in Ayodhya. It planned another *ektamata yatra* in 1995 calling for the worship of *Bharat Mata*, the holy cow, and the river Ganges. It organized a *yatra* in March 1997 to protest prohibitions against Hindus worshipping at the Krishna temple in Mathura and several *yatras* in December 1998 at what it claimed was the site of a Hindu temple at Baba Budrangi, a Sufi shrine in Karnataka.

The VHP has treated Hinduism as a national religion that includes Sikhs but excludes Muslims. It described Hindu activists as *kar sevaks* to conjure their identification with the Sikh volunteers who rebuilt the Golden Temple in Amritsar after it was damaged by the state in 1984. The VHP revived memories of legendary Sikh battles against Muslim rulers to draw a parallel between the state's damaging the Golden Temple and its refusal to allow Hindus to destroy a mosque and build a temple in Ayodhya. It thereby also associated itself with the Sikh martial tradition and sought to assimilate Sikhs into Hinduism.

The VHP's political commitments have shaped its stance on religion. It began to actively recruit *sants* and form religious advisory groups after it decided to play an activist role. It selected and promoted *sants* who shared

---

[20] See, for example, Lloyd Rudolph and Susanne Hoeber Rudolph, "Living with Multiculturalism: Universalism and Particularism in an Indian Historical Context," in Richard A. Shweder, Martha Minow, and Hazel Rose Markus, eds., *Engaging Cultural Differences: The Multicultural Challenge in Liberal Democracies* (New York: Russell Sage Foundation, 2002).

[21] John McGuire and Ian Copland, *Hindu Nationalism and Governance* (New Delhi: Oxford University Press, 2007), 366.

its views. It organized conventions to address politically charged questions, such as constructing temples in Ayodhya, Kashi, and Mathura, unrest in Punjab and expelling Bangladeshi refugees. It has organized its most important activities on religious holidays like Shivratri, the Kumbha Mela, and Divali, as well as to coincide with elections and other important political events.

The BJP has also employed religious symbols and discourses in organizing protest activities. It has planned demonstrations and processions to coincide with important religious holidays like Dussehra, Janmashtami, Ganesh Chatturvedi, Vinayak Chaturthi, and the Kumbh Mela. It has appreciated the importance of meaning-making work in institutional locations outside the formal political domain. *Yatras* also constitute a critical dimension of the BJP's social movement activities.[22] A BJP pamphlet made its political use of religious traditions explicit:

In modern times, the Bharatiya Janata Party is proud to have reinvented the quintessentially Indian tradition of *Yatra* and employed it – as against the imported, videshi concept of "road shows" – as a means of mass political campaign.[23]

Hindu nationalists have insisted that Hinduism is not a religion but a way of life, thereby implying that it is exempt from secular prohibitions on mixing religion and politics. It has claimed that a defining and sometimes troubling feature of Hinduism is its tolerance, which has rendered Hindus passive and vulnerable to Muslim domination.

Refashioning Identities

The most successful social movements have refashioned identities. Environmental and other movements have heightened tribals' grievances and pride in their own identities. *Dalit* movements against caste oppression have increased *dalit* consciousness and self-respect. Similarly, Hindu nationalists have affirmed Hindu pride and solidarity. They have responded to lower castes' experiences of marginalization by including them in ceremonies and campaigns from which

---

[22] The most important was Advani's *rath yatra* in 1990. Other, less successful *yatras*, followed. Murli Manohar Joshi led a 15,000-kilometer *ekta yatra* (unity pilgrimage) from Kanyakumari, on the southern coast, to Srinagar in the north to protest the government's failure to protect Hindus from Pakistani-backed insurgents in Kashmir from December 1991 to January 1992. Four BJP leaders organized *janadesh yatras* (All-India Pilgrimages) that covered 15,000 kilometers across five states from September 11–25, 1993 to oppose the Congress government's attempts to remove religion from public life.

[23] LK Advani, "How the BJP has Modernized the Concept of 'Yatra' in the Indian Tradition," Bharatiya Janata Party Web site, April 6, 2006. Accessed June 25, 2014. http://www.lkadvani .in/eng/content/view/576/334/.

they have traditionally been excluded. They have idealized Hindu women's roles as wives and mothers and accorded them certain freedoms in order to involve them in violent anti-Muslim campaigns. They have heightened Hindu men's anxieties about their masculinity.

The gendering of racial and ethnic differences does not depend on the actual identities of men and women. In patriarchal societies, male victims tend to be feminized. "A male victim," William Ian Miller argues, "is a feminized male."[24] Conversely, a victimizer tends to be gendered masculine and sexually aggressive. Stanley Tambiah describes the symbolic ways members of one community may attempt to incorporate qualities of the other that they envy or fear.

When a minority, or another community, is under attack by a crowd in the name of equalization of entitlements, then the wanton destruction of the lives and property of the "enemy" is inseparably accompanied by the personal appropriation and incorporation of that enemy's status, genius and wealth.[25]

Arjun Appadurai explores the ways majorities affirm their identities and create cultural certainties by seeking to eliminate minorities. His description of majority violence as marking the bodies of others with signs of their own strength is suggestive of the gendered character of ethnic violence.[26]

Hindu nationalists have sought to refashion male identities. BL Sharma stated, "Men are not born. They have to be created. This is a long slow process. After all it takes nine months to create babies so think about how long it takes to create real men. So far men are missing in this country."[27] He then denigrated Hindu men for being effeminate and passive and Muslim men for being overly masculine and predatory.

Gendered images of Muslim male aggression and Hindu vulnerability have repeatedly enjoined Hindu men to engage in anti-Muslim violence. Hindu nationalists' most provocative slogans, speeches, and graffiti concern Muslim men's supposed virility and sexual aggression. These images bear striking resemblances to colonial images of effeminate, weak Hindu men.[28] Notions of Muslim male sexual excess underlie the rigorous measures that Hindu nationalists have advocated to control Muslim family size, prohibit polygamy, and punish rapists.

[24] William Ian Miller, *Humiliation and Other Essays on Honor, Social Discomfort, and Violence* (Ithaca, NY: Cornell University Press, 1993), 55.
[25] Stanley Tambiah, *Leveling Crowds, Ethnonationalist Conflicts and Collective Violence in South Asia* (Berkeley, CA: University of California Press, 1996), 275–6.
[26] Arjun Appadurai, *Fear of Small Numbers: An Essay on the Geography of Anger* (Durham, NC: Duke University Press, 2006), 89–90.
[27] Interview with BL Sharma, Delhi, February 20, 1991.
[28] Joseph Alter argues that *brahmacharyas* demonstrated their capacity for self-discipline in opposition to colonial characterizations of upper-caste Hindu men as emasculated. Joseph Alter, "Celibacy, Sexuality and the Transformation of Gender into Nationalism in North India," *The Journal of Asian Studies*, February 1994, Vol. 53, no. 1, 45–66.

In order to illustrate the ways religious imagery can be deployed to promote Hindu nationalist activism, I explore the crystallization of general themes within a single historical case. The section that follows describes the Ayodhya movement, the most successful and violent Hindu nationalist social movement. It was laden with religious imagery; polarized Hindus and Muslims in part through religious appeals; and organized simultaneously locally, nationally, and globally.

Ayodhya

The VHP's campaign around Ayodhya peaked from 1989 to 1992. The culmination of the movement, the destruction of the mosque in December 1992, resulted from the combined efforts of the BJP, RSS, and VHP. Ostentatiously ignoring Supreme Court directives, the VHP undertook a widely publicized pilgrimage to Ayodhya to construct a platform within the mosque complex in July 1992. Four months later, it announced that it would undertake a massive procession to Ayodhya that would culminate in the construction of a temple at the site. By the end of November, more than 20,000 people had reached Ayodhya. By December 6, ten times that number assembled to perform what was ostensibly a symbolic *kar seva*, although earlier VHP leaders had hinted at more concrete and violent plans. On the morning of December 6, specially trained Bajrang Dal and Shiv Sena activists began attacking the mosque. The central government did nothing to stop the flow of people to Ayodhya and the police on site made no attempt to stop the demolition. RSS organizers encouraged activists to break through the barricades, plant a saffron flag on the mosque, and demolish it with hand tools.

Senior BJP leaders LK Advani and MM Joshi arrived at the site before activists began destroying the mosque.[29] Advani told the gathering to seal the roads to Ayodhya to prevent government forces from intervening.[30] The Liberhan Commission, which later investigated the mosque demolition, reported that the BJP state government had ample prior knowledge that the demolition was planned for December 6. In the immediate aftermath of the destruction of the mosque, the jubilant and unrepentant BJP Chief Minister of UP, Kalyan Singh, spoke of "an approaching revolution" and claimed that "no power on earth can now stop completion of the grand and majestic Ram temple." He proclaimed:

December 6th has found a permanent place in *Hindusthan's* history. It marks the day the masses gave their verdict, removing forever a symbol of slavery. ... The nation's glory and pride returned that day. ... It signals the beginning of a new India, a nation which can take pride in its people and hold its head high.[31]

[29] "News Reports on the Demolition," *The Hindu*. December 7, 1992.
[30] Ibid.
[31] *Indian Express*, January 19, 1993.

The BJP claimed that the Ayodhya movement reflected a groundswell of popular support for the construction of a temple. Its white paper on Ayodhya stated that Sangh Parivar leaders had unsuccessfully begged people not to damage the structure and had even tried to physically restrain the crowds.[32] It described the demolition as an "uncontrollable upsurge of a spontaneous nature" and claimed that the government had not appreciated "the mass passions involved."[33] Bhagwati Prasad, BJP state executive committee member, exclaimed, "We never expected that so many people would come to do *kar seva*. It was impossible to control such an enormous gathering."[34] The BJP's national executive committee meeting of November 9–10, 1990 described the *rath yatra* as "an irresistible movement," "saluted the *kar sevaks* who had traveled long distances ... bowed its heart in tearful homage to the sacred martyrs of Ayodhya," and promised that the "blood of *Ram bhakts* shall not go in vain."[35]

The Ayodhya movement was far from spontaneous. The VHP, with RSS and BJP support, engaged in extensive prior planning and preparation. In April 1984, it demanded that the government return shrines in Ayodhya, Mathura, and Varanasi to Hindus. It threatened to break the locks to the shrine in Ayodhya if the government did not allow Hindu devotees to pray there. That same year, an RSS-affiliated organization, the Ram Janmabhoomi Mukti Yagna Samiti (Committee of Sacrifice to Liberate Ram's Birthplace) launched the *tala kholo* (open the locks) agitation. On September 23, 1984, the VHP organized a procession from Sithamarhi in Bihar that reached Ayodhya on October 6. It cancelled a large demonstration it had scheduled in Delhi because of Indira Gandhi's assassination. Twenty-five processions traveled from various parts of north India to Ayodhya in 1985. Four years later, the VHP announced a much more ambitious agenda to build a costly temple at Ayodhya. In September–October 1989 it organized the *Ram shila puja*, which entailed inscribing "Shri Ram" on several hundred thousand bricks. The VHP secured the support of thousands of religious leaders who established training centers at 213 sites in twenty-two states from June to October 1989. Activists transported the bricks to villages across the country where priests and village elders wrapped them in saffron cloth, worshipped them, and took them to large collection sites. The VHP reported that in UP alone, 78,272 people performed prayers. It strengthened its subdistrict-level organizations and created new bodies within temples to organize *Ram bhajans* (prayers that sing praises of Lord Ram) and publicize VHP activities.

---

[32] *The BJP's White Paper on Ayodhya and the Rama Temple Movement* (New Delhi: Bharatiya Janata Party, 1993), 132.
[33] Ibid., 131.
[34] Interview with Bhagwati Prasad, Lucknow, December 28, 1992.
[35] Bharatiya Janata Party, *Volume 5: Political Resolutions* (New Delhi: Bharatiya Janata Party, 2005), 297.

Public displays [handwritten annotation]

The VHP mobilized mass support by planning activities in which people could participate in person or from overseas. It issued evocative, symbolically rich religious appeals to self-sacrifice, courage, and justice. It identified the Ayodhya movement with the anticolonial nationalist movement by depicting Muslims as outsiders and Hindus as rightful but wronged citizens. It mobilized anger against the UP government which it claimed was anti-Hindu. It made skillful use of the mass media and drew historically marginalized groups into its campaigns. It challenged Hindu men to demonstrate their masculinity by engaging in violence. And it gained the support of the BJP both when the BJP was in opposition and in office in UP.

The *Ram shila puja*, like many of the VHP's activities, allowed people to contribute to temple construction regardless of their social standing and physical location. Those who could not join processions could donate bricks. By gathering bricks from all over the country and from many parts of the world, the VHP implied that ordinary people had built the temple quite literally from the ground up. An article in a VHP journal commemorating the campaign stated, "It is a programme which connects every individual to the national memorial of Shri Ram. In a way it is a memorial which will be built by mass participation brick by brick."[36]

Following the *Ram shila pujas,* the VHP organized the *shilanyas* (November 9, 1989), a foundation-laying ceremony at which activists laid the bricks in an excavated area where they planned to build the temple. In the *Ram jyoti* ceremony that followed, activists lit torches in Ayodhya and used them to light other torches along the way. In November 1990, the VHP organized processions carrying twenty-two urns filled with ashes of activists who had been killed in Ayodhya.

All these actions suggested that millions of Hindus had participated in building the temple with their own hands. They demonstrated that people in far-flung regions could participate in the campaign without traveling any distance, spending much money, or incurring any risk. Simply blessing a brick, lighting a torch, or placing a saffron flag on a rooftop or a sticker on a door signified their commitment. These expressive actions also had instrumentalist goals. The VHP reported having collected $692,000 from UP and $4.6 million nationwide in the course of the *shilanyas.*[37]

The VHP's imaginative ceremonies were modeled on religious observances. The *Ram shila puja* and the *Ram jyoti* procession captured the decentralized spirit of Hinduism in which prayers could be performed over bricks at the roadside rather than by visiting a temple. Similarly, the lighting of the *Ram jyoti* could easily be incorporated into the ritual of lighting the oil lamp at dusk. The VHP transformed the familiar North Indian greeting, "Jai Sita Ram," into the battle cry "Jai Shri Ram," and encouraged people to blow conch shells and fly

[36] BK Kelkar, "Frankly Speaking," *Organiser*, October 8, 1989.
[37] Vishva Hindu Parishad, *VHP Silver Jubilee Special Issue*, 1989–90, 63–4.

saffron flags from their rooftops. The most important of these ceremonies was LK Advani's triumphant *rath yatra*, which left Somnath Gujarat on September 25, 1990, and planned to reach Ayodhya, 10,000 kilometers away, on October 30, 1990. Advani's Toyota van was bedecked with ornaments that transformed it into a splendiferous chariot. Advani assumed the attributes of a mythological hero and many of the activists who accompanied him were clad in saffron and dressed like the monkey god Hanuman. The *rath yatra* stopped frequently en route to participate in religious ceremonies.

Hindu nationalists likened their protests in Ayodhya to *satyagrahas* during the anticolonial struggle. KR Malkani compared Advani's *rath yatra* to Gandhi's salt march.[38] They sought to demonstrate that the BJP was better suited than the Congress Party to lay claims to a nationalist identity, for "the sons of Macaulay," as RSS leader Sudharshan described Congress leaders, had committed the sin of dividing the holy *Bharat Mata*.[39] Advani claimed, "We are taking up the tradition of Hindu nationalism since Congress has abandoned it."[40] Hindu nationalists implied that the struggle for independence remained incomplete because it had not confronted the legacy of Muslim domination. Amit Puri, BJP executive member for UP and convener of its youth wing, asked:

Why is it that we fought so hard against British colonialism which lasted only a couple of hundred years, but we don't undo the damage that our earlier conquerors inflicted on us? We have removed statues of King George and Queen Victoria but for some reason we are reluctant to destroy mosques, the sign of Muslim domination.[41]

Hindu nationalists' opposition to the state was directed both at previous Congress governments and at the state government that Mulayam Singh Yadav headed in UP. Yadav ordered police to keep activists out of Ayodhya and to open fire on those who violated the ban in October 1990. A BJP national executive committee resolution (November 9–10, 1990) compared British government repression and Yadav's attempt to curb Hindutva activists. "Even the British, in all their excesses from 1857 to 1942 ... had not indulged in so much oppression of the people," it stated. Vishnu Hari Dalmia similarly spoke of the "many brothers who sacrificed their lives at Ayodhya when the events of Jalianwallabagh were repeated."

Television, film, and audio cassettes were used to promote the movement. The growth of the mass media, and citizens' ability to consume and participate in it, David Meyer and Sidney Tarrow note, have increased the velocity

[38] Interview with KR Malkani, New Delhi, February 21, 1991.
[39] Interview with Sudharshan, New Delhi, April 3, 1991.
[40] Interview with LK Advani, Jaipur, February 2, 1991.
[41] Interview with Amit Puri, Lucknow, December 30, 1993.

of contentious politics.[42] Video *raths* on trucks bearing generators and large screens would travel to villages in UP, some of which lacked electricity, where hundreds of people would assemble to view the films. The televised *Ramayana* series brought a glorified national hero, Ram, into people's homes every Sunday morning for several years. JK Jain, a businessman, produced propaganda films for the BJP from his studio in Vijay Raje Scindia's compound, and broadcast idealized images of the October 1990 *rath yatra* to Ayodhya. The films portrayed Hindu activists as martyrs who were waging a massive, glorious campaign.

The BJP made excellent use of the print media to popularize the movement. Starting from the period when the Jan Sangh joined the Janata Party and LK Advani served as information and broadcasting minister, the BJP placed sympathetic reporters in vernacular-language newspapers to provide extensive press coverage of the Ayodhya movement. Pramod Mahajan, one of the masterminds behind the *rath yatra*, said that he invited news reporters to cover each leg of the journey to Ayodhya so that it would be well publicized.[43]

At the height of the Ayodhya movement, newspapers were filled with reports and photographs on every action of Sangh Parivar leaders. There was a striking contrast between paltry reports on Muslim victims compared to extensive coverage of Hindutva activists. Whereas press reports of BJP leaders were largely adulatory, reports of the Muslim leadership were highly disparaging. They tended to focus on the most conservative leaders, like Syed Shahabuddin and Syed Ahmed Bukhari, to the exclusion of moderate leaders like Zafrayab Jilani, thereby greatly exaggerating the former's influence over the Muslim community. They also accorded great importance to unrelated incidents of Islamic extremism in neighboring countries.[44]

Media biases were so acute around the time of Advani's first trip to Ayodhya in October 1990 that the Press Council of India censured four Hindi daily papers, *Aaj, Dainik Jagran, Chetna*, and *Swatantra Bharat*, for egregious distortions in their reporting on Ayodhya.[45] One of the most glaring examples was the wildly different assessments of the number of Hindu activists whom the police shot for violating state government orders and traveling to Ayodhya in October 1990.[46] After painstaking investigation, Hemnath Sharma, a reporter for the *Jan Satta*, found that the police had killed thirty-two people; the VHP

---

[42] David S. Meyer and Sidney Tarrow, eds., *The Social Movement Society: Contentious Politics for a New Century* (Lanham, MD: Rowman & Littlefield, 1998), 13.

[43] Interview with Pramod Mahajan, New Delhi, June 12, 1992.

[44] *BJP's White Paper on Ayodhya and the Rama Temple Movement* (New Delhi: Bharatiya Janata Party, 1993), 47.

[45] *Annual Report of the Press Council* (Press Council, 1991).

[46] P. Singh, Venkitesh Ramakrishnan, "When the 'Dead' Come Back," *The Hindu*, May 24, 1991. Accessed July 18, 2014. http://www.hindu.com/thehindu/thscrip/print.pl?file=2010011 5270104600.htm&date=fl2701/&prd=fline&.

placed the estimate at 156, while one Hindi newspaper, *Dainik Jagran*, estimated 300 and another, *Aaj*, estimated 400.[47]

Hindu nationalists' histories of Ayodhya highlighted Hindu victimization and provided extensive, if unreliable, information about the prior existence of a temple at the site of the *babri masjid*. They refused to describe the *babri masjid* as a mosque, and corrected me when I did so, instead referring to it as a *dhancha* (structure). The BJP even claimed that people who used the term were responsible for the demolition on December 6.[48] It stated that those referring to "the masonry structure at Ayodhya as a Mosque ... sow seeds of communal discord."

Had this disputed structure not constantly and wrongly been called by the Congress Party and its allies as a "masjid," the country would have been spared the protest and violence, at home and abroad, in the wake of December 6.[49]

Mosques, in the RSS view, simply represented affronts to Hindus, not Muslim places of worship. Moreover, this reasoning continued, Muslim leaders' willingness to accept a judicial verdict on the Ayodhya dispute showed that Muslims, unlike Hindus, were not guided by faith. An RSS spokesperson commented:

It's good that the Muslims have agreed to abide by the Supreme Court. That means it is not a question of faith for them, but of law. And if it's not a question of faith, they should honor the sentiments of Hindus. No Muslim sentiments are involved in Ayodhya.[50]

Madan Lal (ML) Khurana stated, "For forty-one years *akhand kirtan* and *pujas* [Sikh and Hindu prayers] have been held there."[51] Bal Thackeray, founder of Shiv Sena, declared, "Muslims should draw a lesson from the demolition; otherwise they will meet the same fate. Muslims who criticize the demolition are without religion and without a mission."[52]

Conversely, the VHP claimed that Hindus would reject a legal resolution to the Ayodhya dispute. Giriraj Kishore stated:

The BJP holds that the nature of the controversy is such that it just cannot be sorted out by a court of law. A court of law can settle issues of title, trespass, possession, etc. But it cannot adjudicate as to whether Babar did actually invade Ayodhya, destroyed a temple, and built a mosque in its place. Even when a court does pronounce on such facts, it cannot suggest remedies to undo the vandalism of history.[53]

---

[47] Interview with Hemnath Sharma, Lucknow, January 3, 1991.
[48] Political resolution adopted at the national executive meeting held in New Delhi on December 22–4, 1992, 19.
[49] "VP Flayed for Stand on Temple," *The Times of India News Service*, October 8, 1992.
[50] Interview with MG Vaidya, *The Times of India*, April 14, 2002.
[51] Interview with ML Khurana, New Delhi, March 20, 1991.
[52] Citizens' Tribunal on Ayodhya: Report of the Inquiry Commission, (1993), 211.
[53] Interview with Giriraj Kishore, New Delhi, March 19, 1991.

The VHP sought to demonstrate its inclusive, democratic character by including women, *dalits*, and even Muslims in its activities. A *dalit* laid the first foundation stone at the *shilanyas*. Shri Banu Pratap Shukla described this ceremony in a VHP publication:

> Those who witnessed this scene recalled the old tradition of Shri Ram. This was an explicit example of social equality, social security, social respect prevalent in Hindu society. ... The editors and representatives of the world press saw that untouchability had no social or religious sanction.[54]

An article in *Organiser* described Advani's *rath yatra* to Ayodhya as follows:

> [A]s the roar of the ocean on the morning of September 25th mingled with the chanting of Vedic hymns and cries ... Shri Advani lifted a bow, its arrow pointing to Ayodhya. It was presented by the tribals of Ambaji. The priest of Somnath temple presented him with a *bhagwa dhwaja* [saffron flag]. The fishermen from Dwarka, after presenting a conch, blew it to mark the occasion. The Gohil Samaj of the Kshatriyas presented Advaniji with a sword.[55]

Speakers at a VHP rally on April 4, 1990 included a *dalit*, a Muslim, an OBC, and a woman. Kalka Das, a *dalit* BJP MP from Delhi, said:

> Congress lays claim to the legacy of Ambedkar but it never followed his wishes. We will fight now to realize his vision of social justice for the weaker sections. We will do what other parties have just spoken about.[56]

Arif Baig, a Muslim, spoke of his commitment to Ram culture and recited passages from the *Ramayana*. BJP president MM Joshi described Hindus and Muslims as "blood brothers" and called for fraternity among all Indians. He claimed that once the BJP came to power and built a temple at Ayodhya there would be "a grand national reconciliation."[57] Advani went further, claiming that Muslims wanted the temple built because they wanted the dispute to end.[58]

The VHP framed a violent, exclusionary campaign as selfless, ethical, and inclusive. Processions blasted inspirational music and posters depicted a heroic and awe-inspiring Ram. Injunctions to violence and self-sacrifice were closely intertwined. The Bajrang Dal created a *balidan jatha* (sacrifice brigade), which engaged in guerilla warfare training and planned suicide missions to demolish the mosque. Its founder, Vinay Katiyar, said that this brigade, unlike the ordinary *kar sevaks*, would not be deterred by police bullets.[59]

54 Shri Banu Pratap Shukla, "Shilanyas: A Thrill," *Vishva Hindu Parishad, Silver Jubilee Special Issue*, 1989–90, 66–7.
55 KN Panikkar, "Religious Symbols and Political Mobilization: The Agitation for a Mandir at Ayodhya," *Social Scientist*, July–August, 1993, Vol. 21, no. 242–3, 76.
56 Interview with Kalka Das, New Delhi, March 22, 1991.
57 "BJP's White Paper on Ayodhya and the Rama Temple Movement," *Hindunet*, April 1993. Accessed July 18, 2014. http://www.hindunet.org/hvk/specialrepo/bjpwp/ch1.html.
58 Interview with LK Advani, New Delhi, June 27, 1995.
59 *Indian Express*, November 10, 1992.

Violence occurred at many different points in the campaign. The *Ram shila puja* provoked violence in Kota and Jaipur in Rajashtan, Khargone and Indore in Madhya Pradesh, and several parts of UP. The most serious violence occurred in Bhagalpur, Bihar, where approximately 1,000 people were killed.[60] The *Ram jyoti* processions triggered violence in several places, most significantly in Gonda district, UP, where 100 people were reportedly killed. The route of Advani's procession was marked both by scenes of jubilation and devastation.[61] At various points, the procession incited Hindus to attack Muslim homes and shops. Former BJP general secretary Pramod Mahajan commented that the weapons that the VHP received were sufficient to "liberate the *Ram Janmabhumi* in a day."[62] Advani's arrest on his way to Ayodhya on October 23, the BJP's call for a movement of protest thereafter, and the arrival of Hindu volunteers at Ayodhya on October 30 also provoked violence. From September 1 to November 20, 116 "riots" occurred in which 564 people died. UP alone experienced twenty-four "riots" in which 224 people were killed.[63]

Hindu nationalist violence was replete with gendered imagery. In many different times and places in the course of the Ayodhya campaign, Hindutva activists presented glass bangles to Hindu men who did not attack Muslims, to signify their effeminacy. After the police fired on the men who broke through the picket lines and climbed atop the mosque in 1990, Giriraj Kishore stated in an interview that the wives of military officers gave the police glass bangles and asked, "Are you such cowards that you can't even stand up for the *kar sevaks?*"[64] Anatulla Siddiqui, the state convener of the Janata Dal in Bhopal, reported that the Hindu men who came to his locality refused to comply with orders to destroy his house.[65] Hindutva activists later presented these men with bangles and mocked them for behaving like cowardly women. I was told about similar incidents in Bijnor and Jaipur.

Hindutva activists publically humiliated Muslim men and challenged their manhood. A Muslim man who was a victim of Hindutva violence in Seelampur, East Delhi, told me that the police had dragged him to a police station and interrogated him.[66] To make him speak, they had ripped the hair from his head and beard. When Hindutva activists were uncertain of a man's religious identity, they might pull down his trousers to determine whether he had been circumcised. One of the ugly slogans that circulated during this time

---

[60] K. Chaudhari, "A Commission Divided: Who Was Behind the Bhagalpur Riots?" *Frontline*, August 11, 1995, 33.

[61] People's Union for Democratic Rights, *Cry the Beloved Country* (Faizabad: People's Union for Democratic Rights, 1993), 6.

[62] *Organiser*, October 14, 1990.

[63] *Divided We Stand*, dossier, no page number given.

[64] Interview with Giriraj Kishore, New Delhi, March 19, 1991.

[65] Interview with Anatulla Siddiqui, Bhopal, December 30, 1990.

[66] Interview, Seelampur, Delhi, December 12, 1992.

was: "Landiya log Pakistan jao," or "Circumcised men, return to Pakistan." In Bhopal and Bijnor, many Muslim *imams* and *maulvis* (religious functionaries) were forced to engage in the humiliating act of uttering "Jai Shri Ram" and other Hindu nationalist slogans.

Hindutva activists sought to emasculate Muslim men by rendering them incapable of protecting and providing for their families. In the course of attacks on Muslim neighborhoods, they destroyed the fabric of family life. When they did not raze homes to the ground, they would smash pots, destroy implements, break furniture, and kill animals. In one home I visited in Bhopal, a Muslim man told me that he and his family had fled from their home before it was vandalized. However, mobs knifed his pet dog in his absence.

Hindutva groups repeatedly mobilized Hindu men by depicting India as the ravaged motherland and Hindu women as victims of Muslim male aggression. Rumors that Muslim men had raped Hindu women preceded many attacks on Muslims. In Bhopal, a newspaper reported that eighty Hindu women had been abducted from a hostel and raped, although the hostel warden denied this. Many people claimed that the rumor was a catalyst to anti-Muslim violence on December 7, 1992. In Surat, a rumor that scores of Hindu women had been raped resulted in Hindus looting Muslim shops and burning down Muslim homes from December 7–12, 1992. Rumors that girls from the Kamala Nehru School were kidnapped preceded Jaipur's first "riot" in 1989. A rumor about the molestation of young women preceded a "riot" in Jaipur three years later.[67]

Hindutva activists Sadhvi Rithambara and Uma Bharati incited Hindu men to engage in violence against Muslims and derided those who failed to do so. They addressed Hindu men in their public speeches with vulgarity, familiarity, and condescension. When Uma Bharati told Hindu men to act like lions rather than frogs, she assumed the tone of a wife scolding her negligent husband. Rithambara repeatedly stated that Hindus had been exploited because of their selflessness and passivity.

Discard the cloak of cowardice and effeminacy and learn to sing the song of bravery and heroism! You watched the looting of Somnath temple and stood silent; what did you receive in return for your silence? They took your virility, purity and your greatness to be cowardice and effeminacy. ... Do you want this ugly history to be repeated? If not, you must awaken!

Uma Bharati led massive women's *satyagrahas* on January 6 and 17, 1990, and December 6, 1992. She goaded activists to destroy the *babri masjid* through her rallying cries "Ek Dhaka Aur Lugow" (Strike One More Blow) and "Ram Lala Hum Ayengeh, Mandir Vahin Buneyenge" (Dear Ram, we will come

---

[67] Shail Mayaram, "Communal Violence in Jaipur," *Economic and Political Weekly*, November 13–20, 1993, Vol. 28, nos. 46–47, 2530.

and construct a temple there). Both *sadhvis* recorded cassettes that were so incendiary that the government banned them. In one speech Rithambara called Mulayam Singh Yadav "Mullah (a Muslim religious leader) Mulayam" and compared him to Ravana, the demon king from the *Ramayana* epic, implicitly beseeching Hindus to protect the vulnerable Sita from Muslim male violence.[68] Speaking of politicians, whom she claimed had failed to oppose Singh's use of force against Hindu activists in Ayodhya in October 1990, Rithambara exhorted:

I told them, you fools, it's been nine *lakh* years since Ravana abducted Sita and still today we burn Ravana's effigy. If we could not forget this incident after nine *lakh* years, can we forget the cruelty of Mullah Mulayam after three or four months? If so, the future of Hindus is dark. Youth from UP asked me to give them revolvers so they could take care of Mulayam Singh. But I told them not to waste a bullet on a eunuch; kill him politically instead.

Hindu nationalists engaged in identity-shaping work during the Ayodhya campaign by depicting Hindu and Muslim identities as polarized, antagonistic, and unchanging: Hindus were peace-loving whereas Muslims were aggressive. Hinduism preached tolerance whereas Islam preached fanaticism. Hindu families respected women whereas Muslim families disparaged them. Women activists were well-placed to make these gendered appeals.

The Anti-Globalization Movement

Hindu nationalists began to engage in anti-globalization activism in 1996. The BJP initially opposed economic liberalization, for undermining small-scale Indian enterprises, and cultural globalization, for undermining Indian cultural traditions, but later reversed its stance on economic globalization. The RSS and VHP have opposed globalization, to lesser or greater degrees.

The RSS supports *swadeshi*, labor-intensive industries, and appropriate technology. It calls for primary reliance on domestic capital and human resources and supports trade barriers to protect domestic industry from foreign competition. Govindacharya, a lifelong *swayamsevak* (RSS functionary) who devoted himself to the cause of *swadeshi* after 2000, described the market as an alien system of exchange.[69] He asserted that the *swadeshi* movement sought to change people's lifestyles by rejecting Western consumerism and reviving traditional skills that embodied Hindu cultural and civilizational values. Govindacharya praised the division of labor associated with the caste

[68] Speech delivered at a rally in New Delhi on April 4, 1991.
[69] Interview with Govindacharya, New Delhi, June 24, 2007.

system and family- and kin-based forms of production. He identified the sanctity of the cow with agricultural productivity:

One goal of the *swadeshi* movement is to increase the ratio of cattle to people. Two hundred years ago the ratio of man to cattle was 1:2; today it is 4:1 and in Vidharbha, it is 6:1. Commercialization of agriculture is reducing the need for cattle. When farmers used cattle to plough the land, they reduced costs of production and increased productivity. Today farmers are committing suicide because of the agrarian crisis and cows are dying because they are neglected. It's not enough to call for a ban on cow slaughter. We're teaching people to care for cows and use bullocks in agricultural production.[70]

The RSS rejected wholesale reliance on the state or the market in favor of greater reliance on the family. Muralidhar Rao, all-India convener of the Swadeshi Jagran Manch (SJM, Platform to Promote Swadeshi), argued that strengthening the traditional family would alleviate a variety of ills that India faced. He felt that families' commitments to saving were essential to reducing the costs of welfare and averting economic crises. He associated the breakdown of traditional families with mental illness.[71]

Three RSS-affiliated organizations have contested globalization: the Bharatiya Kisan Sangh BKS, a farmers' organization; the BMS, a workers' organization; and the SJM, which reports that it has 85 million members and is the largest labor union in India.[72] The BMS has opposed the creation of private monopolies and demanded state transparency in the sale of public-sector units. The BKS was founded in 1979 with the goal of emphasizing the "importance and suitability of age-old agriculture technique [*sic*]." It criticizes political parties for exploiting farmers for narrow political gains and claims to be apolitical.[73]

The SJM, the most important of the three organizations, was formed in 1991 to challenge certain facets of globalization and promote *swadeshi*. It has an all-India office in New Delhi and branches in every state. It reports that its strongest units are in Karnataka, Odisha, Rajasthan, Jharkhand, Tamil Nadu, Andhra Pradesh, West Bengal, and Madhya Pradesh. According to Ajay Bharti, the editor of *Swadeshi Patrika*, its English-language newsmagazine for activists has a circulation of 2,000 and its Hindi version has a circulation of 6,000.[74] The SJM echoes leftist critiques of globalization. Muralidhar Rao explained in an interview that by 1991, the United States was seeking to create a unipolar

---

[70] Ibid.
[71] Interview with Muralidhar Rao, New Delhi, November 19, 2008.
[72] http://www.bms.org.in/.
[73] See, for example, "Farmers' Groups Seek Livelihood Security from Political Parties," *The Economic Times*, March 2, 2014. Accessed June 25, 2014. http://articles.economictimes.indiatimes.com/2014-03-02/news/47823930_1_field-trials-livelihood-security-political-parties; http://en.kisansangh.org/static/aimsandobjects.aspx.
[74] Interview with Ajay Bharti, New Delhi, November 19, 2008.

world based on capitalist principles. The SJM has organized campaigns against multinational corporations and "foreign imperialism." In the mid-1990s it launched a major campaign against the energy agreement that the Maharashtra government made with the American firm Enron. It has also organized numerous agitations against the World Trade Organization (WTO), in Rao's words, "for representing the interests of entrenched groups in the West." Rao provided a scathing commentary on the global economic crisis:

The politics of the World Bank and the IMF have been exposed. They have lost legitimacy. The US made imprudent decisions based on faulty monetary and fiscal policies. They have demonstrated that relying on the market does not work. Our position today is much stronger than it was in the past.[75]

The RSS and its affiliates have organized anti-globalization campaigns in many large cities and small towns across the country since the early 1990s. The best-publicized campaigns have protested the presence of multinational corporations like Pizza Hut and Kentucky Fried Chicken. In 1995, the SJM organized a demonstration demanding that Pepsi and Coca-Cola quit India, echoing Gandhi's "Quit India" campaign. Protesters chanted, broke Pepsi and Coke bottles, and burned cardboard cutouts of bottles. MM Joshi, former BJP president, spoke at the rally.

The BJP's views on globalization have dramatically changed. Until about 1991, it distinguished itself from Congress and the RSS by supporting economic liberalization. However, once Congress embraced economic reform, the BJP changed its stance and proclaimed a nationalist commitment to *swadeshi*.[76] LK Advani explained that the BJP had come to support *swadeshi* because economic liberalization had rendered India increasingly vulnerable to foreign exploitation.[77] Jagdish Shettigar, a member of the BJP's economic cell, stated, "We don't think we can do without foreign investment in high tech sectors of the economy. But we support *swadeshi* in the domestic consumer goods sector. And we are critical of the government for ignoring the unorganized sector of the economy."[78] The BJP participated in some well-publicized RSS campaigns against multinational corporations.

After the NDA government was formed, the BJP reverted back to favoring economic liberalization. It took steps to fulfill the government's commitments to the WTO by phasing out quantitative restrictions on imports, including consumer goods. It sought to dispense with state government control over electricity. It allowed foreign companies to invest up to 40 percent in the insurance sector. It authorized the sale of public-sector units to private industrialists and

[75] Interview with Muralidhar Rao, New Delhi, November 19, 2008.
[76] Salim Lakha, "From Swadeshi to Globalization: The Bharatiya Janata Party's Shifting Economic Agenda," in John McGuire and Ian Copland, eds., *Hindu Nationalism and Governance* (New Delhi: Oxford University Press, 2007), 108.
[77] Interview with LK Advani, New Delhi, June 27, 1995.
[78] Interview with Jagdish Shettigar, New Delhi, December 30, 2008.

passed a bill allowing product patents. It permitted foreign direct investment in a number of formerly protected industries, including liquor and tobacco. Several BJP state governments, above all Gujarat under Modi, energetically pursued foreign trade and investment.

The RSS and the VHP strenuously opposed the BJP's pro-globalization stance. Senior leaders, including Praveen Togadia and Ashok Singhal of the VHP, Dattopant (DP) Thengadi, founder of the BMS, and Kunwarhi Jadav, president of the BKS, vociferously challenged the BJP's economic policies. Hasmukh Dave, BMS president, demanded that the government retain control over defense, railways, and oil, and protect local industry.[79] The RSS and affiliated groups planned protests in major cities to pressure the government to scale back reforms. The BMS organized massive rallies in Delhi on November 30 and December 3.[80] The RSS threatened to withdraw support from the BJP if it did not heed RSS warnings. However, the NDA continued to pursue economic reform. In 2001, at the WTO's urging, it reversed its previous policy of protecting consumer goods producers, which especially affected small-scale domestic industries.[81]

The RSS took a strong stand against the NDA government's pro-reform policies. RSS leader KS Sudarshan warned Prime Minister Vajpayee to correct his "anti-Hindutva, anti-*swadeshi*" policies. He gave the government six months to "come back to the nationalist path" and threatened that, "if it failed to do so," the Sangh Parivar "would be forced to take an openly adversarial role."[82] The six-month deadline coincided with the start of the VHP's *Dharma Sansad* in January. Sudarshan said that ministers and public officials who opposed *swadeshi* should be expelled and called for a "second independence movement" to combat the growing influence of foreign "superpowers."[83] At the RSS national council meeting in March 2001, Mohan Bhagwat lashed out at the government's economic policies.[84] He stated that they imposed an "unbearable financial burden" on future generations and could result in "financial disaster." He spoke of the despondency gripping farmers and small entrepreneurs because of imports of foreign goods and "reckless concessions" to foreign companies.[85]

[79] Kay Benedict, "Anti-Reform Axis in Place," *The Telegraph*, September 21, 2002. Accessed July 18, 2014. http://www.telegraphindia.com/1020921/asp/nation/story_1220297.asp.

[80] "BMS State Unit to Join Nationwide Protests," *The Times of India*, October 21, 2001. Accessed July 18, 2014. http://timesofindia.indiatimes.com/city/bangalore/BMS-state-unit-to-join-nationwide-protests/articleshow/1075135000.cms.

[81] Lakha, "From Swadeshi to Globalization: The Bharatiya Janata Party's Shifting Economic Agenda," 110.

[82] Venkitesh Ramakrishnan, "Back to Ayodhya," *Frontline*, June 24, 2010. Accessed June 30, 2014. http://www.frontline.in/navigation/?type=static&page=archive.

[83] "RSS Chief Flays Economic Reform Process," *Deccan Herald*, April 24, 2002.

[84] "Tehelka Tapes 'Appear to Be True' Says RSS," *The Hindu*, March 17, 2001. Accessed June 25, 2014. http://www.hinduonnet.com/thehindu/2001/03/17/stories/02170005.htm.

[85] Ibid.

Sudarshan directed the SJM to organize protests against the NDA government's economic policies, particularly for allowing foreign direct investment in the tobacco and liquor industries, and for retaining certain bureaucrats who opposed *swadeshi*. The SJM opposed the government's preferential treatment of foreign investors, particularly in contrast with its neglect of farmers and small-scale industrialists.[86] The opposition of the SJM and the RSS to disinvestment sharpened in 2002 when the NDA sold shares of public-sector units to private industrialists. They argued that the government should only sell public-sector companies that were operating at a loss, and should retain control over the telecommunications, power, and oil sectors.

Under RSS directives, the BKS, BMS, and SJM organized a giant rally in New Delhi in September 2002 against the government's "anti-people, anti-farmer, and anti small-scale industry policies."[87] They followed this with week-long agitations in Bhopal, Patna, Ahmedabad, Lucknow, and other cities to pressure the government to scale back economic reforms. The SJM questioned the government's desire to "sacrifice the interests of Maruti" [cars manufactured in India] to "promote the interests of Suzuki," [cars manufactured in Japan]. Dave, Jadhav, Rao, and other leaders demanded priority to jobs over growth, a review of economic and disinvestment policies, and rejection of the WTO agreement. SJM leaders went on hunger strikes in May 2003 to protest the government's policy on tariffs. After the BJP's defeat in the 2009 general elections, the RSS ensured that its anti-globalization activists were well represented in the party leadership. Muralidhar Rao joined the BJP national executive to advise Rajnath Singh.

The BKS, BMS, and SJM have all questioned the pro-globalization stance of the BJP government that was elected in 2014. The BKS has opposed an official commission's proposal for field testing genetically modified food crops. The BMS has criticized the government's plan to amend labor laws and has demanded the regularization of contract workers. The SJM has objected to the opening of defense and railways to foreign investors. However, in contrast to earlier years, the RSS is more committed to ensuring the success of the BJP government than to supporting anti-globalization activism.

---

[86] "Vajpayee Govt Is Worse than Rao's," *The Indian Express*, September 29, 2002. Accessed June 25, 2014. http://archive.indianexpress.com/oldStory/10309/. "Be Wary of the Effect, not Process, of Reform," *The Indian Express*, September 29, 2002. Accessed June 25, 2014. http:// archive.indianexpress.com/oldStory/10311/. "National Interest Must Be Above All," *The Indian Express*, September 29, 2002. Accessed June 25, 2014. http://archive.indianexpress.com/oldStory/10310/. "Reforms: Divided Colours of Saffron," *The Indian Express*, September 29, 2002. Accessed June 25, 2014. http://archive.indianexpress.com/oldStory/10307/.

[87] *Hindustan Times*, November 1, 2002. Accessed June 30, 2014. "Centre Giving in to WTO Terms: Manch," *Tribune News Service*, April 14, 2003. Accessed June 25, 2014. http://www.tribuneindia.com/2003/20030415/nation.htm.

Gender and Globalization

The RSS has encouraged women to protect the family from the invasion of market forces and Western cultural influences. Families who respected women's traditional roles as wives and mothers were, in Muralidhar Rao's view, best suited to resisting destructive Western influences. Conversely, women were often the worst victims of globalization.

The Rashtra Sevika Samiti passed a resolution urging Indian industrialists to desist from marketing brand name goods produced by multinational companies. It praised the Campco factory in Mangalore, Karnataka for "turning down a lucrative offer to be bought out by Hindustan Lever Limited."[88] A resolution lamented the adverse effects of economic liberalization on women:

Thousands of women who make a living making curd and butter out of milk have been affected because milk powder and curd is now available in the market. These women and their families will be driven to poverty. And what will happen to the children of this country – a country in which rivers of milk flow – if milk powder from cows affected by the "mad cow" disease is sold here?[89]

Asha Sharma said that women's *shakhas* were encouraging women to buy Indian products to strengthen Indian manufacturing enterprises:

We urge women to buy goods made in India. For instance, we advise them against buying Ariel. We got to hear of an Indian producer which makes Manjula Soaps. It is as good and much cheaper. We spread the word in *shakhas*, urging women to buy Manjula Soaps instead. We should encourage our small industry. Look at Japan, where people have industries within their houses. Chinese and Korean goods have taken over our markets. Chinese battery cells are being sold for Rupees 1 per cell. They are not as good as Indian products but at such a price, who can resist? I am also told that bulb manufacturers have shut down entirely. Our small-scale industry cannot compete with foreign multinationals.[90]

In 2011, Uma Bharati threatened violence against Walmart if it entered the Indian market following the Indian government's decision to allow foreign direct investment in multi-brand retail (up to 51 percent) and in single-brand retail (100 percent). She said:

By giving permission to Walmart to directly invest in the retail sector, the Centre has jeopardized the employment opportunities of *dalits*, poor and backwards ... I would personally set afire the showroom when it opens anywhere in the country and I am ready to be arrested for the act.[91]

[88] Resolution passed at the executive meeting of the Rashtriya Sevika Samiti, February 5, 2000.
[89] Resolution 3, passed at the central executive meeting of the Rashtriya Sevika Samiti, July 26, 2000.
[90] Interview with Asha Sharma, New Delhi, October 12, 2005. In 2005, the exchange rate was $1 USD = 45 Rs.
[91] "I'll Set Walmart Store Afire: Uma," *The Hindu*, November 26, 2011. Accessed June 25, 2014. http://www.thehindu.com/news/national/article2660373.ece.

A Sadhvi Rithambara cassette recording asserts that India has lost its moral bearings. "Things have deteriorated to the point that everything is now bought and sold, minds, bodies, religion, and even the honor of our elders, sisters, mothers, and sons," she cries out. "We cannot auction our nation's honor in the market of party politics." In a sweeping gesture, Rithambara ingeniously links the corruption of the political process, capitalist development, and sexual objectification. Rithambara also interlaces opposition to globalization with anti-minority sentiments.

A country's strength lies not in its skyscrapers, roads, big schemes, nice clothes but in their citizens' character, especially women's decency, their culture. Simultaneously because of this neglect of Indian spiritual development *crores* [i.e., tens of millions] of rejected Hindus became Christians and Mussalmans and we ... Hindus stayed dreaming in our ashrams. As a result, hundreds of Hindus were killed in Kashmir, and the numbers of Hindus has declined in Assam, Manipur, Kerala, Mizoram, Bengal, Bihar.

Hindu nationalist women's organizations have been especially active in opposing Western cultural influences. The BJP Mahila Morcha raided several hundred establishments that were displaying "obscene" publications and pressured the Delhi press commissioner to confiscate them. It blackened billboards that displayed women's bodies in Delhi, Lucknow, and Bhopal. It demanded that the film certification board censor alleged vulgarity in Indian cinema. According to Shashi Ranjan, president of the BJP film cell, "Mainstream cinema is being shamelessly imbued with innuendo and vulgarity which is threatening to strike at the very core of our culture, so steeped in decency and decorum."[92] Activists argue that growth of satellite television has increased "cultural pollution."

After the BJP came to national power briefly in 1998, Sushma Swaraj, minister of information and culture, censored the fashion television channel as well as other programs that broadcast revealing images of women's bodies and required news anchors to dress modestly. She closed an independent radio program that discussed sexual health and supported abstinence-based education. The BJP created the Script and Stage Performances Scrutiny Board to vet all material designed for media distribution.

Kiran Maheshwari, former president of the Mahila Morcha, stated:

Unfortunately, women are being projected in advertisements in ill manners as show pieces with physical exposure. This unethical and offensive presentation of women in advertisements works to their detriment and perpetuates an undesirable gender hierarchy. One of the main reasons for increasing incidents of crime against women is this negative image and these advertisements. ... In the name of secularism, teaching of traditional values, culture and age old principles of social fabric are being denied to our children. TV, cinema and Internet have become a tool to destroy our rich traditions.[93]

[92] *Indian Express,* February 8, 1994.
[93] Interview with Kiran Maheshwari, *Organiser,* December 2, 2007. Accessed June 25, 2014. http://organiser.org/archives/historic/dynamic/modules8369.html?name=Content&pa=showpage&pid=212&page=6.

When asked her views about sex education in schools she responded:

This talk of sex education in school is absurd. What we need is education about our rich traditions, social harmony and skills in the art of life. They are talking about sex education to destroy the institution of family and our social foundation.

The RSS has opposed the impact of globalization on women and the family through a variety of popular publications. One of them, *Nari Siksha* (Women's Education), attacks Western feminism for supposedly destroying the family, which it characterizes as the moral backbone of society. It insists on the sanctity of motherhood and enjoins Hindu women to repudiate Western notions of liberation. An RSS booklet entitled *Adarsh Hindu Ghar* (Ideal Hindu House) rejects the use of the Christian calendar and proposes a ban on birthday cakes and candles in favor of the Hindu practice of lighting *diyas* (lamps) and giving alms to the poor. It considers honeymoons symptomatic of Western indulgence. It advocates collective family prayers in the evenings and a weekly *panchayat* meeting at which family members can resolve their problems.

The RSS has put its principles into practice. Rajnath Singh called for a boycott of beauty pageants and encouraged the ABVP to oppose them. Because Hindutva activists threatened to organize a disruptive protest in Bangalore, the 1996 Miss World beauty contest had to be moved to the Seychelles Islands. The VHP and Bajrang Dal have called for boycotts of hotels that celebrate New Year's Eve and threatened individuals who do so. They have organized annual, violent campaigns on February 14 against shops, cafes, and restaurants that celebrate Valentine's Day in big cities and small district towns. They have harassed young couples in movie theaters, picnic spots, and shops and forced couples whom they assumed were dating to tie *rakhis* (signifying that they are brother and sister), or apply *sindhoor* (a symbol of marriage), and take marriage vows.[94]

These RSS injunctions have encouraged male-dominated organizations like the Bajrang Dal and the ABVP to engage in violent attacks on women who

---

[94] Reports on these incidents appear in: "The Shiv Sena, Including the Groups' Activities and Areas of Operations within India," *RefWorld*, April 29, 2011. Accessed June 25, 2014. http://www.unhcr.org/refworld/country,IRBC,IND,4fc4b12f2,0.html. Harmeet Shah Singh, "Indian Police Target Valentine 'Obscenity,'" *CNN World*, February 10, 2011. Accessed June 25, 2014. http://articles.cnn.com/2010-02-03/world/india.valentines.day_1_maharashtra-obscenity-hindu?_s=PM:WORLD. "Upholding the Law," *The Indian Express*, August 14, 2012. Accessed June 25, 2014. http://www.indianexpress.com/news/uphold-the-law/987898. Suchandana Gupta, "On V-Day, Bajrang Dal Men Force Couple to Get 'Married,'" *The Times of India*, February 15, 2008. Accessed June 25, 2014. http://articles.timesofindia.indiatimes.com/2008-02-15/india/27749916_1_bajrang-dal-moral-police-saffron-brigade. "Bajrang Dal Protests against Valentine's Day," *The Hindu*, February 15, 2008. Accessed June 25, 2014. http://www.hindu.com/2008/02/15/stories/2008021553680500.htm. "Sena, Bajrang Dal Act Spoilers on Valentine's Day," *Rediff News*, February 14, 2008. Accessed June 25, 2014. http://www.rediff.com/news/2008/feb/14vday.htm.

challenge normative ideals of Hindu womanhood. VHP-affiliated organizations have vandalized art that they claim is obscene. They broke into the home
of eminent Muslim artist Maqbool Fida (MF) Hussain and destroyed his paint-
ing of a nude Sita riding on the tail of the monkey god Hanuman in 1996 and
organized another assault on Hussain's art two years later. Although Hussain
left India and renounced his Indian citizenship, the Bajrang Dal and its affiliates attacked galleries where his art was on display in Ahmedabad in February
2006, and in Delhi in August 2008 and January 2011.

The Sangh Parivar has harassed filmmakers like Deepa Mehta who critique
patriarchal Hindu practices. In December 1998, Hindutva activists stoned
movie theaters in several cities that screened Mehta's film, *Fire*, which depicts
a lesbian relationship. Although Mehta obtained the Indian government's
authorization to shoot the film *Water* two years later, 2,000 Hindutva activists
destroyed the film set and one activist threatened to commit suicide to stop film
production.[95] A number of prominent BJP members participated in the protest.
Following consultations with the RSS, BJP Chief Minister of UP Ram Prakash
Gupta stopped the film shooting following consultations with the RSS.[96] Both
Fire and *Water* were controversial because they addressed the subjugation of
Indian women and starred Shabana Azmi, a Muslim feminist, human rights
activist, and Member of Parliament (MP). The uproar over the films reveals
Sangh Parivar's obsession with controlling women's sexuality and hostility to
Muslim women, as well as the complicity of the RSS and the BJP state govern-
ments in creating a repressive cultural and political environment.

The Sri Ram Sena (Lord Ram's Army) was active in numerous Hindutva
attacks: on Christians in Karnataka in September 2008, Hussain's art in
Delhi in August 2008, the Malegaon bomb blasts in September 2006, and
anti–Valentine's Day activities for many years.[97] On January 24, 2009, its
members assaulted women in a bar in Mangalore to oppose women drinking at night in public places. Shortly after this incident, the Bajrang Dal
assaulted people attending a private party. Under pressure from the central
government, the Karnataka government arrested twenty-nine Shri Ram Sena
activists, including Pramod Muthalik, its founder and head. RSS and BJP

[95] "'Water' Shooting Stopped Again, Mehta Asked to Leave Varanasi," *The Hindu*, February 7, 2000.
[96] "No Sentiment Hurting Films, Please, We Are BJP," *Times of India*, February 2, 2000. Accessed June 30, 2014. http://timesofindia.indiatimes.com/articleshow/14446797.cms?. PK Roy, "Water-borne Problems for Sangh Parivar," *The Hindu*, February 13, 2000. http://hindu.com/2000/02/13/stories/0413225c.htm.
[97] "Malegaon Is a *Jhalak*. More Is Possible if Every Woman Picks Up Bombs," *Tehelka Magazine*, February 6, 2009. Accessed June 25, 2014. http://archive.tehelka.com/story_main41.asp?filename=Ne140209malegaon_is.asp. "Saffron Links," *Tehelka Magazine*, February 6, 2009. Accessed June 25, 2014. http://archive.tehelka.com/story_main41.asp?filename=Ne140209saffron_links.asp. "For the Right Price, You Can Get Shri Ram Sena to Organize a Riot Anywhere," *Tehelka Magazine*, May 22, 2010. Accessed June 25, 2014. http://archive.tehelka.com/story_main44.asp?filename=Ne220510coverstory.asp.

leaders supported the prohibition on women going to pubs, however barring Muthalik's attack on the pub in Mangalore, the BJP has refrained from criticizing the Sri Ram Sena.[98]

The RSS position on the growing incidence of rape in India reflects its desire to sequester women. In response to the high-profile gang rape in Delhi in January 2012, Mohan Bhagwat blamed "Western values" for growing sexual violence in urban India and claimed that rapes did not occur in rural India, where traditional values hold sway.[99]

Hindu Nationalist "Terrorism"

Hindu nationalists have engaged in bombings which they attributed to Muslims since 2006. Bomb blasts targeted Muslim civilians at a cemetery in Malegaon on September 8, 2006, killing thirty-seven people; a *dargah* (shrine) in Ajmer, Rajasthan, on October 11, 2007, killing three people; the Mecca Masjid, a mosque in Hyderabad, on May 18, 2007, killing fourteen people; the Samjhauta Express, a train linking Delhi and Lahore, on February 18, 2007, killing sixty-eight people; and Malegaon on September 29, 2008, killing eight people. Thirty-one people have been charged with planning and carrying out these attacks. They include Sunil Joshi, former RSS district leader in Indore; Pragya Singh Thakur, member of the ABVP and the Durga Vahini; and founding member of the Jai Vande Mataram Jan Kalyan Samiti. RSS activist Aseemanand was accused of masterminding most of the attacks. (He is named, but not yet charged, in two attacks in Malegaon, in September 2006 and September 2008). Aseemanand admitted to his role in Delhi and Haryana courts in December 2010. In several interviews with a journalist from the *Caravan*, he claimed that he was acting on orders of Mohan Bhagwat.[100]

In some respects these bomb blasts are antithetical to social movement tactics in that they are covert activities that do not engage in mass mobilization. However, the RSS has planned these attacks while denying responsibility for them to generate fear and hatred of Muslims while claiming that Hindus are victims. Ram Madhav denied that these attacks constituted attacks of "terrorism:"

We do not agree that there is Hindu terrorism. Unlike jihadi terrorism there cannot be Hindu terrorism because there is no religious justification in Hinduism for terrorism.

---

[98] In 1986, Muthalik joined the RSS and became a *swayamsevak*. He joined the VHP in 1993 and became the first Bajrang Dal convener in Karnataka in 1996. He and many of his followers left the Bajrang Dal in 2004 and formed the Sri Ram Sena three years later.

[99] "Rapes Occur in 'India,' not in 'Bharat': RSS Chief," *Hindustan Times*, January 4, 2013. Accessed July 18, 2014. http://www.hindustantimes.com/india-news/newdelhi/rapes-occur-in-india-not-in-bharat-rss-chief/article1-984900.aspx.

[100] Leena Gita Reghunath, "The Believer: Swami Aseemanand's Radical Service to the Sangh," *The Caravan*, February 5, 2014. Accessed December 6, 2014:

We don't subscribe to violence. We welcome investigations but we are confident that there is no Hindu terrorism. If there were some acts of retribution, it's because so many Hindus have been killed in real terrorist violence.[101]

Tarun Vijay, former editor of the RSS journal *Panchajanya*, argued that Islam and Muslims were undermining the core Hindu civilizational values of pluralism and tolerance. "They have assaulted and invaded us so many times that Hindus have become penetrable. Our beliefs and civilizational flow are being influenced by those Semitic views whose values undermine our own." He considered Hindu "terrorism" an oxymoron. He rejected my suggestion that some of these "terrorist" attacks might have been responses to the growth of Hindu nationalism and in particular to the 2002 Gujarat violence:

The terrorist attacks by Islamic militants cannot be seen as a response to the growth of Hindu nationalism because Hindu nationalists have never done anything to Muslims. In 1992, they attacked a symbol of oppression. They did not attack Muslims.

He continued, "These false allegations will have future consequences. They will 'Islamize' Hindus," implying that Hindus would be forced to respond violently to false allegations.[102] The Ayodhya movement promoted discourses of Muslims victimizing Hindus that persisted. If in the 1980s Hindutva activists attributed Hindu victimization to state policy, two decades later they attributed it to the growth of transnational Islamic militancy.

Conclusion

The movements around Ayodhya and globalization were similar in a number of respects. They bridged the chasm between private and political domains and reshaped cultural identities and values. They opposed the state, in one case because of its economic policies, and in the other because of its stance on minority rights. They affirmed values embedded in the community rather than in the marketplace of politics and wealth. They employed nationalist discourses. They recruited groups that have been historically marginalized, lower castes in the case of the temple movement, and tribals and small manufacturers in the case of the anti-globalization movement. They emerged from and strengthened a dense network of organizations. They fruitfully engaged women and appealed to gendered imagery.

They also differed in certain respects. The Ayodhya campaign appealed more to religious values and engaged in greater identity-shaping work than the campaign against globalization. As BJP leader Jagdish Shettigar noted, "these cultural issues have the most appeal."[103] The Ayodhya movement,

[101] Interview with Ram Madhav, New Delhi, November 17, 2008.
[102] Interview with Tarun Vijay, New Delhi, November 18, 2008.
[103] Interview with Jagdish Shettigar, New Delhi, December 30, 1992.

like many other movements, established clear causal connections between a discrete group of victims and the perpetrators of their suffering.[104] It identified Hindus as the victims and the state and Muslim communities as the oppressors. By contrast, the movement against globalization identified multiple victims – Hindu women, workers, peasants, and Indian society – and victimizers – the state, Western markets, and certain Indian intellectuals and artists.

The Ayodhya movement was more successful than the anti-globalization movement in influencing the government, promoting mass mobilization, and forging local-national-global links. The Ayodhya movement brought about the downfall of three governments and helped the BJP attain power at the center and in several states. Until 2004, every government that took office felt compelled to address the Ayodhya dispute. Both Congress and the National Front governments conceded to some of the movement's demands. By contrast, the anti-globalization movement failed to influence the policies of a BJP-led government, let alone governments led by other parties. No party or government of any ideological persuasion has been inclined to oppose globalization.

The temple movement had a dramatic political impact at local, regional, and national levels whereas the movement against globalization was only effective in localities. The Ayodhya movement attained funding and legitimacy for temple construction from diasporic groups. By contrast, the anti-globalization movement was unable to gain diasporic support; Narendra Modi persuaded NRIs to invest in Gujarat. Thus Hindu nationalism was most militant and successful in one of India's most globalized Indian states. The anti-globalization campaign was thus weak in Gujarat, the state in which the BJP has been strongest.

The difference in the success of these two movements is partly explained by the different relations among party, movement, and state in the two cases. The Ayodhya movement had the support of both the BJP and the VHP. Activists succeeded in demolishing the mosque in 1992 when a sympathetic BJP government came to power in UP. By contrast, the BJP did not fully support the RSS campaign against globalization and some BJP state governments and the NDA government opposed it. The NDA government did not cave to nationalist pressures on economic issues. When Ram Madhav was asked at a press conference why the RSS had been relatively silent on the question of *swadeshi* while the NDA government was in office, he responded that *swadeshi* was "far trickier" than Ayodhya or cow slaughter.[105]

At the end of the day, the entire *parivar*, including the BJP, thinks alike on the last two issues whereas on economics our house is divided. A resolution on economic policies

[104] Margaret E. Keck and Kathryn Sikkink, *Activists beyond Borders* (Ithaca, NY: Cornell University Press, 1998), 27–8.
[105] Interview with Ram Madhav, New Delhi, November 17, 2008.

would not only be difficult to phrase but tougher to pass because of the conflicting interests in our ranks.[106]

As a result, whereas the BJP refused to yield to the RSS on economic policy, it made more concessions to the RSS in opposing the Westernization of culture. Tragically, the more successful of the two campaigns was also more violent. Indeed, the Ayodhya movement's religious exhortations and identity-shaping and meaning-making work were suffused with violent words and acts.

Certain Hindu nationalist movements, including the one in Ayodhya, might be described as countermovements that emerge in reaction to movements of subordinate groups and states that represent their interests.[107] Unlike the movements they oppose, countermovements are linked to entrenched interests and organizations and have ties to the established order. They tend to be short, intense, and violent. Countermovements organized by conservative groups often employ the same discourses as the progressive movements they oppose. Hindu nationalist countermovements have given voice to upper-caste anxieties about being victims of the state's preferential treatment of the lower castes and to broader fears of national disintegration and instability amid the growth of ethnic movements in Kashmir, Punjab, and Assam. Govindacharya described majority nationalism as a response to minority nationalism.[108]

Hindu nationalist countermovements also represent a backlash against the political assertions of the conservative Muslim community and the state's acquiescence, at times, to their demands. Their contention that the state has ignored or disparaged Hindu interests echoes the claims of ethnic minorities. Similarly, in its exhortations that Muslims have engaged in ruthless violence against Hindus, the VHP has symbolically aligned Hindus with *dalits* who have been exploited by the upper castes, and women, who have been exploited by men. Thus, as much as the movement around Ayodhya succeeded in employing popular discourses and gaining the support of historically marginalized groups, the movement neither emanated from nor articulated their abiding interests.

---

[106] Radhika Ramaseshan, "Sangh in Spot on Swadeshi Silence," *The Telegraph*, March 16, 2003. Accessed June 25, 2014. http://www.telegraphindia.com/1030316/asp/nation/story_1772944 .asp.

[107] Writings on countermovements include: Meyer and Staggenborg, "Movements, Counter-movements and the Structure of Political Opportunity"; Hayagreeva Rao, Calvin Morrill, and Mayer Zald, "Power Plays: How Social Movements and Collective Action Create New Organizational Forms," in Barry Staw and Robert T. Sutton, eds., *Research in Organizational Behavior: An Annual Series of Analytical Essays and Critical Reviews*, Vol. 22; 237–81. (New York: JAI-Elsevier Science, 2000.) Kimberly B. Dugan, "Just Like You: The Dimensions of Identity Presentation in an Antigay Contested Context," in Rachel L. Einwohner, Daniel J. Meyers, and Jo Reger, eds., *Identity Work in Social Movements* (Minneapolis, MN: University of Minnesota Press, 2008); and Bert Useem and Mayer N. Zald, "Movement and Countermovement Interaction: Mobilization, Tactics and State Involvement," in McCarthy and Zald, eds., *Social Movements in an Organizational Society*.

[108] Interview with Govindacharya, New Delhi, July 24, 2007.

PART II

EXTENSIVE VIOLENCE

4

When Local Violence Is Not Merely Local
A Tale of Two Towns

The conjuncture of party, movement, and state activities provoked anti-minority violence in many towns in northern India in the early 1990s. This chapter explores this conjuncture as well as another, of local and national forces in Bijnor and Khurja, before, during, and after the violence.

I challenge conventional reports on "riots" that often render victims and perpetrators of violence nameless and faceless. I recount their stories to illuminate the complex logics that inform their actions.[1] I explore the displacement of class and caste tensions onto conflicts between particular groups of Muslims and Hindus. Muslims were the victims of Hindu nationalists' attempt to capture the support of *dalits*, whose political affiliations were in flux. Although Hindu nationalists asserted that there had always been fixed and absolute differences between Hindus and Muslims, in fact they worked hard to create Hindu unity by undermining other competing identities. They appealed to *dalits* by promising to protect them from Muslim exploitation and by providing them with symbolic power. They similarly accorded Hindu women recognition and assured them of safety from supposed Muslim aggression. As a result, women and *dalits* played key roles in forging links between party and movement activities.

The BJP was anxious to improve its electoral standing in local political bodies. It had experienced electoral setbacks in both towns, and hoped to stage a comeback by joining the RSS, VHP, Bajrang Dal, and Durga Vahini in the Ayodhya campaign. All these Hindu nationalist organizations sought to win over sympathetic members of the local administration while challenging higher branches of the state.

---

[1] I have used pseudonyms to describe the people I interviewed, with the exception of public officials and leaders of major organizations, whose actions are subject to scrutiny.

FIGURE 4.1. Bijnor and Bulandshahr in Uttar Pradesh.
Map prepared by Andy Anderson, Amherst College, by modifying public-domain
maps from https://commons.wikimedia.org/wiki/Category:Locator_maps_of_districts
_of_Uttar_Pradesh.

The period of militant Hindu nationalist mobilization was intense but
short-lived. A different constellation of parties, movements, and states
quickly curbed anti-minority violence. The OBC-led SP and the *dalit*-led BSP
politicized caste identities, defused Hindu-Muslim polarization, and created
greater opportunities for Muslim political representation. The character of
local administrations and elected bodies also changed under BSP and SP
governments.

Khurja

With a population of 98,610, Khurja is the largest town in Bulandshahr
district. Sixty percent of Khurja's population is Hindu and 38 percent is
Muslim (the rest are Jains and others). A significant proportion of the population in Bulandshahr district – 20 percent (588,683 out of 2,913,122) –
is Scheduled Caste. The most numerous among the Scheduled Castes are
Chamars (436,047, or 15 percent of the population); Balmikis (also known as
Valmikis) constitute 1.7 percent (51,804) and Khatiks 1.3 percent (37,562).[2]
A key goal for Hindu nationalists was to acquire *dalits'* support by alienating
them from Muslims.

---

[2] Registrar General and Census Commissioner of India, Census of India, District Profile, 2011.
Accessed July 9, 2014. http://www.censusindia.gov.in/DigitalLibrary/Archive_home.aspx.

Khurja had been relatively peaceful in the past. However, it experienced two incidents of Hindu-Muslim violence, from December 1990 to February 1991. Seventy-four people died in the first incident (December 15–16, 1990), and twenty-two people in the second (January 31–February 5, 1991). Many more Muslims than Hindus were killed on both occasions. The death toll in the first incident was sixty-two Muslims and twelve Hindus, and in the second, eighteen Muslims and four Hindus.[3]

Several skirmishes preceded the first incident. Balmikis alleged that on December 11, Muslims damaged their temple and refused to repair it, so they collected money and repaired it themselves. Muslims claimed that they found a dead pig in front of their mosque on the same day. Two days later, there was a violent conflict between Muslims and Balmikis in the neighboring township of Jahangirpur. It ended with the VHP and its Hindu (primarily *bania*) supporters setting fire to a Muslim home and killing eleven people who had taken refuge inside.

The tensions further escalated on December 14 when a Hindu stabbed a young Muslim man. Many people blamed a Balmiki woman known as Meerutvali (because she was from the town of Meerut) and her son, Lakshman. I heard several different versions of the story of Meerutvali's role. Some Muslims contended that the BJP had paid Meerutvali 2,500 rupees (approximately $100 in 1991–2) to kill Fareed, the Muslim, in order to provoke further violence. Other Muslims claimed that Meerutvali was settling scores with Muslims over earlier conflicts. By contrast, most Balmikis believed that a Muslim Congress Party worker had implicated Meerutvali because they were competitors for a post on a Congress Party committee. Meerutvali claimed in an interview that the Congress Party worker had framed her. She stated that she had not been near the site of the crime and denied that Lakshman was her son.[4] Although rumors spread that Fareed had died, in fact he recovered after being hospitalized in Delhi. When the police took Lakshman into custody, 400 Hindutva activists surrounded the police station, demanded his release, and exploded two petrol bombs outside the station. The police abdicated their authority to the Sangh Parivar by releasing Lakshman that night.

The following day (December 15), a fight erupted between Balmikis and Muslims in which two Balmikis were killed. A rumor spread that 200 Muslims had congregated at the Muslim-owned Mehboob Pottery, abducted Hindus who were passing by, hacked them to death, and thrown their bodies in the kilns. Shortly thereafter, fifty Hindu men marched to Sarai Sheikh Alam, a neighborhood where many Ansari Muslims lived, and engaged in arson, looting, and murder. Within a two-hour period they killed sixty-two Muslims, in many cases by setting Muslim homes on fire.

[3] Estimates of the number of people killed in Hindu-Muslim violence vary greatly. I have recorded both the official figures and the estimates that I was given by local communities.
[4] Interview with Meerutvali, Khurja, May 11, 1991.

Hari Prasad, a reporter for the *Hindustan* newspaper, stated in an interview that when he visited Sarai Sheikh Alam during the violence, he did not see a single police officer, despite the presence of a nearby police station.[5] The following day the administration deployed troops and made many arrests. Although the violence stopped, tensions remained acute. The administration placed Khurja under curfew. While it issued passes to Hindus, enabling them to move freely through the town, Muslims remained confined to their homes.

Muslims feared more violence and prepared to defend themselves. On January 2, the police discovered that Muslims had stored large supplies of arms and ammunition in a mosque in Sarai Sheikh Alam. Referring to the concealed supply of weaponry, Ali Khan, a Muslim attorney in Khurja, commented, "This would never have happened under ordinary circumstances but they [Muslims] saw that the administration had not protected them so they were determined to protect themselves."[6] The police arrested sixty-eight people on charges of procuring and storing arms. The BJP put pressure on the administration to keep the Provincial Armed Constabulary (PAC), the state armed reserved force, posted in Khurja to protect Hindus.[7]

A series of provocations and rumors preceded the second major incident of violence. On January 29, four Hindus attacked a Muslim fruit vendor at Raniwalla Chowk, near a PAC picket. Shortly thereafter, a bomb blast in a Muslim home killed five people. Some claimed that Balmikis had deliberately detonated the bomb, while others claimed that a Muslim had accidentally done so. Rumors of Muslim aggression circulated rapidly. On January 31, the BJP organized a large protest outside the police station after it claimed to have found fourteen dead cows outside its office. The Sub-Divisional Magistrate (SDM) found only two cow carcasses and, upon investigation, determined that they had not been poisoned but had died of natural causes. Although, as Prasad commented, Muslims would never have risked going to a Hindu neighborhood and poisoning cows during curfew, many people believed that Muslims had poisoned the cows. Other rumors followed. For example, Hindutva activists claimed that a Balmiki boy had disappeared while making a delivery to Muslim street vendors. A college professor who was a BJP member alleged that a Muslim water tank operator had poisoned the town's drinking water. When Prasad challenged him, he admitted that he had no evidence that the water had been poisoned but that he had intended to signal a potential danger. Prasad also reported on a rumor circulating in his neighborhood that 500 Muslims were planning to attack the neighborhood. Therefore, Hindus needed to arm

[5] Interview with Hari Prasad, Khurja, May 10, 1991.
[6] Interview with Ali Khan, Khurja, May 10, 1991.
[7] The predominantly Hindu PAC is widely known to have engaged in extensive human rights violations and in particular anti-Muslim violence. An Additional District Magistrate (ADM) whom I interviewed explained that the PAC was designed to be an anti-dacoit (anti-bandit) force and was ill suited to preventing violence. For example, it did not have rubber bullets with which to disperse crowds.

themselves in self-defense. Upon learning that an RSS member had spread the rumor, Prasad persuaded his neighbors that the rumor was unfounded.

On the evening of January 31, microphones blasted a cassette recording of terrified screams, conveying the impression that people in a neighboring locality were being attacked and slaughtered. The district magistrate (DM) and Senior Superintendent of Police (SSP) scoured the town and determined that no one had been attacked. Meanwhile, however, Muslims armed themselves and fled to the rooftops of their houses. When they refused to lay down their arms, the police opened fire and killed one person. Muslims retaliated by throwing petrol bombs. They also set several Hindu homes in Punjabi *mohalla* (area of town) on fire. Shortly thereafter, Hindus attacked homes in Sarai Sheikh Alam, killing twenty-two people. The administration imposed a curfew on the town and the violence quickly came to an end.

Why Violence?

The BJP had grown significantly in Khurja over the years preceding the violence. Former BJP president in Khurja GS Gupta said that the BJP's membership had soared from several hundred to 2,700.[8] The VHP, which had been relatively inactive in the past, also grew significantly and allied with the BJP. A number of new organizations emerged, including the Bajrang Dal, Durga Vahini, Hindu Yuva Vahini, Hindu Jagran Manch, (Struggle for Hindu Existence), Sriram Seva Samiti, and Sri Ram Janmabhumi Mukti Yagya Samiti. This dense network of interconnected organizations jointly planned religious festivals, community service, and political protests that culminated in violence.

Several people traced the origins of Hindu-Muslim tensions in Khurja to the Ayodhya campaign. Hindutva activists had organized a victory procession when the Congress government unlocked the gates of the *babri masjid* and allowed Hindus to worship at the site. Many activists from Khurja had joined Advani's *rath yatra* to Ayodhya in October 1990 and their families hosted people who were traveling to and from Ayodhya. Eqbal Khan described Muslims' helplessness and fear when Hindu activists passed through Khurja on their way to Ayodhya.[9] On December 15, when violence first occurred, the town was anticipating the arrival of the *asthi kalash*, a procession bearing ashes of the Hindu activists who had been killed in Ayodhya. Rumors caused small conflicts to escalate into more serious ones.

There is extensive evidence that Hindu nationalists played a crucial role in fomenting both violent incidents. Witnesses identified high-ranking BJP members directing crowds to Muslim shops and homes over a two-hour period on December 15. Ram Swarup Bhaia, the district head of the RSS, was later charged with murdering eleven people. Kishori Lal Sahani, a professor at JS

---

[8] Interview with GS Gupta, Khurja, May 9, 1991.
[9] Interview with Eqbal Khan, Khurja, May 10, 1991.

Intermediary College, was arrested and released a few days later. Sahani reportedly attacked the home of one of his Muslim students who survived the attack and testified against him.

Hindu nationalists spread rumors alleging that Muslims were planning to attack and kill Hindus, so Hindus needed to engage in violence to protect and defend themselves. The rumor on December 15 that 200 Muslims had congregated at the Muslim-owned Mehboob Pottery and brutalized Hindus turned out to be fictitious. An investigation team headed by Azad Khan found that the factory had been closed and was empty that day. However, it was some time before the rumor was discredited. And even then, VHP president Durga Dutt Joshi described in gruesome detail how Muslims had chopped the bodies of Hindus into small pieces and stuffed them into the kiln.[10] Just prior to the violence on January 31, rumors circulated about Muslims killing cows, contaminating drinking water, and attacking Hindu neighborhoods.

The BJP sought to improve its electoral performance by polarizing Hindus and Muslims in order to gain Hindu support in Khurja and neighboring constituencies. The BJP had performed poorly in elections to the municipal council, which were held in Khurja in 1988 after a seventeen year hiatus. Of the twenty-one seats on the municipal council, the BJP won four, Congress five, independents ten, and the Janata Dal two. Fourteen of the elected representatives were Hindu and seven were Muslim; many Hindus voted for Muslim candidates. The most heated contest pitted BJP member Elhans against SP candidate Sharma. Both were Hindu. The latter won with significant Muslim support. In 1989, Bhagwan Das Rathore, a Janata Dal candidate, won the parliamentary seat from Khurja with 50 percent of the popular vote. BJP candidate Lakshmi Chand received merely 2 percent of the vote. Two years later, in the aftermath of the violence, the BJP's performance significantly improved. Although Janata Dal candidate Roshan won the election with 42 percent of the vote, BJP candidate Lakshmi Chand received 36 percent of the vote, a significant improvement over his performance in the previous election. The BJP's Harpal Singh won successive Legislative Assembly elections in 1993 and 1996.

The BJP was especially anxious to gain *dalit* support because Khurja was a reserved constituency (in which only Scheduled Castes could be elected). Chamars largely supported the BSP. The BJP revived memories of conflicts between Balmikis and Muslims that had occurred in 1983 and depicted these incidents as part of a long, unbroken history of Hindu-Muslim conflict. The suggestion was triply erroneous: it falsely claimed there had been a continuous history of Hindu-Muslim conflict, labeled as religious what was in fact a class conflict between certain groups of Muslims and certain groups of Balmikis, and masked the BJP's role in exacerbating rivalries.

Conflicts in Khurja have involved subgroups created by the permutations of caste and community identities, for example, lower-caste Hindus and

[10] Interview with Durga Dutt Joshi, Khurja, May 12, 1991.

upper-caste Muslims. The town's *mohallas* are differentiated by caste, class, and community. Among the *dalits*, the better-off Chamars and poorer Balmikis live in different neighborhoods. Khurja's Muslim community is also stratified by class and status. Muslim Pathans and Ansaris are relatively affluent; Gaddis are quite poor. Clusters of Muslim Pathan and Hindu *bania* neighborhoods are located within the main town; poor Gaddi and wealthier Ansari Muslims and Balmikis live on its periphery in close proximity to each other.

What became a conflict between Muslims and Hindus began as a class conflict between relatively affluent Muslims and poor Balmikis. Raj Kumar, one of three Balmiki lawyers in Khurja, reported that only 100 Balmikis in Khurja were educated and many had left Khurja to find government jobs elsewhere.[11] The initial dispute was between two groups in adjoining neighborhoods: Muslims living in Tarinam Teraha and Balmikis in Sarai Matyas. Most Balmikis in this neighborhood worked as sweepers, mainly for Muslim families. Some Balmikis complained that their employers harassed them and withheld wages. They claimed that the residents of Tarinam Teraha had already driven them out of Purana Kabila and were attempting to take over land in Sarai Matyas to construct a market there.

Most Balmikis in Khurja had traditionally been Congress Party supporters. Many resented the BSP because they believed that it favored Chamars. The BJP had been courting them, with mixed results. Raj Kumar said, "The BJP wanted to start the procession to Ayodhya from our temple on October 30th. We asked them to take the procession from some other place and we did not participate. We don't support their campaign in Ayodhya."[12]

However, Balmiki support for the BJP grew when the BJP defended Meerutvali. Balmikis were angry that Muslims blamed her for stabbing Fareed and claimed that she was an innocent woman who had been deemed a troublemaker because she had defended Balmikis. Omprakash Balmiki, a sweeper, said that the BJP supported Balmikis' demands for higher wages and their grievances against their Muslim employers.[13] In the aftermath of the two episodes of violence, Hindutva activists gave Balmikis a new vocabulary to describe their own identities as well as those of their Muslim neighbors. The *pradhan* of the Balmiki *panchayat* proclaimed that Khurja was divided between "Pakistan and Hindustan." Meerutvali said that the government never questioned the veracity of Muslim claims because it continually "appeased" them. Thus, by 1992, Khurja's BJP president, Surender Tiwari, could boast, "the Balmikis are with us."[14]

The BJP was determined to undermine influential Muslim leaders. In Khurja, its main target was Sarwar Hussain, who had been elected to Parliament from

[11] Interview with Raj Kumar, Khurja, May 11, 1991.
[12] Ibid.
[13] Interview with Omprakash Balmiki, Khurja, May 11, 1991.
[14] Interview with Surender Tiwari, Khurja, January 7, 1992.

Bulandshahr on a Janata Dal seat in 1989. He had served as union minister of state for flood and civil supplies under the National Front government. After the Janata Dal split, he remained close to Mulayam Singh Yadav. Hussain's father-in-law, Mahmood Hussain, served two terms as MP. One of Hussain's cousins was a lawyer, his son was an MP, and several of his extended family members were educated professionals. Hindutva activists resented Hussain's political prominence, ties to the ruling party, strong kin network, and lower caste support. They claimed that Hussain had encouraged Muslims to attack Hindus and supplied them with arms and ammunition. According to BJP president Tiwari, Hussain had sent six truckloads of ammunition from Delhi to Khurja; five trucks had reached Khurja. He warned, "Sarwar Hussain has exhorted Muslims to crush Hindus. He is a dangerous man. He is a Muslim first and a human being afterwards."[15] The administration stated that the charge that Hussain had sent arms to Khurja was baseless.

Hindutva activists deeply resented Hussain's political connections in Lucknow and Delhi. RSS member Raj Khurana said that Hussain had pressured the police to file First Information Reports (FIRs, complaints lodged with the police for cognizable offenses) against seventy Hindus in connection with the "riot" even though many of them were innocent. He claimed that Hussain used his political influence to get the chief minister to transfer the DM and several policemen out of Khurja after the violence. Khurana recalled that Hussain disliked the police because they searched Muslim homes and mosques for arms and ammunitions. He said, "For months I didn't dare go near the police *thana* [station]. It was Muslim *raj* [nation] there."[16] Khurana and other Hindutva activists were also angry with Hussain's family for creating a relief camp for Muslim victims in Sarai Sheikh Alam. They regarded this as another instance of Muslims favoring their own community. Indeed, they complained so bitterly that the administration moved the camp to another location. Hindutva activists then set up relief camps for Hindus only.

Sarwar Hussain found the BJP allegations ludicrous but explicable. He said in an interview:

I didn't need to instigate riots to build my political career. I was a Minister in Delhi. Instigating a riot would have hurt my reputation. Riots are the work of people who lack power. They are the work of people who feel they are weak and want to become stronger.[17]

What Hussain actually did was less significant than what he represented to Hindu nationalists – a Muslim who wielded state power and belonged to a rival party that both Muslims and lower-caste Hindus supported.

[15] Interview with Surender Tiwari, Khurja, May 7, 1991.
[16] Interview with Raj Khurana, Khurja, May 9, 1991.
[17] Interview with Sarwar Hussain, Khurja, May 12, 1991.

The violence also resulted from competition between the two main local industries. By way of background, pottery manufacturing grew from a small cottage industry into a source of employment for 40,000 Khurja residents. Although initially Muslims predominated among owners of pottery industries, Hindus replaced them once the industry expanded. By the early 1990s, there were 500 pottery factories in Khurja, of which 396 were registered as independent or self-sufficient units. About 60 percent were owned by Hindus and 40 percent by Muslims. The Pottery Manufacturers' Association (PMA), Khurja's most powerful institution, helped the owners of independent units secure licenses and obtain tax breaks.

The economic interdependence of Hindus and Muslims, through the pottery industry, should have deterred interethnic violence. However, it had the opposite effect for several reasons. First, the PMA promoted a vast underground market that sold coal to Ghaziabad.[18] Because the underground economy depended on state support, PMA officeholders patronized elected officials, bureaucrats, and the police to help them procure coal and escape prosecution. Thus, elections to positions on the PMA were highly politicized and coveted.

PMA members admitted that 75 percent of the profits from the pottery industry came from coal black marketeering. Indicative of the extent of corruption in the industry, according to one informant, was that only 300 of the 500 registered pottery units were functioning; the other 200 only existed on paper.[19] The black market in coal contributed to the growth of criminal networks that produced and sold arms. It also brought into being a *satta*, a gambling enterprise, which took bets on whether a "riot" would occur. People could buy tickets costing 4 to 40 cents from the neighborhood *paan* (betel leaf) or tea stall. Eqbal Khan estimated that people placed bets worth roughly $400 on "riots" taking place.[20] Given that hundreds of thousands of rupees were at stake and that the institution developed after the first episode of violence, many of my informants speculated that the gambling industry helped instigate the second episode of violence.

Second, leadership positions on the PMA were highly coveted and rival groups sought to discredit their opponents by implicating them in violence. Two rival factions, both comprised of Hindus and Muslims, sought control of the PMA. One faction was headed by Raj Kumar Poddar, the other by Raj Khurana. At the time of the first incident of violence, the Poddar group monopolized posts on the PMA. Surender Tiwari estimated that Poddar turned a profit of between $200,000 and $400,000 annually. He attributed its success in part to Sarwar Hussain's patronage.[21] The Khurana group was determined to

[18] See Uma Chakravarty et al., "Khurja Riots 1990–1991: Understanding the Conjuncture," *Economic and Political Weekly*, May 2, 1992, Vol. 27, no. 18, 951–65.
[19] Interview with Surender Tiwari, Khurja, May 9, 1991.
[20] Interview with Eqbal Khan, Khurja, May 10, 1991.
[21] Ibid.

undermine the Poddar group and stall elections to the PMA. Khurana was an RSS member and several pottery owners in his faction were BJP members. The Khurana group spread the rumor about Sarwar Hussain dispatching truckloads of ammunition to Khurja. The Poddar group sought revenge by having members of the Khurana group booked on charges of instigating a "riot." It gave the administration the names of people whom it claimed had engaged in violence. Some people alleged that Hussain had used official connections to ensure that charges were brought against members of the group. The Khurana group responded by bringing charges against members of the Poddar group. Altogether the two groups gave the administration the names of 900 people whom they claimed had precipitated violence; the administration rejected 775 of them, and investigated the remainder.

Third, several pottery owners were RSS and BJP members who engaged in anti-Muslim violence. They were especially determined to undermine Sarwar Hussain, who was involved in both the pottery industry and party politics. Furthermore, both the Poddar and Khurana groups exploited Hindu-Muslim tensions to their own advantage. Although the rival factions' motivations were primarily economic and political, their actions deepened animosities between Hindus and Muslims.

The state was implicated in the violence both by virtue of what it represented to different groups and what its many branches did. The groups that precipitated the violence sought to undermine the state government, which was headed by Mulayam Singh Yadav. The police demonstrated their sympathy for Hindutva activists by refusing to stop the violence and the local administration failed to act decisively to curb it. Once the administration called in the army, declared a curfew, and made arrests, the violence subsided. Fewer people were killed in the second than in the first incident because of quicker and more decisive administrative intervention.

Violence did not occur in Khurja after Hindutva activists destroyed the *babri masjid* in December 1992, in part thanks to the local administration. When tensions began to mount in Khurja, SDM Dimple Varma imposed a curfew that she enforced strictly and impartially. She also detained forty-two people, mostly members of Hindu organizations, on December 13, which Hindutva organizations termed a black day in protest against the central government's decision to remove BJP state governments from office.[22] Moreover, the response of Hindu organizations to the events in Ayodhya was less aggressive than previously. SP Bali, a Khurja resident, described why: "Some of them felt that they had accomplished their job and others were afraid and went into hiding."[23]

Another reason that violence did not recur in Khurja in 1992 was that Muslim leaders were determined to prevent it. Sarwar Hussain said that when

[22] Interview with Dimple Varma, Khurja, January 7, 1993.
[23] Interview with SP Bali, Khurja, January 7, 1993.

he learned that some members of his community were planning to damage a local temple, he organized other Muslims to protect it. He also dissuaded Muslims from organizing a demonstration protesting the destruction of the mosque in Ayodhya. He commented: "I was able to convince them [Muslims] that peace-loving Hindus throughout India and the world were speaking out on our behalf so there was no reason for us to put ourselves in danger."[24] According to Hussain, only 10 percent of Hindus in Khurja responded to the BJP's call to observe a black day.

To summarize, the conjuncture of local and national events, within and outside political institutions, facilitated the Khurja violence. Some groups in the pottery industry exploited community tensions to acquire institutional power and amass profits. Ideology had little to do with their actions. For many Balmikis, tensions centered not on the temple/mosque dispute but on their relations with Muslim employers. Hindu nationalists recast class tensions as Hindu-Muslim conflicts to gain the support of Balmikis and turn them against Muslims.

The violence in Khurja also reflected contestation over access to state power. Members of the BJP and its affiliates could influence members of the police force but not the more impartial officers of the Indian Administrative Service (IAS). Their resort to violence reflected their frustration at being unable to influence the state government, anger at those who did, and political ambitions. At the same time, the state government's opposition to the BJP and the important role of certain Muslim leaders limited the extent of the violence.

Bijnor

Bijnor is located in a largely rural district bearing the same name in western UP. Seventy-six percent of the district's population lives in rural areas and 24 percent in urban areas.[25] Given the dearth of private-sector employment, public-sector jobs are highly coveted. The major source of nonagricultural employment is a nearby sugar mill.

Bijnor has a population of 115,381, of whom 66 percent are Muslim and 32 percent Hindu (2 percent are Jains and others). While the vast majority are Muslim, Hindus are economically dominant. Hindus work as traders, shopkeepers, and small business owners; Muslims work as rickshaw drivers, artisans, and craftspeople. Remittances from the Gulf have not made their way back to Bijnor and created a Muslim bourgeoisie, as in some other localities. Twenty-one percent of Bijnor district is Scheduled Caste (655,806 out of

---

[24] Interview with Sarwar Hussain, Khurja, January 8, 1993.
[25] Uttar Pradesh 2001 Census Data, *Office of the Registrar General and Census Commissioner, India*, http://www.censusindia.gov.in/PopulationFinder/Population_Finder.aspx.

3,131,619). The most numerous Scheduled Castes are Chamars (571,454), followed by Balmikis (42,135) and Bhuiyars (18,353).[26]

The three Muslim civic organizations in Bijnor – the Mujahedin-e Islam, formed in December 1989, the Adam Sena, formed in September 1990, and the Muslim Youth Federation, formed in October 1990 – are relatively weak, even by the BJP's reckoning. By contrast, Hindu nationalist organizations have steadily grown. LP Jain, owner of a clothing store, became president of the BJP in Bijnor in 1990.[27] He reported that the BJP had 600 members, including 35 active members in the town, and 9,000 members, including 400 active members in the district. He said that the BJP had strong vertical ties with district and ward offices and collaborated extensively with the VHP and its affiliates.

Raghuvir Singh, the VHP president for Bijnor, stated that the VHP had 300 full-time members and a large number of supporters.[28] He claimed that three events contributed to the VHP's rise in the 1980s: the UP government's decision to authorize Hindus to worship at the *babri masjid*, Rajiv Gandhi's overturning the Supreme Court verdict on Shah Bano, and VP Singh's designating Prophet Mohammed's birthday a national holiday. He said that the VHP had organized a *Virat Hindu Sammelan* (Grand Hindu Conference) in Bijnor in March 1989 that 30,000 people had attended. This was the first time that he could remember Hindu-Muslim tensions in the town.

Sangh Parivar activists frequently collaborated with the Shiv Sena and Arya Samaj in Bijnor. Ram Gopal, the town's Shiv Sena president and the owner of a tent shop, reported that the Shiv Sena had a membership of 15,000 in Bijnor district. "There are big differences between the BJP and the Shiv Sena," he said. "We do what we say we'll do. They just talk."[29] But regardless of Gopal's qualms about the BJP, he participated in its activities. The Arya Samaj had been active in Bijnor since the early twentieth century. Shri Krishnamurthi, Arya Samaj president for the town and senior vice president for UP, said that its work centered on social reform, particularly on improving the conditions of *dalits* and Hindu women.[30] However, Krishnamurthi said that the Arya Samaj had begun to work closely with the RSS and had become increasingly committed to preserving and defending Hindu culture. "Brothers often disagree, but when a family is attacked from the outside, they band together in self-defense," he said.

Bijnor experienced Hindu-Muslim violence from October 30 to November 3, 1990. Eighty-seven people were killed, according to official sources, and between 198 and 300, according to unofficial estimates.[31] I first visited Bijnor

---

[26] Registrar General and Census Commissioner of India, Census of India, District Profile, 2011. Accessed July 9, 2014. http://www.censusindia.gov.in/DigitalLibrary/Archive_home.aspx.
[27] Interview with LP Jain, Bijnor, May 2, 1991.
[28] Interview with Raghuvir Singh, Bijnor, May 2, 1991.
[29] Interview with Ram Gopal, Bijnor, April 25, 1991.
[30] Interview with Shri Krishnamurthi, Bijnor, June 7, 1991.
[31] Estimates of casualties vary widely. Official estimates, according to Raj Kumar, the former DM are: 87 persons killed, 127 injured (of which 42 were identified as serious injuries and 85 as

six months after the violence and returned periodically over succeeding months and years.[32] On each occasion, I interviewed Hindus and Muslims from a range of backgrounds. Although their accounts about what had transpired differed in important respects, they all agreed that the violence on October 30 was the culmination of a sequence of events that dated back several years. The incidents concerned municipal council elections in November 1988, conflict over a plot of land on August 25, 1990, the banning of Ram devotees (*Ram bhakts*) from Bijnor on October 4, 1990, and a rally that the UP chief minister organized on October 9, 1990.

The Municipal Council Elections

I discuss local elections in Bijnor at some length because they laid the foundation for the violence that followed. The BJP's success in the 1988 municipal council elections was the culmination of its efforts to implant itself in Bijnor. In the 1987 elections, it had only won thirty-three seats for the chairs of the block-level councils. The following year it captured seventy-four seats. Similarly, while in 1987 the BJP won twenty-eight seats in the *zila parishads* (district councils), the following year it won 110 seats. It was equally successful in the municipal council elections.

The municipal council, an elected body, is responsible for urban planning, economic development, and social service delivery. The government regards municipal councils as branches of government. To ensure that they are representative of their communities, it reserves a quota of municipal council seats for Scheduled Castes and women. Until the passage of the 74th Amendment Act in 1992, the state government could dissolve municipal councils if it considered them derelict in carrying out their responsibilities. The Act circumscribed the state government's control over municipal bodies.

Many residents of Bijnor traced Hindu-Muslim tensions back to 1988, when Zafar Khan (a Muslim) was elected chair of the municipal council. Khan was a well-educated, sophisticated lawyer who appeared to be the obvious choice for municipal council chair. The other contender for the position, Sandip Lal

---

simple injuries), and 1,038 cases of arson and looting. Kumar noted that the previous DM had reported that only 36 people were killed; after he had been replaced, many more people had come forward and filed reports. The DM had no record of how these figures broke down by religious community. However all unofficial estimates, including those of Hindu nationalists, report much higher casualties, mostly among Muslims. Nandaji, RSS *pracharak* in Bijnor, estimates that 14 Hindus and 184 Muslims were killed. According to KL Joshi, a reporter for the *Dainik Jagran* who toured Bijnor right after the riots, 75 Hindus and 225 Muslims were killed and 400–500 people were injured.

[32] For earlier accounts of the Bijnor violence, see my "When Local Riots Are Not Merely Local: Bringing the State Back in, Bijnor 1988–92," *Economic and Political Weekly*, October 1, 1994, Vol. 29, no. 40, 2605–21, and Patricia Jeffery and Roger Jeffery, "The Bijnor Riots, October 1990," *Economic and Political Weekly*, March 5, 1994, Vol. 29, no. 10, 551–8.

128 *Extensive Violence*

(a Hindu), was a poor alternative to Khan. He was relatively uneducated and was reputed to be corrupt. After the violence, even Hindutva activists admitted that he and his sons had acquired vast wardrobes by looting Muslim shops. Lal was also considered a political opportunist. From the time he became active in politics in 1985 until 1992, he shifted party allegiance seven times. Outraged that the SP had not nominated him to contest the 1991 Legislative Assembly elections, Lal had produced explosives that he planned to detonate in the SP candidate's home.[33] However, the bomb exploded in Lal's own home.

The *Bijnor Times* newspaper backed Lal and characterized Khan in its editorials as a "communal" man because he had collected funds for Muslims whose family members had been killed in the Meerut violence in May–June 1987 and had brought back two Muslim bodies for burial in Bijnor. Khan defended his actions. He stated that the families of the young victims were friends and neighbors, and that he considered it appropriate to honor the dead with proper burials.

The municipal council consisted of twenty-four members; eighteen were elected – eleven Muslims and seven Hindus. Unlike the Muslims, many of the Hindu elected members were political activists. Ram Gopal was the local Shiv Sena president, Raghuvir Singh, the local VHP president, and Tilakwala, head of the Bajrang Dal. (He acquired his nickname from the enormous *tilak* – red mark – on his forehead.) Three of the other six municipal council members were nominated to reserved seats for women and Scheduled Castes; the remaining three were ex-officio and included a Member of the Legislative Assembly (MLA), an MP, and the chair. A core group of elected members plotted to undermine Khan by alleging that he was misusing public funds and political office to serve partisan ends by discriminating against Hindus. Singh alleged that Khan had allocated 80 percent of the municipal council's funds on sanitation and street lighting to Muslim neighborhoods and only 20 percent to Hindu neighborhoods.[34] He also claimed that Khan had allotted 95 percent of the land under the council's control to Muslims and only 5 percent to Hindus for a *dharamsala* (religious sanctuary for the poor). Furthermore, he asserted that Khan sought to ensure that Muslims would monopolize office. Although customarily, if the municipal council chair was a Muslim, the chair would appoint a Hindu as vice chair, he said that Khan had appointed Mustafa Aziz, a Muslim, as vice chair. Moreover, according to Singh, save for one exception, Khan had appointed Muslims to all the other key posts on the municipal council. Through these actions, Singh falsely claimed, Khan was trying to build his career as a Muslim leader.

Singh reported that over the previous three years, Khan's Hindu opponents had frequently tried to remove him from office. They gained the support of

[33] Interview with local intelligence officer, Bijnor, May 3, 1991.
[34] Interview with Raghuvir Singh, Bijnor, May 2, 1991.

two of Khan's allies on the municipal council: Tej Malwa, a *dalit,* and Ashraf Hasan, a Muslim. However, the chief minister of UP intervened to protect Khan by changing the nominated members; the opposition in turn brought charges of undue interference against the chief minister. It also brought charges against the DM for refusing to hear its no-confidence motion. Khan's opponents simultaneously pursued another strategy. They coordinated with Deepak Mehra, the editor and proprietor of the *Bijnor Times,* to discredit Khan and pave the way for his defeat in the municipal council elections. Although Mehra was not a BJP supporter, he allied with Hindu groups in this instance.

The *Bijnor Times* was replete with stories that denigrated Khan. For example, it provided extensive coverage of the rape of a Muslim woman by police constables while she was in custody, and decried Khan for failing to defend her. It praised two Muslim men, Ashraf Hasan and Niaz Zaidi, for organizing a demonstration in protest. Coverage of rape and other atrocities against women was otherwise conspicuously absent from the *Bijnor Times.* Through this biased coverage, the *Bijnor Times* implicitly contrasted "good Muslims" with "bad Muslims" like Khan.

Zafar Khan responded to these charges during several lengthy interviews.[35] First, he convincingly demonstrated that he had not displayed favoritism toward Muslim wards. Khan showed me a letter that he had sent to the eighteen elected municipal council members authorizing them to oversee sanitation for their wards. He also showed me one set of ledgers on street lighting and another on sanitation, both of which covered the period from 1989 to 1991. Ward supervisors, most of whom were Hindus, had signed these ledgers every month, certifying that they had consented to perform certain tasks and had done so. In defense of his claim that he had not favored Muslims, Khan clarified the process whereby officers were selected for the municipal council's subcommittees. The entire council, not the chair alone, elected the vice chair. Khan favored a Hindu vice chair and proposed Pyare Lal for the post. He also proposed Radhika Seth, a Hindu who had been nominated to fill a seat reserved for a woman, as assistant vice chair. However Pyare Lal and Radhika Seth refused the appointments. In what he later regarded as poor judgment, Khan then entrusted the council with selecting the vice chair. He continued:

The meeting that day went on for a long time and we were unable to decide on a vice chair before we adjourned. So we scheduled another meeting. The day before this meeting I dropped in at Pyare Lal's house. I found my opponents assembled there. They had met without me and made Wajid Khan the vice chair and Sharif Mujahid [both Muslims] the assistant vice chair in order to discredit me and divide my supporters.

---

[35] Interviews with Zafar Khan, Bijnor, April 25 and 26 and May 3, 1991.

Khan did not let the matter rest. He appealed to the commissioner in Moradabad to nullify the decision on grounds that he had been deliberately excluded from the meeting. The commissioner decided that the resolutions had no legal standing. By acting on their own, he said, municipal council members were undermining the chair's fiscal and administrative authority. The district government counsel, whom Khan consulted, said that members had to be informed about municipal council meetings at least three days in advance. If the chair was absent, he had to appoint a presiding officer in his place. In the absence of such measures, meetings of even a majority of municipal council members had no legal standing.

However, Khan faced insuperable obstacles. KL Joshi and Seth turned against him. The other four Hindu members of the municipal council had long been his bitter opponents and he judged that appointing one of them vice chair would have been counterproductive. The press widely publicized the fact that Zafar Khan's two principal lieutenants were both Muslim. Once it attained power in UP, the BJP state government provided institutional support for Hindutva activists. In August 1991, six weeks after coming to office, the state government dismissed Khan from the municipal council and temporarily suspended elections.

The allegation that Khan had appointed Muslims to all the other influential posts on the municipal council proved equally unfounded. Every year the chair appoints council members to serve as subcommittee conveners to oversee construction, lighting, taxation, health and sanitation, and cultural and recreational activities. In his first year as chair, Khan appointed Muslims to five of the ten posts and Hindus to the other five. In his second year as chair, he appointed eleven Hindus and seven Muslims. He made these appointments although he was aware that several of the Hindus he appointed were attempting to undermine him. He provided me an account of his allocation of posts on the municipal council during his first two years as chair (see Table 4.1).

Khan reported that his opponents had brought two no-confidence motions against him by enlisting the support of a majority of the twenty-four municipal council members. Among those who signed the motions was Kanshi Ram, an ex-officio, nonvoting member of the Bijnor municipal council and a voting member of the municipal legislative council. At the council's request, the DM authorized Kanshi Ram to vote at its meetings. As a result, the no-confidence motion would have had the support of thirteen municipal council members. The opposition was therefore confident that the state administration would support its no-confidence motion against Khan.

When Khan learned of the ploy, he provided evidence that Kanshi Ram, as an ex-officio member, did not have voting rights on the municipal council. However, it turned out that even with Kanshi Ram's support, the motion would have been disqualified because his opponents had excluded Khan from

TABLE 4.1. *Bijnor Municipal Council*

Post	1st year	2nd year
OCTROI (a tax on goods for local use)	Nikhil Sharma (Hindu)	Mustafa Aziz (Muslim)
Health and sanitation	LK Chaudhury (Hindu)	Surendra Bishnoy(Hindu)
Convener of music conference	Rakeshwar Pal (Hindu)	Rakeshwar Pal (Hindu)
Kavi sammelan	Ram Gopal (Hindu)	SL Rajagopal (Hindu)
Kavali	Praveen Kashyap (Hindu)	Praveen Kashyap (Hindu)
Wrestling	Avdesh Khannna (Hindu)	Avdesh Khannna (Hindu)
Mushera	Zaidi (Muslim)	Zaidi (Muslim)
Tax	Sharif Ahmad (Muslim)	Raffudin (Muslim)
Lighting	Rais Ahmad (Muslim)	Niaz Ahmad (Muslim)
Construction	Niaz Ahmad (Muslim)	Sharif Ahmad (Muslim)

Source: Compiled by author.

voting. By including Khan and excluding Ram, support for the no-confidence motion fell from thirteen to eleven. To prevent the recurrence of such an incident, Khan informed Chief Minister Mulayam Singh Yadav, who replaced the three nominated members. This incident increased Khan's opponents resentment at Yadav.

In June 1990, Khan's opponents again tried to disqualify him by recruiting the newly nominated members. They succeeded in gaining the support of Chandra Shamber, a *dalit*. However, Khan got the nominated members disqualified by demonstrating that they had missed three consecutive meetings. Once again the chief minister replaced the nominated members and foiled the no-confidence motion. At this stage, because his rivals could not defeat Khan through institutional means, they decided to take to the streets.

The Banning of Ram Devotees

Bijnor became embroiled in the Ayodhya campaign on the heels of the municipal council dispute. The VHP had planned a *Ram jyoti* procession to traverse the state with burning torches that activists had lit in Ayodhya. In anticipation, Chief Minister Mulayam Singh Yadav banned the procession and had the bridge over the Ganges River, which provided the only entry point into town, cordoned off. Hindutva activists and their supporters from Bijnor arrived at the riverbanks on October 4, a day before schedule. What subsequently transpired was recounted by Durga Vahini activist Rani Bansal.

I was stunned when I learned that the *Ram jyotis* were at the barricades and could not enter Bijnor. I dropped everything and ran from one house to the next calling women to join me. Women poured out of their houses with babies in their arms. Some of them had gathered stones, sticks, whatever we could find. I did not even have time to put on my *chappals* (slippers) – I marched twelve kilometers in my bare feet. Along the way we kept calling people out to join us. By the time we reached the bridge there must have been ten thousand of us. We did not need any leaders to tell us what to do. We tore down the barricades and threw them into the river. The police just stood by and watched. No one tried to stop us.[36]

Bansal's romanticized recollection of the event, including her account of police inaction and her inflated estimate of the number of people in attendance, conveys women's excitement in defying state orders. More reliable accounts suggest that 1,200–1,500 people gathered at the bridge. In what became a victory procession, the group marched back to town with the Ram devotees. Ashok Varma reported that DM RS Yadav told him, "There is nothing we can do. There are far too many people here for us to stop them."

Women like Rani Bansal, who had previously been politically inactive, came to see themselves as influential activists. A woman in her mid-forties and mother of two, she presented a portrait of middle-class sobriety. During our interview in her home, she sat in a comfortable chair, two well-groomed Pomeranian dogs by her side, next to a large display case filled with ornaments. She told me that the VHP had created a local chapter of the Durga Vahini because it believed that the nation was in danger and women should rise to its defense. Her activism gave her self-confidence. Bansal commented, "We used to be ignorant and afraid but we have stood up." The incident provided a precedent for Hindu women's subsequent activism in Bijnor.

The Disputed Plot of Land

On August 25, 1990, Khan's opponents, joined by other Hindutva activists, alleged that Khan's anti-Hindu prejudices had surfaced in a dispute over a vacant plot of land in a Hindu neighborhood in the center of town. They intended to replicate the VHP's actions in Ayodhya by building a temple on the site. Tilakwala commented, "We wanted to build a temple on the land just as our leaders did in Ayodhya. We used to think of it as the same struggle and we even described it that way."[37]

Nandaji, an RSS leader, claimed that the land belonged to a Hindu man who was living in Lucknow.[38] When he failed to pay his rent, the municipal council threatened to take it over, whereupon he paid his back rent. However, Nandaji claimed, Khan cancelled the lease anyway and allotted the land to a Muslim.

[36] Interview with Rani Bansal, Bijnor, August 24, 1991.
[37] Interview with Tilakwala, Bijnor, May 3, 1991.
[38] Interview with Nandaji, Bijnor, April 24, 1991.

Singh added a sensational twist to the story: the new Muslim tenant planned to open a butcher shop to sell beef. In the meanwhile, he said, the municipal council had denied Hindus' request to build a *dharamsala* on the land.

Rummaging through municipal council files, Khan pulled out the property registry. On it was a plot plan for the land adjoining a mosque. The records indicated that the municipal council did in fact own this land. It had leased out a small parcel of it to someone from Lucknow but regained possession when the man ceased to pay rent. Khan produced letters from various groups and individuals seeking to rent the land. Overall, Khan had authorized more requests from Hindus than from Muslims. In the case of the disputed land, it had only received one request for rental and that was from a Muslim; as mandated by the council rules, a majority of its members approved his lease. Had the chairman tried to usurp the council's powers by making a unilateral decision, his detractors would certainly have publicized this. Nowhere in the files was there a letter from Hindus requesting authorization to build a *dharamsala* on this land.

Early on the morning of August 25, a small group of Hindus occupied the disputed land and declared their intention of constructing a temple on it. Among them were militant young activists of the Bajrang Dal and Shiv Sena, joined by older RSS and BJP members. Tilakwala provided a vivid account of the events. His excitement was palpable:

We got up early in the morning and went to the land carrying statues of Vishnu and Lakshmi. When we arrived there we installed our idols, lit incense, and began reciting the Ramayana. Later in the day we began constructing the temple wall.

Muslims came to the mosque for prayers. Some of my friends were afraid of a fight and left but most of us stayed on. In fact we began to read the Ramayana even louder. By 8 P.M. the crowd had grown. Many important Hindus of the town joined us. All the time we heard rumors that Muslims were gathering arms and planning to attack us. We had come heavily armed ourselves. I heard the Muslims shouting threatening slogans.

A little while later, Muslims began throwing stones at us. At midnight the SDM, ADM, and the police arrived at the spot. Muslims began stoning them and hit a policeman; the police were enraged and opened fire. They killed two Muslims. Then the police took our statues and destroyed the wall we had been building.

The next day the police took us to the office to bring charges against us but Hindu lawyers went on strike to protest our arrests. Hindu shopkeepers supported the protest by closing down their shops for two days. Outside the police office Hindus organized people to court arrest: first women and children, then men. The women told the officers: "If you won't allow us to have our temple, we will read the Ramayana here," and they performed prayers right outside the police office. Kalyan Singh came from Lucknow to encourage us.

At 2.30 P.M. I ran home and told my mother, "The tension is building *ama* [mother]. We cannot contain it." She gave me her blessings and told me to be careful.[39]

---

[39] Interview with Tilakwala, Bijnor, May 3, 1991.

Tilakwala spoke of the bravery of women who continued to recite prayers after the police arrived. He claimed that the police had engaged in brutality against the devotees and commented, "I did not stand for this. After all I too have drunk my mother's milk," a reference to his masculinity. He commented, "Even our *sants* [religious leaders] tell our women, 'Don't just sit there praying to Ram, get up and fight.' We tell even our girls to keep weapons, not just for show but to use." When the police arrived, he said, he and his friends found shelter in the home of a Hindu woman.

Nandaji provided additional details:

Muslims were angry when they heard rumors that Hindus had captured their *dhancha* [a reference to the *babri masjid* in Ayodhya]. That was why they collected stones and armed themselves. But we felt secure because we were in a Hindu locality and we knew that our community would support us. In the morning we must have been twenty-five people, but by evening there were hundreds there with us. Even the policemen who had arrested ten Shiv Sena activists secretly told us that they were on our side and we believed them.

Khan reported that he wanted to avoid confrontation at all costs. He refused to accompany a group of Muslims to the disputed land on the afternoon of the 25th. The group then invited Niaz Zaidi, a more radical Muslim leader, who consented. Concerned that relations between the two communities would further deteriorate, Khan agreed with the administration that the Hindu activists held in custody should be released. The administration did so and took temporary control of the disputed land. To many Hindus this in itself constituted a victory, for their actions had prevented a Muslim who had been allotted the land from acquiring it.

What lessons can be derived from examining the series of disputes involving challenges to Khan's leadership? First, they demonstrate the close relationship between the struggle over economic resources and political power. In seeking to build a temple on municipal council land, Hindus were not only seeking control over a piece of property but also political control. Second, Hindu activists in Bijnor conflated the municipal government with the state government headed by Mulayam Singh Yadav. They projected their hatred of Yadav onto Zafar Khan.

Mulayam Singh Yadav's "Communal Harmony Rally"

Mulayam Singh Yadav convened "communal harmony" rallies on October 9 in many parts of UP, including Bijnor. The purpose, he stated in an interview, was to assure Muslims that he would prevent Advani's *rath yatra* from entering the state and would do everything to ensure Muslims' safety.[40] However, the rally in Bijnor resulted in three deaths – two Hindus and one

Muslim – thirty looted shops, and ninety-five arrests.[41] Everyone I interviewed agreed that the rally had inflamed Hindu-Muslim relations, but for
different reasons.

Mulayam Singh Yadav's sharpest critics, all upper-caste Hindus, contended
that he had so fired Muslims' passions and fears that those attending the rally
filled their trucks with stones as they left the rally. A few miles outside Bijnor,
Muslims attacked the car of Janardhan Agarwal, the VHP district president.
Agarwal described the incident as follows:

> I was on my way to Kiratpur with my family when I saw a mob heading towards Bijnor.
> They surrounded my car. They threw stones at the car and damaged it. They would
> have killed me if Hindus had not come to my rescue. Meanwhile, rumors circulated that
> I had been killed. Naturally there was some reaction.[42]

The *Bijnor Times* provided flagrantly biased accounts of Mulayam Singh
Yadav's rally on October 11, 1990. It reported that the police had killed and
injured 100 people, thereby inflating the number of the casualties and conflat-
ing injuries and deaths. A more reliable account by another newspaper, *Dainik
Jagran*, reported that three people had been killed that day.

Many Muslims and Hindus denied that Mulayam Singh Yadav's speech had
been inflammatory. They claimed, as did a report in the *Pioneer* newspaper,
that he had urged Muslims to remain peaceful.[43] However, they acknowledged
that in the climate of fear that Hindu nationalists had created, many Hindus
felt threatened by the sheer presence of thousands of Muslims from outside the
district. Anticipating this, Ashok Varma recalled, he had opposed the rally in
his editorials and predicted that it would foment violence.[44]

Interestingly, Sandip Lal, a supporter of Mulayam Singh Yadav and opponent of Khan, was the principal local organizer of the event. He denied that
Yadav's speech had been inflammatory. What was provocative, he asked,
about Yadav stating that he would protect the mosque in Ayodhya? What was
provocative about stating that he would abide by a court verdict on the status of the mosque? What was provocative about ensuring Muslims' safety?
Lal held Hindu nationalists responsible for the violence. After calling for a
boycott of the rally, they arranged for ten truckloads of Hindus to come to
Bijnor from surrounding towns on October 9. These people fanned out to all
the major access points to prevent Yadav supporters from entering the town.
Once Mulayam Singh Yadav began speaking, they set fire to his effigies. When
the rally was over, they lined the main roads and attacked Muslims as they
returned home.

[41] In a grossly exaggerated estimate, the *Bijnor Times* reported that 200 people had been killed as
a result of the rally. *Bijnor Times*, October 11, 1990.
[42] Interview with Janardhan Agarwal, Bijnor, May 11, 1991.
[43] *Pioneer*, October 13, 1990.
[44] Interview with Ashok Varma, Bijnor, April 24, 1991.

Several respondents confirmed Lal's tale of Hindu nationalists' complicity. Among the most revealing was Tilakwala, who boasted of the bonfires that the Bajrang Dal and Shiv Sena had lit to burn the chief minister's effigy. "We shouted slogans calling Mulayam Singh a donkey," he laughed, "and we carved his name on a donkey's back!" According to local intelligence sources, Hindu nationalists had been planning for weeks to obstruct Mulayam Singh Yadav's rally. They also feigned an attack on Agarwal and then circulated rumors that he had been kidnapped and killed.

The October 9 rally intensified Hindu-Muslim animosities. Shopkeepers, a key BJP constituency, closed their shops for four days to protest the rally. When the police arrested Hindus, the Shiv Sena and its affiliates organized demonstrations outside the administrative headquarters in Bijnor to protest the allegedly anti-Hindu character of the government. Support for Hindu organizations grew when the administration dropped all charges against those who had been arrested for vandalism, looting, and violence.

The "Riot"

Hindu nationalists arranged for thousands of activists to converge in Ayodhya on October 30. Following Mulayam Singh Yadav's orders, the police arrested 637 activists throughout the state. Because the local jail could not accommodate all those who were arrested, the police held them in a girls' intermediate college.[45] The next day the detained activists launched a protest against conditions in the college and demanded better food, sanitation, and amenities. Ashok Varma reported that he had inspected the college and considered these activists better housed, fed, and clothed than the large majority of prisoners. Furthermore, the term imprisonment was highly misleading, for security at the girls' college was minimal.[46]

That evening activists tried to escape from the college. The police opened fire and rumors spread that they were gunning down Hindu activists by the dozen. The *Bijnor Times* reported that the police had injured 100 detainees and had refused to bandage their wounds. Not even the British, it editorialized, had employed such brutality against prisoners. A reporter found that the police had killed one person and injured three others.[47] On October 27 and 28, many shopkeepers closed their stores to protest the ill treatment of Hindu activists. Some of them removed their wares in anticipation of violence.[48] The following day several hundred people marched from the Arya Samaj temple to the DM's office, where they engaged in a "jail *bharao*

[45] *The Bijnor* Times, October 21, 1990.
[46] Interview with Ashok Varma, Bijnor, April 24, 1991.
[47] Interview with Kishori Lal, Bijnor, April 24, 1991.
[48] Interview with intelligence officer, Bijnor, May 3, 1991.

andolan." Women were at the forefront of this protest and the one that followed.

Tensions ran high in Bijnor on October 30, the day Hindu activists reached Ayodhya. The VHP had organized a large group of women to assemble outside the Arya Samaj temple for morning prayers. Hundreds of Hindu activists who had been detained en route to Ayodhya attended. Around 11 A.M., a police officer rushed to the temple with news he had heard over the BBC: Hindu activists had reached Ayodhya, placed their flag on the mosque, and started to demolish it. Within an hour, several hundred people marched through Bijnor in a victory procession, shouting slogans about their determination to build a temple in Ayodhya. From 200 to 250 women were among them, according to Bansal. The procession headed toward *ghanta ghar*, a clock tower in the center of town where the road forked, dividing Muslim and Hindu quarters. The group disagreed over which way to proceed. The more militant members prevailed and the procession marched through the Muslim quarters.

Muslim families congregated on their rooftops and watched the procession with horror. The Hindu demonstrators shouted ugly, provocative slogans, including: "Musalmaan keh doh istaan, Pakistan aur kabristan" ("The two places for Muslims are Pakistan and the graveyard"); "Tel lugake Dabar ka, masjid girao Babar kah" ("By applying Dabar [a brand name] oil eradicate Babar's mosque"); and "Hindu bachche Ram ka, Musalman haram kah" ("Hindus are the children of God; Muslims are bastards"). At some point along the way, Muslims began to pelt stones at the people in the procession who responded in kind.

The *Bijnor Times* held Muslims responsible for violence. It reported that Muslims had hurled stones from their rooftops at a peaceful Hindu procession, forcing Hindus to respond in kind. The report stated: "It has become clear that today's rioting was pre-planned. Until the 30th morning the fight was between the government and majority community; no one thought that the minority community would get involved." To remove any ambiguity from this account, an article on November 1 entitled "Riots Pre-Planned" stated that the "riot" could not have been spontaneous for it would have been illogical for people to attack a peaceful procession. It noted that the first shop to be burned down belonged to a Hindu and that the violence emanated from the Muslim quarter. The *Bijnor Times* echoed the views of Hindutva activists, who were its major informants. LP Jain and Raghuvir Singh claimed that Muslims planned the violence by gathering stones on their rooftops to attack the procession. They neglected to mention the coarse threats from Hindutva activists.

When Fazlul Hyder, a Muslim doctor, saw that Hindu women at the forefront of the procession on October 30 were caught in the crossfire, he provided them shelter in his clinic. The account that follows was provided by Habib Ansari, a Muslim veterinarian.

Hyder was the most humane and secular minded person. He kept his clinic open that day because he felt that people should resist attempts to divide the two communities. That was also why he took those women into his clinic. But a rumor spread that Hyder had abducted Hindu women; some angry Hindu men broke into the clinic and murdered him.

When Muslims carried Hyder's body back to *mohalla* Charshiri where he had lived, people went out of their minds with grief and rage. A group of Muslims marched to Bartwan [a neighboring Hindu locality] and attacked the Hindus there. Once the violence started, some other Muslims joined in because they wanted to settle scores with a Hindu from Bartwan who had been having a love affair with a Muslim woman. Several hours later the Muslims had killed twelve people in Bartwan.[49]

Significantly, Muslim violence in Bartwan was directed at the Jogi OBC community. Upper-caste Hindus later plied the victims with relief. Hindu nationalist violence against Muslims in Bijnor, as in other parts of the country, was designed to gain lower-caste support.

Some of the most extreme violence occurred in the predominantly Muslim B42 Charshiri. I asked Abdul Shamim, who lived along the route of the procession, to describe the violence that he had witnessed. He recounted:

The PAC arrived here on October 31st around 2:30 P.M. Some boys from the Bajrang Dal and Shiv Sena were identifying our houses. One of the PAC members was holding a gator [an instrument used to spray pesticides in the fields] which was filled with petrol. They systematically went from one house to the next, spraying houses with petrol and setting them on fire.

There is a *masjid* across the street where about nine Muslims had taken shelter. I saw the PAC march in, drag people onto the streets, and beat them badly. None of these people tried to escape. Two men whom they had beaten severely just lay there. But the SDM ordered the PAC to open fire. The PAC did not want to shoot them because their bodies were covered with bruises so instead they poured kerosene on seven men and set them on fire.[50]

Shamim took me to Abdul Chowduli, who lived a few houses away. We found the old man sitting in bed, which I was told he rarely left. Tears streamed down his face as he spoke:

They killed both of my sons, my only two sons. I am a widower and now I have no one in this world ... they killed both of my sons ... The SDM and sub-inspector of police came to my house and searched for arms. We have no arms but I had collected 40,000 rupees ($1,600 at the time) for my older boy's wedding; he was to be married on June 5th. That was all the money I had. They took the money, hauled my sons out of the house and shot them.

When the sub-inspector who had been searching my house leaned over, his identification card fell out of his pocket. I kept it and made copies of it. Then I wrote to the prime

[49] Interview with Habib Ansari, Bijnor, April 25, 1991.
[50] Interview with Abdul Shamim, Bijnor, April 25, 1991.

minister and enclosed a photocopy of the ID card. I said, "This officer has killed my son. I saw him shoot my son with my own eyes. What sort of a government do you run?" The government gave me 100,000 rupees ($4,000) compensation.[51]

Chowduli gave me a copy of the ID card bearing a picture of a clean-cut young man who must have been his son's age. For several weeks I carried it around with me and often stared at the photograph, searching for an explanation for these murders. After I imagined that I had surely heard the worst and could not bear to hear more, other people told similar stories. Within the same *mohalla* lived a widower named Habib Afshar.

When we heard that the PAC was invading Muslim homes and killing innocent people, we wanted to run away. But where could we go? A curfew was in force and the police had been given shoot on sight orders – which meant that any Muslim roaming the streets would be at great risk. So we could not run away. We were trapped in our houses like prisoners.

On the 31st afternoon, PAC officers and Rampal and Jaspal [two local Hindu men] broke into my house. They looted my house and took all my savings. Then they dragged my son out of the house, tied his feet to a *bhel gari* [ox-drawn cart] and took off. Once we could leave the house safely, we searched the stinking, decaying corpses for my son. I could not give up hope until I found his body near the railway crossing. He was my only son. He lived with me. He supported me. He was my reason to live.[52]

I visited a small, isolated, and extremely poor Muslim *mohalla*. I wound my way through a long, dirty, narrow cobblestone path lined on both sides by high walls and entered a small house where I met a woman and her five-year-old daughter. The child sitting by her mother's side looked haunted and terrified. Her mother spoke:

It happened on the 31st afternoon. Four PAC men entered my house and said they had learned we were storing arms so they had come to search my house. Then they made all of us leave the house except for my fourteen year old girl. They spent the whole night in the house violating my daughter. [She breaks into uncontrollable sobs.] I was outside, banging on the door, throwing my whole body against the door, trying to get in. The next day they brought her out to the courtyard and locked me inside. They doused her with kerosene and burned her to hide all proof of rape and murder.

My home has become like a prison now. I wanted to run away but I had no place to go and for days I lay awake all night afraid that they would come back and attack us.

I spoke with the *imam* of Norrani mosque near B24 *mohalla* Charsiri, a frail and saintly man. His mosque was one of four that were destroyed during the violence. He reported:

On the 31st afternoon the PAC barged into my house. My daughters Tasleen and Nusrat were with me. They stripped Nusrat and took her to the other room. Then the

[51] Interview with Abdul Chowduli, Bijnor, April 25, 1991.
[52] Interview with Habib Afshar, Bijnor, April 26, 1991.

SDM entered the house. I thought that he would stop the PAC but instead the SDM was shouting orders: "Shoot, shoot, shoot!!" They seemed to have lost their senses. The SDM shouted at us, "We have destroyed your chairman Zafar Khan and now we will destroy all your *imams!*" After they left my house I watched them from my courtyard. Twenty-one Muslims were killed in this *mohalla* and five are missing; I saw the PAC kill three of them with my own eyes. And I saw that the SDM was goading them on.

Although most of the violence was confined to urban Bijnor, some occurred in the surrounding villages, above all in Rampur Bakli, about a mile east of Bijnor. Because of its large number of permanent homes, Bakli bore greater resemblance to a town than a village; however, most of its residents derived their livelihoods from agriculture. Bakli contained 256 houses, 106 Muslim and 150 Hindu. According to Sharma from the *Dainik Jagran*, 17 people were killed, 15 were missing, and 620 were injured; 21 houses were burned and 66 looted; 223 people were arrested. Sharma reported that, although he did not have precise figures concerning each community's losses, Muslims suffered far more than Hindus.

I interviewed a Muslim family who owned about six acres of land and a spacious house surrounded by a large courtyard. A woman from this family said:

There is no history of communal violence here – not at all. When we heard news of the tensions in Bijnor we wanted to leave but our Hindu neighbors persuaded us to stay on. They said, "Whatever happens in Bijnor, you know you are safe here." At the time we believed them but now we feel that they deceived us.

On the first night hordes of people descended on the village. Most of them had come from the town. With them were some PAC members. They went to the Hindu homes and asked for help. Our neighbor Rakesh was helping them.

When the Muslims saw this, most of them ran away. Some went to Bakshwala [a neighboring village]; some hid in the fields. We left at that time too. Those who remained here were killed. After about four days, the police found us and escorted us back to our houses. What a sight we found when we returned.[53]

The woman walked me through her compound. The granary had been set on fire and all the grain had been destroyed. She then took me to the field where the tube well had been damaged and the plough dismantled, making it impossible to cultivate the land. Inside her house, a storeroom had been ransacked and money and jewelry stolen. The agricultural equipment had been damaged and because the family could not afford to repair it, cultivation had virtually come to a standstill. The theft of their savings meant having to postpone their son's marriage. I asked this woman to describe what happened:

It all began with Mulayam Singh's rally on October 9th. We did not attend; in fact we were opposed to it but it made people very angry. Then there has been this whole temple/mosque issue. Frankly we don't care whether a mosque or a temple stood there.

[53] Interview with Ghazala, Bijnor, May 3, 1991.

What does it matter to us? And it didn't matter much to our neighbors either until recently. But now they have changed. Now we no longer trust them and we can never trust them again. Because when the mobs came here, hindus became Hindus.

The killings were not random: the major targets were young men, many of whom were soon to be married. Families reported the loss of money, jewels, and clothing they had been accumulating for their sons' marriages. In losing their sons, parents were deprived of the principal income earners in the family and of the possibility of grandchildren. The perpetrators of violence deliberately targeted Muslim men across the class spectrum. They burned their rickshaws (bicycle-drawn taxis), looted their shops, and smashed their agricultural equipment.

This does not mean that there was complete polarization between the two communities. I heard stories of Muslims taking in Hindu children who were playing on the streets when the violence broke out and stories of Hindu families hiding their Muslim neighbors. Once the violence was over, some Hindus felt responsible and guilty. Ashok Varma said, "When the curfew was lifted and we faced each other we were ashamed. We could not keep blaming other people for what we had done."[54]

The local administration's responsibility for the violence changed from passivity when it first began, to aggression, when it was underway. From August 25 to October 30, the state was indecisive, unprepared, and relatively inactive in face of provocation by Hindu organizations. For example, although Khan notified the police at 10:30 A.M. on August 25 that Hindu militants had occupied municipal council land early that morning, they did not arrive for eleven hours. By this time, the gathering had become larger, more vociferous, and harder to disperse. As if to compensate for their earlier inaction, police opened fire, killing two Muslims who had been entirely peaceful. Similarly, when crowds rushed to the Ganges River to bring back the *Ram jyotis*, the police and government officials did not even attempt to stop them. Rani Bansal reported that several police watched impassively as the crowds dismantled the barricades. The combination of Mulayam Singh Yadav's bravado, when he claimed that not even a bird would enter the state, and his inability to control the local police, encouraged Hindutva activism.

Given the backdrop of August 25 and October 4, the administration was surprisingly unprepared for the October 9 rally. According to several informants, fights broke out because the administration had not made adequate security arrangements along the major roads leading to Bijnor. During the several hours that the rally lasted, the administration could have deployed more forces. After the rally, although about twenty-five Muslim shops and eight Hindu shops had been looted and destroyed, the police made few arrests.

[54] Interview with Ashok Varma, Bijnor, November 15, 2008.

Some people argued that the administration was unprepared because Bijnor had no history of Hindu-Muslim violence. However, this ignores the violent incidents that had occurred on August 25, October 4, and October 9. There was also other evidence that violence was likely. Fearing violence, schools and colleges that had closed on August 25 had not reopened. On October 27, Hindutva activists held a huge meeting in front of an Arya Samaj temple to plan a procession three days later. According to one official, Shiv Shankar, the ADM was present but made no attempt to disband the meeting, despite the ban on public assemblies.

Government inaction from October 30 to November 3 had particularly damaging consequences. Four sources reported that leading administrators failed to respond to requests to stop the procession. Ashok Varma saw the procession assembling outside the temple on October 30 and asked DM RS Yadav to disperse it.[55] An intelligence officer reported that when he realized that the procession could no longer be halted, he asked Yadav to prevent it from passing through the Muslim quarters.[56] Yadav responded that he could not do so because women and children headed the procession. Zafar Khan asked a senior police officer the morning before the procession to place Bijnor under curfew. "The SP [Superintendent of Police] was evasive," Khan reported. "He said he would discuss it with the DM." But the DM was nowhere to be found as tensions mounted and he did not impose a curfew until 1:30 A.M. on October 31, about fourteen hours after he was asked to do so.

MN Kapur, one of the few officers who remained posted in Bijnor after the October violence, provided an eyewitness account of what transpired. Kapur reported that he had accompanied the Deputy Superintendent of Police (DSP) to the temple where crowds had gathered on the 30th morning.

When I saw the huge mob assembled there I pleaded with the ADM and the DSP. "Call off the procession or there will be trouble." The DSP replied, "We have discussed matters with the Hindu leaders and they have assured us that nothing will go wrong." I said, "Even if the leaders are responsible, they cannot say what others will do." But no one would listen to me.[57]

Shortly after the procession began, officials witnessed Muslim violence against Hindus. According to Ashok Varma, when the police saw this, they sought revenge. "At that stage," Varma said, "Hindu organizations were no longer necessary."[58]

[55] Interview with Ashok Varma, Bijnor, April 25, 1991.
[56] Interview with intelligence officer, Bijnor, May 3, 1991.
[57] Interview with MN Kapur, Bijnor, June 6, 1991.
[58] Interview with Ashok Varma, Bijnor, April 25, 1991.

From October 31 to November 3, violence took on a wholly different character. It was no longer perpetrated by one community against the other but rather by the state against Muslims. During this phase, district administrators, the police, and above all the PAC, which had arrived from its headquarters in Moradabad, targeted, looted, and destroyed Muslim shops. They searched out Muslim men and women and tortured and shot them. The most serious violence took place after the administration declared a curfew following Muslims' attacks on Hindus, when PAC and government officials forced their way into Muslim homes. Sharma reported that whereas Muslims observed the curfew out of fear, Hindus roamed through the town, looting Muslim shops. The state was complicit by redefining public spaces as Hindu. During the curfew, it distributed passes to Hindus so that they could move about freely whereas Muslims were trapped inside their homes. Ironically, the Hindu activists who were detained at the girls' intermediary college were freer than Muslims to wander through the streets at night.

As Hindu activists marched through the heart of Bijnor, they drove Muslims off the streets and onto the rooftops or into their houses. The activists did not simply seek to confine Muslims to ever smaller spaces: they demonstrated that there were no safe spaces for Muslims and certainly none that they could share with Hindus. The alternatives for Muslims were death or departure. The strategy apparently bore fruit: six months after the violence, many Muslim homes remained boarded up. Friends and neighbors reported that former residents had either relocated to other parts of town or left permanently. Hindus' appropriation of what had traditionally been a shared public space found its corollary in their attempt to establish political dominance.

The violence in Bijnor ended when the state government intervened. Chief Minister Mulayam Singh Yadav transferred three administrative officers who had participated in the violence and replaced them with administrators who were considered extremely secular; the new DM Ram Kumar, was a *dalit* and the ADM and SDM were Muslims. Kumar reported that whereas the previous administration had distributed only 35 percent of the compensation that the central government had authorized for victims, his administration distributed the remainder.[59] Similarly, the previous administration downplayed the casualties and made only seventy-five arrests, although many more people were implicated in the violence. The *Bijnor Times* and local radio station reported that on November 1, the inspector general of police announced that 1,000 people had been arrested in connection with the violence. Four days later the SSP issued a correction and announced that 326 people had been arrested.

There were no reports of Hindu-Muslim tensions in Bijnor under the new administration. Kumar described the precautionary measures he had taken,

---

[59] Interview with Ram Kumar, Bijnor, June 7, 1991.

such as relying heavily on peace committees composed of local residents and intelligence officers.

During *asthi kalash*, VHP workers toured the state, carrying urns containing ashes of the *kar sevaks* who had been killed in Ayodhya. In other parts of the state this provoked riots so we maintained very tight security to make sure that they could not enter our town. We faced an even more dangerous situation on April 16th when Muslims observe *Eid* [one of the major Muslim festivals]. The BJP had planned a rally that day. We put our forces on alert. We created thirteen police assistance centers in the town and encouraged people to report to them if there was any trouble. We did not allow the BJP to pass through Muslim localities and we banned loudspeakers and provocative slogans. The pillar of a mosque was damaged in Nagina. At night we posted officers to guard the spot and quietly repaired it. By the morning Muslims went to Nagina for prayers and did not even notice the damage.

In July 1992, Parameswaran Iyer, a South Indian, was posted to Bijnor as DM; the ADM was a Muslim. The two officers acted preemptively to defuse tensions. Upon learning of the destruction of the mosque in Ayodhya in December 1992, Iyer immediately called in the national army. He declared a curfew in sensitive neighborhoods, made several preventive arrests, and demanded that all arms be deposited in his office. Small factories in the villages bordering Bijnor and Moradabad had made a lucrative business of producing low-cost petrol bombs and other explosives. The previous administration had freely issued licenses to arms dealers. Iyer brought 125 cases against illegal arms manufacturers.[60]

The fact that simple measures were so effective in 1993 tragically suggests that the losses two years earlier might have been averted. Iyer involved both Hindus and Muslims in peacekeeping efforts by organizing meetings in various localities, posting Hindus and Muslims alongside the armed forces on picket lines, and meeting with Muslims to reassure them they could trust the administration. Certain symbolic measures were highly effective. For example, when Hindu groups damaged a mosque in Bijnor, the administration made them pay for repairs and announced that a builder would be available at all times to repair other mosques or temples that were damaged. Officials roamed the towns in cars with loudspeakers to demonstrate that they were closely monitoring the situation.

Parties, Movements, and States in Khurja and Bijnor

Party and social movement organizations, with state support, bear major responsibility for the violence in Bijnor and Khurja. Explaining the violence requires understanding the roles of the BJP, VHP and its affiliates, and the local administration.

---

[60] Interview with Parameswaran Iyer, Bijnor, January 1, 1993.

The violence in both towns reflected Hindu activists' ability to mobilize resentment toward state institutions and give voice to popular expectations and demands of the state. It also reflected class tensions between certain groups of *dalits* and better-off Muslims, whom Hindu nationalists framed as "communal." One of the BJP's major targets was the 20–21 percent of *dalits* in both towns. Achieving their support required remarkable involvement of civil society groups in redefining the identities of both Hindus and Muslims.

Parties

The BJP sought to change the arithmetic of electoral politics to its advantage and to prevent the further growth of the SP and the BSP. An OBC himself, Mulayam Singh Yadav was a strong supporter of the government's decision to implement the Mandal Commission recommendations, which supported reserved seats in government, educational institutions, and employment for OBCs. Upper-caste youth had organized violent protests against reservations for OBCs in both Khurja and Bijnor. Having lost the support of the Yadav community to Mulayam Singh Yadav, the BJP sought the support of Jats, a prosperous agricultural community that was not entitled to government-mandated quotas. According to Nandaji, enlisting Jats in the Ayodhya campaign was a way to secure their electoral support.

In the past we have never had much following among the Jats in western UP, though the Jats participated in a few *shakhas* here and there. Most Jats supported Chowdhury Charan Singh and voted only for Jats. But we started working among Jats during the *Ram Janmabhoomi* struggle. We told them, "Hinduism is bigger than Jatism" and they followed us. But once we had Jat support, we began to lose the *harijans* [*dalits*].[61]

Most *dalits* worked for Jat farmers as agricultural laborers, for long hours at low wages. They distrusted any party that the Jats supported. The BSP's attempt to forge an alliance between *dalits* and Muslims against the upper castes posed a serious threat to the BJP. *Dalit* support was especially important to the BJP in Khurja where a Legislative Assembly seat was reserved for Scheduled Castes.

"One could say that both Mayawati and BSP were born in Bijnor," commented OP Gupta, former principal of the Vardhaman PG College in Bijnor.[62] Mayawati launched her political career when she was twenty-seven by contesting the 1985 parliamentary elections from Bijnor. Although she came in third, she received a considerable 65,000 votes. Newspapers described Mayawati's distinctive and appealing campaign style as she bicycled through the town, stopping along the way and talking to ordinary people over endless cups of

[61] Interview with Nandaji, Bijnor, September 21, 1991.
[62] "Bijnor Remembers a Young Mayawati," *Hindustan Times*, April 15, 2007. Accessed June 30, 2014. http://www.hindustantimes.com/india-news/bijnor-remembers-a-young-mayawati /article1-216077.aspx.

tea. The BSP won eleven out of eighteen seats in municipal council elections in 1988. Recognizing that it needed greater Muslim support, it nominated several Muslim candidates to contest the 1989 Legislative Assembly election. Three of them won. The BSP attacked the BJP for its upper-caste character and for generating conflict through its Ayodhya campaign. The BSP polled 9.9 percent and the BJP 7.6 percent of the vote. Despite a Janata Dal wave, Mayawati defeated a seasoned rival, the BJP candidate Mangal Ram Premi, and was elected MP from Bijnor.

In many ways Mayawati's appeals inverted those of the BJP. She too polarized communities in order to achieve electoral advantage but her major rivals were upper-caste Hindus. I attended a rally where Mayawati railed against the BJP.[63] "If the BJP comes to power," she cried out, "we will be cleaning the sewers again! [a reference to the demeaning labor that certain *dalits* perform] But it can't come to power. There are too few of them and too many of us." She concluded, "Musalman-Harijan bhai-bhai, yeh Hindu yuhan kaseh eye eh?" ("Muslims and Harijans are brothers, how do Hindus fit in here?") Mayawati's rhetorical style resembled that of Hindutva activist Sadhvi Rithambara, in that it was impassioned, exclusionary, and often vulgar. Like Rithambara, Mayawati, as a *dalit* woman from a poor background, seemingly represented the subaltern. Hindutva activists in Bijnor and Khurja saw both Yadav and Mayawati as powerful and dangerous. They depicted Yadav as brash, condescending, and opportunistic and Mayawati as shrill, uncouth, and irrational. Rani Bansal described Mayawati as a woman of "bad character" in contrast to women of "good character" who were part of the Sangh Parivar. Attacks on the personal character of Mayawati and Yadav were designed to generate hostility toward them and make them seem life-sized and vulnerable.

The BJP swept the polls in the 1991 elections. Its candidate in Bijnor, Mangal Ram Premi, won with 247, 465 votes (47.2%). All seven BJP candidates from Bijnor won the Legislative Assembly elections; the BJP won 53 percent of the popular vote while opposition parties shared the remainder. In a few constituencies, the BJP gained the support of OBCs who had been excluded from the Mandal recommendations. The Chandpur constituency, for example, which had traditionally supported Ajit Singh, elected a BJP candidate by a wide margin. In Khurja, in the aftermath of the violence, a BJP candidate, Harpal Singh, won successive Legislative Assembly elections in 1993 and 1996.

The BJP's success partly lay in its ability to refashion *dalit* identities. It captured *dalit* support by exacerbating class tensions between *dalits* and Muslims in several towns that had experienced violence in the early 1990s. One of these was the industrial town of Ghaziabad, twelve miles from Delhi. On January 26, 1990, violence there claimed fifteen lives, twelve Muslims and three Hindus. The PAC killed two Muslims and *dalits* killed the others. Tensions between

---

[63] The rally took place in Bijnor on June 7, 1991.

Muslims and Balmikis in Ghaziabad were long-standing. The two communities lived in close proximity to one another and had clashed several times in the past, most significantly over control of Kela Bhatta, an area sandwiched between them. Land values were high in Ghaziabad because of its close proximity to Delhi and there was what one informant described as a big land mafia in town. The *Dinam Times*, a Hindi newspaper, provided the following account of relations between the two communities in Ghaziabad.

The Balmikis are poor and have no latrines in their homes. They say that their women are sometimes harassed by Muslims when they go out early in the morning and late at night. But Muslims say that the Balmikis allow their pigs to roam the streets and go into their homes and mosques. There was a scuffle last year for this reason.

A clash between Balmiki and Muslim boys marked the start of the violence. It escalated a few hours later when the BJP and its affiliates organized Balmikis to attack Muslims. Because relations between the two communities had always been fraught, it appeared to be spontaneous, thereby masking the BJP's role.

In Khurja, whereas Chamars were committed to the BSP, the Balmikis represented an important potential vote bank for the BJP. By heightening class tensions between Balmiki workers and their Muslim supporters, the BJP was able to gain significant Balmiki support.

The BJP pursued various strategies to gain *dalit* support in Bijnor. It fostered tensions between *dalit* and Muslim municipal council members and favored *dalits* in allocating municipal council land. It also sought, unsuccessfully, to enlist *dalits* in the Ayodhya campaign. Pralad Balmiki from Raiteen *mohalla* asked why his community should help construct a temple from which they would be excluded. The BJP's most successful strategy was to heighten class tensions between Balmikis in Raiteen *mohalla* and Muslims in Charshiri *mohalla*.[64] Mohan Kumar said that Muslims expected Balmikis to say *salaam* when they went past the mosque and to turn down their music when Muslims were doing *namaz* (prayers). The Balmikis were angry that Muslims built a slaughterhouse near their *basti* (slum). He appreciated the BJP's recognition of their grievances. Balmikis' antipathy to Muslims deepened after October 30, when Muslims from the neighboring *basti* set their homes on fire. As Hindutva activists plied them with propaganda and relief, *dalits* came to see Muslims in a new light – not just as local adversaries but as a national threat.

Hindutva activists were especially threatened by Hindu and Muslim leaders who transcended their prescribed identities and acquired cross-caste and community support. Both Mayawati and Mulayam Singh Yadav demonstrated the compatibility of lower-caste and Muslim interests. In Khurja, Sarwar Hussain represented a threat because both Muslims and Hindus had elected him to a party that represented OBCs and Muslims. Fazlul Hyder, the Muslim doctor whom Hindutva activists murdered, refused to be intimidated

64 Interview with Pralad Balmiki, Bijnor, June 7, 1991

by Hindu nationalists and attended his clinic on October 30. In a further act of transgression, he offered protection to several Hindu women.

Far from being a leader of Muslims, Zafar Khan was elected to the municipal council in Bijnor as a result of extensive *dalit* support. He was also one of the BSP's most prominent leaders in Bijnor and, as he acknowledged, he paid for it.

What were the real sources of Hindu resentment against me? I helped the BSP forge a powerful *dalit*-Muslim combination in this area. When Mayawati first won the elections in 1985, she did not have Muslim backing. But by 1989 she won because of it. This was what Hindus resented most. During the riot, in many areas *dalits* provided protection to Muslims. This has been one of the BSP's major achievements.

In Bijnor in 1991, while Hindus voted overwhelmingly for the BJP, the Muslim vote was divided, in part because Zafar Khan and his Muslim supporters temporarily left the BSP. Khan alleged that the BSP had not provided much assistance to Muslims after the violence and failed to promote local leaders. Moreover, several observers noted that while the violence promoted a large Hindu turnout, Muslims stayed away from the polls out of fear.

Social Movements and Civil Society
A large network of Hindu nationalist organizations contributed to the buildup of tensions and subsequent violence. In Khurja, they not only included well-known RSS affiliates but also relatively unknown organizations. In Bijnor, the Arya Samaj and Shiv Sena joined forces with Sangh Parivar-affiliated groups. The membership of some of these organizations overlapped. For example, Tilakwala was both district president of the Bajrang Dal and president of the ABVP.

Hindu nationalist organizations developed broad civil society networks as their members drew family and friends into their social and political activities. These organizations included professors, lawyers, shopkeepers, and other groups that had "respectable" occupations. Many individuals in these organizations had ties to powerful local institutions, including colleges, municipal councils, industrial boards, and the bureaucracy. The vernacular press highlighted and exaggerated the strength of Hindu nationalist groups. It covered every event in the Ayodhya campaign and often glorified Hindutva activists. Hindu nationalists cultivated a rapport with newspaper reporters, many of whom were already sympathetic to their goals.

The growth of towns like Bijnor and Khurja in western UP created a large market for newspapers, especially among the predominantly Hindu middle and lower middle classes. One Urdu newspaper and five Hindi papers, the *Amar Ujala, Bijnor Times, Dainik Jagran, Chingari,* and *Nav Bharat Times,* had a combined circulation of several hundred thousand in the town of Bijnor alone. While a few journalists in both towns provided balanced reports on Hindu-Muslim relations, most were highly partisan toward Hindu nationalists.

Nor was their intervention exclusively editorial. Several newspaper proprietors became candidates for positions on the municipal council.

The violence in Khurja and Bijnor originated in small local disputes that came to acquire – or, rather, were made to acquire – a wholly different meaning and significance. In Khurja, the first incident of violence in December 1990 laid the groundwork for the next in January–February 1991. Tensions around the actions of one woman ignited class conflicts among Muslims and Hindus and power rivalries among leaders of the pottery association. Hindu nationalists provided discourses for interpreting local conflicts as part of broader causes and outcomes.

In Bijnor, the "riot" was the culmination of a series of earlier conflicts. Each incident entailed greater participation by more diverse individuals and groups. The first struggle was confined to members of the municipal council. Zafar Khan's opponents included Ram Gopal, Shiv Sena president, Raghuvir Singh, the local VHP president, and Tilakwala, the head of the Bajrang Dal, as well as others, like Deepak Mehra and Sandip Lal, who were not Sangh Parivar members. Deepak Mehra, the *Bijnor Times* editor, opposed Khan's election as chair because Mehra had struck a deal with Sandip Lal. If elected, Lal had promised to allot land to the *Bijnor Times* group. Although Mehra was a communist and Sandip Lal a member of the SP, they shared an enmity to Khan. This illustrates how the BJP was the beneficiary of the common short-term interests of ideologically diverse individuals.

Hindutva activists became increasingly organized after the struggle over the chairmanship of the municipal council in Bijnor. They enlisted the Shiv Sena, Bajrang Dal, and VHP to occupy municipal council land on August 25. However, they still needed greater community support, particularly because male leaders were planning to be away in Ayodhya. Nandaji reported that the RSS had encouraged women to play leadership roles because it anticipated that men would be imprisoned or in Ayodhya.[65] On October 4, the Durga Vahini, Mahila Morcha, and Rashtra Sevika Samiti jointly planned a procession to the Ganges to escort activists from Ayodhya to Bijnor. Hindu women remained active thereafter. Ritu Chandra, Mahila Morcha secretary, said that they organized protest marches from October 27 to October 29 demanding the release of detained Hindutva activists. They also slipped into the college to bring food to activists. Hindu women went door to door asking people to participate in the procession on October 30. Ritu Chandra reported that about 500 women assembled that morning and led the procession through the Muslim quarter of the town.

Hindutva activists drew on repertoires of protest that other social movements have employed to confront injustice and inequality. They participated in processions, demonstrations, hunger strikes, and door-to-door campaigns, courted arrest, and surrounded government buildings. By the time the violence

[65] Interview with Nandaji, Bijnor, April 24, 1991.

occurred in Bijnor and Khurja, movement leaders were able to draw in Hindus who had previously been inactive.

Pervasive, vicious rumors contributed to politicizing Hindu men and women. Although we tend to speak of "rumors spreading" in the passive tense, as if they spread of their own accord, Hindu nationalists systematically disseminated rumors to polarize Hindus and Muslims. In Khurja, they circulated rumors that Lakshman had been murdered; fourteen cows had been slaughtered; the town's water supplies had been poisoned; people were being killed in neighboring *mohallas*; and Muslims were planning to attack Hindu neighborhoods. In Bijnor they circulated rumors that Muslims had kidnapped and killed the VHP president; many *kar sevaks* had been killed in detention; and Fazlul Hyder had abducted Hindu women. Only Hindus could dispel these rumors and several newspaper reporters in both Bijnor and Khurja attempted to do so. But most people could not afford to ignore rumors that appeared to put their families and themselves at risk. Rumors help explain why Hindus who were not ideologically committed to the BJP engaged in violence against Muslims and considered their actions defensive rather than aggressive.

Neither the causes nor the repercussions of the violence in Bijnor and Khurja were merely local. The activists who perpetrated violence depicted local individuals and events as epitomizing larger political forces. The notion that Zafar Khan and Sarwar Hussain were anti-Hindu recalled a key theme in the Ayodhya campaign concerning the anti-Hindu biases of sixteenth-century Muslim rulers. National Muslim leaders Syed Shahabuddin and Javed Habib furnished Hindu nationalists with examples of "Muslim fundamentalists." But the threat was made more palpable when it was linked to the immediate threats allegedly posed by men like Sarwar Hussain in Khurja and Zafar Khan in Bijnor. Similarly, the BJP evoked images of Muslim men as sexual predators and Hindu women as their victims by claiming that Fazlul Hyder was molesting Hindu women in his clinic in Bijnor and that Muslim men were sexually harassing Balmiki women in Khurja.

Events in Khurja and Bijnor and in Ayodhya were linked in temporal sequence through metonymy and metaphor.[66] The timing of key incidents in Bijnor coincided with events of national and statewide significance, such as Mulayam Singh Yadav's rally, the procession of Ram devotees, and Hindutva activists' arrival in Ayodhya. Several Hindu nationalist activities, including protests against government orders to ban processions of *Ram jyotis* in Bijnor, replicated their actions in Ayodhya. In both settings, Hindu nationalists claimed that the police had engaged in repression against their activists. Most strikingly reminiscent of Ayodhya were Hindutva activists' actions in Bijnor

---

[66] As Veena Das describes in the case of Hindu violence against Sikhs in 1985, Hindus made Sikhs imitate the fate of the assassinated prime minister. Veena Das, "Introduction," in Veena Das, ed., *Mirrors of Violence: Communities, Riots and Survivors in South Asia* (New Delhi: Oxford University Press, 1990), 26–7.

on August 25. They occupied land adjoining a mosque where they created a makeshift temple, brought idols to the spot, and worshipped them. By replicating its actions in Ayodhya in towns like Bijnor, the BJP made its larger objectives locally meaningful. The Ayodhya campaign placed towns like Khurja and Bijnor on the Hindu nationalist map.

Hindutva slogans and aphorisms claimed that Muslims did not belong in India, for their true loyalties were pan-Islamic. Why else would they cheer for Pakistan during cricket matches? Why did they sell sweets in the streets when Pakistan defeated India? Processions would call out, "If you want to remain in India, you will have to become a Hindu," "Hindustan is for Hindus," "If you stay in Hindustan, you must say Vande Mataram," "We should abolish *namaz* five times a day," and "What place is there for Muslims amid the children of Ram?"

The notion that Muslims did not belong in India legitimated Hindutva activists' attempts to gain control over Muslims' land, mosques, and homes. Their most spectacular claims involved the *babri masjid* in Ayodhya and mosques in Kashi and Mathura. But they attacked Muslim burial grounds, shops, and homes in many places. They pressured Muslims to vacate positions of power. In Bijnor, as in many other towns that experienced violence, a Hindu procession deviated from the officially prescribed route and marched through a Muslim locality. Such invasions of Muslims' physical space, often during Muslim prayer times, implied that there were no safe places for Muslims.

The State

Hindus and Muslims in Khurja and Bijnor agreed that the state was sufficiently powerful to instigate, prevent, and stop violence. However, both groups claimed to be victims of state biases. Hindutva activists repeatedly claimed that the state was biased against Hindus and favored minorities, thereby justifying Hindus taking the law into their own hands. By contrast, Muslims characterized the state as biased in favor of Hindus and tacitly allowing or actively precipitating anti-minority violence.

Both antipathy toward the state and a desire to obtain state power reflect an appreciation of its centrality to people's everyday lives. Atul Kohli notes:

[T]he more control a government has over its people's access to life chances in a society, especially in a society in which alternative routes to satisfactory livelihood are scarce, the more the everyday struggles of livelihood take on a political character. Getting one's children admitted to a school, getting a loan to buy an irrigation pump, getting a job on a new public-works project, helping a relative get a job in the municipal government – all of these require the influence of someone in power.[67]

---

[67] Atul Kohli, *Democracy and Discontent: India's Growing Crisis of Governability* (New York: Cambridge University Press, 1990), 198.

The dearth of nonagricultural employment in Bijnor and Khurja meant that people prized public-sector jobs, which they obtained by connections to political officials. Even Khurja's underground economy depended on state patronage. Caste-based reservations for OBCs increased upper-caste anxieties about gaining admission to colleges and securing public-sector employment. With the Janata Dal in national office and the SP in power in UP, many upper-caste Hindus felt that the state was doubly biased against them.

To appreciate how the state was implicated in the violence necessitates conceptualizing the state as a plural rather than a single entity and recognizing the distinctive roles and different popular perceptions of its roles nationally, federally, and locally. One local branch of the state is elected, and includes municipal councils, while another is comprised of civil servants under the direction of the IAS. The DM bears overall responsibility for the maintenance of law and order at the district level. A parallel line of authority is the police force under the supervision of the SSP. A third branch of the state consists of members of the Legislative Assembly, whose constituencies include towns like Bijnor and Khurja, where they sometimes reside.

To further complicate matters, the local state was neither wholly autonomous nor a cohesive, unitary actor. There were sometimes conflicts between the SSP and the DM. The local bureaucracy and the police force were susceptible to contending pressures of civil society groups on the one hand and the SP-led UP government on the other. Conflicts were especially evident within the police hierarchy. At the apex of the organization was the SSP, who was selected from the highly competitive national Indian Police Force. Under his or her authority, members of the police were drawn from the UP police service who were close to civil society activists. This explains why higher-ranking police officers complied with the chief minister's orders to prevent Hindutva activists from reaching Ayodhya and arrested them when they attempted to do so. By contrast, the local police in Bijnor and Khurja not only failed to stop the violence but sometimes attacked Muslims themselves.

Hindu nationalists sought allies in the local administration but bitterly opposed the national and state governments. The BJP had unseated Prime Minister VP Singh and undermined the National Front government in November 1990. The ruling party had factionalized and Mulayam Singh Yadav, who remained chief minister of UP, characterized the BJP as a sectarian, anti-Muslim party and took decisive actions to stop the Ayodhya campaign. In contrast to Yadav, local administrators, especially the police and bureaucrats in Khurja and Bijnor, prevaricated when the violence broke out.

In Bijnor, Hindutva activists repeatedly claimed that the state wrongfully apprehended innocent and devout Hindus. Thus, on August 25 they organized a protest against the arrest of ten people who had occupied municipal council land. Women who participated in the rally to bring *Ram jyotis* to Ayodhya on October 4 considered the state's actions unjust. When the police opened fire to deter Hindu activists from leaving the girls' intermediary college where they were being detained, women protested what they described as state tyranny. In each incident, Hindu nationalists identified what has historically been an important catalyst for movements, namely state repression against civilian populations.

The BJP popularized the view that the Congress government "pampered" minorities. Upper-caste Hindus saw Sarwar Hussain in Khurja and Zafar Khan in Bijnor as dangerous products of the state's "appeasement" policies. Both men were powerful local leaders with larger political ambitions and connections. In Khurja, Hussain personified the power and reach of the state; he exercised influence over several major institutions, including the PMA, the local administration, and the police. He was also able to rectify some of the damage that Muslims had suffered by collecting funds for Muslim victims of violence.

Hindu activists blamed Zafar Khan for the Bijnor violence although he had opposed and even boycotted Mulayam Singh Yadav's rally. He was not at the site of the violence on October 30. In fact, he had provided shelter to two Hindus who were caught in the crossfire. Nonetheless, Superintendent of Police Praveen Singh ordered Khan arrested in compliance with the DM's orders. After a new administration took over in Bijnor, it assigned Khan a full-time bodyguard because he received so many death threats.

Khan represented a threat because, as municipal council chair, he exercised control over both material and symbolic resources. He could sanction or withhold funds for municipal facilities, and authorize or prevent the construction of a temple on municipal council land. Khan's opponents were enraged that he outsmarted them by identifying their violations of established procedures. When Khan's opponents failed to discredit him, they forcibly appropriated municipal council land in the name of religion.

Yet contrary to the allegations of Hindu activists, the local state did not protect minorities. In both Bijnor and Khurja, the administration was slow to respond to warnings that violence was likely. Bureaucrats failed to take preventive measures to stop the violence and several even engaged in it. The police did not stop Hindutva activists from attacking Muslim shops and homes and sometimes even encouraged them to do so. The PAC, acting on police orders, engaged in egregious anti-Muslim violence.

Imagining the state in the plural helps explain why Hindus and Muslims held strikingly different views of the state. While both groups blamed the state for the violence, they each spoke of a different state. Muslims who accused the state of not protecting them from violence and indeed often enabling it spoke primarily of the local administration. By contrast, upper-caste Hindus referred primarily to the national and state governments, which they claimed were anti-Hindu and appeased Muslims. They resented the fact that Zafar Khan appealed to Mulayam Singh Yadav to invalidate the charges his opponents on the municipal council brought against him and that Sarwar Hussain pressured the chief minister to involve the SSP in controlling the local police. They also believed that Sarwar Hussain had played an important role in getting Mulayam Singh Yadav to transfer bureaucrats and the police after the first episode of violence. The UP government may well have changed the composition of the administration in Khurja as it did in Bijnor as a routine matter in the aftermath of violence. The ruling party controls the appointments of IAS officers and can transfer them at will. However, the BJP depicted these actions as willful attempts to undermine Hindu interests, thereby fueling Hindus' fear and resentment of the state government.

Hindu nationalist mobilization emerged in reaction to the growing power of the lower castes and the state's recognition of their interests. It temporarily halted but did not stop the growth of lower-caste parties. By the late 1990s, it competed unsuccessfully with the BSP and SP in attracting lower-caste electoral support and did not even try to compete for Muslim support. Muslims voted for whichever party was most likely to defeat the BJP. Zafar Khan and other Muslims in Bijnor rejoined the BSP once it broke ranks with the BJP and increasingly nominated Muslim candidates. As the BJP declined, its affiliated civil society organizations also became weaker and more disorganized.

The Later Years

Khurja

Khurja's political landscape changed dramatically as the BJP declined and the BSP grew.[68] By 2007, BSP leaders were elected to all the major municipal posts. Rajeev Bansal, formerly a BJP member, was elected mayor, and Anil Kumar was elected to the Legislative Assembly in 2002 and reelected in 2007. Surender Nagar was elected MP in 2009. In the 2012 elections, the Congress Party's candidate, Banshi Singh Pahadiya, defeated the BSP's candidate, Horam Singh.

Both the BSP and the BJP ceased to mobilize identity-based movements. The BSP achieved cross-caste support. It recruited upper castes and Muslims into the party and nominated them for political office. It began to address inequalities and poverty among Muslims. Buoyed by its electoral success and its strong ties to state bodies, it changed from a movement-party to a governing party.

[68] For insightful treatments of the BSP's growth in Uttar Pradesh, see Sudha Pai, "From Dalit to Savarna: The Search for a New Social Constituency by the Bahujan Samaj Party in Uttar Pradesh," in Sudha Pai, ed., *Political Process in Uttar Pradesh: Identity, Economic Reforms, and Governance* (Delhi: Pearson Longman, 2007), 221–3; and Christophe Jaffrelot, "The Rise of the Other Backward Classes in the Hindi Belt," *The Journal of Asian Studies*, February 2000, Vol. 59, no. 1, 86–108.

Faced with the growth of lower-caste parties, the BJP was no longer able to mobilize support by polarizing Hindus and Muslims. Some old-time Hindutva activists were critical of the BJP's growing moderation. Ram Swarup Bhaia reported that he had retired from political life and devoted himself to *seva* (service). Naren Chatterjee, a VHP member, said that he had become disillusioned by the BJP when its coalition governments in UP had done nothing to create a Hindu *rashtra* (state). Many upper-caste Hindus who had formerly supported the BJP ceased to do so. Suren Mehta, like many other Brahmins, felt that the BSP did much more than the BJP for its core constituency. He claimed that whereas the BJP had ceased to represent upper-caste interests because it sought lower-caste support, the BSP remained committed to its *dalit* base.

Khurja also witnessed the growth of a few radical Muslim and Hindu organizations. Both Hindu and Muslim activists forged ties to criminal networks associated with the black market in coal. Khurja was close enough to Delhi to be a hideout from which to plan attacks on the national capital. One organizations in Khurja was affiliated with the Indian wing of Lashkar-e-Taiba (Army of the Pure), the Tanzim Islahul Muslimeen, or the Organization for the Improvement of Muslims. In July 1998, the police uncovered a bunker that it had constructed in a pottery kiln to conceal explosives, arms, and ammunition. The police arrested three members of the Abdul Karim "Tunda" cell, led by Abdul Sattar, including Faisal Hussain, to whom local residents had given a forged passport. Another, Abu Sayeed, was living in the home of a local Muslim, Mohammad Sadique in Khurja.[69] The police discovered that Abu Sayeed had created a factory under the name of Paras Industry to provide cover for his activities.

These discoveries brought Khurja's Muslim community under suspicion and in the years that followed, the press spread rumors that it was harboring terrorists. The *Dainik Jagran* newspaper published several inflammatory stories, including one entitled "Terrorists Hoisted Pakistani Flag in Khurja." It alleged that hundreds of people, including terrorists and members of the outlawed SIMI, had assembled to hoist Pakistan's national flag at a *madrasa* on August 14, 2003, Pakistan's independence day. Hazi Abdul Aziz, chairman of the *madrasa*, filed a complaint on September 23, 2009, which alleged that the news had been fabricated and that no such event had taken place at the *madrasa*. An inquiry commission of the Press Trust of India heard the case and determined that the report had indeed been fabricated and censured the *Dainik Jagran* editor and reporter.[70]

[69] For additional information, see Praveen Swami, "Unending War," *Frontline*, January 14–27, 2006, Vol. 23, No. 1, and Praveen Swami, "Harnessing Hate," *Frontline*, July 29, 2006. Accessed June 25, 2014. http://www.frontline.in/static/html/fl2315/stories/20060811003912800.htm.
[70] "AMU Issues Notice to Dainik Jagran for False News," *Radiance Viewsweekly*, December 20, 2011, Vol. 49, No. 34. Accessed July 21, 2014. http://www.radianceweekly.com/282/7927/ruining-innocent-livesguilt-of-investigating-agencies/2011-11-20/inside-india/story-detail/amu-issues-notice-to-dainik-jagran-for-false-news.html.

New anti-Muslim organizations emerged, independent of the RSS and affiliates. Satyender Kumar Malik founded and led a Hindu "terrorist" organization, the Arya Sena (Noble Army), which in early 2000 masterminded bomb blasts in four mosques and one *madrasa* in the Saharanpur and Dehradun districts of UP. Investigations uncovered the existence of the Arya Sena after one of its members, Narendra Giri, shot and seriously injured Shamim Ahmad, *imam* of Sarkadi Kumar mosque in Topri village on June 4, 2002. The Central Bureau of Investigation (CBI) found that a police constable created the Arya Sena to fight Islamic "terrorism" and strengthen Hindutva forces.[71]

The Arya Sena created a factory that manufactured arms in an *ashram* in Khurja. The police wrongfully accused a Muslim man of doing so, even though the Arya Sena had left leaflets at the sites it destroyed. The leaflets claimed that the Arya Sena sought to make India a Hindu *rashtra*, create "Akhand Bharat" ("Undivided India" including Pakistan and Bangladesh), and teach Muslims a lesson.[72] Local residents organized demonstrations demanding that the district authorities apprehend the culprits and punish them under the provisions of POTA.

Most Muslims feared and despised militancy and were drawn to the BSP because Mayawati expressed support for Muslim victims of Hindu nationalist aggression and opposed characterizing all Muslims as "terrorists." Tanvir Ansari stated that the BSP was ready to defend Muslims against charges of "terrorism." He cited a speech that Mayawati had delivered in Lucknow in October 2008, in which she called for a ban on the BJP because its main objective was to create "communal disturbances."

Muslims became increasingly committed to holding public office. Mujahid Ansari was elected chair of the municipal council in Bulandshahr district. Razia Saleem Khan defeated a BJP candidate and was elected a second term as chair of the Khurja municipal board. Khan was one of several women who were elected to chair local governing bodies in Bulandshahr district. Muslim families expressed increasing desire to improve their social and economic conditions. Members of the Waqf Board, district officials, and BSP and SP members publicized the availability of government programs to promote education and employment for minorities.

Bijnor

When I returned to Bijnor in 2008, I found a statue of Bhimrao (BR) Ambedkar, the *dalit* author of the Constitution, in town square. It symbolized *dalits'*

---

[71] Danish A. Khan, "Cop Running Saffron Terror Gang in Saharanpur Region," *The Milli Gazette*. Accessed July 21, 2014. http://www.milligazette.com/Archives/01072002/0107200298.htm.
[72] "Blasts in Saharanpur," *The Milli Gazette*, Vol. 3, no. 11. Accessed July 21, 2014. http://www .milligazette.com/Archives/01062002/0106200262.htm. "Blasts in Saharanpur Mosque," *The Times of India*, May 14, 2002. Accessed July 21, 2014. http://timesofindia.indiatimes.com/city /lucknow/Blasts-in-Saharanpur-mosque/articleshow/12804204.cms.

capture of public space. The major axis of conflict was no longer between the BSP and the BJP but rather between the BSP and the SP. Hindus and Muslims agreed that while violence had not recurred and surface relations between the two groups had improved, they harbored painful memories of the past. Suman Tyagi, an active BJP member commented, "The divide is there. Muslims will not forget the time that Hindus rose up and taught them a lesson. They are determined to keep us out of power."[73] Hamid Sultan, a Muslim, said, "Just one drop of water on a pan of hot oil is what it would take for things to flare up again."[74]

However, most people felt that Hindu-Muslim violence was unlikely to recur. Both the BSP and BJP had ceased to promote enmity between communities and had become more inclusive. As a result, many committed activists who had once fully supported the BJP or the BSP had become more critical of their respective parties. Tensions between the SP's OBC supporters and the BSP's *dalit* supporters had also grown. Muslims were not the victims of either conflict. Most believed that their interest lay in defusing identity politics.

As a result of anti-incumbency sentiment, the presence of several small parties, and a split in Muslim votes, the BJP and BSP alternately won the Legislative Assembly seat in Bijnor: the BJP's Mahendra Pal Singh in 1993, BSP's Reza Gazafar in 1996, BJP's Kunvar Bhartendra in 2002, BSP's Shahnawaz in 2007, and BJP's Bhartendra in the 2012 Assembly elections. The successful candidates won by relatively narrow margins – between 1,000 and 1,800 votes in each of these elections. The SP and the Rashtriya Lok Dal were more successful in the parliamentary than the Legislative Assembly elections. The parliamentary seat went to the BJP's Mangal Ram Premi in 1996, the SP's Omwati Devi in 1998, and the BJP's Sheeshram Singh Ravi in 1999. In 2004, the Bijnor parliamentary seat was reserved for Scheduled Castes. The SP and Rashtriya Lok Dal formed an alliance and their candidate Munshi Ram was elected. The BJP, which had won the previous elections, only received 14 percent of the vote in Bijnor in 2004.

As the BJP adopted a more moderate stance and sought a broad spectrum of support across caste and community lines, it alienated many of its once committed followers. When I asked Yogendra Kishan of the RSS whether the Bajrang Dal, Shiv Sena, and the VHP remained active in Bijnor, he replied:

We are still doing a lot of social work here but we don't do much political organizing. We don't meet as often. We are much less organized than we were before. Our party supported us before but it no longer does. We expected the BJP to reward us when it came to power. Look at the CPM government in West Bengal. It realizes it has an obligation to its grassroots workers. But the BJP forgot about us. I didn't even bother voting in the last elections.[75]

---

[73] Interview with Suman Tyagi, Bijnor, November 15, 2008.
[74] Interview with Hamid Sultan, Bijnor, November 16, 2008.
[75] Interview with Yogendra Kishan, Bijnor, November 15, 2008.

Sriram Madhup, a disgruntled BJP member commented, "BJP members no longer feel great commitment to the party. BJP officials don't do anything for their
constituencies. It's all talk."[76]

Tyagi worried that as the BJP abdicated its Hindu nationalist commitments,
Muslims had become more assertive:

The Muslims here are more confident now. They never used to wear *topis* (caps). They
tried to hide the fact that they were Muslims. Now they want to assert it.

Muslim leaders here have become more powerful. They are getting money from
Pakistan. They influence their community because most Muslims here are poor, uneducated and gullible.[77]

Madhup commented, "This UP government has given *harijans* and Muslims
confidence. It has ordered that schools should close on Ramzan. Muslims are
being elected to the Legislative Assembly."

The BSP grew significantly by mobilizing across caste and community lines.
While it continued to measure electoral success through caste calculations, it
became more committed to creating a strong party organization that extended
down to the grassroots level. While keeping religion out of politics, it cultivated
devotion to the party. Tyagi commented cynically, "People said we were bringing religion into politics. But they have made Ambedkar into a God."

The BSP's inclusion of Brahmins and Thakurs generated new sources of
discontent. Bhupendra Singh founded a radical *dalit* organization, the Vishva
Dalit Parishad, which opposed the BSP for giving tickets to Brahmins, Thakurs,
and other upper castes. At the same time, the BSP's politicization of caste also
led Muslim organizations like the All India Pasmanda Front to demand eligibility for reserved seats. Habib Ansari, one of its members, criticized Mayawati
for not pursuing the Sachar Committee recommendations, especially when the
government had identified Bijnor as a district with a significant concentration
of minorities.

Most Muslims continued to oppose the BJP and supported either the SP or
the BSP. Zafar Khan commented sadly:

If Muslims survive it will only be by allying with the *dalits*. A Muslim party has no
chance of success. Our decision about which party to support depends on two considerations: whether the party is likely to be elected and whether it will steer clear of an
alliance with the BJP.[78]

Hamid Sultan concurred, "Muslims don't necessarily vote for Muslim candidates. They vote for whichever candidate can defeat the BJP. Muslims have a
negative influence. They can keep some candidates out but they can't exercise
real leadership."[79]

[76] Interview with Sriram Madhup, Bijnor, November 17, 2008.
[77] Interview with Suman Tyagi, Bijnor, November 15, 2008.
[78] Interviews with Zafar Khan, Bijnor, November 15 and 16, 2008.
[79] Interview with Hamid Sultan, Bijnor, November 15, 2008.

However, both the BSP and the SP had at different times allied with the BJP, and Muslims were divided between these two parties. Sultan had more faith in Mulayam Singh Yadav than he had in Mayawati. He had come to distrust the BSP after it allied with the BJP and he especially questioned Mayawati's ties to Narendra Modi. Zafar Khan defended the BSP. He believed that Mayawati recognized that she needed Muslim support and could only achieve it by addressing Muslims' interests. He claimed that BSP MLAs had overseen increased investment in the town's infrastructure and had formulated a broad-based strategy of economic development. He believed that Mayawati had distanced herself from Modi and no longer needed to ally with the BJP. She had also become increasingly committed to Muslim political representation. He pointed out that the BSP had nominated fourteen Muslim candidates to run in the 2007 assembly elections. One of them, Shahnawaz Raza, was elected from Bijnor.

Khan said that class and caste conflicts had overshadowed Hindu-Muslim tensions. He described Mahendra Singh Tikait's attack on Mayawati at a rally that Tikait had recently organized near there.

Tikait held a big rally on March 30th 2008. Ajit Singh was sitting on the dais. Tikait hurled abuses against Mayawati. He was very derogatory. Mayawati had him arrested. Tikait called on his people to retaliate. For four to five days it seemed that there would be a war.

The incident brought to light simmering caste and class tensions in the region.[80] Tikait expressed the resentment of land-owning Jats at the growing power of *dalits* and Mayawati's response reflected *dalits'* increased assertiveness. Mayawati's decision to have Tikait arrested for making anti-*dalit* remarks infuriated his Jat supporters. His arrest led to a major confrontation between 300 police officers and Tikait supporters at his village, Sisauli. Twenty-five policemen and at least two farmers were injured. Nine people, including Tikait's younger son Surendra, were arrested.

However, none of these tensions resulted in large-scale violence. Cohesive identities had become fractured. Caste politics did not give rise to the kinds of animosities and antagonisms that had been associated with Hindu-Muslim violence. Compared to the BJP, the BSP had weaker ties to committed civil society activists and was less willing to foster violence. Furthermore, Muslims as well as Hindus came to see caste as cross-cutting the Hindu-Muslim divide.

An equally significant change was the impact on towns like Bijnor and Khurja of the national government's recognition of socioeconomic inequalities between Hindus and Muslims. Following the release of the Sachar Committee Report, the UPA government identified districts in which minorities comprised

---

[80] For additional details, see Sudha Pai, "The New Old Story of Bijnor," *The Indian Express*, April 3, 2008. Accessed June 25, 2014. http://archive.indianexpress.com/news/the-new-old-story-of -bijnor/ 291820/.

at least 25 percent of the population, were especially disadvantaged and lacked infrastructural facilities. It identified ninety such districts, of which twenty-one were in UP. They included Bijnor and Bulandshahr (where Khurja is located). The government designated these Minority Concentrated Districts (MCDs) and allotted them funding and facilities through a Multi-Sectoral Development Plan.

Critics charged that the plan failed to allot adequate resources to MCDs and was implemented in a top-down fashion without sufficient consultation with community leaders. Although these criticisms may be apt, the plan had two positive consequences. First, research that the government commissioned into the conditions of minorities in these districts revealed the extent to which Muslims lagged behind Hindus according to most socioeconomic indicators and with respect to the benefits they received from government entitlements. Surveys of Bijnor and Bulandshahr districts showed that, compared to Hindus, Muslims had less access to credit facilities, suffered higher levels of indebtedness, and experienced more illness and landlessness.[81] In Bijnor, 63 percent of Hindus and 50 percent of Muslims were literate and 30 percent of Hindus and 26 percent of Muslims were employed. In Khurja, literacy rates were 63 percent for Hindus and 45 percent for Muslims and 40 percent of Hindus and 34 percent of Muslims were employed. As this information became more widely known, it became harder to characterize Muslims as "pampered minorities." It also became harder to characterize Muslims on the basis of their religious rather than their class identities.

Second, the Congress-led government's recognition of Muslims' socioeconomic conditions and its plans to rectify inequalities encouraged the BSP to compete with Congress for Muslim support by similarly addressing class inequality among minorities. The BSP formed "Muslim Bhaichara" (Brotherhood) committees in many districts, including Agra, Meerut, and Devipatan. Mayawati promised that if the BSP came to power nationally, it would support reservations for Muslims. She also announced plans to improve the conditions of Muslims, including financial grants to *madrasas*, the creation of government schools in Muslim-dominated areas, self-employment schemes to create jobs for minorities, and the promotion of the Urdu language. That these plans have yet to be implemented is evident from the continuing poverty and lack of opportunities for Muslims in Khurja and Bijnor. Yet the fact that these schemes were created suggests how much state and party discourses had changed, making Muslims less vulnerable to violence.

---

[81] See reports by the Giri Institute of Development Studies: YP Singh, *Baseline Survey in the Minority Concentrated Districts Of U.P. (Report of Bulandshahr District)*, sponsored by the Ministry of Minority Affairs, Government of India (Lucknow: Giri Institute of Development Studies, 2008).

Hindu-Muslim violence resulted from the separate and combined activities of political parties, the state, and civil society groups. Conversely, violence diminished in subsequent years not simply as a result of the actions of the state or any other single institution but rather as a result of changes in relations among movements, parties, and the state government, this time under the control of the lower castes.

5

Gujarat

The Perfect Storm

Ethnic violence – in 1969, 1981, 1985, 1990, 1992–3, and 2002 – has lasted longer and been more destructive in Gujarat than in any other state in postindependence India. Bhikhu Parekh observes that Gujarat has "the dubious double distinction of having the highest per capita deaths in the country and causing the highest number of casualties in a single cluster of riots."[1] Five hundred and twenty-four people were killed amid Hindu-Muslim violence in 1969.[2] About 500 people were killed in Ayodhya-related events from September 1990 to January 1993.[3] Official estimates are 1,180 and unofficial estimates are 2,000 deaths in February-March 2002.[4]

Thus for some scholars, 2002 was another event in a familiar series of violence. Based on a longitudinal database of "riots" in India, Steven Wilkinson identifies the continuities between 2002 and earlier times in Gujarat and other states:

The Gujarat violence has been so truly awful that it is perhaps necessary to remind ourselves that seen in the context of the previous major riots in India, the recent events have not been exceptional. In all the largest communal riots since independence ... state governments from various political parties have, as in Gujarat, delayed taking action to

---

[1] Bhikhu Parekh, "Making Sense of Gujarat," *Seminar*, May 2002. Accessed June 26, 2014. http://www.india-seminar.com/2002/513/513%20bhikhu%20parekh.htm.

[2] Pingle Jagmohan Reddy, Akbar S. Sarela, and Nusserwanji K. Vakil, "Report: Inquiry into the Communal Disturbances at Ahmedabad and other Places in Gujarat on and after 18th September 1969." Gujarat: (India) Commission of Inquiry on Communal Disturbances, 1971: 179.

[3] Asghar Ali Engineer, ed., *The Gujarat Carnage* (New Delhi: Orient Longman, 2003).

[4] Biggs and Dhattiwala estimate that 984 people were killed. Michael Biggs and Raheel Dhattiwala, "The Political Logic of Ethnic Violence: The Anti-Muslim Pogrom in Gujarat, 2002," *Politics and Society*, 2012, Vol. 40, no. 4, 483–516. Their estimates and others exclude the people who died in the Godhra train fire.

stop the violence for days or even weeks. In most of these riots, as in Gujarat in the past month, minorities suffered disproportionately.[5]

Others argue that March 2002 constituted India's first pogrom and that the scale and intensity of the violence were unprecedented.[6] No single "riot" claimed as many lives as the one in February–March 2002; at least 495 people were killed in just three days.[7] Moreover, the brutality of the violence was unparalleled. Depicting the violence as exceptional risks ignoring its analogs and the quotidian acts of violence that "ordinary" people routinely commit.[8] However, depicting the 2002 violence as part of a continuum may not adequately acknowledge the magnitude of the suffering and the conjuncture of events that caused it.

Clearly there were continuities between 2002 and earlier years: the rumors, biased press reports, police inaction or complicity, and responsibilities of Hindu nationalists. The systematic destruction of mosques and marking out of Muslim homes and shops so that the assailants knew which properties to destroy were all part of an earlier repertoire. All too familiar was the targeting of prominent Muslim leaders – Kadir Peerzada and Mohammad Surti in 1992 and Congress MP Eshan Jaffrey in 2002.

The Ayodhya campaign and, in particular, the Surat violence in 1992 laid the groundwork for Hindu nationalist violence in 2002. Haresh Bhatt, a Bajrang Dal leader who was elected MLA from Godhra in 2002, admitted to training activists who destroyed the *babri masjid* in 1992.[9] Narendra Modi, the general secretary of the BJP in Gujarat at the time, was the chief architect of the 1990 *rath yatra* and the *ekta yatra* the following year.

This chapter suggests that the violent conjuncture in 2002 sets it apart from previous violence in Gujarat and violence in other parts of the country. It begins by exploring the continuities and differences between two periods in which Hindu-Muslim violence has been most extensive in Gujarat: 1969 and 2002. I argue that the state, political parties, and civil society organizations/ social movements all bore responsibility for the violence both times. However, by 2002, the character of these organizations and relations between them had

[handwritten margin note: What led to the violence]

[5] Steven Wilkinson, "Putting Gujarat in Perspective," *Economic and Political Weekly*, April 27, 2002. Accessed June 26, 2014. http://www.epw.in/system/files/pdf/2002_37/17/Putting_Gujarat_in_Perspective.pdf.

[6] Paul Brass, "The Gujarat Pogrom of 2002," *Social Science Research Council*, March 26, 2004. Accessed June 26, 2014. http://conconflicts.ssrc.org/gujarat/brass.

[7] Biggs and Dhattiwala, "The Political Logic of Ethnic Violence," 487.

[8] Two good attempts to link the quotidian and the extraordinary are Parvis Ghassem-Fachandi, *Pogrom in Gujarat: Hindu Nationalism and Anti-Muslim Violence in India* (Princeton, NJ: Princeton University Press, 2012); and Arafaat Valiani, *Militant Publics in India: Physical Culture and Violence in the Making of a Modern Polity* (New York: Palgrave MacMillan, 2011).

[9] Ashish Khetan, "The Sting in the Story," *Tehelka Magazine*, September 8, 2012, Vol. 9, No. 36. Accessed July 18, 2014. http://archive.tehelka.com/story_main53.asp?filename=Ne080912Coverstory.asp.

changed. Gujarat in 2002 represented the perfect storm – if perfect can be used to describe the mobilization of hatred. There was an unprecedented convergence of forces that heightened Hindu nationalist militancy and violence: an active RSS presence within civil society; high levels of coordination between the RSS, VHP, BJP, and militant Bajrang Dal; a cohesive political party; a BJP state government with ties to the bureaucracy and law enforcement agencies; and an NDA government at the center. The boundaries that generally distinguish civil society organizations and the state had eroded by 2002 and were never fully reestablished.

The second section places Gujarat in comparative perspective and asks why the BJP was more activist and militant here than in UP. I explore differences in the character of political parties, caste politics, and relations between the state and national governments in the two states. Unlike UP, Gujarat does not have a tradition of low-caste or leftist movements. By participating in anti-Congress movements, the Gujarat BJP gained upper-caste and middle class support. Unlike UP, the BJP in Gujarat did not face serious caste tensions either within the party or within the electoral arena. The national government sanctioned the BJP government in UP in 1992 but not in Gujarat in 2002.

The third and fourth sections explore the ways the BJP has surmounted the opposition it has faced both within the Sangh Parivar (section three) and from other civil society activists (section four.) Section three analyzes Hindutva activists' hostility to Narendra Modi's leadership as a result of the BJP government's economic policies and sanctioning of the VHP. The RSS supported the BJP and enabled it to withstand these challenges, pursue its ideological agenda, and retain powerful and remunerative positions in civil society organizations and government bodies. As section four describes, secular NGOs have opposed the Gujarat government in the courts and through their work with Muslim victims. Although they have achieved some success, they cannot rival RSS-affiliated organizations, which are founded in earlier social movements and have ties to the state and a political party.

1969 and 2002

On September 18, 1969, two Hindu *sadhus* were herding their cows to the Jagannath temple complex in Ahmedabad when they encountered Muslims celebrating the annual Urs festival. One of the cows injured a Muslim woman and her two children and damaged Muslims' pushcarts. Muslim youth attacked and injured the *sadhus* and damaged the temple windows. One of the priests engaged in a protest fast until a fifteen-member Muslim delegation issued an apology. Disrupting the temporary calm, some Hindus damaged a *dargah* near the temple. When Muslims protested, large groups of Hindus attacked and killed Muslims and burned down their homes, shops, and mosques. On September 20 and September 24, groups of Hindus stopped trains leaving

Ahmedabad and killed Muslim passengers. The violence only ended when the army took charge of Ahmedabad.

On February 27, 2002, a train carrying VHP members who were returning from Ayodhya stopped at Godhra. About twenty minutes later, a coach caught on fire, killing fifty-nine people, of whom at least thirty were VHP supporters or activists. The VHP destroyed a mosque at Signal Falia, attacked Muslims at almost every station en route, burned seven buses and Muslim shops, and brought the charred bodies to parade them around Ahmedabad that night. Its Gujarat *bandh* on February 28 resulted in massive attacks on Muslim homes, shops, and neighborhoods in Ahmedabad and surrounding cities, towns, and villages. A second round of violence, which began on March 15, coinciding with the *shiladaan* (donation of a carved stone) in Ayodhya, continued until March 20 in Ahmedabad, Vadodara, Bharuch, Bhavnagar, and Rajkot. The Bajrang Dal called on Hindus to protest after newspapers erroneously reported that Muslims had attacked *Ram bhakts*. Isolated attacks on Muslims occurred in late April, June, and July.[10]

There are several similarities between the 1969 and 2002 violence. The RSS and its affiliates played key roles; the violence was electorally-motivated; and the press spread provocative, false rumors.

The Role of the Sangh Parivar

With respect to the RSS, in September 1969, Jan Sangh and RSS members created the Hindu Dharma Raksha Samiti (HDRS, Committee for the Defense of the Hindu Religion). Under its auspices, fifty-seven Jan Sangh members undertook a fast demanding the suspension of a police officer who had kicked the *Ramayana*, a sacred Hindu text, on September 4. RSS leader Nanaji Deshmukh visited those fasting on September 15 and the RSS organized rallies across Ahmedabad. From September 18 on, the Jan Sangh and its affiliates mobilized Hindus to engage in violence against Muslims. The government-appointed Reddy Commission stated that RSS and Jan Sangh members distributed voter registration lists that identified Muslim homes and properties that they subsequently destroyed.

By 2002, the RSS had implanted itself in the state. Narendra Modi, an RSS *pracharak*, became national general secretary of the BJP and chief minister of Gujarat; SS Bhandari, another RSS *pracharak,* became governor; and Gordhan Zadaphia, VHP member, became minister of state for home affairs. The BJP state government appointed RSS and VHP members as prosecutors, office bearers, and political officials.

The RSS, BJP, and VHP went into action immediately after the Godhra train fire in 2002. Senior officials of these organizations and two government ministers, Ashok Bhatt and Pratap Singh Chauhan, participated in a VHP meeting

[handwritten in right margin: Similar to what happened in Rwanda]

---

[10] "Incidents of Post-Godhra Violence," *Sabrang*. Accessed June 26, 2014. http://www.sabrang .com/tribunal/vol1/convio.html.

at Lunavada to plan a *bandh*.[11] Gujarat BJP president Rajendrasingh Rana announced the BJP's support for the *bandh* and informally told the VHP that it had until the evening of the 28th to retaliate.

The comments that senior RSS, VHP, and BJP members made in the aftermath of the violence were virtually indistinguishable. "Every action has an equal and opposite reaction," said Narendra Modi. "It had to be done," said Keshavram Kashiram Shastri, chairman of the Gujarat unit of the VHP.[12] The RSS issued a resolution on March 17 that stated: "Let Muslims understand that their real safety lies in the goodwill of the majority."[13] A few weeks later, Ashok Singhal described the violence as a "victory for Hindu society." Whole villages had been "emptied of Islam." "We were successful," he said, "in our experiment of raising Hindu consciousness, which will be repeated all over the country now."[14]

Electoral Motivations

The violence was electorally profitable both in 1969 and in 2002. The Jan Sangh fielded fifty-five candidates and won two seats for the first time in municipal corporation by-elections in October 1969. The BJP had experienced electoral defeats prior to March 2002. Two years earlier, it lost elections to twenty-three out of twenty-five district *panchayats*, a majority of *taluka panchayats*, and, for the first time in years, municipal corporations in Ahmedabad and Rajkot. It also lost by-elections in September 2001 for the State Assembly and for Parliament. The BJP continued its downward slide after Modi replaced Keshubhai Patel as chief minister. It lost two Assembly seats in three by-elections in February 2002. To increase the BJP's chances of winning the forthcoming Assembly elections, Modi attempted to force early elections in July, eight months ahead of schedule, but the Election Commission did not allow this. When elections took place in December 2002, Muslims were still in relief camps and Hindu nationalist sentiments were still running high.

The BJP won 50 percent of the vote in 2002, a 5 percent increase over 1998. It performed especially well in fifty-two out of the sixty-five constituencies in which the violence occurred. Hindu nationalists precipitated the least violence in constituencies or districts where the BJP had sufficient support to win the

[11] "An Inquiry into Carnage in Gujarat," *Sabrang*. Accessed June 26, 2014. http://www.sabrang .com/tribunal/vol2/compgovt.html.

[12] Sheela Bhatt, "It Had to Be Done, VHP Leader Says of Riots," *Rediff News*, March 12, 2002. Accessed June 26, 2014. http://www.rediff.com/news/2002/mar/12train.htm.

[13] "Hate Speech," *Outlook India*, November 22, 2002. Accessed June 26, 2014. http://www .outlookindia.com/printarticle.aspx?218024.

[14] Pankaj Mishra, "The Other Side of Fanaticism," *New York Times*, February 2, 2003. Accessed June 26, 2014. http://www.nytimes.com/2003/02/02/magazine/the-other-face-of-fanaticism .html?pagewanted=all&src=pm.

elections and the most violence in constituencies or districts where it needed to improve its electoral performance.[15]

The Role of the Media

The Gujarati press contributed to the escalation of violence in both 1969 and 2002. The headlines of the front-page story in the *Jai Hind* dated September 19, 1969 read "Fanatical Attack on the Jagganath Temple."

A fanatical (infuriated) group attacked three Sadhus and severely beat them. A Sadhu who was attacked by a knife received injury on the leg and his leg was bleeding profusely ... the Sadhus ran for safety in the temple, but the mob chased the Sadhus and it is said that they entered the inner part of the temple. Other Sadhus who ran to inquire were also severely beaten and some fell to the ground.... The intention of the mob was clear from the way the mob had unrestrictedly attacked and beaten up the Sadhus. The passing of the cows caused them no hardship but the mob has some other fanatical motive also.[16]

The *Jan Satta* and *Gujarat Samachar* also carried inflammatory reports. The *Sandesh* reported on September 20 that several (presumably Hindu) women had been stripped and raped in public.[17] It later retracted the report. That afternoon there was a round of killings and rapes of Muslim women. The Reddy Commission stated that press reports of injuries and damage to the temple were highly exaggerated and violated all press code rules.

The HDRS circulated pamphlets with provocative titles like: "Hindus Beware," "A Public Meeting Condemning the Heinous Attack on the Jagannath Temple of Hindus," and "Total Strike in Protest against the Attack by Communal Muslims on Jagannath Temple." The pamphlets exaggerated the damage to the temple and injuries to *sadhus* and called on the Hindu community to "associate in large numbers with the programs of the HDRS."[18] False rumors preceded the violence – the *sadhu* who was injured at the Jagannath temple had died in the hospital, cows were being slaughtered, and the dead body of a young (presumably Hindu) girl had been found.

Rumors of Muslim male aggression against Hindu women were a catalyst for the violence that followed the Godhra train fire in 2002. The *Sandesh*'s front-page story on February 28 reported that "religious fanatics" had kidnapped ten to fifteen Hindu women by snatching them from the train. Headlines read: "Ladies ran away to save lives and miscreants caught them," and "Two distorted dead bodies of the women who were kidnapped from the Sabarmati Express,

[15] Biggs and Dhattiwala, "The Political Logic of Ethnic Violence," 505.
[16] Reddy, Sarela, and Vakil, "Report: Inquiry into the Communal Disturbances at Ahmedabad and other Places in Gujarat," 104–5.
[17] Ghanshyam Shah, "Communal Riots in Gujarat: Report of a Preliminary Investigation," *Economic and Political Weekly*, January 17, 1970, Vol. 5, nos. 3-4-5, 17.
[18] Reddy, Sarela, and Vakil, "Report: Inquiry into the Communal Disturbances at Ahmedabad and other Places in Gujarat," 107.

found, breasts of both women cut off." These stories suggested that women had been repeatedly raped.[19] On March 1, the *Sandesh* reported that Muslims had abducted two Hindu women from a train, gang raped, mutilated, and killed them, and dumped their bodies in Kalol near Godhra. It later reported that a third body had been found. Although the police investigated the story, searched the village, and found the story baseless, the *Sandesh* did not publish retractions, corrections, or clarifications.[20] The *Gujarat Samachar* published a story stating that the *Sandesh* article was false, but did not acknowledge that it had published equally fictitious stories of Muslim men raping Hindu women. With the exception of one story in *Gujarat Today*, no Gujarati-language newspaper reported the extensive rapes of Muslim women that independent investigations documented.

The Scale and Brutality of the Violence
The scale and brutality of the violence, including sexual violence in 2002, far surpassed 1969.[21] The 1969 violence primarily affected Ahmedabad and to a lesser extent Sabarkantha, Junaghad, and Rajkot. The 2002 violence crossed rural-urban lines, spread from slums to posh middle-class localities, and occurred in thirty-seven cities. Gujarat's additional director general of police (intelligence) informed the Election Commission of India that twenty out of twenty-six districts, 151 towns and 993 villages, covering 154 out of 182 Assembly constituencies in the state and 284 out of 464 police stations experienced violence.[22]

There were some reports of rape during earlier periods of violence, including Surat in 1992. The VHP and Bajrang Dal had long been obsessed by Muslims' sexuality.[23] Their publications describe Muslim men as sexual predators and Hindu women as their victims. They made strenuous efforts to break up Hindu-Muslim romantic and marital relations. The BJP government replaced the Violence against Women police cell with a cell that monitored intercommunity marriages in 1995.

[19] Syeda S. Hameed, Ruth Manorama, Malini Ghose, Shebha George, Mari Thekaekara, and Farah Naqvi, "How the Gujarat Massacre Has Affected Minority Women: The Survivors Speak," *Fact Finding by a Women's Panel Sponsored by Citizen's Initiative, Ahmedabad,* April 16, 2002. http://www.geocities.com/shrawan_k_s/Communalism/Gujrat/TheSurvivorsSpeakX.html.htm, annexure 1.6.
[20] Kamal Mitra Chenoy, SP Shukla, KS Subramanian, and Achin Vanaik, "Gujarat Carnage 2002: A Report to the Nation: An Independent Fact Finding Mission," April 10, 2002. Accessed June 26, 2014. http://www.sacw.net/Gujarat2002/GujCarnage.html.
[21] In 2002, some 200,000 people were displaced from their homes; the economic damage was more than a billion US dollars. Wilkinson, "Putting Gujarat in Perspective." Nearly 500 mosques were destroyed. "The Gujarat Pogrom of 2002."
[22] Sidharth Vardarajan, *Gujarat: The Making of a Tragedy* (New Delhi, India: Penguin Books), 329.
[23] Tanika Sarkar, "The Semiotics of Terror," *Economic and Political Weekly,* July 13, 2002. Accessed June 26, 2014. http://www.epw.in/commentary/semiotics-terror.html.

Nitesh, a former Bajrang Dal member, described policing interfaith couples.[24] He said that the Bajrang Dal tracked marriages between Hindus and Muslims that dated back twenty years and abducted Hindu women who had married Muslim men. The police would visit the homes of interfaith couples and threaten to brand the men Pakistani agents if they did not separate.[25] He believed at the time that he was protecting Hindu women from sexual violence and enjoyed feeling strong and having good connections to the police.

Niyaza Bibi, a Muslim who was living in Siyasat Nagar, a temporary relief colony, said that Bajrang Dal activists began stirring up tensions between men and women in her village in 2001. Hindu neighbors ceased to invite her to their religious festivals. Her daughter said that Bajrang Dal boys would taunt and harass her and her friends when they left school. Niyaza spoke to the principal of the school, who told her that he was afraid to ask the men to leave. The tensions kept growing. Finally, she and her family left the village unharmed when a young Hindu boy who was a family friend alerted them to the likelihood of violence; he could not prevent the subsequent destruction of her house.

In Upendra Baxi's terms, the emergence of a new and horrifying "rape culture" in 2002 set Gujarat apart from mass violence in other times and places in India.[26] Sexual violence against women was extreme, of a kind unseen since Partition, more than half a century earlier. Women in relief camps described being molested, raped, stripped, and brutalized. The Concerned Citizens' Tribunal reported that as many as 250 women and girls were subject to "gross sexual crimes."[27] After the attacks, officials refused to provide proper medical examination, destroyed evidence, and misfiled or refused to file FIRs, making it much harder for victims and their families to subsequently pursue legal cases.[28] Sexual violence against Muslim women dishonored, humiliated, and terrorized the entire Muslim community and prevented Muslims from regaining control over their lives.

Hindu nationalists increasingly described Muslims as being disloyal to India after Pakistan shot down a plane carrying Gujarat chief minister Balwantrai Mehta, and the Indo-Pakistan war in 1965. RSS leader MS Golwalkar and Jan Sangh leader Balraj Madhok delivered fiery speeches in which they identified

[24] Interview with Nitesh (pseudonym), Ahmedabad, November 21, 2008.

[25] Hameed et al., "How the Gujarat Massacre Has Affected Minority Women," 34.

[26] Upendra Baxi, "The Second Gujarat Catastrophe," *Economic and Political Weekly*, 37, no. 34 (2002): 3519–31. Accessed June 26, 2014. http://www.epw.in/special-articles/second-gujarat-catastrophe.html.

[27] Concerned Citizens' Tribunal, "Crime against Humanity: An Inquiry into the Carnage in Gujarat." Vol. 2, 108. Gujarat, 2002. http://www.sabrang.com/tribunal/.

[28] Human Rights Watch, "Compounding Injustice: The Government's Failure to Address Massacres in Gujarat," *Human Rights Watch*, July 2003, Vol. 15, No. 3(C). Accessed June 26, 2014. http://www.coalitionagainstgenocide.org/reports/2003/hrw.jul2003.vol15.no3c.pdf, 43.

Muslims with Pakistan and called for their "Indianisation" in 1968 and 1969, respectively.

By 2002, the Sangh Parivar was claiming that Gujarati Muslims had direct ties to Pakistani intelligence and to international "terrorist" groups. Although the causes of the Godhra train fire remain disputed, the reigning view, expressed by the Banerjee Commission, is that it was an accident.[29] Nonetheless, Chief Minister Modi and Home Minister LK Advani declared the fire a premeditated act of "terrorism" either by the Pakistani government or by "*jihadis*."[30] Gordhan Zadaphia, a minister at the time, claimed that the BJP government had received privileged intelligence information that the Pakistani Inter-Service Intelligence (ISI) had preplanned the Godhra violence.[31] Echoing a widely-held view, he described the Hindu violence against Muslims that followed as a spontaneous expression of outrage. He said, "People were so angry about what happened in Godhra that they could not contain their anger. What happened next would not have happened if Muslims had not preplanned Godhra."

Hindu nationalist leaders linked Godhra to past Partition violence. Zadaphia said:

Godhra has always been a very communal place. The Nawab of Junagadh wanted to join Pakistan after Partition. Muslims in Godhra maintained strong ties to Pakistan. There is even a street in Pakistan called Godhra. When people saw the charred bodies on the trains, it reminded them of the dead bodies on trains from Pakistan after Partition.

In Gujarat, bordering Pakistan, Godhra was a much more effective symbol of supposed Muslim tyranny than Muslims' destruction of the sixteenth-century *babri masjid* in Ayodhya.

The claim that international "terrorists" were responsible for the fire was bolstered by the post-9/11 environment. VHP vice-president for Gujarat, Jaideep Patel, compared the Sangh Parivar's response with that of Western countries to "terrorist" attacks:

We have been tolerating this kind of aggression for five hundred years. The US and Britain don't tolerate it so why should we? Naturally there was a reaction when 5,000 Muslims gathered at the station platform in Godhra, bearing arms and petrol. When the train arrived, four hours late, they killed sixty people in the one bogey that was carrying kar sevaks from Ayodhya.[32]

Throughout the 2002 election campaign, the Sangh Parivar invoked memories of Hindus killed in the Godhra massacre and a "terrorist" attack on

---

[29] "India Godhra Train Blaze Verdict: 31 Convicted," *BBC News*, February 22, 2011. Accessed June 26, 2014. http://www.bbc.co.uk/news/world-south-asia-12534127.
[30] Siddharth Varadarajan, *Gujarat: The Making of a Tragedy*, 5.
[31] Interview with Gordhan Zadaphia, Ahmedabad, January 8, 2007.
[32] Interview with Jaideep Patel, Ahmedabad, January 9, 2007.

the Akshardham temple in Gandhinagar that killed thirty-three people on September 24. An election poster in Godhra featuring Chief Minister Modi and Pakistan president Pervez Musharraf suggested that a vote against Modi was tantamount to a vote for "terrorism." When Modi took a *gaurav yatra* through Gujarat in anticipation of the elections in September 2002, he defended the killings at Naroda Patiya saying, "It should be remembered, they occurred because of the Godhra carnage."[33]

The Role of the State

State actions were crucial determinants of the scale and brutality of the violence in 1969 and 2002. Whereas the state failed to act decisively and quickly to stop the violence in 1969, it bore more direct responsibility for the violence in 2002.

The Reddy Commission criticized the police for failing to disperse the crowds, delaying imposing curfew, and arresting more Muslims than Hindus in 1969. It criticized the government for only calling in the army at the chief secretary's insistence and for not placing the army in charge of the entire city. However, it emphasized that the government's negligence and the consequences that followed were unintentional.[34] The government's weakness was partly a result of factionalism in the Congress Party. Just two months before the violence, Congress split into Congress O, which was led by Morarji Desai, and Congress I, which was loyal to Indira Gandhi. To retain power, Congress O allied with the Jan Sangh which impaired its ability to investigate and stop the violence.

There is extensive documentation of the roles that cabinet ministers, the police, and bureaucrats played in the 2002 violence. Indeed, there was no previous "riot" in which the government was as patently partisan as it was in Gujarat in 2002. It allowed a public funeral procession for the Godhra train victims, permitted the VHP to call a *bandh* on February 28, provided voter registration and sales tax data that identified Muslim homes and property, and instructed the police not to assist Muslim victims. In the days following the violence, the government ignored 150 FIRs that named Sangh Parivar members. The 2,500 people who were arrested did not include any of them. Meanwhile the police arrested 134 people, almost entirely Muslims, under the draconian antiterrorism Act. Although the UPA government revoked POTA, it did not call for the release of Muslims who were arrested under its provisions. By 2010, of the 134 persons who were initially accused, 104 were formally charged, 5 died, 14 were released on bail, and 85 remained in jail in Gujarat, despite a 2005 review committee ruling that POTA did not apply to them, a 2008 Supreme Court ruling

[33] Darshan Desai, "Dark Descent," *Outlook India*, September 23, 2002. Accessed July 21, 2014. http://www.outlookindia.com/article/Dark-Descent/217313.

[34] Reddy, Sarela, and Vakil, "Report: Inquiry into the Communal Disturbances at Ahmedabad and other Places in Gujarat," 214.

granting their release, and a 2009 Gujarat high court ruling that POTA charges did not apply to the accused and they should be granted bail.[35]

Eyewitnesses and human rights reports named several BJP ministers and MLAs as being responsible for the violence. BJP MLA Shankar Chaudhary was arrested on murder and rioting charges in 2005. Seven years later, the Supreme Court convicted senior BJP leader and MLA Mayaben Kodnani for precipitating the horrific violence in Naroda Patiya. Kodnani became a minister of state while she was under investigation in 2007. (In a 2008 interview, Kodnani described herself as committed to uplifting women and claimed that Modi's support for her demonstrated that women did not face discrimination when the BJP was in power.[36]) Among the thirty-one others whom the Court found guilty of murder, attempted murder, and conspiracy were former Bajrang Dal convener Babu Bajrangi; BJP member of the Ahmedabad Municipal Corporation Kishan Korani; and BJP and VHP leaders Bipin Panchal and Ashok Sindhi. Still under Supreme Court investigation are VHP leaders Jaideep Patel and Praveen Togadia, former Minister of State for Home Affairs Gordhan Zadaphia, BJP spokesperson and Urban Development Minister IK Jadeja, and BJP MLAs Kalu Malivad, Mehsana Anil Patel, and Madhu Srivastava.

The government's attitude filtered down to the civil service. A former cabinet secretary, TSR Subramanian, said, "There is no civil service left in Gujarat."[37] Harsh Mander resigned from the civil service in anger in 2002. The police and Home Guards, an armed body deployed to stop Hindu-Muslim violence, were filled with RSS members.[38] The chief minister directed the home secretary to assume the powers of the director general of police and to post suitable officers in key locations.[39] RB Shreekumar, an Indian Police Service officer who directed the Gujarat State Intelligence Bureau from April to September 2002, reported that the chief minister, senior bureaucrats, and police officers had instructed him to conceal information about government functionaries' direct and indirect complicity and to submit false reports about Muslim extremist leaders.[40] A study based on Shreekumar's affidavit charted the professional trajectories of police chiefs in twenty-nine police districts. It found that police were likely to be promoted in police districts in which anti-Muslim violence was extensive and demoted in police districts in which no Muslims were killed.[41]

[35] "2010 Human Rights Reports: India," *Bureau of Human Rights, Democracy and Labor*, April 8, 2011. Accessed June 26, 2014. http://www.state.gov/j/drl/rls/hrrpt/2010/sca/154480.htm.

[36] Interview with Maya Kodnani, Ahmedabad, November 22, 2008.

[37] KS Subramanian, *Political Violence and the Police in India* (New Delhi: Sage Publications, 2007), 269.

[38] Chenoy et al., "Gujarat Carnage 2002: A Report to the Nation," 21–3.

[39] Subramanian, *Political Violence and the Police in India*.

[40] "Gujarat Riot Muslims 'Eliminated,'" *BBC Online*, April 14, 2005. Accessed June 26, 2014. http://news.bbc.co.uk/2/hi/south_asia/4445107.stm.

[41] Biggs and Dhattiwala, "The Political Logic of Ethnic Violence," 503.

Opposition parties pressed the NDA government to invoke Article 356 of the Constitution, which enables the central government to intervene in states experiencing serious internal strife. LK Advani insisted that the state government was capable of restoring order on its own and supported early elections in Gujarat. Prime Minister Vajpayee informed the Rajya Sabha that the Centre had considered and rejected the option of dismissing the Narendra Modi government.

Former President of India Kocheril Raman Narayanan advised Prime Minister Vajpayee to send the army to Gujarat, "How many instances of the serial killings could have been avoided if the Army had resorted to shooting against rioters? The slaughter could have been avoided if the Army was given the freedom to stem the riots."[42] The army finally arrived in Ahmedabad on March 1, but the violence continued for more than thirty-six hours because the state government failed to utilize the armed forces or provide them with information regarding the locations of violence.

Whether Narendra Modi was directly responsible for the 2002 violence remains unresolved. His accusers claim that he allowed the VHP to bring the charred remains of the Hindu victims of the Godhra train fire to Ahmedabad, permitted it to organize a *bandh*, told police officers to allow Hindus to engage in "revenge killings," placed two cabinet officials in police control rooms to carry out his directives, penalized nonpartisan police officers and rewarded compliant ones, and appointed biased public prosecutors. Court deliberations about Modi's culpability have been inconclusive.

In 2009, the Supreme Court asked a Special Investigation Team (SIT) that it had formed the previous year to investigate a criminal complaint against Modi that Zakia Jaffrey (the widow of Ehsan Jaffrey) had filed in 2006 but the Gujarat police had ignored. The SIT concluded in February 2012 that there was not enough prosecutable evidence to bring charges against Modi. Critics note that the SIT failed to consider all the evidence and that there were discrepancies between the findings of the SIT and Raju Ramachandran, the chief court-appointed prosecutor. [43] Aside from the SIT's failings, it is unlikely that Modi would have been prosecuted because Indian Criminal Law requires proof that the accused carried out, or directly conspired to carry out, the crime. By contrast under International Criminal Law, a head of state who could have prevented a crime, but chose not to, can be found guilty.

[42] "Gujarat Riots a BJP Conspiracy: KR Narayanan," *The Hindu*, March 2, 2005; *Indian Express*, May 5, 2005; *Indian Express*, March 3, 2005. http://www.iptindia.org/wp-content/pdf/report/COMMUNALISM-IN-ORISSA.pdf. Coalition against Genocide, "Genocide in Gujarat," 3. March 2, 2005. Accessed June 26, 2014. http://www.coalitionagainstgenocide.org/reports/2005/cag.02mar2005.modi.pdf.

[43] Manoj Mitta, *The Fiction of Fact Finding: Modi and Godhra* (Delhi: Harper Collins India, 2015) and Gautam Appa, "How Many Clean Chits for Modi? Accessed November 25, 2014. http://blogs.lse.ac.uk/indiaatlse/files/2014/03/chit-e1395678970149.jpg.

Relief and Rehabilitation
After the 1969 violence, the government opened three camps that senior government officials regularly visited and subdivisional officers oversaw.[44] It made arrangements for food, medical facilities, and rehabilitation. Still, relief measures were inadequate, according to the Reddy Commission, not because of government unwillingness but because of the magnitude of the problem.[45]

By contrast, the state government continued to persecute Muslims in the aftermath of the 2002 violence. Narendra Modi delivered a speech on September 9, 2002, in which he asked:

> What should we do? Run relief camps for them? Do we want to open baby-producing centers? We are five and they are twenty-five. Gujarat has not been able to control its growing population and poor people have not been able to get money.
>
> There's a long queue of children who fix tire punctures. In order to progress, every child in Gujarat needs education, good manners and employment. That is the economy we need. For this, we need to teach a lesson to those who are increasing the population at an alarming rate.[46]

The government's relief, resettlement, and rehabilitation measures were seriously inadequate. Initially, the state government announced that the families of Hindus killed in Godhra would receive $4,094 whereas comparable Muslim families would receive half that amount. Following public opposition to this double standard, it decided to provide a single sum of US $2,047 to all victims. However, the government's disbursement of financial compensation was excrutiatingly slow; nor did it include everyone who was eligible or the amounts they were entitled to. State provision of medical and food supplies was inadequate and sanitary conditions were abysmal.[47] In February 2012, the Gujarat High Court issued a contempt notice to the Modi government for failing to compensate fifty-six people whose shops were destroyed during the violence. It also ordered the government to fund repairs of nearly 500 religious buildings.

The national government decided to pay each bereaved family $511, those who had been disabled and whose houses had been destroyed $1,023, and those whose dwellings had been damaged $209. It said it would bear the entire cost of rehabilitating orphans and widows. The Gujarat government reduced its compensation to $1,023 after the national government provided relief and ordered that all refugee camps should be closed down by October 30, 2002, leaving

[44] Reddy, Sarela, and Vakil, "Report: Inquiry into the Communal Disturbances at Ahmedabad and other Places in Gujarat," 203.

[45] Ibid., 222.

[46] "Modi's Anti-Minority Speech Aired," *The Tribune*, September 15, 2002. Accessed June 26, 2014. http://www.tribuneindia.com/2002/20020916/nation.htm#4.

[47] Smita Narula, "'We Have No Orders to Save You': State Participation and Complicity in Communal Violence in Gujarat," New York: Human Rights Watch Report, April 2002, Vol. 14, No. 3, 6.

200,000 people homeless. In 2006 it returned unspent funds to the national government.

In 2007, according to civil society activist Hanif Lakdawala, 5,000 Muslims were still living in makeshift camps with limited access to schools, urban amenities, and jobs.[48] A survey by the Aman Biradari NGO in 2006 identified eighty-one functioning relief colonies, all but six of which Muslim organizations had established.[49] By denying that these colonies existed, the Gujarat government refused to recognize their residents as internally displaced persons. According to civil society activist Gagan Sethi, this designation would have provided them rights and protection under both human rights and international humanitarian law and entitled them to UN assistance.[50]

I visited two relief colonies in 2008. One was in Citizens Nagar, Ahmedabad, where Muslim organizations, Jan Vikas, and Action Aid had provided facilities to 116 families. The colony adjoined a rough, unpaved road near a paint factory that emitted toxic fumes and polluted the water. Garbage and sewage that was dumped there from Ahmedabad created a mountain of solid waste. The stench was overwhelming. There were no street lights, sewage services, or drinking water facilities in the neighborhood.

I spoke to a group of women who had previously spent six months in the Shah-e-Alam camp. They were afraid to return to their villages and unable to afford the cost of rebuilding their homes that had been destroyed in 2002. One of them said that she had filed an FIR against men in the village and they had threatened to kill her if she returned. Another woman said that Hindus had taken over the family land. Taunted and harassed in the village, she and her family had returned to Ahmedabad.

These women's lives were extremely precarious because of their lack of income, assets, and employment. They said that the government had provided them compensation for death and injuries to family members but not for their material losses. Although they didn't have title deeds or leases to their temporary homes, the police hounded them to pay house taxes. Some of their male family members traveled several hours each day to find work as casual laborers, often unsuccessfully. Hindus who had employed them in the past were reluctant to do so. A few of the men who owned their own businesses – *paan* stalls, rickshaws, and pushcarts that sold vegetables – had lost their equipment and thus their incomes. Several of the women who had worked in the past, doing tailoring and laundry, were too far from their employers to keep these jobs. Food was expensive because these women didn't have ration cards that provide staples to low-income families at subsidized rates.

---

[48] Interview with Hanif Lakdawala, Ahmedabad, January 9, 2007.
[49] Harsh Mander, "Inside Gujarat's Relief Colonies: Surviving State Hostility and Denial," *Economic and Political Weekly*, December 23–9, 2006, Vol. 41, No. 51. Accessed June 26, 2014. http://www.epw.in/system/files/pdf/2006_41/51/Inside_Gujarats_Relief_Colonies.pdf.
[50] Interview with Gagan Sethi, Ahmedabad, January 14, 2007.

The women said that their children often got sick because of the filth and pollution. They walked long distances to get pails of clean drinking water. They discouraged their children from drinking even boiled water that was available locally so the children became dehydrated. There were no medical facilities in the area. The school had closed so the children were on the streets all day. Some of the women worried that the older children would become involved in criminal activities and that their sons might become "terrorists." The children could see that their parents were denied citizenship rights, including ID cards that enabled them to vote. Families were subjected to degrading and humiliating conditions on a daily basis.

I also visited a group of Muslim refugees in Siyasat Nagar, near Chandola Lake, where the Jamaat had constructed 172 homes. The families in Siyasat Nagar were slightly better off than those in Citizens Nagar. They had ration cards, valid voter IDs, and electricity connections. However, although they had proof that they were long-time residents of Gujarat, the police constantly harassed them and claimed that they were illegal immigrants from Bangladesh. They were also among the first to be interrogated when crimes occurred in Ahmedabad. Ignoring a Supreme Court ruling that residents should be forewarned of demolitions, the Ahmedabad Municipal Corporation ordered the police to demolish 172 houses, a *madrasa*, and a school in Siyasat Nagar. The administration claimed that it had demolished the colony to create a rapid bus transit project through the area although it had approved NGO plans to provide housing for Muslims there. The residents, having no place to go, camped out on the streets.

To summarize, 1969 and 2002 mark the starting and end points on a continuum. The RSS and its affiliates played leading roles on both occasions, their motivations were in part electoral, and the press provoked further violence. However, the violence was far more extensive and brutal in 2002 than in 1969. Some state officials were complicit and the state government continued to victimize Muslims after 2002 through institutional means. Although the 2002 violence may have been exceptional, it precipitated quotidian violence long after the killings had ceased.

Gujarat in Comparison

The BJP has at different times been extremely powerful in both UP and Gujarat, as a party, state government, and participant in social movements. Both UP and Gujarat are important to the BJP's national ambitions, UP because of its historic importance to the Congress Party and Gujarat as a laboratory for Hindu nationalism. Indeed, one might argue that the BJP sought to make Gujarat what UP once represented to the Congress Party. The BJP spokesperson for Gujarat, IK Jadeja, said proudly:

What happens in Gujarat happens in the rest of the country ten to fifteen years later. The anti-Congress wave began in Gujarat and then spread to the rest of the country. Gujarat developed a two-party system before the rest of the country. Gujarat is also leading the way in development.[51]

However, there are striking differences in the BJP's electoral trajectory in the two states. In UP, the BJP received 30–33 percent of the vote in the 1991, 1993, and 1996 Assembly elections; by 2002, it received only 20 percent of the vote and its share of the vote has since declined even further. By contrast, in Gujarat, the BJP's performance steadily improved, from 27 percent of the vote in 1990 to 50 percent in 2002, to 49 percent in 2007 and 48 percent in 2012 (see Figure 5.1). The BJP has generally relied on multiparty coalitions to govern UP, whereas it has ruled Gujarat alone but for a few months, from March to October 1990. Whereas BJP governments have been constrained by their coalition partners in UP, they have had a free hand in formulating policies and making political appointments in Gujarat.

Differences in the character of political parties and in party-movement alliances in the two states partly explain why anti-minority violence has been greater in Gujarat than in UP. A strong socialist movement in UP laid the foundations for the OBC-led SP and a *dalit* movement that presaged the BSP's emergence. By contrast, the absence of lower-caste and leftist movements and the strength of upper-caste movements in Gujarat enabled the BJP to create a coalition of upper and middle castes. Whereas in Gujarat the BJP consolidated the support of upper and middle castes in the mid-1980s, in UP it only sought to do so in the early 1990s by conjoining support for Mandir with opposition to Mandal.

The BJP is stronger, opposition parties are weaker, and there are fewer caste and factional divisions within the BJP in Gujarat than in UP. Whereas lower-caste parties have challenged and influenced the BJP in UP, the only party that has opposed the BJP in Gujarat, the Congress Party, has become its pale reflection. Muslims have become increasingly politically active in UP but not in Gujarat. Lower-caste parties have sought greater Muslim support in UP, than Congress and the BJP have in Gujarat. Leftist parties and movements have been weak in Gujarat historically. The communists have never received more than 1 percent of the vote. The three socialist parties – the Samyukta Socialist Party, Socialist Party, and Praja Socialist Party – secured 8 percent of the vote in the first two elections but declined thereafter as their members joined other political parties. There have been few *adivasi* and *dalit* struggles protesting discrimination and demanding land rights, forest resources, and higher wages. The upper and middle castes have led the major social movements: the

---

[51] Interview with IK Jadeja, Ahmedabad, January 11, 2007.

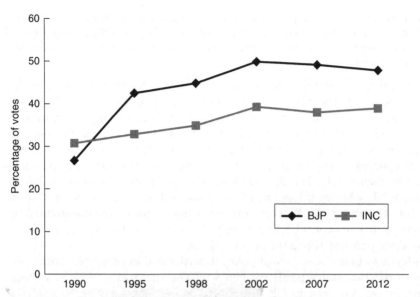

FIGURE 5.1. Gujarat Legislative Assembly Election Results.
Source: Election Commission of India, *Statistical Report on the General Election, 1990–2012 to the Legislative Assembly of Gujarat,* New Delhi: Election Commission of India. Assessed July 21, 2014. at: http://eci.nic.in/eci_main/StatisticalReports/SE_1990/StatRep_GJ_90.pdf
http://eci.nic.in/eci_main/StatisticalReports/SE_1995/StatisticalReport-GUJ95.pdf
http://eci.nic.in/eci_main/StatisticalReports/SE_1998/StatisticalReport-GUJ98.pdf
http://eci.nic.in/eci_main/StatisticalReports/SE_2002/StatReport_GUJ2002.pdf
http://eci.nic.in/eci_main/StatisticalReports/SE_2007/StatReport_DEC_2007_GUJARAT_after_IC.pdf
http://eci.nic.in/eci_main/StatisticalReports/SE_2012/Reports_Index%20Card_ECIApplication_GujaratState_CEO.pdf
Compiled by author, permissions not necessary.

Mahagujarat movement for the creation of Gujarat, Nav Nirman movement, anti-reservation protests, and Ayodhya movement.

The BJP's growth in Gujarat rests on the combined support of the upper and middle castes as well as segments of the lower castes. As the 1931 census and subsequent estimates suggest, Gujarat has a relatively small proportion of upper castes and a significant number of middle castes (the Patidars). At the lower end of the caste hierarchy, it has a relatively small proportion of *dalits* and a large proportion of tribals.

Whereas in UP, OBCs and *dalits* have asserted their own caste identities and interests, in Gujarat, the middle, backward, and lower castes have sought upward mobility through Sanskritization, in other words claiming upper-caste status. Kolis have identified with Kshatriyas, Patidars, who were once considered Shudras, with Brahmins and Vanias, and *dalits* and *adivasis* with caste Hindus.[52] Religious groups like the Swaminarayan sect facilitated this process by including middle, backward, and upper-caste members. The BJP's approach was assimilationist. It actively recruited the Patidars in the 1970s and *dalits* and *adivasis* from the 1980s on. It offered Patidars, who evolved from sharecroppers into landowners after the land reforms, the status and power that they lacked and *dalits* and tribals recognition and material rewards. The early, rapid development of capitalism in Gujarat created a Jan Sangh constituency of middle-class Patidars.

Hindu nationalists acquired increased support from the upper castes, the middle castes, rich peasants, and farmers through their participation in the Nav Nirman anticorruption movement, and two large protests against reservations.[53] They initiated *bandhs* against traders suspected of hoarding food in the Saurashtra region. They gained urban middle-class support in Rajkot, Ahmedabad, and Vadodara by organizing agitations against rising prices and by subsequently opposing the Congress government's State of Emergency (1975–7).[54]

The alliance between the Patidars and the BJP became stronger after the Congress Party returned to power in 1980 under Chief Minister Solanki, who created a coalition that he termed KHAM – Kshatriyas, Harijans, Adivasis, and Muslims. Patidars, whom KHAM excluded, feared losing power. Unlike the Janata Party and the SP in UP, the Gujarat Congress Party lacked deep roots among the lower castes. Solanki did not heed Achyut Yagnik's warning that his strategy made him susceptible to right-wing opposition.[55] The upper castes in Ahmedabad organized another major anti-reservation protest in 1985 when Solanki sought to increase reserved quotas. Many incidents of anti-Muslim violence took place when the BJP called for a statewide *bandh* against Solanki in March 1985. Although the Solanki government withdrew its proposal to increase reservations, the BJP and the ABVP continued the agitation until Solanki resigned on July 6, 1985.[56]

---

[52] Kanbis Sanskritized by changing their caste identity to Patidars. (The name is derived from *patis*, holders of parcels of land.) Patidars adopted the surname Patel (traditionally used to refer to village headmen) and adopted upper-caste Hindu ritual practices. Ghanshyam Shah, "The BJP and Backward Castes in Gujarat," *South Asia Bulletin*, 1994, Vol. 14, no. 4, 296. Also see David Pockock, *Kanbi and Patidar: A Study of the Patidar Community of Gujarat* (London: Oxford University Press, 1972).

[53] Ghanshyam Shah, "The 1975 Gujarat Assembly Election in India," *Asian Survey*, March 1976, Vol. 16, no. 3, 271.

[54] Suchitra Sheth and Achyut Yagnik, *Shaping of Modern Gujarat: Plurality, Hindutva and Beyond* (New Delhi: Penguin Books, 2005), 254.

[55] Interview with Achyut Yagnik, Ahmedabad, November 22, 2008.

[56] Howard Spodek, "From Gandhi to Violence: Ahmedabad's 1985 Riots in Historical Perspective," *Modern Asian Studies*, 1989, Vol. 23, no. 4, 767–8.

The BJP acquired new bases of support in the rural areas. The Sangh Parivar's agrarian affiliate, the BKS, launched a rural agitation in Gujarat for relaxing land laws, abolishing minimum wages, debt relief, higher floor prices for crops, better credit facilities, and electrical power at subsidized prices.[57] Rich farmers were at the forefront and lower-caste, middle, and marginal farmers supported the movement.[58]

The Sangh Parivar actively mobilized support for the Ayodhya campaign in both states but with greater dividends in Gujarat than in UP. Advani's *rath yatra* started in Gujarat and planned to end in UP in September–October 1990. The movement generated anti-Muslim violence in both states, in Gujarat during a *yatra* in 1986, a *Ram-janki shobha yatra* in 1987, the *Ram shila puja* in 1989, and *rath yatra* in 1990. The Congress-led national government dismissed the BJP government in UP after the destruction of the *babri masjid*, which contributed to its subsequent electoral reversals. By contrast, the BJP was not in office in Gujarat during the Ayodhya movement and the Surat violence occurred after the destruction of the *babri masjid*. The BJP came to power in 1995 and remained in office thereafter.

The 1990s witnessed the emergence of a multiparty system in UP and a two-party system in Gujarat. Moreover, the parties that emerged in UP in the 1990s were founded on lower-caste support. In Gujarat, the Janata Dal-BJP, Janata Dal (Gujarat)-Congress, and Congress held office at different times between 1990 to 1995. However, third parties, which had always been weak in Gujarat, became even weaker after 1995. The Janata Dal included the BJP in a coalition government headed by Chimanbhai Patel in 1990. One faction of the Janata Dal that rechristened itself the Janata Dal-Gujarat recognized the BJP's growing power and merged into the Congress Party. The Janata Dal was decimated in the elections.

In both UP and Gujarat, the party high command turned against former chief ministers who left or were expelled and formed breakaway parties of their own (Keshubhai Patel and Shankersinh Vaghela in Gujarat and Kalyan Singh in UP). In both cases, militant activists accused the dominant party leadership of having reneged on its ideological commitments. However, unlike UP, the BJP in Gujarat remained highly cohesive, centralized, and ideologically committed. The BJP in both UP and Gujarat adopted a more militant posture after 2002 to counteract their electoral setbacks, restore party unity, and placate the RSS and VHP. This paid off electorally in Gujarat but not in UP.

In UP, Muslims became increasingly politically active in the aftermath of the destruction of the *babri masjid*. By contrast, in Gujarat, Muslims (9 percent of the state's population) lack an effective political voice. Muslim organizations,

[57] Nikita Sud, *Liberalization, Nationalism and the State in India* (New Delhi: Oxford University Press, 2012), 147.
[58] Harish Khare, "Unending Struggle of Gujarat's Political Soul," *Seminar*, October 1998, No. 470, 17–23.

like the Muslim League and the Majlis, have always been weak. Muslims have been underrepresented in *panchayats*, cooperatives, government schemes, and NGOs. Both Congress and the BJP have nominated few Muslims to run for political office so their representation in the Legislative Assembly is extremely low. The BJP did not nominate a single Muslim to run for the Legislative Assembly elections in 2012 or for the parliamentary elections in Gujarat in 2014.[59]

To summarize, in UP the Ayodhya movement enabled the BJP to leapfrog to success but it experienced a rapid decline thereafter. Caste consciousness and conflicts resulted in deep-rooted factionalism within the BJP and undermined its electoral success. By contrast, the BJP in Gujarat won over the upper, middle, and lower castes and tribals. Strong *dalit* movements and parties that undermined the BJP's success in UP were absent in Gujarat. Caste identities and conflicts damaged the internal workings of the BJP as well as its standing relative to other parties in UP. By contrast, in Gujarat, upper-caste BJP members did not express caste hostility toward Modi and Modi did not highlight ~~his~~ OBC identity.

Party-Movement Tensions

The BJP in Gujarat was deeply factionalized until 2002. After that, Narendra Modi centralized power within the party and the state, thereby reducing party factionalism but provoking a new set of tensions within the Sangh Parivar. Dissident members of the RSS, BJP, and VHP claimed that the party and government had reneged on their Hindu nationalist commitments and sold out to big business. Thus, even in Gujarat, where the BJP has close ties to the RSS and the VHP, party-movement relations were strained. Ironically, Modi's strong leadership was responsible both for discontent within the Sangh Parivar and for party and government strength. The BJP was able to subdue internal opposition because it was organizationally strong, ideologically committed, and intertwined with the state. Modi removed rebels from the BJP and the parties they have formed have been relatively ineffective. The RSS has played a key role in enabling the BJP to forge strong ties to local administrators and networks of civil society organizations.

From 1995 to 2002 three different chief ministers presided over BJP governments: Keshubai Patel (March 1995 to October 1995), Sureshchandra Mehta (October 1995 to September 1996), and Narendra Modi (2001–14). Following President's rule (September 1996 to October 1996) and two elections, the BJP returned to power with Keshubhai Patel as chief minister in March 1998. It replaced Keshubhai Patel with Narendra Modi after the BJP's defeat in the

[59] "Election Results 2014 – West: Congress Swept into Arabian Sea as BJP Washes 4 States in Saffron," *Indian Express*, May 16, 2014. Accessed July 21, 2014. http://indianexpress.com/article/india/politics/live-election-results-2014-gujarat-rajasthan-maharashtra-goa/.

by-elections in October 2001. The 2002 violence enabled the BJP to regain electoral strength and patch up rifts within the party. The frequent rotation of BJP chief ministers underscores the extent of factionalism within the Gujarat BJP. It also demonstrates extensive involvement by RSS and national BJP leaders in backing Patel against Vaghela, replacing Patel with Mehta, and replacing Patel, who resisted vehemently, with Modi.

Modi exerted control over a lean administration. The Cabinet comprised just eleven ministers of state and seven cabinet ministers who shared over thirty-seven portfolios. Modi retained eight portfolios: Home, Industry, General Administration, Climate Change, Ports, Information and Broadcasting, Narmada, and Kalpasar. Three ministers in the administration, Anandiben Patel, Saurabh Patel, and Nitin Patel, were Modi loyalists.[60] Modi exercised control over the Finance Ministry by virtue of his close ties to Nitin Patel.

The Legislative Assembly's power diminished after 2002. Modi had a reputation for discouraging debate on the Assembly floor. According to government records, after Modi became chief minister in October 2001, the State Assembly only met for 327 days during its entire term, which was less often than any Assembly that had lasted a full term since Gujarat was formed in 1960.[61] The Assembly met an average of forty-nine days a year under Keshubhai Patel and just thirty days a year under Narendra Modi.

Modi's relations with important Sangh Parivar leaders, including Keshubhai Patel, Gordhan Zadaphia, Suresh Mehta, AK Patel, Kashiram Rana, Sanjay Joshi, and Haren Pandya, were tense.[62] Some BJP leaders, who believed that Modi had sidelined them, vociferously opposed him. Sixty-two BJP MLAs blamed the BJP's poor performance in the Lok Sabha in 2004 on Modi's dictatorial style, and unsuccessfully appealed to the national BJP to replace him.[63] Two previous chief ministers and one minister resigned from the BJP to form their own parties. After the BJP expelled Vaghela in September 1995 he formed the Rashtriya Janata Party with the support of forty-seven BJP MLAs. After being forced out, Zadaphia formed the Mahagujarat Janata Party in 2008, which he later merged into the Gujarat Parivartan Party (GPP) that

---

[60] Anandiben Patel became chief minister in 2014 after Modi was elected prime minister; the cabinet ministers remained the same with one new addition, Jaydrathsingh Parmar.

[61] Sumit Khanna, "No. 1 CM Modi has Lowest Average Assembly Sittings," July 19, 2012. Accessed June 30, 2014. http://www.dnaindia.com/india/1717128/report-no-1-cm-modi-has-the-lowest-average-assembly-sittings.

[62] Haren Pandya was murdered in Ahmedabad in 2003 while serving as home minister. His wife contends that the Gujarat government murdered him. http://indiatoday.intoday.in/story/jagruti-haren-pandyas-wife-to-contest-gujarat-polls-keshubhai-patel-gujarat-parivartan-party/1/235242.html.

[63] Anosh Malekar, "The War Within: Keshubhai Patel Gathers Ranks to Take on Narendra Modi," *Caravan*, September 1, 2012. Accessed July 21, 2014. http://www.caravanmagazine.in/perspectives/war-within.

Keshubhai Patel formed in 2012. Zadaphia claimed that Modi's centralization of power was undermining the party.

> The BJP is withering away as an organization. The party has become a slave to the government. Party workers are like bonded laborers. Keshubai was different. He consulted with all ministers and senior party members before arriving at a decision.[64]

Several RSS and BJP leaders shared Zadaphia's views. Veteran RSS leader Pravin Maniar stated, "In 2000, on the insistence of RSS top brass, I brought in Narendra Modi as chief minister. But during his tenure, he has finished all saffron organizations, and now the time has come to oust him from the post."[65] An article in the RSS *Panchjanya* stated that Modi needed to "relook at his style of functioning and organization capabilities." It urged the BJP not to decide hastily on Modi as its candidate for prime minister in the 2014 elections. An editorial in the BJP magazine *Kamal Sandesh*, in a barely veiled critique of Modi, stated that leaders should be faithful to the RSS and BJP tradition of placing individuals at the service of the party. "The system is maintained by those who function in the party. Party doesn't function on the basis of any individual's contribution alone but on the basis of everyone's contribution."[66] These writers were especially angered by Modi's removing Sanjay Joshi, RSS *pracharak* and BJP general secretary in Gujarat, from all posts in 2005. Six years later, the national BJP made Joshi BJP coordinator for the UP Assembly elections and appointed him to the national executive. However at Modi's behest, the national party demanded Joshi's resignation in June 2012.[67] LK Advani later resigned from all posts in the BJP in opposition to Modi's chairmanship of the BJP election committee.[68]

Movement activists challenged the BJP government's neoliberal policies. The GPP and BKS were angered by the government's appropriation of agricultural land to create Special Economic Zones, inattention to the plight

---

[64] Interview with Gordhan Zadaphia, Ahmedabad, November 25, 2008.
[65] Malekar, "The War Within."
[66] P. Jha, "Come Together and Unite to Build a Strong Organisation," *Kamal Sandesh*, June 1, 2012. Accessed June 30, 2014. http://www.bjp.org/images/kamal_sandesh/ks_e_june_1_15_2012.pdf.
[67] "Who Is Sanjay Joshi," *Hindustan Times*, June 8, 2012. Accessed July 21, 2014. http://www.hindustantimes.com/india-news/newdelhi/who-is-sanjay-joshi/article1-867841.aspx."Narendra Modi wins again, Sanjay Joshi quits BJP, RSS steps in," *IBN Live*, June 8, 2012. Accessed July 21, 2014. http://ibnlive.in.com/news/narendra-modi-wins-again-sanjay-joshi-quits-bjp-rss-steps-in/265010-37-64.html
[68] "BJP Patriarch LK Advani Resigns after Narendra Modi Made Poll Chief," *The Indian Express*, June 10, 2013. Accessed July 21, 2014. http://archive.indianexpress.com/news/bjp-patriarch-l-k-advani-resigns-after-narendra-modi-made-poll-chief/1127265/."LK Advani resigns from all positions in BJP," *Times of India*, June 10, 2013. http://timesofindia.indiatimes.com/india/LK-Advani-resigns-from-all-positions-in-BJP/articleshow/20519578.cms."Rift in BJP wide open after Advani's resignation from party posts," *Hindustan Times*, June 10, 2013. Accessed July 21, 2014. http://www.hindustantimes.com/india-news/newdelhi/rift-in-bjp-wide-open-after-advani-s-resignation-from-party-posts/article1-1073929.aspx

of poor farmers, and failure to adequately invest in rural development.[69] The BKS and the Gujarat Khedut Sangharsh Samiti campaigned against the BJP in the 2004 parliamentary elections.[70] Zadaphia criticized the government for courting large businesses like Tata to build the Nano car, while suppressing trade union activity and failing to create jobs for unemployed local youth. He also claimed that Modi had rescinded his Hindu nationalist commitments.

> Modi used to be committed to protecting Hindus. Now that Modi has ambitions to take power in Delhi, he is trying to present himself as a secular leader.... We are angry that the government has not taken stronger action against *jihadis*. Modi destroyed temples in Maninagar, Ahmedabad and Surat. We organized *dharnas* to demand that the government stop this. Modi claimed he had but actually he has continued the demolitions.[71]

An RSS member in Ahmedabad openly criticized Modi, in part because he had violated Gujarat's prohibition of alcohol.

Modi won the elections in 2002 because of all the work we did to get him elected. But over the last five years he has ignored the people who helped get him elected. He has stopped talking to us. He has allowed the police to destroy temples to build bigger roads. He has allowed alcohol in SEZs. He told the police to raid Swaminarayan temples because they hadn't paid their electricity bills. Modi used us to gain power but he doesn't need us anymore.

Some BJP officials stoked Hindu-Muslim tensions against their government's wishes. In Vadodara, Mayor Sunil Solanki and municipal corporation members claimed that a 200-year-old *dargah* was obstructing the flow of traffic. Muslim community members met with them and agreed that the structure surrounding the *dargah* that protruded onto the road should be demolished but wanted to preserve the *mazar*, the most sacred part of the *dargah*. Although Solanki assured Muslims that they could arrive at an agreement, he ordered the police to demolish the *dargah* while negotiations were under way on May 1, 2006. Violence broke out in which six people (four Muslims and two Hindus) were killed and twenty-five people were seriously injured.[72]

The Bajrang Dal sought to invoke connections to Ayodhya by claiming that the *dargah* was a mini *babri masjid* although in fact both Hindus and Muslims visit *dargahs*. Nalin Bhatt, twice minister in BJP governments in Gujarat and a party general secretary, was at the site of the demolition and responsible for

---

[69] "Days after Modi, Keshubhai also Courts RSS," *Times of India*, October 24, 2012. Accessed June 30, 2014. http://articles.timesofindia.indiatimes.com/2012-10-24/india/34707637_1_gujarat-parivartan-party-keshubhai-patel-rss-worker.

[70] Sud, *Liberalization, Hindu Nationalism and the State in India*, 36.

[71] Interview with Gordhan Zadaphia, Ahmedabad, November 25, 2008.

[72] "Vadodara Flares up as Old Dargah Demolished, 4 Die," *The Indian Express*, May 2, 2006. Accessed June 30, 2014. http://archive.indianexpress.com/news/vadodara-flares-up-as-old-dargah-demolished-4-die/3621/.

planning it. Bhatt was under Supreme Court investigation for his role in the 2002 violence. When I interviewed him four months after the BJP had expelled him from the party in September 2006, he stated that the city government had demolished the *dargah* because it was angered that the state government was appeasing Muslims and forfeiting Hindu interests. He said, "BJP claims to be a party with a difference. But today it's no different than Congress. It is betraying Hindus. We wanted to show that we are still committed to the people who elected us."[73] NV Patel, Vadodara's party chief and vice president of the state-level BJP, also fully defended the city government's decision to demolish the *dargah*. Indeed, he claimed that ISI agents had instigated local Muslims to protest.[74] Echoing the BJP's refusal to describe the *babri masjid* as a mosque, he refused to call the *dargah* anything but a grave in the middle of the road. In contrast to his actions in 2002, Modi toured the violence-hit areas of Vadodara and appealed to people to maintain calm.[75] The state government called in the army on May 3.

The VHP became increasingly hostile to the BJP, although there were divisions in its ranks. Ashok Singhal differed with Modi at times but largely supported him. By contrast, Praveen Togadia was angry that Modi dropped Gordhan Zadaphia from the Council of Ministers, booked Gujarat VHP joint secretary Ashwin Patel for sedition after the police suspected that he was responsible for setting off bomb explosions in 2008, destroyed unauthorized temples, and evicted the BKS from government quarters after it launched a farmers' agitation.[76]

VHP activists had multiple grievances against the BJP government. In 2007, the BJP decided not to re-nominate several VHP members who had run for the 2002 Assembly elections. They included VHP joint secretary Niraj Jain, and, among sitting MLAs, secretary Ramila Desai, organizing secretary Ramesh Mistry, and Bajrang Dal national president Haresh Bhatt, who was elected from Godhra. Under pressure from the Supreme Court, the Modi government reopened cases against VHP and Bajrang Dal workers who had participated in the 2002 violence. The Gujarat government also investigated the VHP's powerful ally, Asaram Bapu, and two of his associates for attempting to murder a man who had testified against him before the government-appointed DK Trivedi Commission in December 2009. A group of religious leaders formed the Hindu Jagran Manch to protest Modi's failure to protect *sadhus* and *mahants*.[77]

[73] Interview with Nalin Bhatt, Vadodara, January 12, 2007.
[74] Interview with NV Patel, Vadodara, January 12, 2007.
[75] Vinay Kumar, "Army Deployed in Vadodara," *The Hindu*, May 4, 2006. Accessed June 30, 2014. http://www.thehindu.com/todays-paper/army-deployed-in-vadodara/article3128471.ece.
[76] Ajay Umat, "Once Hindutva Twins, Narendra Modi and Praveen Togadia no Longer Conjoined," *The Times of India*, February 9, 2014. Accessed June 30, 2014. http://articles.timesofindia.india times.com/2013-02-09/india/37007205_1_ashwin-patel-hedgewar-bhavan-maninagar.
[77] *Gujarat Samachar*, October 20, 2007, 15.

The VHP retaliated during BJP election campaigns. The government alleged that the VHP had distributed anti-BJP pamphlets a few days before the municipal council elections in 2005 and ordered the police to search the VHP office in Ahmedabad for incriminating material. Abiding by directives from Praveen Togadia rather than Ashok Singhal, the VHP did not campaign for Modi in the 2007 Legislative Assembly elections.[78] Uma Bharati's Bharatiya Janshakti Party, another splinter group from the BJP, joined VHP members in campaigning against Modi. Twenty-four VHP-affiliated *sadhus* in Vadodara organized a demonstration where they shouted slogans like "Death to Narendra Modi" and carried placards that read, "Who is Narendra Modi? Murderer of forty-eight *Pujaris*" (Hindu temple priests); "Who is Narendra Modi? Killer of One lakh [one hundred thousand] *gau mata*" (cows); "Who Is Narendra Modi? Murderer of four hundred *Sadhus*."[79] VHP members opposed Modi again in the 2012 elections. They warned tribal voters that the BJP was distributing unauthorized leaflets in the VHP's name and they should not be swayed by its appeals.[80]

And yet the BJP regained power in 2007 and 2012. Forty-four percent of Gujarat's population is urban and the BJP won an impressive 60 percent of the urban vote in the 2012 elections. Dissident parties performed poorly. The GPP won only two seats and 3.6 percent of the vote in the 2012 Legislative Assembly elections. Its claim that the BJP government discriminated against Patels was not electorally popular. Modi made eight Patels (four Kadva Patels and four Leuva Patels) government ministers. It appointed RC Faldu, a Leuva Patel, to serve a second term as president of the Gujarat BJP. Before that Parshottam Rupala, a Kadva Patel, served as party president.[81] The BJP also made gains among two large OBC communities, the Kshatriyas and Kolis, in the 2012 elections.[82]

---

[78] Radhika Radaseshan, "Sangh not for Modi, Cadres Free to Be," *The Telegraph*, December 4, 2007. Accessed June 30, 2014. http://www.telegraphindia.com:80/1071204/asp/nation/story_8625939.asp.

[79] *Gujarat Samachar*, Vadodara edition, December 10, 2007, 16, and on Togadia's opposition to Modi, "VHP not to Support Modi in Elections," *The Hindu*, August 6, 2007. Accessed June 30, 2014. http://www.hindu.com/2007/08/06/stories/2007080660471400.htm, and on Singhal's support for Modi, see "Shot in the Arm for Modi as VHP Declares 'Full Support,' " *The Indian Express*, November 10, 2012. Accessed June 30, 2014. http://newindianexpress.com/nation/article1335056.ece.

[80] Manas Dasgupta, "BJP Tries to Reap Harvest of VHP Hard Work in Tribal Areas," *The Tribune*, December 12, 2012. Accessed June 30, 2014. http://www.tribuneindia.com/2012/20121213/nation.htm#2.

[81] Class and rural-urban differences have created tensions within the Patel community. The Leuva Patels oppose Modi but the Kadva Patels do not. While the Leuva Patels' influence is rural, Kadva Patels' influence is urban.

[82] Yogendra Yadav, "Narendra Modi Is Popular, but Is He Democratic?" *The Economic Times*, December 21, 2012. Accessed June 30, 2014. http://articles.economictimes.indiatimes.com/2012-12-21/ news/35953538_1_gujarat-verdict-fair-election-narendra-modi.

The BJP skillfully combined appeals to globalization, Hindu nationalism and Gujarati subnationalism. It won accolades from large industrialists and the urban middle classes for Gujarat's economic growth. A 2012 election survey found that a majority of the electorate, including those who voted for Congress, credited the BJP government for Gujarat's development. Gujarat has long been an industrialized state and growth rates under the Modi government were not significantly higher than they were in the prior two decades. Although Gujarat is widely believed to attract more foreign direct investment than any other state, it ranked sixth on this measure in 2011, far below the leading state of Maharashtra.[83] Furthermore, Gujarat's human development indicators are relatively poor.[84]

The BJP government in Gujarat has formally distanced itself from the VHP, but some of its own officials share the VHP's views. VHP activists aptly note that the government has reigned them in and complied with the Supreme Court and other national government agencies that have been investigating those who were charged with inciting violence. As a result, the state government has become far more powerful than the party or the movement.

Modi has yet to express regret or remorse for the 2002 violence against Muslims. In a 2013 interview, he commented,

If someone else is driving a car and we're sitting behind, even then if a puppy comes under the wheel, will it be painful or not? Of course it is. If I'm a chief minister or not, I'm a human being. If something bad happens anywhere, it is natural to be sad.

Modi's comment belies his consistent refusal to acknowledge the government's responsibility for the violence. His comment also reveals a degrading view of Muslims. Street dogs, to which he compared Muslims, are reviled in India.[85] The government's attitude has perpetuated the Hindu-Muslim divide. The CSDS survey showed that fewer people wanted to see the guilty punished in 2012 than a decade earlier. At the same time, a majority of those surveyed were more pessimistic about the likelihood of "communal peace" than five years earlier.[86]

[83] Vinod Jose, "The Emperor Uncrowned: The Rise of Narendra Modi," *Caravan*, March 1, 2012. Accessed November 25, 2014. http://caravanmagazine.in/reportage/emperor-uncrowned.

[84] See, for example, Aseema Sinha, *The Regional Roots of Developmental Politics in India: A Divided Leviathan* (Indiana: Indiana University Press, 2005); Atul Kohli, *Poverty amid Plenty in the New India* (Cambridge, UK: Cambridge University Press, 2012); and Nikita Sud, "Constructing and Contesting an Ethno-Religious Gujarati-Hindu Identity through Development Programmes in an Indian State," *Oxford Development Studies*, 2007, Vol. 35, no. 2, 131–48.

[85] Shruthi Gottipati and Annie Banerjee, "Modi's 'Puppy' Remark Triggers New Controversy over 2002 Riots," *Reuters*, July 12, 2013. Accessed June 30, 2014. http://in.reuters.com/article/2013/07/12/narendra-modi-puppy-reuters-interview-idINDEE96B08S20130712.

[86] "Gujarat Assembly Election 2012: Pre-poll Survey by Lokniti," *Center for Studies in Developing Societies Poll*. Accessed July 21, 2014. http://www.lokniti.org/pdfs_dataunit/Questionairs/gujarat-prepoll-2012-survey-findings.pdf.

The BJP government's power also rests on two other axes. The first is the close links between the state government, the local government, the national BJP, and transnational groups. The RSS supported Modi against his rivals within the Gujarat BJP prior to both the 2007 and 2012 elections. It recognized that Modi was the most promising BJP candidate for reelection in Gujarat and for prime minister. Modi has enormous support among the influential Gujarati diasporic community. The BJP regularly wins elections to local government bodies, from municipal corporations to district, block, and village *panchayats*. From 2004 to 2012, the BJP consistently polled more than 50 percent of the vote in municipal corporation and district *panchayat* elections.

The second axis is the link between the state government and a powerful network of RSS-affiliated civil society organizations, which predate the 2002 violence. The RSS began making inroads into the state before Modi became chief minister. In January 2000, the BJP Gujarat government, with the NDA government's support, removed a ban on state government employees participating in the RSS and VHP. It provided the RSS with free electricity, water, and land. From 1999 on, the RSS installed the chairman of the state public service commission, and the vice-chancellor of Gujarat University. It also pressured the BJP government to appoint RSS-affiliated Arun Oza senior government pleader in the Ahmedabad High Court, to represent the government in all legal matters. Oza's appointment established the Sangh Parivar's supremacy over political affairs in Gujarat.

To summarize, the factionalized Gujarat BJP (1995–2002) became highly unified once Modi became chief minister. Although Modi was considered authoritarian, he captured the support of the urban middle classes through his pro-business policies without abdicating his commitment to Gujarati identity and Hindu nationalism. However, the BJP's strength does not simply rest on Modi's leadership qualities. The BJP has forged vertical ties to the national party and to local networks of civil society organizations and state administrators. The RSS is a beneficiary of linkages both to the national government and to the grassroots level.

NGOs and Civil Society Associations

There has been a vigorous debate about the ability of NGOs – alternately described as social action, voluntary, and nonparty groups – to effect social change.[87] Many scholars saw NGOs as promising alternatives to leftist parties that had ignored the problems of *dalits*, tribals, women, and other marginalized

[87] NGOs are strong in Gujarat. According to official records, Gujarat had 761 registered NGOs in 2002. Ghyanshyam Shah, "Civil Society and the Poor at an Impasse," (unpublished report prepared for the Center for the Study of Developing Societies, Delhi), 57. An independent estimate identifies 550 NGOs in Gujarat and 175 in Ahmedabad. TK Oommen, *Reconciliation in Post Godhra Gujarat: Role of Civil Society* (New Delhi: Pearson Longman, an imprint of Pearson Education, 2008).

groups.[88] However, by the 1980s, observers began to question NGOs' transformative potential. They feared that the state (the Janata government and later the Congress government) was co-opting NGOs by engaging them in development work. They worried that NGOs had become donor dependent and driven. Prakash Karat, general secretary of the CPM, made a scathing critique of NGOs for denying the importance of parties and fragmenting the left.[89] Although the CPM position has softened, some left-leaning scholars have continued to argue that donor dependence has made NGOs increasingly bureaucratized, professionalized, and depoliticized.[90]

Most discussions and debates have explored the relationship between left-leaning NGOs, political parties, and social movements. They have not analyzed the challenges that secular organizations face when they compete with state-supported conservative, religious NGOs. This section evaluates critiques of NGOs in a context in which right- and left-wing NGOs compete for resources and legitimacy on highly unequal terms. Secular left NGOs have not been weakened by dependence on the state or international funding but by the absence of potential allies among leftist parties, social movements, and state governments. The contrast with Hindu nationalist organizations could not be greater.

Hindu Nationalist Civil Society Associations

With the decline of Congress and its patronage networks, most importantly the Textile Labor Association, the Sangh Parivar began patronizing a wide range of civil society organizations, from the Rotary Club and Lion's Club to business, trade, industrial groups, caste associations, and religious organizations. The BJP acquired authority over a vast network of cooperative institutions, including the Gujarat Cooperative Milk Marketing Federation, Gujarat State Cooperative Housing Finance Corporation, and most sports cooperatives including cricket, chess, swimming, and rifle shooting. It has made significant headway in capturing the agriculture produce marketing committees, the fisheries' cooperative union, and the saltpan workers' cooperative. Amit Shah,

---

[88] Rajni Kothari, "Non-party Political Process," *Economic and Political Weekly*, February 4, 1984, 216–24. Accessed June 30, 2014. http://www.epw.in/system/files/pdf/1984_19/5/special_articles_the_non_party_political_process.pdf. Harsh Sethi, "Groups in a New Politics of Transformation," *Economic and Political Weekly*, February 18, 1984, 305–16. Accessed June 30, 2014. http://www.epw.in/system/files/pdf/1984_19/7/special_articles_groups_in_a_new_politics_of_transformation.pdf. DL Sheth, "Grassroots Initiatives in India," *Economic and Political Weekly*, February 11, 1984. Accessed June 30, 2014. http://www.epw.in/special-articles/grass-roots-initiatives-india.html.

[89] Prakash Karat, "Action Groups/Voluntary Organizations: A Factor in Imperialist Strategy," *The Marxist*, April–June 1984, Vol. 2, No. 2, 51–63.

[90] Sangeeta Kamat, *Development Hegemony: NGOs and the State in India* (New Delhi: Oxford University Press, 2002), 21.

Modi's close associate, chaired the Gujarat State Financial Corporation and the Ahmedabad District Cooperative Bank, which enabled the BJP to increasingly gain control of the Gujarat State Cooperative Bank.[91]

Cooperatives have provided RSS members with access to funding and remunerative employment. They have also enabled the RSS to forge links between the state and civil society that cross-cut caste and class, and rural and urban lines. By acting as intermediaries between the state and local communities, the RSS and its affiliates have helped people get ration cards, electricity, and jobs.[92] Recipients of municipal services are indebted to BJP politicians and regularly vote for them in elections.

Hindu nationalists have also created a network of civil society organizations among subaltern groups. The BJP formed *dalit* and tribal cells in 1980 and a Kshatriya Samaj in the late 1980s. The RSS formed a *dalit* organization, the Samajik Samrasta Manch (SSM or Social Assimilation Platform), in 1983. The VHP created the Bharat Sevashram, Hindu Milan Mandir, and *ekal vidyalayas*, one-teacher schools in tribal areas. The Sangh Parivar-affiliated Vikasan Foundation raised money for these schools in India and abroad.[93] One of the central goals of these organizations was to encourage tribals and *dalits* to assimilate into caste Hinduism. The VHP's Jaideep Patel stated in an interview that the Vanvasi Kalyan Ashram had converted 15,000 tribals from Christianity; he had personally converted 4,500 tribals in a single day.[94] In these mass conversion ceremonies, tribals vowed to give up alcohol, gambling, and cigarettes and not to lie or convert again. The VHP's claim that it was rescuing tribals from forced conversions by Christians provided justification for anti-Christian violence.[95]

The Sangh Parivar has also provided extensive social services to *adivasi* and *dalit* communities.[96] It organized relief camps and distributed food grain, medicines, and clothes to tribal and *dalit* victims of the drought in 1985–6 and of

---

[91] "Amit Shah's Return to Gujarat Set to Boost Modi's Prospects," *India Today*, October 18, 2012. Accessed June 30, 2014. http://indiatoday.intoday.in/story/gujarat-assembly-polls-2012-narendra-modi-amit-shah-tulsi-prajapati-encounter-case/1/225302.html.

[92] See Ward Berenschot, *Riot Politics: Hindu-Muslim Violence and the Indian State* (New York: Columbia University Press/Hurst, 2012).

[93] "The Foreign Exchange of Hate," IDRF and American Funding of Hindutva. 2002. Accessed June 30, 2014. http://stopfundinghate.org/sacw/index.html.

[94] Interview with Jaideep Patel, Ahmedabad, January 9, 2007.

[95] The BJP, RSS, Bajrang Dal, VHP, and Hindu Jagran Manch all engaged in attacks on Christians in Gujarat in the late 1990s. From January 1998 to February 1999, the Indian Parliament reported that 94 out of 116 attacks on Christians across the country occurred in Gujarat. The worst violence was in the Dangs in southwest Gujarat. Claiming that Christians had been converting tribals to Christianity, Hindutva activists harassed Christians on spurious charges, disrupted Christian ceremonies, and attacked churches, Christian-owned shops, and missionary schools.

[96] Seth and Yagnik, *The Shaping of Modern Gujarat*, 225, and Ornit Shani, *Communalism, Caste and Hindu Nationalism: The Violence in Gujarat* (New York: Cambridge University Press, 2007), 159.

caste violence in 1985. It helped find jobs for *dalits* who had become unemployed when the textile mills closed.

RSS-affiliated NGOs rely heavily on international funding to promote their ideological agendas. Between 2000 and 2002, funding for religious organizations rose by 37.8 percent, from $63.11 million to $86.89 million. The Swaminarayan sect and, in particular, the Bochasanwasi Shree Akshar Purushottam (BAPS) and the Swaminarayan Sanstha, were beneficiaries. BAPS received $6.3 million and went from being twenty-sixth to first on the list of foreign-funded organizations. International organizations like the India Development and Relief Fund (IDRF) provided extensive funding to Sewa Bharati, a wing of the Sangh Parivar, after the 2001 earthquake in Bhuj, Gujarat.[97] Sewa Bharati used these funds to reconstruct Hindu rather than Muslim houses, schools, and temples. [98] About a quarter of the funds from Sewa International United Kingdom for reconstruction and rehabilitation went to schools run by the RSS-affiliated Vidya Bharati.[99]

NGOs' use of international funding depends on government authorization.[100] Thus, civil liberties activist Zakia Jowhar commented wryly that Gujarat had no real NGOs, only GOs (Government Organizations).[101] While allowing the RSS and its affiliates to fundraise abroad, the Gujarat government has restricted international funding for left and secular NGOs. The government stopped World Bank payments to nearly 2,500 women's self-help groups in rural areas. Several activists said that tax authorities and the Gujarat charity commissioner had singled out secular NGOs for investigation.[102] Scrutiny of NGOs that work among poor and marginalized groups is likely to increase. A classified document that the Intelligence Bureau submitted to Prime Minister Modi charged that many foreign-funded NGOs were "negatively impacting

[97] "A Factual Response to the Hate Attack by the India Development and Relief Fund," Accessed July 18, 2014. http://www.letindiadevelop.org/thereport/.
[98] Nalini Taneja, "More on RSS Foreign Funds – The Awaaz Report," *People's Democracy*, March 4, 2004. Accessed June 30, 2014. http://www.stopfundinghate.org/resources/news/UK/030704PeoplesDemocracy.htm.
[99] Awaaz – South Asia Watch Ltd. "In Bad Faith? British Charity & Hindu Extremism," Report Summary, London, 2004. Accessed July 18, 2014. http://www.sacw.net/DC/CommunalismCollection/ArticlesArchive/British_charity_and_Hindu_extremism_a_report_summary.pdf.
[100] The Indian Social Action Forum (INSAF), a national coalition of 700 social movements and NGOs in fifteen states, petitioned the Supreme Court to strike down rules that give the government unchecked powers to block access to foreign funding for organizations that it deemed political. On April 30, 2013, the Home Ministry froze INSAF's bank account because its activities are "prejudicial to the public interest." A large number of activists signed a petition protesting the government's decision. Harsh Mander et al., "Attacking INSAF," *Economic and Political Weekly*, Vol. 48, No. 24, June 15, 2013.
[101] Interview with Zakia Jowhar, Ahmedabad, November 24, 2008.
[102] Human Rights Watch, Discouraging Dissent: Intimidation and Harassment of Witnesses, Human Rights Activists, and Lawyers Pursuing Accountability for the 2002 Communal Violence in Gujarat. New York: Human Rights Watch, 2002.

economic development" by engaging in activism against corporate exploitation. It stated, "These foreign donors lead local NGOs to provide field reports
which are used to build a record against India and serve as tools for the strategic foreign policy interests of Western governments."[103]

Hindu nationalists have attacked left and secular NGOs for being elitist outsiders who lack a commitment to *asmita* (Gujarati pride). NV Patel, BJP leader
from Vadodara, claimed that human rights activists were defending "terrorists"
and ignoring the human rights violations of the majority population.[104] Jaideep
Patel stated that certain well-known activists (whom he named) had links with
Pakistani intelligence services.[105] Gordhan Zadaphia contrasted "pseudo" NGOs
that received international funding with "real NGOs" like the Swaminarayan
sect.[106] These pseudo NGOs were privileged whereas he and other Hindu activists came from simple backgrounds, he said. Chief Minister Modi famously
mocked "pseudo-secular five star NGOs" that were rife with incompetence, corruption, favoritism toward minorities, and lack of accountability.[107]

Left and Secular NGOs: Restorative Justice

The increased availability of international funding in the 1980s and 1990s
enabled NGOs to work with disadvantaged communities around health, education, land, wages, and environmental issues. Influenced by social movements,
they spoke of empowerment and conscientization and engaged in participatory
action-oriented research.

Among this group of NGOs, Achyut Yagnik founded SETU (Center for Social
Knowledge and Action), a research and advocacy organization, in 1982, as an
offshoot of the New Delhi-based Lokayan. SETU provides a bridge between
knowledge and action by facilitating communication between activists, policy
makers, and underprivileged communities. Gagan Sethi established Jan Vikas
in 1987 to foster participatory approaches to development and capacity building. Hanif Lakdawala founded Sanchetana in 1982 to work with urban slum
dwellers, particularly around community health. Sanchetana's Institute for
Initiatives in Education (IFIE) addresses education, unemployment, poverty,

---

[103] Amitav Ranjan, "Foreign-aided NGOs Are Actively Stalling Development, IB Tells PMO in
a Report," *The Indian Express*, June 7, 2014. Accessed July 23, 2014.: http://indianexpress
.com/article/india/india-others/foreign-aided-ngos-are-actively-stalling-development-ib-
tells-pmo-in-a-report/; and "Modi Government's Message to NGOs in India: Big Brother Is Watching
You," *Forbes*, http://www.forbes.com/sites/meghabahree/2014/06/16/modi-governments-
message-to-ngos-in-india-big-brother-is-watching-you/.
[104] Interview with NV Patel, Vadodara, January 12, 2007.
[105] Interview with Jaideep Patel, Ahmedabad, January 9, 2007.
[106] Interview with Gordhan Zadaphia, Ahmedabad, November 23, 2008.
[107] Dionne Bunsha, "A Spat in Gujarat," *Frontline*, November 5, 2005. Accessed June 30, 2014.
http://www.hindu.com/thehindu/thscrip/print.pl?file=20051118002604800.htm&date=fl2223/
&prd=fline&.

and gender inequality in the Muslim community. Cedric Prakash and other Jesuit priests formed Prashant, a Centre for Human Rights, Justice and Peace in 2001 to advocate for Christian and *dalit* communities. Harsh Mander formed Sneh Samudaya as part of Action Aid to provide relief and rehabilitation for victims of the earthquake in Kutch in 2001. Janpath was founded in 1992 to coordinate NGO activities. Several organizations addressed gender inequality. In Ahmedabad they included Sahr Waru Women's Action and Resource Unit and the Self Employed Women's Association (SEWA). In Vadodara, Olakh sought to cultivate women's leadership and Sahiyar provided livelihood support for women, education and health awareness for adolescent girls, and legal and other support for victims of rape and domestic violence.

The year 2002 was a turning point for many of these NGOs. They demanded restorative justice by seeking relief and rehabilitation for the victims and repairing damaged relations between Muslims and Hindus. When violence broke out in Vadodara, Trupti Shah reported that the Shanti Abhayan (SA) and People's Union for Civil Liberties (PUCL) formed peace committees and organized around-the-clock vigils in localities where they had contacts with both communities.[108] A team of PUCL-SA activists met with the police commissioner and secured curfew passes. They gave their names and phone numbers to the police and to people in the affected areas. Shah was especially proud that activists kept out intruders and maintained stability in Tandalja, a neighborhood on the western outskirts of Vadodara (populated by about 40,000 people, 60 percent Muslims and 40 percent Hindus at the time of the carnage; many Hindus have since left.)[109] However, these efforts were less successful after March 15 as the violence intensified. The police commissioner refused to issue the activists curfew passes and the police, who were often complicit in the violence, would not respond to their calls.

Secular activists were less able to maintain peace on the streets of Ahmedabad than of Vadodara in February and March 2002 because of the larger size of the city and the greater severity of the violence. The police did not stop Hindutva groups from attacking peace activists who organized a meeting at the Indian Institute of Management in Ahmedabad on March 3, at Ishwar Bhavan on April 3, and at Gandhi Ashram on April 7. The violence of February and March 2002 revealed the far greater strength of Sangh-affiliated NGOs than secular NGOs in Ahmedabad. Cedric Prakash quoted Modi as having said that there were so few human rights activists in Gujarat that he could ship them out on one boat into the Arabian Sea. Prakash acknowledged that Modi's estimate was not much of an exaggeration.[110]

In the aftermath of the violence, many secular activists in Ahmedabad engaged in critical self-reflection about the weaknesses and limitations of

---

[108] Interview with Trupti Shah, Vadodara, Ahmedabad, January 12, 2007.
[109] Ibid.
[110] Interview with Cedric Prakash, Ahmedabad, January 13, 2007.

NGOs. Gagan Sethi criticized secular civil society organizations for not working closely with local institutions like schools, *panchayats*, and primary health centers. As a result, he argued, these institutions were susceptible to RSS influence and became party to attacks on Muslims.[111] He encouraged NGOs not to limit their work to the aftermath of violent attacks but to make more sustained and long-term efforts to forge Hindu-Muslim solidarities.

Prior to the violence, few NGOs included Muslims on their staff or worked on safeguarding minority rights. According to Zakia Jowhar, a member of the Sahr Waru and Social Action Forum, activists who were committed to eradicating rural poverty excluded Muslims.[112] The proportion of Muslims, *dalits*, and *adivasis* on the governing boards of NGOs was very small.[113] Not a single Muslim organization was listed among the recipients of foreign funding in Gujarat.

Several existing organizations, including SETU, Prashant, Jan Vikas, Sanchetana's IFIE, Sahr Waru, Olakh, and Sahiyar redirected their energies in the aftermath of the 2002 violence. New organizations emerged. Action Aid formed Aman Samudhaya and Shabnam Hashmi, KN Panikkar, and Harsh Mander founded Act Now for Harmony and Democracy (ANHAD) in Delhi in March 2003. ANHAD has organized people's tribunals and creative campaigns to challenge religious nationalism and promote secular values. The umbrella coalition, the Citizens' Initiative, brought together thirty-four NGOs to offer relief, legal aid, and livelihood training for victims of the violence.

NGOs have provided goods and services to the people who have been housed in relief camps since 2002. Many, like Trupti Shah, had not planned to get involved in this work but felt compelled to do so because of the inadequacy of government services. Several secular NGOs have engaged in peace-building efforts with local communities. For example, Olakh created collectives of Hindu and Muslim women in two urban slums in Vadodara and neighboring villages. Jan Vikas worked with young people who were both victims and perpetrators of violence in seven districts. NGOs also produced extensive documentation of the violence that, in the absence of government records, would have gone unrecorded. Women's organizations like Sahiyar and Sahr Waru investigated sexual violence. These reports provided the basis for demands for compensation to the victims, legal trials, and the creation of people's tribunals.

NGOs that have fought for minority rights in Gujarat have not become bureaucratized and professionalized. Rather, they have depended on the extraordinary dedication and courage of activists like Cedric Prakash, Harsh Mander, Mukul Sinha, Nirjari Sinha, Trupti Shah, Gagan Sethi, Achyut Yagnik, Shabnam Hashmi, Hanif Lakdawala, Girish Patel, Teesta Setalvad, Zakia Jowhar, and Sheba George. These activists have taken risks that have subjected them to harassment, threats, and arrests.

---

[111] Gagan Sethi, speech at conference on "The Fascist State," Ahmedabad, November 23, 2008.
[112] Interview with Zakia Jowhar, Ahmedabad, January 13, 2007.
[113] Shah, "Civil Society and the Poor at an Impasse," 67.

Far from being donor-driven, secular NGOs have sought to influence donors' agendas and address the problems of minorities. For example, the donor development agency CARE had worked in India for fifty years, mainly on disaster relief projects. At the advice of local NGOs, and based on its success in working with local communities, CARE, with support from the Netherlands Embassy, started the Gujarat Harmony Project, which included eight NGOs, a charitable trust, and a feminist collective.[114]

However, even high-profile, nonconfrontational NGOs that have lavish international funding are vulnerable to state sanction. The experiences of SEWA are revealing. SEWA began as the women's wing of the Textile Labor Association in 1972 but became an independent union of women in the informal sector of the economy in 1981. It organizes women vendors, home workers, construction laborers, and forest dwellers, among other groups. Thirty percent of its 519,309 members in Gujarat are Muslim.[115] It is not only the largest, most visible, and most respected NGO in Gujarat but a poster child of women's NGOs internationally.

SEWA, which describes itself as both an organization and a movement, was well-placed to fight for minority rights in 2002. Forty thousand SEWA members were affected by the violence; 10,000 of their homes were destroyed. However, according to Mirai Chatterjee, SEWA's director of social security, SEWA members debated the appropriate course of action and the majority felt that SEWA should influence government officials through private channels rather than by confronting them outright. She said,

We wanted to be able to support our members and we were worried about exposing them to repression if we took a strong public stand. Two bombs were planted on our premises to send us a warning. So we decided to work between the lines.[116]

SEWA concentrated on relief work: providing child and health care facilities, psychological counseling, and other forms of assistance to women so they could rebuild their lives. They were especially active in working with widows and children.

SEWA's caution did not protect it from state sanction. In 2005, the state government charged SEWA with poor performance, financial irregularities, and nepotism in administering a seven-year $15 million loan from a UN agency. SEWA ordered an independent audit which dispelled these charges. However, the state government demanded that SEWA return some of the funds it had received. In October 2005, SEWA decided to withdraw from twenty state government-sponsored projects. According to Mirai Chatterjee, the BJP government sought to undermine SEWA by spreading false rumors about its

---

[114] Sara Ahmed, "Sustaining Peace, Re-building Livelihoods: The Gujarat Harmony Project," in *Gender and Development*, 2004, Vol. 12, No. 3, 94–102.
[115] http://www.sewa.org/.
[116] Interview with Mirai Chatterjee, Ahmedabad, January 13, 2007.

activities, trying to co-opt its members, and bringing fabricated charges against it. Chatterjee claimed that the government wanted to make an example of SEWA because it was the largest civil society organization in Gujarat and, as a cadre-based organization, it directly competed with Sangh-affiliated NGOs.[117]

Left and secular NGOs are at a distinct disadvantage in Gujarat. Unlike RSS-affiliated NGOs, secular NGOs lack the ability to get jobs, housing, and municipal services for their constituencies. Nor can NGOs mobilize demonstrations on the scale of political parties in their election campaigns. Although left-leaning activists have sometimes supported secular Congress Party candidates, the Gujarat Congress Party is a poor ally. It failed to protect its own members and some of its members participated in the 2002 violence. Activists have sought the support of the national Congress Party, and in particular Sonia Gandhi, but this has not had an impact on Congress policies in Gujarat.

The only other alternative is for NGOs to form their own parties. The Jan Sangharsh Manch formed the New Socialist Movement Party in 2007 with Amrish Patel as the party general secretary and Mukul Sinha as the party chairman. Three candidates including Mukul Sinha contested and lost the Legislative Assembly elections from Ahmedabad in 2007.

Legal Advocacy and Retributive Justice

NGOs have also engaged in legal advocacy or what some activists term retributive justice: bringing the accused to trial and representing Muslims who were convicted under POTA and through "fake encounters." A number of organizations, including Citizens for Peace and Justice, the Centre for Social Justice, Alliance in Defense of Democracy, Jan Vikas, Lok Adhikari Sangh, Human Rights Law Network, Commonwealth Human Rights Initiative, and Nyayagrah (people's resistance to secure justice using the law) have engaged in struggles for legal justice. They have investigated officials and activists charged with inciting violence in 2002, secured compensation for the victims, demanded witness protection, protested Muslims' eviction from relief colonies, defended Muslims falsely convicted of "terrorism," and provided victims with an awareness of their legal rights.

Legal battles have been drawn out and victories have occurred years after the crimes were committed. Lawyers have negotiated the most favorable settlements outside Gujarat without the involvement of the victims and their families. Thus, some scholars are skeptical that struggles for legal justice adequately address violence on the scale that Gujarat experienced. For example, Ratna Kapur argues that transitional justice systems entrust the state with finding solutions to the problems it has created.

The story of the Gujarat riots and subsequent efforts to address the harms and injuries through prosecution and apology does not pay attention to the institutional and

[117] Interview with Mirai Chatterjee, Ahmedabad, January 13, 2007.

discursive mechanisms within a democratic polity that can produce moments of extreme violence, moments that cannot be written off as aberrational and deviant ... the Gujarat riots of 2002 cannot be addressed exclusively within a prosecutorial or reparations framework that seeks to prosecute individual wrongdoers who carried out such atrocities and provide compensation to those who suffered.[118]

Kapur argues that legal trials often re-victimize victims. She cites the example of Zaheera Sheikh, who testified in the Best Bakery case. On March 1, 2002, Hindutva activists burned down a small bakery in Vadodara, killing fourteen employees, nine of whom were members of the Sheikh family. Citizens for Justice and Peace represented nineteen-year-old Zaheera Sheikh, a family member, who witnessed the violence and filed an FIR. Zaheera Sheikh feared reprisals and retracted her testimony. The Hindus who attacked her family, the social justice group that cast her as a pawn of the Hindu right, the Muslim community that said she was lying, and the Supreme Court that sentenced her to a year in prison for perjury, all victimized Sheikh. These acts of condemnation fail, Kapur argues, to address "the broader discursive context within which the real Zaheera Sheikh has to live and survive."[119]

Kapur's poignant account of re-victimization could be told about many Muslims who relive their tragic losses in prolonged legal cases. Johanna Lokhande, an activist from Aman Samudhaya, described a different kind of re-victimization of people in relief colonies. She was disturbed by "victim tourism" in which survivors remained trapped in the past by repeating their stories to the activists, scholars, and journalists who visited these colonies. And yet, set against stories of Sheikh and others are stories that activists tell of men and women who regained hope and confidence when they learned to advocate on their own behalf.

Some organizations, such as Jan Vikas's Center for Social Justice and Nyayagrah, which the Lawyers' Collective and Aman Biradari created, have organized legal awareness campaigns and provided free legal services for victims to seek retributive justice themselves. Thousands of people have refused bribes and intimidation and pursued charges against Sangh Parivar members.

If legal recourses affirm the power of the state, they also expose myths of state impartiality, mine fissures within it, and exploit opportunities for change.[120] Secular NGOs have also formed links to sympathetic national bodies such as the National Commission for Minorities, the National Human Rights Commission (NHRC), the Planning Commission, and the Supreme Court. The NHRC played an especially important role in moving the CBI and the Supreme Court to reopen cases that the Gujarat courts had not investigated

---

[118] Ratna Kapur, "Normalizing violence: Transitional justice and the Gujarat riots," *Columbia Journal of Gender and the Law*, 15(3), 2006, 3.

[119] Ibid., 15.

[120] Thomas Hansen, "Governance and Myths of State in Mumbai," in CJ Fuller and Veronique Benei, eds., *The Everyday State and Society in Modern India* (Delhi: Social Science Press, 2000), 31–67.

or investigated improperly. Although the High Court acquitted the accused in the Best Bakery case, the NHRC appealed to the Supreme Court to retry the case outside Gujarat. In 2012, the Bombay High Court acquitted five and upheld life imprisonment for four people.

Mukul Sinha, a High Court advocate and activist with Jan Sangharsh Samiti, waged a major legal battle against the BJP government by presenting evidence to the government-appointed Nanavati Commission, knowing it was biased but accurately assuming the case would attract the national government's attention.[121] The evidence consisted of cell phone tower records that showed top-ranking government officials had ordered the police to leave the sites of violence, ignoring people's pleas for help in 2002. Two years later, the Supreme Court called for a review of 2,000 cases that the Gujarat government had mishandled. The SIT, which the Court created, recommended the establishment of fast track courts, appointment of additional public prosecutors, cancellation of bail, and transfer of cases outside Gujarat. Some of the most significant judgments implicated government officials, police officers, and Sangh Parivar members.

Legal activists have also challenged the Gujarat government's representation of Muslims as "terrorists." Mukul Sinha represented petitioners in the Sohrabuddin Anwarhussain Sheikh, Tulsiram, Prajapati, and Ishrat Jahan Raza encounter cases. The Gujarat government alleged that it had killed Muslims in these and other cases because they were members of the Lashkar-e-Taiba "terrorist" organization and were plotting to kill Chief Minister Modi, LK Advani, Praveen Togadia, and Jaideep Patel. A lengthy process of investigation revealed that the deputy inspector general of police in Ahmedabad, DG Vanjara, was responsible for these murders. Following the Gujarat government's attempts to stall the case, in November 2011, the CBI found that the police had killed a nineteen-year-old college student, Ishrat Jahan Raza, and three other men in June 2004.

In another case, the state police claimed to have killed underworld criminal Sohrabuddin Anwarhussain Sheikh on November 26, 2005 because he was associated with Lakshar-e-Taiba and the Pakistani intelligence agency. The state government's lawyer, KTS Tulsi, later admitted before the Supreme Court that the Gujarat police had staged the gun battle that killed Sheikh. The CBI subsequently revealed that the police had raped and murdered Kausar Bi, Sheikh's wife, and is currently investigating the death of Tulsiram Prajapati, a friend of Sheikh and a witness to Kausar Bi's murder.

Kapur's analysis fruitfully calls attention to the many ways the Gujarat violence was unexceptional. As I have argued elsewhere, Hindu nationalist militancy and violence are products of democratic processes.[122] The question in this context is whether strengthening democratic processes and state authority

[121] Interview with Mukul Sinha, Ahmedabad, November 26, 2008.
[122] Amrita Basu and Srirupa Roy, eds., "Introduction," in *Beyond Exceptionalism: Violence, Religion and Democracy in India* (New Delhi: Seagull Press, 2006).

simply reproduce the conditions that caused the violence. Sentencing those who organized and executed the violence cannot challenge the myriad ways Muslims in Gujarat have been degraded, humiliated, and marginalized. What legal advocacy has done is to expose the Gujarat government's thin understanding of democracy or, in Harsh Mander's words, the Gujarat government's violation of its own laws.[123] It has also challenged the amnesia that the government has promoted in celebrating "vibrant Gujarat" by demonstrating the refusal of victims and activists to forget.

Activists across the Gujarati political spectrum have sought to effect social and political change through parties and on the streets. However, left-wing activists have been far less successful than their opponents. The death of a leading left-wing activist and the election of his adversary as prime minister of India are symbolically significant. Thousands of Mukul Sinha's devoted friends and political allies mourned his death on May 12, 2014 and vowed to keep his memory alive. Millions celebrated Narendra Modi's victory two days later and decided – either explicitly or implicitly – to bury his past.

Mukul Sinha and Narendra Modi could not have differed more in their personalities, ideologies, and goals. Sinha was a labor organizer and legal activist. His personal and political commitments were unconstrained by region, religion, and class. The only thing that Sinha and Modi shared was a commitment to political activism on the streets and in the corridors of power. Sinha devoted immense efforts to proving Modi's constitutional, if not criminal, responsibility for the 2002 Gujarat violence.

Both Sinha and Modi entered the world of politics not through established political institutions but through civil society activism. Both believed in working through the state, in Sinha's case by testifying before a government-appointed commission of inquiry and engaging in legal advocacy. Both men believed that social movements were most likely to be effective when tethered to political parties. However, while Sinha was defeated in the 2007 Assembly elections, Modi's activism enabled him to retain power in Gujarat until he became prime minister of India.

The death of Sinha and election of Modi as prime minister have important implications for Gujarat's minorities. Sinha was one of the major advocates for families of the victims of the 2002 violence and in encounter killings thereafter. Since his death and Modi's election, the Gujarat High Court granted bail to Maya Kodnani, a former minister who was convicted in the Naroda Patiya massacre, and DG Vanzara, a senior police officer accused of staging a series of fake killings at the BJP's behest. The Gujarat government reinstated GP Singhal, a police officer accused in the Ishrat Jahan case, and transferred out of Gujarat and demoted two police officers who investigated the Ishrat Jahan and Sohrabuddin Sheikh cases, and concluded that the police had killed them on false pretexts of their being "terrorists."[124]

---

[123] Interview with Harsh Mander, Delhi, July 24, 2007.
[124] https://www.indiastudygroup.org/thematic-briefings/3-september-thematic-appointments. However, there is still uncertainty about Ishrat Jahan's political affiliations. Praveen Swami,

Conclusion

The 2002 violence was unprecedented in its scale, brutality, and enduring consequences. The episodic influenced the quotidian. The character of daily life in Ahmedabad changed in far-reaching ways. Many Gujarati Hindus I interviewed felt that even if the BJP and its allies had "gone too far, Muslims had to be taught a lesson." If Hindu nationalists had long depicted Muslims as outsiders, after 2002 they branded Muslims actual or potential "terrorists." Muslims found it difficult to rent or buy homes within less than fifteen kilometers of Ahmedabad. Gujarati subnationalism became inseparable from Hindu nationalism.

Harsh Mander commented that two English words entered the Gujarati vocabulary after 2002: border and compromise. Border, he said, referred not to the national border but to a community-enforced border between Hindus and Muslims in Ahmedabad. Compromise referred to a tacit understanding that Muslims could return to their homes and resume their lives as long as they did not seek recompense or justice.[125] The Modi masks and speeches on cell phone rings, repressive vegetarianism that landlords, restaurants, and hotels enforced, exclusion of Muslims from Hindu-dominated neighborhoods and jobs, and punishing living conditions of Muslim victims have all persisted.

It is unusual for all the forces responsible for violence – the party, state, and civil society groups – to be independently powerful and aligned. Indeed, the boundaries between Hindu nationalist party and state, civil society organizations and social movements, and local and state government agencies eroded during the violence. Although the roles of national and state governments were clearly differentiated, the BJP government in Gujarat enjoyed continuous support from the national BJP when the NDA was in office. This alignment of societal and political forces was partly responsible for the BJP's resilience in face of opposition from both the Sangh Parivar and secular activists. Add to this an international community that brands Muslims "terrorists" and you have the perfect storm.

"Ishrat Jahan: The Inconvenient Story No One Wants to Tell," *First Post*, June 13, 2013. Accessed December 9, 2014. http://www.firstpost.com/politics/ishrat-jahan-the-inconvenient-story-no -one-wants-to-tell-867173.html.

125 Interview with Harsh Mander, Ahmedabad, November 22, 2008.

PART III

EPISODIC VIOLENCE

6

Per-desh (handwritten)

Uttar Pradesh

Movements and Countermovements

UP is politically important to compare to texas or cali? (handwritten marginal note)

Dalit leader Kanshi Ram famously commented, "The road to Delhi passes through UP (Uttar Pradesh)."[1] UP is of enormous importance to Indian politics. It commands 80 out of 547 seats in the lower house of Parliament and 31 out of 245 seats in the upper house of Parliament. Many prominent nationalist leaders and seven of India's fourteen prime ministers have been elected from UP.[2] With a population of 200 million people, UP would be the fifth largest country in the world. Not surprisingly, political scientists have studied UP extensively.[3]

[1] Kanshi Ram, *The Chamcha Age: An Era of Stooges*, Privately Printed, 1982. Accessed July 1, 2014. https://archive.org/details/TheChamchaAge.

[2] They include Jawaharlal Nehru, Lal Bahadur Shastri, Indira Gandhi, Rajiv Gandhi, Charan Singh, Vishwanath Pratap Singh, Chandra Shekhar, and Atal Bihari Vajpayee. Narendra Modi is from Gujarat but was elected to Parliament from UP as well as Gujarat.

[3] Important works on UP politics include Atul Kohli, *The State and Poverty in India: The Politics of Reform* (Cambridge, UK: Cambridge University Press, 1987); Kanchan Chandra, *Why Ethnic Parties Succeed: Patronage and Ethnic Head Counts in India*. Cambridge Studies in Comparative Politics (New York: Cambridge University Press, 2004); Ashutosh Varshney, *Ethnic Conflict and Civic Life: Hindus and Muslims in India* (New Haven, CT: Yale University Press, 2002); Zoya Hasan, *Dominance and Mobilisation: Rural Politics in Western Uttar Pradesh, 1930–1980* (New Delhi: Sage Publications, 1989) and *Quest for Power: Oppositional Movements and Post-Congress Politics in Uttar Pradesh* (New Delhi: Oxford University Press, 1998); Sudha Pai, ed., *Political Process in Uttar Pradesh: Identity, Economic Reforms, and Governance* (New Delhi: Pearson Longman, 2007), *Dalit Assertion and the Unfinished Democratic Revolution: The BSP in Uttar Pradesh* (New Delhi: Sage Publications, 2002), *Uttar Pradesh: Agrarian Change and Electoral Politics* (New Delhi: Shipra Publications, 1993), and *Agrarian Relations in Uttar Pradesh: A Study of the Eastern Districts* (New Delhi: InterIndia Publications, 1986); Paul Brass, *Factional Politics in an Indian State: The Congress Party in Uttar Pradesh* (Berkeley: University of California Press, 1965), *Language, Religion, and Politics in North India* (Cambridge, UK: Cambridge University Press, 1974), *Caste, Faction, and Party in Indian Politics*, Vol. 1: *Faction and Party* (New Delhi: Chanakya Press, 1984), *Caste, Faction, and Party in Indian Politics*, Vol. 2: *Election Studies* (New Delhi: Chanakya Press, 1985), *Theft of an Idol: Text*

This chapter explores why Hindu nationalist militancy and violence in UP have been intermittent, and more specifically, why they peaked in the early 1990s, declined, and have since periodically reemerged. The Jan Sangh and BJP pursued moderate and militant strategies at different periods of time. I differentiate four major phases with particular attention to the least studied last two. In the first, starting in the late 1960s, the Jan Sangh formed coalitions with diverse political parties and movements that sought to unseat the Congress government. When it was unable to advance Hindu nationalist goals, it disrupted the coalitions it had formed. In the second phase, from the late 1980s until 1992, the BJP joined forces with a militant VHP-led movement and gained power independently. During the third phase (1993–2002), the BJP pursued a moderate strategy of coalition-building and increasing lower-caste representation within the party and its governments. Although many observers predicted that the days of militant Hindu nationalism were over, the BJP reverted to an activist role during the fourth phase, from 2002 on. Hindu nationalist militancy and violence were designed to overcome factionalism within the party and placate the RSS and radical activists.

This alternation between an aggressive, anti-minority posture and an inclusive, coalitional, moderate stance is puzzling. There was ample reason for the BJP to consistently pursue far-reaching Hindu nationalist goals. The RSS had strong support in UP among Hindu refugees from what became Pakistan.[4] The Ayodhya dispute, which had reverberations in Gujarat in 2002, could well have continued to ignite Hindu-Muslim violence in UP. With the Congress Party's decline and the subsequent emergence of lower-caste parties, the BJP seemed the best representative of upper castes. However, the upper castes that deserted Congress to support the BJP in the wake of the Mandal-Mandir controversy did not remain loyal to the BJP.[5]

Set against these potential assets are multiple obstacles to Hindu nationalist militancy. First, UP lacks a distinctive regional cultural identity. The British created UP through a process of conquest and annexation that spanned three quarters of a century.[6] UP acquired its current designation after independence.

and Context in the Representation of Collective Violence. Princeton Studies in Culture/Power/ History (Princeton, NJ: Princeton University Press, 1997), and *The Production of Hindu-Muslim Violence in Contemporary India.* Jackson School Publications in International Studies (Seattle, WA: University of Washington Press, 2003).

[4] Paul Brass, "Uttar Pradesh," in Myron Weiner, ed., *State Politics in India* (Princeton, NJ: Princeton University Press, 1968), 90.

[5] According to the 1931 census, the last census to provide information about states' caste composition, Hindu upper castes comprise about 20 percent (of whom 9.2 percent were Brahmins and 7.2 percent Rajputs), Scheduled Castes 21 percent (of whom 12.7 percent were Chamars), and Other Backward Classes 42 percent (of whom 8.7 percent were Yadavs). Scheduled Tribes were only 0.06 percent of the population.

[6] They acquired Benares in 1775, followed by lower Doab, Rohilkhand, and the Gorakhpur region in 1801, upper Doab and Bundelkhand in 1803, and Kumaon, except for Tehri Garwhal, in 1815. Their last major territorial acquisition was the province of Oudh, which they annexed in 1856. The British did not administer the territories that comprised UP as a single unit until the merger of Oudh (then called the North Western provinces) in 1902.

In November 2000, state boundaries were reconfigured once again when Uttaranchal became the state of Uttarkhand. UP's lack of distinctive identity has prevented the BJP from adopting its regional cultural traditions. By contrast, the BJP has benefited from identifying with Gujarati sub-nationalism in Gujarat, Rajput culture in Rajasthan, and Pahari cultural traditions in Himachal Pradesh.

2. Lower-caste movements and parties are stronger in UP than in Gujarat and Rajasthan, a second reason for the weakness of Hindutva. Social movements and political parties have emerged in sequential fashion, initially among more secure and better-off groups like farmers and OBCs, and later among more vulnerable groups like *dalits* and Muslims. The Jan Sangh and the BJP initially grew by forging ties to social movements among peasant proprietors and OBCs. With the decline of the Congress Party in UP, the Janata Dal captured the support of these groups. The Ayodhya campaign broadened the BJP's caste constituency to include a large swath of lower-caste groups but could not halt the development of lower-caste movement-parties. By 1996, OBCs and a majority of Muslims were supporting the SP and most *dalits* were backing the BSP. The Jan Sangh and the BJP often had to form alliances with ideologically diverse movements and parties. This enabled them to attain power, but not to pursue their programmatic goals.

3. Third, the BJP's need to broaden its social base created serious internal caste tensions that weakened it, especially after 2002. The RSS and some BJP leaders feared that Kalyan Singh, an OBC, was undermining upper-caste dominance. There were also tensions between upper-caste Brahmin and Rajput leaders. When the BJP marginalized and expelled Kalyan Singh, it lost a committed Hindu nationalist movement leader. Its inability to function as an effective movement-party in UP differed from Gujarat, where Narendra Modi, an OBC leader, had the support of the RSS and the upper castes. Not until the 2014 elections, when Narendra Modi ran for Parliament from UP, did the BJP engage in Kalyan Singh's earlier strategy of appealing both to OBCs and to Hindu nationalist ideals.

4. Fourth, the BJP's organizing abilities declined because it became increasingly factionalized. A key to the BJP's success in the late 1980s and early 1990s, according to Shyam Nandan Singh, its general secretary for UP, was the strength of the party organization at the district, block, and village levels.[7] Neither the UP Jan Sangh nor the BJP experienced significant factionalism or defections until 1999. Party members tended to be more committed to the BJP as a whole than to charismatic party leaders or their personal success. As a result, the BJP could participate in coalitional arrangements without fearing the attrition of its membership or the dilution of its ideology. In Kalyan Singh's apt description, "the party with a difference became a party of differences."[8] Leadership rivalries reflected two different

---

[7] Interview with Shyam Nandan Singh, Lucknow, January 4, 1992.
[8] Interview with Kalyan Singh, Lucknow, July 16, 2007.

conceptions of the BJP: while some of its leaders were committed to maintaining a disciplined cadre-party that had strong ties to the RSS, others favored a catch-all party. The BJP expanded rapidly by incorporating many members who lacked Hindu nationalist commitments.

Fifth, Hindu nationalists became less militant as Muslims became a more significant political force. Hindu nationalists could organize the Ayodhya movement and spearhead anti-Muslim violence when Muslims were fearful of asserting their political interests. In the early 1990s, the SP under Mulayam Singh's leadership gained Muslim votes by challenging the BJP's anti-Muslim policies. Many political parties courted Muslims by nominating Muslim candidates to run for political office and supporting the UPA government's endorsement of limited reservations for Muslims (through a sub-quota of 4.5 percent within the existing 27 percent reservation for OBCs). Most parties have not treated Muslims as a religious community or negotiated exclusively with Muslim religious leaders. Although the BJP has periodically revived anti-Muslim appeals and violence, it has also sought Muslim support.

Phase 1: The Jan Sangh's Faltering Start

The most successful opposition parties and movements in UP from 1952 to 1989 identified and challenged the Congress Party's exclusionary policies. The Jan Sangh was not among them. Nor could the Jan Sangh compete with Congress for upper-caste or Hindu support. Allying with other political parties entailed electoral gains but threatened to dilute the Jan Sangh's distinctive platform. Thus it adopted a dual strategy of allying with parties that represented farmers and OBCs and later undermining the coalitions it formed with them.

The Jan Sangh was unable to emulate the Congress Party's broad-based coalition, which included upper castes, Scheduled Castes, Muslims, and the rural poor. Its social base was confined to Brahmin, Rajput, and Vaishya upper-class elites. It drew between 20 and 50 percent of its Legislative Assembly membership in 1952, 1957, and 1962 from former *zamindars* and *taluqdars*.[9] Of the forty-nine Jan Sangh MLAs who were elected in the 1962 UP Legislative Assembly elections, 49 percent were former *zamindars* or *taluqdars*.[10] OBCs represented a potentially powerful source of opposition to Congress because it excluded and underrepresented them.[11]

[9] Paul Brass, "Politicization of the Peasantry in a North Indian State: I," *The Journal of Peasant Studies*, July 1980, Vol. 7, no. 4, 413.

[10] Christophe Jaffrelot, *The Hindu Nationalist Movement in India* (New York: Columbia University Press, 1998), 190.

[11] In the 1962 general elections, Congress gave tickets to only 27 OBCs as opposed to 260 upper castes. Angela Sutherland Burger, *Opposition in a Dominant-Party System: A Study of the Jan Sangh, the Praja Socialist Party, and the Socialist Party in Uttar Pradesh, India* (Berkeley, CA: University of California Press, 1969), 202. This continued into the 1970s. Although the Congress government decided against creating reservations for OBCs, the Janata government issued an

The Jan Sangh hitched its fortunes to two major social movements that opposed Congress in different ways in the mid-1960s. One challenged Congress governments' exclusion of lower castes and the other demanded more government support for agrarian cultivators. The two movements coexisted and collaborated in their early years. Socialist leader Ram Manohar Lohia organized lower-caste Yadavs, Kurmis, and Lodhs in eastern and central UP to oppose the marginalization and underrepresentation of the lower castes. Over time the OBC movement aligned with descendants of the Socialist Party, which implemented reservations when they came to power. To represent agrarian cultivators, Charan Singh formed the Bharatiya Kranti Dal (BKD) in 1969. The BKD primarily sought to represent the Jat community but because Jats only constituted 1.2 percent of UP's population, it emphasized the common interests of rural cultivators. The BKD organized a powerful movement demanding greater state support and higher remunerative prices for farmers and better terms of trade between rural and urban areas.

Given the Congress Party's strength, the Jan Sangh performed best in 1967 and 1977 when it forged alliances with opposition parties and movements that represented farmers and OBCs. The Jan Sangh's share of the vote increased from 16.5 percent to 22 percent between the 1962 and 1967 Legislative Assembly elections. It declined to 18 percent in 1969 when it split off from the BKD. The Janata Party (which included the Jan Sangh) won an extraordinary 83 percent of the vote in 1977. When the BJP contested the elections alone, its share of the vote was 10-11 percent in the 1980 and 1985 elections. Thus the Jan Sangh and the BJP were electorally weak in the absence of social movement allies.[12]

From 1967 to 1989, power alternated between Congress and a coalition of parties including the BKD, interspersed with frequent periods of President's rule. The Jan Sangh played a major role in both the formation and dissolution of these coalition governments. It allied with the BKD and other parties in the 1967 elections and participated in the Samyukta Vidhayak Dal (SVD),

---

order for modest reservations for OBCs, and Scheduled Castes and Tribes in state services and industrial training institutes in August 1977. However, the Jan Sangh opposed the scheme, withdrew support from the Janata government, and switched its support to the Congress (O), which froze the reservation schemes that the Janata government had proposed.

[12] Election Commission of India, *Statistical Report on the General Election, 1962–1985 to the Legislative Assembly of Uttar Pradesh*, New Delhi: Election Commission of India. Accessed July 16, 2014. http://eci.nic.in/eci_main/StatisticalReports/SE_1962/StatRep_UP_1962.pdf. http://eci.nic.in/eci_main/StatisticalReports/SE_1967/Statistical%20Report%20Uttar%20Pradesh%201967%20.pdf. http://eci.nic.in/eci_main/StatisticalReports/SE_1969/Statistical%20Report%201969%20Uttar%20Pradesh.pdf. http://eci.nic.in/eci_main/StatisticalReports/SE_1974/Statistical%20Report%20Uttar%20Pradesh%201974.pdf. http://eci.nic.in/eci_main/StatisticalReports/SE_1977/Statistical%20Report%20Uttar%20Pradesh%201977.pdf. http://eci.nic.in/eci_main/StatisticalReports/SE_1980/Statistical%20Report%20Uttar%20Pradesh%201980.pdf. http://eci.nic.in/eci_main/StatisticalReports/SE_1985/Statistical%20Report%20Uttar%20Pradesh%201985.pdf.

✗ OBCs = Other Backward Classes ✗

the first non-Congress government in UP. Tensions between the BKD and the Jan Sangh emerged when Charan Singh dismissed several ministers whom he claimed the Jan Sangh had promoted to gain greater control over the SVD. The Jan Sangh and its allies turned against Charan Singh, forcing him to resign. The SVD government collapsed, and the center imposed President's rule.

Relations between the BKD and the Jan Sangh subsequently improved. In 1974, the BKD, Jan Sangh, Socialist Party, and four other parties merged to form the Bharatiya Lok Dal (BLD), which joined the Janata Party. However, tensions between the BLD and Jan Sangh recurred because the Jan Sangh objected to the BLD's support for reservations for OBCs while the BLD objected to Jan Sangh members' ties to the RSS.[13] Jan Sangh members left the Janata Party and formed the BJP in 1980.

Phase 2: Hindu Nationalist Militancy

The BJP won enough votes and elected enough MLAs to form the government in 1991. It became the largest party in the state by participating in both a countermovement and a social movement. First, it organized a countermovement against the National Front government, which it was officially supporting, when Prime Minister VP Singh decided to implement the Mandal Commission recommendations and reserve 27 percent of government posts for OBCs.[14] Anti-Mandal protest enabled the BJP to gain the support of upper-caste Jats, who were excluded from Mandal benefits, and OBC Lodhs, Kurmis, and Sainis, who feared that Yadav OBCs would reap the benefits of reservations. Indeed, many observers have described "Mandir" (or temple, a shorthand for the Ayodhya movement) as a response to "Mandal" (the National Front government's implementation of the Mandal Commission report). Second, the BJP joined the VHP in the Ayodhya movement and thereby gained the support of *dalits* as well as upper-caste Thakurs, Banias, and a large segment of Brahmins.

The BJP also grew as a result of divisions within other parties and movements in UP. The Janata Party was factionalized between supporters of Prime Minister VP Singh and Mulayam Singh Yadav, who was UP chief minister from 1989 to 1991, 1993 to 1995, and 2003 to 2007. Yadav claimed in an interview that VP Singh had tried to undermine him by excluding him from

---

[13] Paul Brass, "Congress, the Lok Dal and the Middle Castes: An Analysis of the 1977 and 1980 Parliamentary Elections in Uttar Pradesh," *Pacific Affairs*, Spring 1981, Vol. 54, no. 1, 5–41, p. 16.

[14] The Janata Dal competed against the BJP in many parts of the state. As a result, the BJP won only 13 percent of the vote (57 seats), compared to Congress, which won 22.1 percent (94 seats), and the Janata Dal, which won 47.8 percent (208 seats) in the Legislative Assembly elections in 1989. Accessed August 27, 2014. http://eci.nic.in/eci_main/StatisticalReports/SE_1989/ Statistical%20Report_%20UP_1989.pdf.

negotiations with the BJP and VHP over the Ayodhya dispute and that VP Singh had stalled curbing the VHP's activities in order to save his government.[15] Lohia's disciple and a strong supporter of reservations for OBCs, Yadav criticized the BJP for being an upper-caste, "fascist" party because of its virulent anti-Muslim stance.

The BJP also profited from a split between the farmers' and OBC movements and the emergence of the Bharatiya Kisan Union (BKU), a farmers' organization that Mahendra Singh Tikait, a rural Jat leader from the prosperous cane- and wheat-growing region of western UP, created after Charan Singh's death in 1987. The BKU organized massive demonstrations in 1987 and 1988, including a twenty-four-day siege of Meerut demanding higher prices for sugar cane, reduced water and electricity rates, and cancellation of farmers' debts. Although the BKU claimed to represent farmers' interests, it mainly represented Jat farmers and relied on Jat leadership of caste councils (*khap panchayats*). *Dalits* who worked as laborers for Jat farmers distrusted the BKU.

The BJP was ideologically closer to the farmers' movement, which represented secure, prosperous groups, than to the Janata Dal, which represented OBCs. It needed to ally with the farmers' movement to broaden its class base from landlords to peasant proprietors. The BKU enabled the BJP to organize in western UP and gain the support of prosperous Jat farmers who had voted for the Janata Dal in the 1989 elections. Although the BKU shared the BJP's opposition to reservations for OBCs, for which Jats were not eligible, it did not share the BJP's anti-Muslim stance and had historically quelled Hindu-Muslim tensions in western UP.[16] Meanwhile, the alliance between the BKU and the BJP fostered tensions between the BKU and the Janata Dal.[17]

The Ayodhya movement enabled the BJP to expand its caste and class constituencies by appealing to a common Hindu identity. Lurking beneath the surface of the BJP's success was opposition to the Mandal Commission, which the upper castes opposed because it threatened their political dominance, and because it would empower their OBC employers. However, the BJP's militant movement-based expansion was short-lived because of deep-rooted tensions within the party over its stance toward the lower castes.

---

[15] Interview with Mulayam Singh Yadav, January 5, 1992. Yadav left the Janata Dal, joined Chandra Shekhar's Janata Dal (Socialist Party), and remained chief minister of UP with the backing of Congress after the National Front government fell in April 1991.

[16] Dipankar Gupta, "Country-Town Nexus and Agrarian Mobilisation: Bharatiya Kisan Union as an Instance," *Economic and Political Weekly*, December 17, 1988, Vol. 23, no. 51, 2688–96.

[17] Zoya Hasan, "Shifting Ground: Hindutva Politics and the Farmers' Movement in Uttar Pradesh," in Tom Brass, ed., *Farmers' Movement in India* (London: Frank Cass, 1994), 187 and Staffan Lindberg, "Farmers' Movements and Cultural Nationalism in India: An Ambiguous Relationship," *Theory and Society*, December 1995, Vol. 24, no. 6, 837–68.

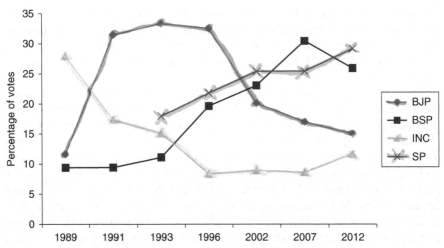

FIGURE 6.1. UP Legislative Assembly Election Results.

Source: Election Commission of India, *Statistical Report on the General Election, 1989–2012 to the Legislative Assembly of Uttar Pradesh,* New Delhi: Election Commission of India. Assessed July 16, 2014. Articles can be found at:

http://eci.nic.in/eci_main/StatisticalReports/SE_1989/Statistical%20Report_%20UP_1989.pdf

http://eci.nic.in/eci_main/statisticalreports/SE_1991/Stat_Rep_UP_91.pdf

http://eci.nic.in/eci_main/StatisticalReports/SE_1993/StatisticalReport_UP_1993.pdf

http://eci.nic.in/eci_main/StatisticalReports/SE_1996/StatisticalReport-UP96.pdf

http://eci.nic.in/eci_main/StatisticalReports/SE_2002/Stat_rep_UP_2002.pdf

http://eci.nic.in/eci_main/StatisticalReports/SE_2007/StatReport_AS_2007_UTTAR_PRADESH.pdf

http://eci.nic.in/eci_main/StatisticalReports/AE2012/Stats_Report_UP2012.pdf

Compiled by author, permissions not necessary.

[handwritten: moderate approach]

[handwritten: 93-03]

[handwritten: tokenized minorities]

Phase 3: The Post-Ayodhya Decline of Hindutva

The BJP realized that pursuing a militant anti-minority stance would cement ties between *dalits*, OBCs, and Muslims, but would not attract lower-caste adherents. Muslims had become increasingly active in demanding political representation and had lost interest in the Ayodhya dispute. Thus, the BJP fell back on its earlier strategy of forming and undermining alliances with ideologically dissimilar parties. In 1995, the BJP saved the BSP government by allying with it, only to withdraw support, which led to the government's collapse four months later. The BJP allied with the BSP two of the four times the BJP occupied office and all four BJP governments relied on defections from other parties (see Figure 6.1). UP's one-party dominant system became a fragmented

TABLE 6.1. *Governments in Uttar Pradesh*

Chief Minister/Governments	Duration
Mulayam Singh Yadav, Janata Dal	December 5, 1989 to June 24, 1991
Kalyan Singh, BJP	June 24, 1991 to December 6, 1992
President's rule	December 6, 1992 to December 4, 1993
Mulayam Singh Yadav, SP	December 4, 1993 to June 3, 1995
Mayawati, BJP-BSP	June 3, 1995 to October 18, 1995
President's rule	October 18, 1995 to March 20 1997
Mayawati, BJP-BSP	March 21, 1997 to September 21, 1997
Kalyan Singh, BJP	September 21, 1997 to November 12, 1999
Ram Prakash Gupta, BJP	November 12, 1999 to October 28, 2000
Rajnath Singh, BJP	October 28, 2000 to March 8, 2002
President's rule	March 8, 2002 to May 3, 2002
Mayawati, BSP	May 3, 2002 to August 29, 2003
Mulayam Singh Yadav, SP	August 29, 2003 to May 13, 2007
Mayawati, BSP	May 13, 2007 to March 7, 2012
Akhilesh Yadav, SP	March 15, 2012–

Source: Compiled by author.

multiparty system in 1989. The BJP ruled intermittently until 2002, mostly by allying with other parties or appropriating their members. After that, two parties alternated in office. The BSP achieved power in 2002 and 2007 and the SP in 2012. The BSP and the SP could govern without the BJP (see Table 6.1). The fragmentation of the multiparty system mirrored the BJP's internal factionalism. One source of tension was between those who favored a smaller, more ideologically pure party as opposed to those who favored a larger, more amorphous party. As the BJP grew by precipitating defections from other political parties, it came to include leaders who did not share its core philosophical commitments. The RSS opposed the transformation of a once-disciplined, hierarchical cadre party into a large, unruly party of rival leaders. The other source of tension was caste-based. In seeking greater support from the lower castes, the BJP threatened the RSS and senior BJP leaders, who feared that the lower castes would gain power within the party. The growth of the BSP and the SP and Muslims' increased demands for political representation accentuated the BJP's internal dilemmas.

Caste Tensions within the BJP

The BJP recognized the need to include the lower-castes to achieve electoral success. Its general secretary KN Govindacharya encouraged it to engage in "social engineering" by inducting lower-caste members into the party's executive committee and nominating them as electoral candidates. Reversing its earlier stance, the BJP publicly supported quotas for both Scheduled Castes and OBCs and dropped Hindu nationalist appeals from its 1996 election campaign. Kalyan Singh increased the BJP's popularity among non-Yadav OBCs, the so-called Most Backward Classes (MBCs), and certain *dalits*, like Balmikis and Pasis, who resented Chamar-Jatav domination of the BSP. Kalyan Singh persuaded the BJP's national executive committee to nominate OBC candidates in 190 out of 420 constituencies in the 1996 elections. More than 29 percent of OBCs voted for the BJP in the parliamentary elections in 1996 and 30.6 percent in 1998.[18]

The national government placed UP under President's rule because no party won a clear majority in the 1996 Assembly elections. The BSP and BJP formed the government with an agreement to rotate the chief minister's post between Mayawati and Kalyan Singh. Upon becoming chief minister, Singh challenged the BSP's commitment to protecting the lower castes from upper-caste violence by asking district administrations to ensure that the Scheduled Castes and Tribes (Prevention of Atrocities) Act, commonly known as the Harijan Act, was not used against political opponents. BSP leader Kanshi Ram called for a mass agitation in protest and the BSP withdrew from the coalition government. Two days later, twenty-six MLAs left the BSP and joined the BJP government.

The BJP government pursued a number of Hindu nationalist goals. The State Education Board rewrote nearly twenty-five textbooks. State Education Minister NK Gaur, a former RSS *pracharak*, introduced *kulp*, a scheme to promote moral education, celebrate Hindu religious festivals, and observe the birth and death anniversaries of Hindutva stalwarts like Keshak Baliram Hedgewar and Shyama Prasad Mukherjee. The government made *kulp* compulsory for all primary schools in the state and ordered public schools to implement it.[19] A government order tried to make singing Vande Mataram, a Hindu nationalist hymn, mandatory in schools, however the National Commission for Minorities intervened and prevented this. The BJP government introduced a Religious Buildings and Places bill, which required district magistrate authorization for the construction of new places of worship and demolition of existing structures. Ram Prakash Gupta repeatedly claimed that the bill was necessary because *madrasas* were sanctuaries for Pakistan's intelligence forces.[20]

[18] Jasmine Zerinini-Brotel, "Options in Uttar Pradesh," *Seminar*, August 1999. Accessed July 20, 2014. http://www.india-seminar.com/1999/480/480%20zerinini-brotel.htm.

[19] "Education BJP Style: Saffronisation of Books – III," *Ganashakti*. Accessed July 1, 2014. http://ganashakti.tripod.com/981214/week_feature2.htm.

[20] Venkitesh Ramakrishnan, "Convulsions in Uttar Pradesh," *Frontline*, April 15–28, 2000, Vol. 17, no. 8. Accessed July 22, 2014. http://www.frontline.in/static/html/fl1708/17080320.htm. The UP Loktantrik Congress, which was a member of the ruling coalition, boycotted a cabinet meeting on April 4, 1998 to demonstrate its opposition to the bill.

The government did not stop the Bajrang Dal and the VHP from organizing attacks on Christians in many parts of the state in 1998.[21] In the early years of the Ayodhya movement, Kalyan Singh was an ideal party, movement, and government leader. After becoming chief minister of UP in 1991, he oversaw government acquisition of 2.77 acres of land adjoining the *babri masjid* complex. He replaced district officials in Faizabad and approved the VHP's decision to replace the priest at the site of worship. Kalyan Singh, along with national party president MM Joshi, and many ministers and newly elected MLAs traveled to Ayodhya and took oaths to build a temple there.[22] Kalyan Singh affirmed his commitment to building a temple in Ayodhya when he was chief minister in 1997.

However, RSS and upper-caste BJP leaders resented the large representation of OBCs among the BJP MLAs who were elected in 1996 and among ministers (twenty-five out of ninety-two) in the BJP Cabinet in 1997.[23] They were also furious that Kalyan Singh created an enormous cabinet of ninety-one ministers, forty-five of whom had defected from other political parties. Thirty-three of the ministers (including three BJP ministers, Hukum Singh, Rakesh Dhar Tripathi, and Sri Ram Sonkar) faced criminal charges.[24] The RSS objected that the BJP's expansion undermined its ideological commitments and ethical character. Rajendra Singh commented that the BJP had lost its moorings and become an imitation of Congress.[25]

Prominent upper-caste BJP leaders, like Rajendra Singh, Lalji Tandon, and Kalraj Mishra, lobbied to replace Kalyan Singh with an upper-caste leader.[26] In May 1999, thirty-three BJP MLAs threatened to resign unless the BJP president expelled Singh; prominent lower-caste leaders like Uma Bharati and Ganga Charan Rajput rallied to his defense.[27] Singh and his supporters

[21] Attacks on Christians occurred in Kanpur on March 16, Robertsgang on August 15 and September 26, Baghpat on September 23 and October 7, and in Amaun, Udham Singh Nagar district on September 26. Praveen Swami, "A Catalogue of Crimes," *Frontline*, January 30–February 12, 1999. Accessed July 1, 2014. http://www.frontline.in/navigation/?type=static &page=flonnet&rdurl=fl1603/16030130.htm.

[22] Gulab Singh Parhar, VHP president for UP, described a ceremony in Ayodhya on June 26, 1991 that 10,000 people attended at which the BJP affirmed its commitment to building a temple in Ayodhya. Interview with Gulab Singh Parhar, Lucknow, January 4, 1992.

[23] Christophe Jaffrelot and Gilles Verniers, "Castes, Communities and Parties in Uttar Pradesh," *Economic and Political Weekly*, August 11, 2012, Vol. 47, no. 32

[24] Venkitesh Ramakrishnan, "The Great Lucknow Circus," *Frontline*, 89-93. November 15–28, 1997. Accessed July 1, 2014. http://www.frontline.in/static/html/fl1423/14230040.htm.

[25] "Factions Unreconciled: The RSS Intervenes in the BJP's Affairs in UP," *Frontline*, February 7, 1997, 14. The RSS also faced another challenge, of curbing the political ambitions of its *pracharaks*. Rajendra Singh criticized the *pracharaks* whom the RSS had deputed to the BJP for succumbing to casteism, corruption, and nepotism. This partially vindicated Kalyan Singh, who had long contended that RSS upper-caste organizational secretaries and *pracharaks* favored members of their own caste in party recruitment and promotion.

[26] "Uttar Pradesh Crisis to Hurt BJP at Federal Level," *Bangalore Deccan Herald*, May 10, 1999.

[27] Senior BJP leader Om Prakash Singh, a Kurmi and a strong supporter of Kalyan Singh, was forced to resign as BJP state secretary. He and other OBC leaders complained of being excluded

circulated pamphlets that denounced the BJP for its upper-caste elitism and plastered Lucknow with graffiti that read "Jo Kalyan ko mitayega, hum use mita denge" ("He who dares to remove Kalyan will be wiped out by us") and "Kalyan nahin to desh nahin" ("No Kalyan, no state").[28] Kalyan Singh complained that the BJP had not consulted him in selecting candidates for the 1999 parliamentary elections and that it had lobbied against the candidates he supported.

Factional rivalries based on BJP leaders' personal ambitions, tensions between the RSS and the BJP, and caste divisions within the BJP, hurt the BJP in the 2002 elections. It was reduced to 20 percent of the vote and 88 seats, from 33 percent of the vote and 174 seats in 1996.[29] The BJP's decisions about political appointments were determined by factional rivalries. Initially, it made Ram Prakash Gupta, a Bania RSS-backed leader, chief minister in order to avoid antagonizing two more powerful contenders for the position, Kalraj Mishra, Public Works minister, and Lalji Tandon, Urban Development minister. However, when Gupta proved an ineffective leader, the BJP replaced him with Rajnath Singh and made Mishra state party president in 2000. When Mishra resigned from the post of party president in 2002, he said that the BJP had lost the election because of infighting among its leaders.[30] There were several instances of BJP MPs – Ram Nagina Mishra in Padrauna constituency, Kishan Lal in Hathras, Sheela Gautam in Aligarh, and Ashok Pradhan in Khurja – undermining candidates from their own party.[31]

There were also tensions between the RSS and the BJP. When the BJP nominated Ravindra Jaiswal in Varanasi under pressure from the RSS, other party members campaigned against him, saying that he was an outsider. When the BJP did not renominate 40 of its 158 MLA incumbents for the 2002 elections, citing their dubious loyalty to the party or nonperformance in office, they objected and blamed the RSS for influencing the BJP's decision.[32] The BJP expelled sixteen rebel candidates, who then organized violent protests and demonstrations in front of its headquarters.[33]

from important party decisions."Acid Test for BJP," *Frontline*, February 15, 2002. Accessed July 1, 2014. http://www.frontline.in/navigation/?type=static&page=archive.

[28] Kalyan Singh did not refute the remarks of his close associate Sachchidanand Sakshi Maharaj, who claimed that the "Brahmin troika," Atal Bihari Vajpayee, Murli Manohar Joshi, and Kalraj Mishra, were plotting his downfall, or his description of Kalyan Singh and Mulayam Singh Yadav as natural allies.

[29] Statistical Report on General Election, 2002 to The Legislative Assembly of Uttar Pradesh, Election Commission of India, New Delhi. Accessed July 1, 2014. http://eci.nic.in/eci_main/StatisticalReports/SE_2002/Stat_rep_UP_2002.pdf

[30] "Kalraj Mishra Resigns as UP BJP Chief," *Express India*, June 1, 2002. Accessed July 21, 2014. http://expressindia.indianexpress.com/news/fullstory.php?newsid=11065.

[31] *Jansatta*, April 17, 2002.

[32] *The Indian Express*, New Delhi, January 14, 2002.

[33] JP Shukla, "Storms of Protest in BJP," *The Hindu*, New Delhi, January 20, 2002. Accessed July 1, 2014. http://hindu.com/2002/01/20/stories/2002012001330800.htm.

Relations among upper-caste BJP leaders, particularly between Rajnath Singh, a Rajput, and Kalraj Mishra, a Brahmin, were also fraught. Several candidates who were Rajnath Singh supporters lost the election and alleged that a Brahmin organization, the Sarva Brahmin Samaj, had mobilized opposition to Rajput candidates. The Rajput Mahasabha distributed pamphlets that it claimed were designed to counter Sarva Brahmin Samaj propaganda.[34] Brahmins were disaffected by the growth of Rajput leadership and voted for the strongest Brahmin candidate rather than for the BJP in several constituencies.[35] In some instances, Banias also voted against the BJP.[36] The BJP sought to maintain upper-caste dominance. All the posters for the 2002 elections depicted upper-caste but not OBC leaders. Ashok Yadav, a government minister, vetoed Rajnath Singh's proposal to recruit MBC members to government jobs and got an interim stay from the High Court. As a result, many OBCs deserted the BJP. Kalyan Singh formed the Rashtriya Kranti Party.[37] Although it won only three seats, it took Lodh support away from the BJP in the Kanpur region and in several districts in western UP.[38] Furthermore Kurmis, who had voted for the BJP in the early 1990s, shifted their support to the Apna Dal, a Kurmi party that was formed in 1995.[39] The Apna Dal only won three seats but adversely affected the BJP in eastern UP. This fracturing of the political loyalties of Kurmis and Lodhs broke the axle around which the BJP's OBC base had revolved.[40]

The BJP also lost Jat support in western UP, where the Jats were numerically preponderant, between the 1996 and 2002 Assembly elections. The BJP's electoral pact with the Rashtriya Lok Dal in 2001 to gain Jat support incurred the opposition of some Jat BJP members. Furthermore, the BJP lost the support of its former ally, Mahendra Singh Tikait, the leader of the BKU, who

---

[34] *Hindustan Times*, February 28, 2002.

[35] For instance, in Kanpur, Dehat, Kannauj, and Farrukhabad constituencies, Brahmins voted for Brahmin candidates from the SP and the BSP rather than the BJP. In Bareilly, the Brahmin Mahasabha supported the Brahmin Congress candidate over the BJP's Bania candidate, "Sabak Na Seekne ka Khamiyaja," *India Today* (Hindi edition), March 6, 2002.

[36] Many Banias were angered by Rajnath Singh's expulsion of Naresh Agarwal from the Cabinet. In Khurja constituency, the Vaish Sabha supported the Rashtriya Kranti Party Bania candidate. Naresh Agarwal took a segment of Banias with him when he joined the Samajwadi Party. *Times of India*, February 17, 2002 and February 19, 2002 and *India Today*, March 13, 2002.

[37] KV Prasad, "Kalyan all Set to Take on BJP," *The Hindu*, February 9, 2002. Accessed July 1, 2014. http://www.hindu.com/2002/02/09/stories/2002020903250900.htm.

[38] "Kalyan Floats New Party, Ends Speculation on Returning to BJP," *DNA India*, January 5, 2010. Accessed July 1, 2014. http://www.dnaindia.com/india/report-kalyan-floats-new-party-ends-speculation-on-returning-to-bjp-1331184.

[39] Besides Lodhs, Kurmis, and Yadavs, nearly half (49.7%) of the OBCs voted for the BJP in 1996. CSDS Data Unit, given in VB Singh, "Uttar Pradesh Chunav ke Nateeje: Kucch Shankaye Bhari Umeede," *Naya Sangharsh*, January–March 1997, 54–62.

[40] Jasmine Zerinini-Brotel, "The BJP in Uttar Pradesh: From Hindutva to Consensual Politics," in Thomas Blom Hansen and Christophe Jaffrelot, eds., *The BJP and The Compulsions of Politics in India* (New Delhi: Oxford University Press, 1998), 80.

supported the Indian National Lok Dal (INLD).[41] The consequent split in the Jat vote affected the erstwhile Jat-Rajput alliance in certain regions, such as the Meerut-Bijnor belt.[42]

In an attempt to capture more OBC votes and gain a competitive edge over other parties, the BJP re-inducted Kalyan Singh in February 2004, just ahead of the parliamentary elections. MM Joshi commented, "Kalyan Singh's return to the party had created an atmosphere of confidence among party workers, and also in the people." Kalyan Singh said he had left all bitterness behind and that returning to the BJP was like "coming home."[43] However, the BJP performed poorly in the 2004 parliamentary elections. It won only 22.2 percent of the votes and ten seats. The upper castes resented Kalyan Singh's return and more Rajputs voted for Congress than for the BJP. Nor could the BJP attract Muslim or non-Yadav OBC support. Only 2.6 percent of Muslims voted for the BJP in the 2004 elections.[44]

Kalyan Singh continued to feel marginalized by upper-caste BJP leaders. He accused the BJP of "humiliating" and "suffocating" him and said that he had made a huge "political blunder" because there was no place for OBC leaders in the BJP.[45] Singh left the BJP and formed the Jan Kranti Party (JKP) to fulfill the BJP's unkept promise of building a Ram temple in Ayodhya.[46] Kalyan Singh's departure not only signified and deepened factionalism in the BJP, but also deprived the BJP of a movement leader. In a 2007 interview, Singh stated, "I have no regrets that the *dhancha* was destroyed. It was a symbol of slavery. Babur ordered the demolition of our temple and the construction of the mosque to humiliate *crores* of Hindus." He said that the BJP had wholeheartedly supported the VHP-initiated movement and that Hindus were disappointed that a Ram temple had not yet been built. "The temple will be built. It's a matter of faith, not a matter that the courts can resolve."[47]

The tensions within the BJP around Kalyan Singh's leadership exemplified a contradiction at the heart of the movement that had catapulted it to power. The Ayodhya campaign was led by an OBC and sought to increase lower-caste

---

[41] Purnima S. Tripathi, "In a Cleft Stick," *Frontline*, February 1, 2002. Accessed July 1, 2014. http://www.frontline.in/static/html/fl1902/19020320.htm.

[42] The BJP was also at odds with the Rashtriya Lok Dal and the INLD over the creation of a separate state, Harit Pradesh, in western UP. Ajit Singh and Chautala's INLD supported its creation and the BJP opposed it. Harit Pradesh contained a large Muslim population and thus a large Muslim electoral bloc.

[43] "Kalyan's Revolving Door Politics," *The Indian Express*, November 16, 2009. Accessed July 1, 2014. http://archive.indianexpress.com/news/kalyan-s-revolving-door-politics/541952/.

[44] Sanjay Kumar, "The Prospects," *Seminar*, no. 571, March 2007. Accessed July 1, 2014. http://www.india-seminar.com/2007/571/571_sanjay_kumar.htm.

[45] Interview with Kalyan Singh, Lucknow, July 16, 2007.

[46] The JKP did not win any of the 208 seats it contested and received only 1.24 percent of the vote in the 2012 Assembly elections.

[47] Interview with Kalyan Singh, Lucknow, July 16, 2007.

support for the BJP. However, although the BJP's upper-caste leadership wanted lower castes' electoral support, it was less enthusiastic about their becoming party leaders and BJP government officials.

The Challenge of Dalit Parties and Movements

Both the BSP and the BJP are movement-parties. Far from seeing elections and activism as antithetical, they have combined rabble-rousing movement activity with savvy electoral strategizing. These movement-parties have pursued their goals by both challenging and joining state institutions. However, the constituencies, ideologies, and goals of these two movement-parties differ. The BSP's rise and the BJP's decline are almost inversely correlated, especially in the Assembly elections in 1991, when the BSP won 9.4 percent and the BJP 31.5 percent of the vote and in 2007, when the BSP won 30.4 percent and the BJP 17 percent of the vote.

The BSP in UP grew out of a long tradition of *dalit* activism that challenged caste discrimination and violence and sought increased *dalit* education, employment, and political representation.[48] The immediate predecessor to the BSP is a social movement organization, the *Dalit* Shoshit Samaj Sangharsh Samiti (DS-4), Committee to fight for the Community of the Exploited and the Oppressed, which Kanshi Ram founded in 1981. The DS-4 held *yatras, jagrans* (people's parliaments), and cycle rallies across the state and organized migrant urban *dalit* slum dwellers. In 1984, Kanshi Ram founded the BSP, a political party (although Mayawati and Kanshi Ram referred to it as a mission or a movement). Building on the DS-4's legacy, BSP party workers traveled through the state on bicycles to politicize *dalits*.

The DS-4 and the VHP engaged in similar forms of political organizing to forge local-national ties. They sent activists to different regions of the country and had them converge at a central location at an appointed date. In November 1983, the VHP organized the *ektamata yatra*, a 100-day campaign that entailed three different processions traveling through the country to Delhi. From March to April 1983, the DS-4 organized a 3,000-kilometer cycle rally across several states. The following year it organized an even larger procession of cyclists that converged on Delhi.

---

[48] The Nava Maveshi movement mobilized Chamars in the 1950s to reject demeaning caste occupations. Badri Narayan, *The Making of the Dalit Public in North India, Uttar Pradesh, 1950–Present* (New Delhi: Oxford University Press, 2011). The Republican Party (RPI) (1954–71) initially organized the Jatavs in urban areas and later rural *dalits* around land to the tiller and minimum statutory wages in western UP. Jagpal Singh, "Amdekarisation and the Assertion of Dalit Identity, Socio-Cultural Protest in Meerut District of Western Uttar Pradesh," *Economic and Political Weekly*, July 4, 1998. Accessed July 1, 2014. http://www.epw.in/system/files/pdf/1998_33/40/ambedkarisation_and_assertion_of_dalit_identity.pdf. One of the RPI's successors, the Dalit Panthers of UP, formed by Rahulan Ambedekar in 1981, rejected electoral participation in favor of social and cultural activism.

(margin handwriting: OBCs advocating in the BSP)

Both the BJP and BSP have combined religious and political themes by conferring religious authority on secular figures and inventing religious ceremonies. If Hindu nationalists have elevated the significance of the Hindu deity Ram, *dalit* activists have worshipped their own gods and constructed temples named after famous *dalits* like Valmiki, BR Ambedkar, and Ravi Das.[49] Both parties have claimed civic spaces for *dalits* and Hindus, respectively. To symbolically challenge *dalits'* historic exclusion from the public sphere, the BSP has memorialized Ambedkar by installing statues of him in town and city squares and naming libraries and schools also after him. It has commemorated Ambedkar's birthday with festivals where activists sing songs, shout slogans, organize skits, read stories, and take out processions. BSP governments have renamed districts, universities, and stadiums after important *dalit* leaders.[50]

The BJP's short-lived government in 1991 and 1992 proposed that the town of Mughalsarai, in eastern UP should be renamed Deen Dayal Nagar and that other towns with Muslim names should be given Hindu names, but the central government prevented this. Rajnath Singh, while chief minister of UP, suggested that Allahabad be renamed Tirthraj Prayag. BJP MP Varun Gandhi pledged to replace statues of Mayawati with statues of Lord Ram if the party regained power in UP.[51] The BJP's 2012 vision document stated, "If BJP comes to power, statues of Kabir, Sant Ravidas, martyr Uda Devi, Jhalkari Bai, Bijli Pasi, and other great personalities of all sections will be installed in memorials and parks constructed during Mayawati regime."[52]

Both BJP and the BSP governments have pursued core ideological commitments. BSP governments have addressed anti-*dalit* violence by fast-tracking investigations, lengthening jail sentences for those convicted of crimes against *dalits*, and providing monetary compensation for victims. They have engaged in large-scale transfers of district magistrates, superintendents of police, and principal secretaries to ensure *dalit* representation in the administration. While in office in 1995 and 1997, the BSP government engaged in development activities among *dalit* communities by strengthening the Ambedkar Village Program.[53]

[49] Badri Narayan, "Inventing Caste History: Dalit Mobilisation and Nationalist Past," *Contributions to Indian Sociology* 38, no. 1–2 (2004): 193–220.
[50] Nicolas Jaoul, "Dalit Processions, Street Politics and Democratization in India," in Julia C. Strauss and Donald Cruise O'Brien, eds., *Staging Politics: Power and Performance in Asia and Africa*. International Library of Political Studies: 18. (London: I. B. Tauris, 2007), 179–83. A BSP government renamed the university in Agra Dr. Bhimrao Ambedkar University and the university in Kanpur Chhatrapati Shahuji Ji Mahraj University. It created a new district called Dr. Bhimrao Ambedkar Nagar. It installed five twelve-foot bronze statues of Ambedkar in Udhyan Park in Lucknow.
[51] "BJP Will Replace Maya's Statues with Lord Ram's: Varun Gandhi," *The Indian Express*, May 20, 2010. Accessed July 1, 2014. http://archive.indianexpress.com/news/bjp-will-replace-maya-statues-with-lord-rams-varun-gandhi/621331/.
[52] Bharatiya Janata Party (Uttar Pradesh) Press Statement, Lucknow, January 16, 2012. For highlights of the vision document, see Nitin Gadkari, *Hamare Sapnon Ka Uttar Pradesh*.
[53] The program designates one village in each block in which *dalits* form at least 30 percent of the population as eligible for special government assistance, such as the construction of link roads,

However, important differences between the two movement-parties explain greater Hindu nationalist than *dalit* militancy. First, senior leaders of the BJP, unlike the BSP, feared that expanding its social coalition and political leadership would destroy the party. Kanshi Ram recognized that *dalits* could only attain power by building a broad social coalition. He claimed that 85 percent of the population, the *bahujan samaj* (majority of people), was united by its subjugation to upper caste domination. Of the BSP's candidates for political office in 1999, 8 percent were Muslim and 27 percent OBC.[54] It then called for *sarvajana*, the inclusion of Brahmins.[55] From 2002 to 2007, the BSP performed better among upper castes, *dalits*, and Muslims than any other party.

Second, compared to the BSP, the BJP has both gained and lost more by having stronger ties to a separate social movement organization. The VHP contributed handsomely to the BJP's early success but ceased to consistently do so in later years. VHP leader Praveen Togadia, who had previously campaigned vigorously for the BJP stated, "The voters in UP were looking for the party with a difference, unfortunately the BJP could not appreciate that.... If the BJP had projected Hindutva with greater intensity, there was no reason why it should not have picked up 225 seats."[56]

The BSP's movement wing is relatively weak. Kanshi Ram created the Backward and Minority Castes Employees' Federation (BAMCEF) in 1978 as a "nonpolitical" organization of government employees. Although BAMCEF organizes mass contact campaigns in poor *dalit* neighborhoods, it is not a social movement organization and its members, who are government employees, cannot participate directly in BSP election campaigns. Instead, BAMCEF engages in social work, trains educated *dalits* for leadership and employment, and constitutes a think tank for the BSP. BAMCEF has always supported the BSP.

Dalit activists have questioned the BSP for prioritizing party-building over grassroots social movement activity aimed at social transformation. They have criticized the BSP for its hierarchical centralized structure, attempts to thwart radical movements, and opportunistic alliances with the BJP. Younger generations of *dalits* feel that the BSP should invest less money in building statues and more in improving *dalits'* material conditions. Echoing their views, Sudha Pai argues that the BSP "once eulogized as a social movement that would introduce social revolution and transformation ... later got converted into an

school buildings, and drinking water and the provision of loans for *dalits* to construct homes and start businesses for a period of two years.

[54] Christophe Jaffrelot, *India's Silent Revolution, The Rise of the Low Castes in North Indian Politics* (New Delhi: Permanent Black), 401.

[55] Christophe Jaffrelot, "The Bahujan Samaj Party in North India: No Longer Just a Dalit Party?" *Comparative Studies of South Asia, Africa and the Middle East*, 1998, Vol. 18, no. 1, 35–52.

[56] *The Times of India*, October 14, 1996.

opportunistic political party interested in the capture of state power."[57] Pai contends that although the BSP successfully combined party and movement attributes in its early years, the party increasingly dominated the movement and came to believe that it could emancipate *dalits* exclusively through electoral means.[58]

However, even *dalit* activists who criticize the BSP believe that BSP governments serve their interests. The BSP's success has brought about visible improvements in *dalits'* status and confidence.[59] The increased presence of *dalits* in administrative positions has enabled activists to gain a sympathetic hearing from local officials and provided *dalits* with new roles as intermediaries between the public and administration.[60] If from one perspective the BSP has betrayed the goals of more radical *dalit* activists, from another perspective the BSP has been true to the vision of the major *dalit* leaders who considered political power the key to *dalit* empowerment. BR Ambedkar believed that *dalits* could compensate for their lack of resources by using their strength in numbers to elect *dalit* officials. Kanshi Ram famously commented, "We have a one point program – take power."[61]

The Growth of Muslim Politics

The emergence of a more politically engaged and assertive Muslim community in UP made it harder for Hindu nationalists to scapegoat Muslims and cast them as religious zealots. Muslims were heartened by the SP's defense of their rights and opposition to the BJP in the early 1990s. They were deeply affected by the publication of the Sachar Committee Report documenting the significant economic, educational, and political disadvantages they face and advocating reservations for Muslims.[62]

Muslims have become increasingly aware of their potential electoral impact. They can significantly affect electoral outcomes in about 130 of 403 Assembly seats. They comprise 20 percent of the electorate in about seventy

[57] Sudha Pai, *Dalit Assertion and the Unfinished Democratic Revolution: The BSP in Uttar Pradesh* (New Delhi: Sage Publications, 2002), 2.
[58] Ibid., 19–20.
[59] Craig Jeffrey and Jens Lerche, "Stating the Difference: State, Discourse and Class Reproduction in Uttar Pradesh, India," *Development and Change* 32, no. 4, (2000): 872.
[60] Nicholas Jaoul, "Political and 'Non-political' Means in the Dalit Movement," in Sudha Pai, ed., *Political Process in Uttar Pradesh: Identity, Economic Reforms and Governance* (New Delhi: Pearson Longman, 2007), 192.
[61] Ram, *The Chamcha Age*.
[62] For example, the commission found that in UP in 2001 literacy rates were 58 percent for Hindus and 48 percent for Muslims and the mean years of schooling for children ages 7–16 was 2.6 percent for Muslims and 3.9 percent for Hindus (not including Scheduled Castes and Scheduled Tribes). Poverty levels for Muslims were significantly higher in rural than in urban areas and Muslims tended to be concentrated in villages that were most lacking in schools, hospitals, bus stops, and regular roads.

seats and 30–45 percent of the electorate in thirty-six seats: twenty in western UP, ten in eastern UP, five in central UP, and one in Bundelkhand.[63] Muslim voting patterns can also decisively influence at least twenty-one parliamentary seats in UP.

Muslims have increasingly pressured parties to address their economic and political interests rather than their religious identities. For example, Muslim leaders opposed the SP's announcement that all government-run or government-aided schools and colleges would end their classes by noon on Fridays to enable Muslim students and teachers to offer *namaz*. They stated that if the state government seriously intended to improve Muslims' welfare, it should devise plans for their educational and economic advancement instead of creating discord between Muslims and Hindus.[64] As a result the SP withdrew the order.

Muslims have formed numerous political parties in UP, including the United Democratic Front, People's Democratic Front, Secular Ekta Party, Ulema Council, Peace Party, Rashtriya Inquilab Party, Parcham Party, and Millat Party. Of these, the most significant is the Peace Party. Most Muslim parties do not hope to win Legislative Assembly elections but rather to voice their interests, influence other parties, and put forward their political demands. Zafrayab Jilani commented:

In these elections these parties won't amount to much. But the secular parties must heed their warning. The feeling of isolation among Muslims is over. If these parties don't pay attention to their genuine needs, both in terms of development and share in decision-making, the community will head towards a secular platform of its own.[65]

The Rashtriya Inquilab Party, which three-time BSP MP Ilyas Azmi formed, calls for lifting restrictions under Article 341 on inclusion of Muslims in the Scheduled Caste list, separate reservations within the OBC quota, and increased Muslim political representation.

Mohammed Ayyub, who formed the Peace Party out of disillusionment with Congress, commented:

For the past two decades each time there is an election, the Congress remembers reservations. Then it warns us if we don't vote for the Congress, the BJP will come to power. We want to tell them: let the BJP come to power. We want the Samajwadi Party and the Congress to get a setback.[66]

---

[63] Rana Ayyub, "The Vote that Counts," *Tehelka Magazine*, December 24, 2011. Accessed July 1, 2014. http://www.tehelka.com/the-vote-that-counts-2/.

[64] "Bukhari Calls to Fight for Rights of Muslims," *Tribune News Service*, March 18, 2006. Accessed July 2, 2014. http://www.tribuneindia.com/2006/20060319/nation.htm#2.

[65] Smita Gupta, "Muslim Mood in UP," *Economic and Political Weekly*, May 16, 2009. Accessed July 2, 2014. http://www.epw.in/system/files/pdf/2009_44/20/The_Muslim_Mood_in_Uttar_Pradesh.pdf.

[66] Rana Ayyub, "The Vote that Counts."

Javed Siddiqui formed the Association for Welfare, Medical, Educational, and Legal Assistance of Muslims after two of his sons were charged with being members of the Indian Mujahideen and planning the 2008 Delhi bomb blasts. He asked, "Where were the Congress and Samajwadi MLAs when our sons were being tortured and taken from one jail to the other? Where was Digvijay Singh? Why are we remembered only around elections?"[67]

As Muslims have formed their own parties, the SP, BSP, and Congress have sought to attract Muslim voters by supporting the community's educational advancement and political representation. Even the BJP has courted Muslim support. In November 2011, Rajnath Singh announced that the BJP was committed to creating a sub-quota for thirty-five Muslim sub-castes within the broader OBC quota. That year both Uma Bharati and LK Advani encouraged Muslims to join their *yatras*.

Phase 4: Return to Militancy

[handwritten annotations: 2002+ · BJP returned to activist role · Radicalism e military]

The BJP reverted to a militant stance in 2002 to regain the support of party workers who opposed its alliances with lower-caste parties and placate the RSS and the VHP, which blamed its electoral defeats on its retreat from Hindutva. In 2002, as in 1991 and 1992, the BJP was in power in UP and its ties to the VHP and its affiliates were relatively strong. Discarding the veneer of moderation, the BJP defended the Hindu Yuva Vahini (HYV) and its militant leader Yogi Adityanath, although he derided and undermined the BJP. Characterizing it as a party that engages in doublespeak, Adityanath campaigned for Hindu Mahasabha candidate Radha Mohan Das Agarwal, who defeated the BJP candidate, ex-Minister Shiv Prakash Shukla, by a wide margin in the 2002 elections.[68] Adityanath was rumored to have campaigned against BJP candidates, who were defeated in the 2009 parliamentary elections.

And yet the major RSS, VHP, and BJP leaders have paid obeisance to Adityanath. In 2003, Deputy Prime Minister Advani accepted Adityanath's invitation to Gorakhpur and high-ranking Sangh Parivar leaders, including RSS head Rajjubhaiyya and VHP leader Ashok Singhal, attended a forum that Adityanath organized. Sangh leaders attended a three-day *mahasammelan* (spiritual gathering) that Adityanath hosted on December 22–24, 2006, although it conflicted with the BJP's three-day national executive and national council meetings in Lucknow. The *mahasammelan* proclaimed a commitment to pursuing the Hindu nationalist goals that it said the BJP had abandoned.[69]

---

[67] Ibid.
[68] Atiq Khan, "Yogi's Revolt may Hit BJP," *The Hindu*, March 28, 2007. Accessed July 2, 2014. http://www.hindu.com/2007/03/28/stories/2007032805111200.htm.
[69] Subhash Gatade, "The Yogi and the Fanatic: Will Eastern UP Be the Next Gujarat?" *People's Democracy*, February 11, 2007. Accessed July 2, 2014. http://archives.peoplesdemocracy.in/2007/0211/02112007_gatade.htm.

Adityanath criticized the BJP for inducting four men whom the BSP had expelled because they faced corruption charges. He was especially enraged that the BJP accepted former BSP Family Welfare Minister Babu Singh Kushwaha, and made him a candidate for the 2012 elections. Adityanath threatened to quit the party, campaign against these candidates, and float a new political outfit if the BJP did not reverse its decision. BJP leaders complied and withdrew Kushwaha's candidacy.

Adityanath's violent anti-Muslim campaigns escalated in 2002, the same year as the Gujarat violence and the VHP's renewal of the Ayodhya campaign. Adityanath described himself as the next Narendra Modi and repeatedly threatened to turn Gorakhpur into Godhra and UP into Gujarat. One of Adityanath's slogans was "UP bhi Gujarat banega, Padrauna shuruaat karega" ("UP will also become a Gujarat and the process will start in Padrauna"). Adityanath's close associate, Radha Mohan Das Agarwal), stated, "Gorakhpur is a Hindu rashtra. Yogijee is both its president and prime minister."

Human rights organizations reported that the HYV had engaged in arson, looting, and killings on many occasions. Two of the most serious episodes occurred in Mau in October 2005 and in January 2007. Tensions between Hindus and Muslims in Mau had been recurrent but ran especially high in October 2005, when the Hindu festival of Dussehra and the Muslim festival of Ramzan coincided. On October 13, Muslims reciting prayers in a mosque objected that they were being disrupted by Hindu prayers on loudspeakers. Some members of the BJP and the administration met and decided to postpone the Hindu ceremony until October 29 to defuse tensions. The controversy would have ended at this point, but on October 14 HYV and Hindu Mahasabha activists blockaded the streets to protest the postponement of the ceremony and accused BJP leaders of neglecting Hindu interests. The crowd exchanged provocative slogans and pelted stones at each other. Some HYV members opened fire. According to official information, eight people (equal numbers of Hindus and Muslims) were killed and thirty-seven people were injured.

An investigation team claimed that the HYV and its leader, Yogi Adityanath, had incited violence.[70] However, BJP leaders supported the HYV. Its national vice president, Kalyan Singh, state president Keshari Nath Tripathi, and leader of the opposition in the state legislature, Lalji Tandon, claimed that the government's appeasement of Muslims was responsible for the violence and blamed Muslim strongman and SP MLA Mukhtar Ansari for provoking it. Lalji

---

[70] Vibhuti Narain Rai and Roop Rekha Verma, "Mau Riots: An Exclusive Citizens Report," Accessed July 22, 2014. https://www.google.com/search?sourceid=navclient&ie=UTF-8&rlz=1 T4RNLC_enUS550US550&q=Roop+Rekha+Verma+Vibhuti+Narain+Rai%2c+Mau+Riots%3a+An+Exclusive+Citizens+Report.

Tandon asked, "How can Hindus, who are merely 25 percent of the total population in Mau, indulge in violence? It was stage-managed. It was instigated by a criminal-turned-politician and had the backing of the local administration."[71]

The HYV instigated even more serious anti-Muslim violence in Padrauna, the Legislative Assembly constituency in which Adityanath was planning to field candidates, in late January 2007. A fight broke out on January 26 in which a Hindu man was badly injured and subsequently died and four Muslim men were injured. Adityanath started a *dharna* at the site and his followers burned down a nearby *mazaar*. The police intervened, imposed a curfew, and arrested Adityanath as well as the people who had assaulted the HYV worker. BJP and HYV activists set fire to vehicles, trains, and government offices to protest Adityanath's arrest. HYV workers sent out thousands of SMS messages that read, "Katua mara jayega, Baap-baap chillayega" ("The circumcised one will be finished off, he will cry out for his father"). Padrauna witnessed unprecedented arson and looting from January 30 to January 31. All Muslim-owned shops on the main market were looted and gutted and many Muslim homes were burned to the ground. BJP members joined in the protests demanding Adityanath's release and called on shopkeepers to close their shops in protest.[72]

The BJP supported Adityanath despite his violent and illegal actions and his criticisms of the party. Although Adityanath may have opposed particular BJP candidates, he shared and promoted the BJP's larger and more enduring ideological commitments. Furthermore, Adityanath won successive parliamentary elections from the Gorakhpur constituency in 1998 (at the age of twenty-six, making him the youngest MP), 1999, 2004, 2009, and 2014.

Adityanath gained a mass following by tethering religious and political causes, engaging in charitable work among poor and lower-caste groups, and exploiting local conflicts. He created a vast network of civil society organizations including the Hindu Jagran Manch, Kesariya Sena, Kesariya Wahini, Krishna Sena, Sri Ram Shakti Prakoshtha, Gorakhnath, Purvanchal Vikas Manch, Hindu Mahasabha, and most importantly, the HYV. Because lower caste movements were weak in the region, Adityanath was able to recruit *dalits* through his leadership of the Gorakhnath temple complex. Adityanath gained the reputation of being a Hindu Robin Hood. He created organizations

---

[71] "Mulayam Says No Judicial Probe into Mau Riots," *The Hindu*, November 24, 2005. Accessed July 2, 2014. http://www.hindu.com/2005/11/24/stories/2005112405660500.htm.

[72] In Deoria, for example, former BJP MLA Surya Pratap Shahi and his supporters encouraged a *bandh*. When the police took Shahi into custody, BJP members staged a *dharna* in the city. In Ballia, BJP workers forced closure of shops and other establishments during a *bandh* to protest the arrests of MP Adityanath and other party leaders. "Gorakhpur under Curfew, Violence in Nearby Areas," *Outlook News*, February 1, 2007. Accessed July 2, 2014. http://www.outlook india.com/news/article/Gorakhpur-under-curfew-violence-in-nearby-areas/447726. "Curfew in UP Town, BJP MP Held," *Rediff News*, January 29, 2007. Accessed July 2, 2014. http://www .rediff.com/news/2007/jan/29up.htm.

for footpath dwellers, woodcutters, and unemployed youth. The HYV was alert to local disputes and, whenever possible, cast them as Hindu-Muslim conflicts.

The RSS increasingly managed the BJP's affairs in UP after 2002. It appointed three senior *pracharaks*, including Narendra Modi, to oversee the 2002 Assembly elections. Fifty RSS activists from Madhya Pradesh traveled through UP to collect information that would help the BJP in the elections.[73] The RSS played a major role in candidate selection. In Jewar, Bulandshahr, and Hapur Ghaziabad, BJP tickets went to RSS functionaries rather than BJP incumbents.[74] The RSS backed militant leaders like Adityanath and Varun Gandhi. It encouraged the BJP to make Vinay Katiyar its UP state president. Katiyar, an RSS *pracharak* and former Bajrang Dal president, actively participated in the events associated with the destruction of the *babri masjid* in December 1992. He was outspoken in criticizing the NDA government for seeking to curb the VHP's *shiladaan* program. After becoming party president in 2002, Katiyar affirmed the BJP's commitment to building a temple in Ayodhya.

The VHP announced that it would turn UP into a laboratory for experiments to promote Hindutva, including a campaign against "the Muslim mentality of jihad." Praveen Togadia stated that in the aftermath of Godhra, "the time had come to cash in on this awakening in the country in general and UP in particular."[75] The BJP strengthened its ties to the VHP, supported some of its long-standing demands, like temple construction in Ayodhya, and questioned the authority of democratic institutions like the Election Commission. Banners on the BJP headquarters in Lucknow urged people to participate in a conference of *sadhus*. The VHP's *chetavani yatra* called on people to elect a government that would construct the temple. BJP candidates and district unit members participated in the *yatra* as it wound its way through UP.[76]

The BJP adopted a militant posture in the 2002 Assembly elections. Following the NDA government's introduction of POTA, the UP government stated it would create its own antiterrorism law. The BJP's election campaign sought to depict UP as a microcosm of a nation endangered by "terrorism" and Pakistani aggression. During a campaign meeting, Rajnath Singh said, "Whoever says Pakistan *zindabad*, UP will send him to jail. Why is there so

---

[73] *India Today*, January 14, 2002.

[74] The RSS supported the candidacy of Horam Singh, the incumbent, although he had been accused of accumulating wealth beyond his means and of cross-voting in the legislative council elections. In Hapur, Ghaziabad, the ticket went to Ramswaroop Bharati, a local RSS functionary, and not the incumbent, Jayaprakash, whom the RSS opposed. *Amar Ujala* (Meerut), January 18, 2002.

[75] Amita Verma, "BJP to Test War on Jihad in UP," *Asian Age*, June 7, 2002. Accessed July 2, 2014. http://www.milligazette.com/Archives/1506200/1506200235.htm.

[76] *Hindustan Times*, January 21, 2002.

much fuss about banning SIMI? What is wrong with putting a terrorist in jail for two to three years?" He identified national security as the biggest electoral issue. "If the BJP wins here, the Centre will get strength. If not, Musharraf will tell the world that Atalji's campaign against terrorism has no popular support."[77] The BJP printed extensive campaign material on the issue of "terrorism." Election posters asked: "Will you hand over the state to the supporters of the pro-Laden SIMI? The decision is yours." The BJP showed films that warned that Muslim fundamentalist outfits and Pakistan would become stronger if Mulayam Singh was elected.

However, militant Hindu nationalism was electorally unpopular in 2002. With 20 percent of the vote, the BJP placed last among the three major parties. The electorate was less worried about "terrorism" than about the criminalization of politics, unemployment, and poor infrastructural facilities during BJP rule (1997–2002). A trader in Mathura summed up the mood: "There's been no electricity, the roads are a mess. Terrorism is a subject for intellectuals."[78] Voters from four villages in Hapur constituency – Jharouti, Shampur, Dadayra, and Mallakpur – and Arjun *mohalla* in Hapur boycotted the polls to protest the lack of *pucca* (paved) roads in the area.[79]

The BJP, once again under Kalyan Singh's leadership, pursued a militant stance in the 2007 Assembly elections. Rajnath Singh campaigned against "minority appeasement," namely reservations for Muslims.[80] He refuted charges that the BJP had dropped the temple issue and insisted that it remained committed to building the Ram temple. Kalyan Singh declared that the BJP would oppose the "growing Islamisation of Indian politics."[81] The VHP's Ashok Singhal, declared that Kalyan Singh was the "undisputed choice of the Hindu Samaj" and had full VHP backing. He also announced that the VHP would establish committees to screen candidates and advise Hindu voters how to cast their votes.[82]

The BJP published lurid newspaper ads that accused its opponents of shielding "terrorists," opposing Saraswati Vandana, and appeasing Muslims. One of them depicted a neighborhood with Islamic flags with the slogan "kya inka irada pak hai?" ("Is their intention pure?") hoisted from every

[77] *Times of India*, February 16, 2002.
[78] Simta Gupta, "BJP terror card fails to turn up trumps," *Times of India*, February 13, 2002. Accessed July 2, 2014. http://timesofindia.indiatimes.com/india/BJP-terror-card-fails-to-turn-up-trumps/articleshow/808500.cms?.
[79] *Amar Ujala* (Meerut), January 19, 2002.
[80] "Rajnath Singh Criticizes UPA's 'Minority Appeasement' Policy," *The Hindu*, June 26, 2006. Accessed July 2, 2014. http://www.thehindu.com/todays-paper/tp-national/tp-karnataka/rajnath-singh-criticises-upas-minority-appeasement-policy/article3124527.ece.
[81] "BJP Strikes at Islamisation of Indian Politics," *Asian Age*, September 28, 2006. Accessed July 2, 2014. http://www.hindunet.org/hvk/articles/1106/170.html.
[82] "VHP to Establish 'Hindu Rashtra' Singhal," *One India News*, February 11, 2007. Accessed July 2, 2014. http://news.oneindia.in/2007/02/11/vhp-to-establish-hindu-rashtra-singhal-1171211738.html.

and public displays in Ireland

housetop.[83] When asked whether it intended to suggest a pun on the word "Pak," the BJP initially denied it, but Kalyan Singh later said, "Whatever we have stated in the advertisement is the truth. There is nothing objectionable in it."[84]

On the eve of the 2007 Assembly elections in UP, the BJP produced and distributed a virulently anti-Muslim CD entitled *Bharat ki Pukar* (The Call of India). The CD describes Muslims as a treacherous anti-Hindu community that will kidnap, forcibly marry, and convert Hindu women; kill cows while pretending to care for them; and organize anti-national activities through *madrasas*. The CD's hero is a schoolteacher (*masterji*) who warns Hindus to act before it is too late. The *masterji* dies for the cause of Hindu nationalism. At his funeral, one of the mourners warns:

This time if you don't vote for the BJP, disaster will strike this country. The country will be destroyed. The BJP is a party that thinks about the country. It thinks about the Hindu religion.... All other parties are agents of the Muslims.

That day is not far away when we will be afraid to even call ourselves Hindu, and you will never be able to find a Sohanlal, Mohanlal, Atmaram or Radhekrishan anywhere. Wherever we look, we will only see Abbas, Naqvi, Rizvi, and Maulvi.

During the Mulayam regime, *iftaars* were organised on the Ganga ghats in Haridwar, insulting Hindu religion. Textbooks approved by the UPA government say goddess Durga was fond of liquor, Aurangzeb was a living saint, Lord Ram and Krishna were fictitious characters, Guru Gobind Singh was a Mughal employee.[85]

Senior state party leaders Lalji Tandon and Keshari Nath Tripathi released the CD amid great fanfare on April 3, four days before the first round of polling, but withdrew it when it provoked a controversy. Tandon stated that he had no prior knowledge of the CD's contents and the BJP could not take responsibility for it.[86] However, the producers claimed that senior BJP officials had approved the CD prior to its release. The list of credits included Atal Bihari Vajpayee, LK Advani, Rajnath Singh, and other BJP leaders.

Following directives from the Election Commission, the police lodged a complaint against Lalji Tandon, Rajnath Singh, and other BJP leaders who were associated with the CD for inciting "communal" tensions. Rajnath Singh and LK Advani organized protest demonstrations and courted arrest in

---

[83] Praful Bidwai, "BJP Plumbs the Lower Depths Elections," *Khaleej Times*, April 14, 2007. Accessed July 2, 2014. http://www.khaleejtimes.com/kt-article-display-1.asp?xfile=data/opinion/2006/December/opinion_December102.xml&section=opinion.

[84] "BJP Says Ad Targets Anti-national Outfits," *Outlook India*, April 1, 2007. Accessed July 2, 2014. http://www.outlookindia.com/news/article/BJP-says-ad-targets-antinational-outfits/464631.

[85] "Hindutva Overdrive Gone Wrong? BJP Pulls Out Its Hate-Muslim CD," *The Indian Express*, April 5, 2007. Accessed July 2, 2014. http://expressindia.indianexpress.com/story_print.php?storyId=27552.

[86] Interview with Lalji Tandon, Lucknow, July 16, 2007.

Lucknow. Although the official BJP position was that it had not sanctioned the CD, Rajnath Singh stated:

Now a CD has become the centre of a controversy and the clamour from all our opponents is that the BJP should be derecognized. Why are we being subjected to this? Because we tell the truth. It is more important for the BJP to tell the truth than to win elections. Those who castigate us as communalists are the ones who are demanding religion-based reservations for Muslims. The BJP will never give in to the politics of minority appeasement. We will never allow religion-based reservation to be implemented. We will ensure equal respect for all communities, all religions.[87]

On the eve of the polls, top VHP leaders, including Ashok Singhal, visited Varanasi to mobilize Hindu support; on February 11–13, 2007, a VHP conference in Allahabad decided to install an idol of Ram in every village in the state. The VHP launched statewide *yatras* to drum up support for candidates who accepted its agenda.

The BJP supported some very militant candidates in the 2009 parliamentary elections, despite the electoral unpopularity of a militant approach in the previous Assembly elections. Varun Gandhi contested the parliamentary elections from the Philbhit constituency in UP. He delivered incendiary speeches in which he stated:

This is not the [Congress symbol] "hand" this is the hand of the "lotus." It will cut the throat of the [derogatory reference to a Muslim] after the elections.... Varun Gandhi will cut.... Cut that hand, cut it, cut it.

Go to your villages and give the call that all Hindus must unite to save this area from becoming Pakistan....

If someone slaps you, what do you do? [They say] turn the other cheek.... I haven't heard a stupider thing. If someone slaps you, you should cut off [expletive] his hand, so he can never slap anyone later.

If any wrong element raises his hand on a Hindu ... I swear on the Gita that I will cut off that hand![88]

India's Election Commission alleged that Varun Gandhi's "highly derogatory" references and seriously provocative language was "wholly unacceptable."[89] Chief Minister Mayawati invoked the National Security Act against Gandhi and had three FIRs filed against him. Gandhi was imprisoned on March 27, 2010 for two weeks.

---

[87] Venkitesh Ramakrishnan, "Two-man Army," *Frontline*, May 4, 2007. Accessed July 2, 2014. http://www.hindu.com/thehindu/thscrip/print.pl?file=20070504006401400.htm&date=fl2408/&prd=fline&.

[88] "EC Notice for Varun Gandhi Hate Speech," *The Indian Express*, March 18, 2009. Accessed July 2, 2014. http://www.outlookindia.com/news/article/EC-Notice-for-Varun-Gandhi-Hate-Speech/655997.

[89] "BJP Refuses to Drop Varun Gandhi," *BBC News*, March 23, 2009. Accessed July 2, 2014. http://news.bbc.co.uk/go/pr/fr/-/2/hi/south_asia/7958450.stm.

Despite the directives of the Election Commission, the BJP retained Varun Gandhi as its candidate and accorded him a central role in its election campaigns. Yogi Adityanath strongly endorsed Varun Gandhi's views and toured the state with him in preparation for local party meetings. Reminiscent of its response to the CD and like the VHP, which often challenged the authority of the courts, BJP spokesperson Balbir Punj held that the Election Commission had "no authority to give such a direction to a political party."[90] Rajnath Singh said that Gandhi's prosecution was politically motivated and denied that his speeches had inflamed Hindu-Muslim relations.

The BJP persisted in its attempt to revive movement politics. It had Uma Bharati lead a campaign against the UPA government's failure to save the Ganges River from pollution. The Ganga *yatra* began in West Bengal in September 2012, passed through five states, and ended in UP, where RSS leaders organized prayers and public meetings at fifty-four places. Most of these areas have significant OBC populations and Bharati appealed to their shared caste backgrounds. She also campaigned for the construction of the Ram temple in Ayodhya and sought to rally opposition to the central and state governments' "Muslim appeasement" policies. However, Bharati's Ganga *yatra* exposed fissures in the BJP. Many senior BJP leaders opposed an OBC leader from another state campaigning in UP and boycotted the *yatra*.

The BJP's renewed militancy failed to pay electoral dividends in the 2007 and 2012 Legislative Assembly elections. Its share of the popular vote declined from 20.8 percent in 2002 to 16.9 percent in 2007 to 15 percent in 2012. It was unable to profit from anti-incumbency sentiment or forge alliances with other parties. It was unable to regain the support of upper-caste voters or expand its lower-caste following.[91]

However, the BJP performed unprecedentedly well in the 2014 parliamentary elections in UP. It won seventy-one out of eighty seats (42 percent of the vote, a 25 percent increase over 2009) and its ally Apna Dal won two seats (1 percent of the vote). Anti-incumbency sentiment and Modi's promises of development partly explain the BJP's success. Twenty percent of the electorate believed that the BJP was more capable than any other party of achieving economic development, including better roads, schools, electricity, and drinking water supplies. Young voters were especially receptive to these appeals.

The BJP was able to regain the support of upper-caste voters and a significant section of Jats, non-Jatav *dalits*, and Kurmi OBCs partly as a result

[90] Ibid.
[91] CSDS Team, "Special Statistics: 2012 State Elections Sixteenth Assembly Elections in Uttar Pradesh," *Economic and Political Weekly*, April 7, 2012. Accessed July 2, 2014. http://www.epw.in/system/files/pdf/2012_47/14/Sixteenth_Assembly_Elections_in_Uttar_Pradesh.pdf.

of allying with the Apna Dal, to which it had lost three seats in 1996.[92] It accorded important roles to its OBC leaders, Uma Bharati and Kalyan Singh. Its candidates included twenty-five OBCs, seventeen *dalits*, sixteen Brahmins, and fourteen Rajputs. Reversing its earlier position, the BJP promised increased reservations for OBCs.

The BJP also owed its success to a climate of Hindu-Muslim tensions resulting from serious anti-minority violence in Muzaffarnagar in August and September 2013. It resulted in at least sixty-two (forty-two Muslim and twenty Hindu) deaths, ninety-three injuries, and the displacement of more than 50,000 people. Twelve of the fourteen people the police arrested for engaging in anti-Muslim violence in Muzaffarnagar were BJP leaders, and independent investigators claim that Hindu nationalists orchestrated extensive violence.[93] The BJP benefited from a split in Muslim votes because Muslims were disillusioned by the SP government's handling of the issue.

The BJP gained upper caste and Jat votes by making explicit anti-Muslim appeals. Amit Shah, who masterminded the UP campaign, delivered an inflammatory speech in Muzaffarnagar district in April 2014, urging Jats to vote against the SP, BSP, and Congress because, he claimed, they had pandered to Muslims and discriminated against Hindus. Shortly thereafter, Shah addressed a gathering of Jat leaders in Bijnor and stated that Mayawati, in her eagerness to win the votes of a particular community (*varg vishesh*), had violated the honor of his assembled audience's sisters and daughters (*jo behen-betiyon ... ki aabru pe haath dalta hai*) by allotting nineteen Lok Sabha tickets to that community and only seventeen tickets to *dalits*.[94] Shah was clearly referring to the nineteen Muslims the BSP had nominated to run for the parliamentary elections and suggesting that Muslims (*varg vishesh*) had violated the honor of Hindu women.

[92] Mirza Asmer Beg, AK Verma, and Sudhir Kumar, "A Saffron Sweep in Uttar Pradesh," *The Hindu*, May 23, 2014. Accessed November 25, 2014. http://www.thehindu.com/opinion/op-ed/a-saffron-sweep-in-uttar-pradesh/article6037683.ecedu.

[93] Ellen Barry and Suhasini Raj, "Amid Modi's Centrist Shift, an Aide with a Turbulent Past Rises," *New York Times*, July 5, 2014. Accessed November 26, 2014. http://www.nytimes.com/2014/07/06/world/asia/amid-modis-centrist-shift-an-aide-with-a-turbulent-past-rises.html and Centre for Policy Analysis, "Muzaffarnagar 2013: Violence by Political Design," Report of an Independent Fact Finding Group," September 17, 2013. Accessed July 22, 2014. http://kafila.org/2013/09/18/muzaffarnagar-2013-violence-by-political-design-centre-for-policy-analysis/.

[94] Mukul Kesavan, "Amit Shah's Speeches in UP Belie the Promise of a New BJP," *The Telegraph*, April 10, 2014. Accessed July 22, 2014. http://www.telegraphindia.com/1140410/jsp/opinion/story_18171718.jsp#.U879YMZOWFE. Also see Pervez Iqbal Siddiqui, "Two FIRs Lodged against Amit Shah for Hate Speech," *Times of India News*, April 7, 2014. Accessed July 22, 2014. http://timesofindia.indiatimes.com/news/Two-FIRs-lodged-against-Amit-Shah-for-hate-speech/articleshow/33355533.cms, and "FIR against Amit Shah for 'Hate Speech,'" *The Hindu*, April 7, 2014. Accessed July 22, 2014. http://www.thehindu.com/news/national/fir-against-amit-shah-for-hate-speech/article5879656.ece.

The BJP fielded three candidates who were charged with inciting violence against Muslims in Muzaffarnagar the previous year. One of them, Sanjeev Balyan, who had been imprisoned for twenty-seven days, won a landslide victory. Balyan made his platform clear in his election speeches. "Wherever we will find people belonging to the Muslim community, by killing them, we will get our revenge.... I will not talk of development; this is not the time to talk development. The verdict from this area must be one-sided. You know what to do. There is nothing more for me to say."[95] The BJP government that was formed in 2014 appointed Sanjeev Balyan junior minister for agriculture. It made Amit Shah president and Varun Gandhi, Uma Bharati, and Kalyan Singh vice presidents of the national BJP and Kalyan Singh and Yogi Adityanath, both of whom were elected to Parliament, members of the national executive.

The BJP resorted again to incendiary fears of Muslim male sexual predators in campaigning for by-elections for eleven assembly seats and one parliamentary constituency in UP in September 2014. It chose Yogi Adityanath to head its campaign. Adityanath alleged that Muslims were organizing an international conspiracy to seduce and corrupt Hindu girls. He said in a television interview that he would "not tolerate what is happening to Hindu women in the name of love jihad." One of his videos asked supporters to convert 100 Muslim women through marriage every time a Muslim man married a Hindu. [96]

The Allahabad High Court gave the UP government ten days to respond to a petition to drop the term "love jihad" and take action against Adityanath. Although the UP government informed the Court that there was no evidence of "love jihad" in the state, the BJP was not deterred.[97] Adityanath defied state orders and organized a large public rally and senior BJP leaders endorsed his views.[98] The VHP, Hindu Jagran Manch, ABVP, and the Bharatiya Janata Yuva Morcha, all participated in the campaign to fight "love jihad" in UP. One

---

[95] Vandita Mishra, "BJP Candidate says 'this Time It's about Swabhiman, not Sadak,'" *The Indian Express*, April 14, 2014. Accessed July 23, 2014. http://indianexpress.com/article/india/politics/lok-sabha-election-bjp-candidate-says-this-time-its-about-swabhiman-not-sadak. Ellen Barry and Suhasini Raj, "Amid Modi's Centrist Shift, an Aide With a Turbulent Past Rises," *New York Times*, July 5, 2014. Accessed July 23, 2014. http://www.nytimes.com/2014/07/06/world/asia/amid-modis-centrist-shift-an-aide-with-a-turbulent-past-rises.html.

[96] Praful Bidwai, "Spreading Fear through Stereotypes: The Politics of 'Love Jihad,'" *The Daily Star*, Thursday, September 11, 2014. Accessed November 26, 2014. http://www.thedailystar.net/politics-of-love-jihad-40364.

[97] Senior Superintendent of Police Shalabh Mathur and State Police Chief AL Bannerjee found no evidence of a "love jihad" conspiracy and stated that the concept was designed to foster fear and divisions between Hindus and Muslims. Reuters reported that police in UP had found no credence to these allegations. Rupam Jain Nair and Frank Jack Daniel, "'Love Jihad' and Religious Conversion Polarise in Modi's India," *Reuters*, September 5, 2014. Accessed November 26, 2014. http://in.reuters.com/article/2014/09/05/india-religion-modi-idINKBN0GZ2OC20140905.

[98] Bidwai, "Spreading Fear through Stereotypes."

of their goals was to prevent young women from using cell phones and the Internet to prevent their "falling into the love jihad trap."

Conclusion

The BJP has been most successful when it has overcome factionalism, had close ties to the RSS and its affiliates, and captured the support of both upper and lower castes. The BJP has also fared best when Muslim votes have been splintered among political parties. The challenge for the BJP has been to simultaneously increase lower-caste representation in the party and government and attract lower-caste votes while retaining RSS support. The late 1990s marked a low point for the BJP because of its strained relationship with the RSS, and caste tensions within the party, particularly between upper- and lower-caste leaders. The BJP's militancy and violence were designed to placate the RSS, overcome factionalism, and attract a broad caste constituency. Electoral incentives do not explain the BJP's shift in orientation. It pursued a militant stance in anticipation of the 2002 elections and thereafter, despite the fact that its share of the vote in the Assembly elections plummeted from 33 percent in 1996 to 21 percent in 2002 to 15 percent in 2012.

It is difficult to predict the future of the BJP and militant Hindu nationalism in UP in the aftermath of the 2014 elections; psephologists debate how well parliamentary elections predict Legislative Assembly election results – and vice versa.[99] Given the importance of caste-based movements and parties and the likely increasing political participation of the Muslim community in UP, the BJP will always have to grapple with upholding Hindutva without alienating its core upper-caste leadership and the RSS.

However, one important development in the 2014 elections was the Sangh Parivar's willingness to accept OBC Narendra Modi as a movement, party, and government leader. In the past, the BJP had recognized that OBCs were effective movement activists but was less willing to accept them as party and government leaders. When Kalyan Singh left the BJP in 2009, he intimated that the BJP had used him and other OBC leaders without according them real power. "Why is it that mass-based leaders like Uma Bharati in Madhya Pradesh, Babu Lal Marandi in Jharkhand, ML Khurana in Delhi and I have been cast aside by the BJP?" he asked.[100] When the BJP dismissed Kalyan Singh, it made another OBC movement leader, Vinay Katiyar, party president and brought OBC leader Uma Bharati to UP to organize a movement around the Ganges

[99] "The Significance of State Legislative Assembly Elections Politics" November 2013. Accessed July 22, 2014. http://www.ukessays.com/essays/politics/the-significance-of-state-legislative-assembly-elections-politics-essay.php?cref=1. Sandeep Shastri, KC Suri, and Yogendra Yadav, eds., *Electoral Politics in Indian States: Lok Sabha Elections in 2004 and Beyond* (New Delhi: Oxford University Press, 2009).
[100] Atiq Khan, "Kalyan Singh Quits BJP," *The Hindu*, January 21, 2009. Accessed July 2, 2014. http://www.thehindu.com/todays-paper/kalyan-singh-quits-bjp/article378889.ece.

River in advance of the elections. The BJP recognized that Kalyan Singh, Vinay Katiyar, and Uma Bharati could mobilize mass support both because of their militancy and their ability to attract lower-caste supporters. However, it did not fully accept their political leadership. Caught between its support for a movement strategy and its upper-caste prejudices, the BJP alternately expelled and re-inducted Kalyan Singh and Uma Bharati.

The BJP's strategy in the 2014 elections was both innovative and familiar. Under Narendra Modi's guidance, the BJP replicated Kalyan Singh's strategy of appealing both to Hindu nationalism and to the lower castes. (Not surprisingly, Kalyan Singh rejoined the BJP after the 2014 elections.) This time, however, the BJP followed in the tradition of many previous Congress prime ministers for whom UP was a microcosm of India, by linking Hindu nationalism to Indian nationalism. This time the RSS and the BJP accepted the undisputed leadership of a charismatic OBC leader. This time the RSS mended factional tensions within the BJP so that the party was highly unified. This time the BJP did not nominate any Muslim candidates and, for the first time in UP's history, no Muslims were elected to Parliament from UP. This time the BJP rewarded its most militant leaders and selectively mobilized groups like Jats who had recently engaged in anti-Muslim violence. This time the BJP won an unprecedented victory and was acclaimed for having relinquished its militancy to purse a path of moderation.

7

Himachal Pradesh

The Party Rules

There are good reasons to expect Hindutva movements to flourish in Himachal Pradesh (HP). The two-party system, in which power alternates between the BJP and Congress, has been associated elsewhere with party polarization over minority votes.[1] RSS members have exercised considerable influence over BJP governments (1990–2, 1998–2003, and 2007–12). The large majority of the state's population, about 56 percent, is upper-caste Hindu (Rajputs 28 percent, Brahmins 20 percent, and Vaishyas/Khatris 8 percent). The lower castes have not opposed the BJP through parties or movements.

However, Hindutva movements are relatively weak in HP. Some explanations are plausible if not wholly persuasive. One is that Muslims constitute such a small proportion of the population – 2 percent – that Hindus – 95 percent – do not see them as a threat, electorally or otherwise.[2] However, demographic factors are not decisive. The Sangh Parivar has engaged in considerable violence against Christians, who are less numerous than Muslims.

Another possible reason concerns HP's relatively small role in national politics. Because it holds only four parliamentary seats, HP is less apt than Gujarat or UP to form a laboratory for Hindu nationalism. However, this small state is important to the national BJP. Three of the major leaders in HP, Shanta Kumar, Jagdev Chand, and Prem Kumar Dhumal, are nationally prominent and have served on the BJP's national executive committee. While Modi was BJP general secretary, he directed HP's 2003 and 2007 election campaigns and supported the expulsion of Shanta Kumar and his replacement by Modi's ideological ally,

---

[1] See Steven I. Wilkinson, *Votes and Violence: Electoral Competition and Ethnic Riots in India* (New York: Cambridge University Press, 2004), 143–4.

[2] The remainder of the population is 1 percent Sikh, 1 percent Buddhist, and 0.09 percent Christian. "Socio-Cultural Aspects" of 2001 Census Data, Office of the Registrar General and Census Commissioner, India. Accessed July 2, 2014. http://www.censusindia.gov.in/Census_Data_2001/ Census_Data_Online/Social_and_cultural/Religion.aspx.

Prem Kumar Dhumal.[3] Moreover, HP has been drawn into national waves of Hindutva activism, including the Ayodhya movement and anti-Christian violence.

Three other explanations for the dearth of Hindutva activism are more compelling. First, neither religion nor caste undergird strong movements or parties in HP. As one commentator notes, Hinduism in HP is not "the Hinduism of the Vedas" but "the Hinduism of the masses."[4] Religious practices in the northern region of the state represent a mix of Shaivite Hinduism, Tibetan Buddhism, and pre-Buddhist Bon traditions. Hindus and Buddhists pray in each other's temples and consult each other's priests. In the upper hill regions, village gods and goddesses are more popular than the major Hindu deities.

The BJP has largely respected the state's distinctive regional and cultural traditions. Radha Raman Shastri, minister of education in the BJP government (1990–2), spoke of his commitment to promoting and preserving regional culture:

Pahari [mountain] culture is born of this soil and suits this soil. People here don't like rigidity and dogma so we have to be flexible to remain popular with the masses. We have to respect their language, food, and cultural traditions.... I have tried to promote the use of Pahari [also the regional language]. I created the first Pahari-Hindi dictionary.[5]

The upper castes dominate politics but caste loyalties do not directly translate into party affiliations. The upper castes support the BJP in the "new HP" (part of Punjab until 1966) and the Congress Party in the "old HP." OBCs, 11 percent of the population, do not vote as a coherent bloc and have not created their own party.[6] Scheduled Castes (25 percent of the population) vote for both parties but more for Congress than for the BJP.

Second, the strongest social movements address environmental and economic issues and want the state to play a larger role in fostering development and protecting vulnerable communities. Similarly, contestation between Congress and the BJP concerns economic and environmental policy. The political economy of the region partly explains this. More than 93 percent of the state's population is rural; 71 percent is employed in agriculture. Land reforms created relatively equitable patterns of land distribution. After HP achieved statehood, Congress transferred land under long-term occupancy (through the Himachal Pradesh Ceiling on Land Holding Act and the Tenancy and Land Reforms Act, 1972). By 2003, half of all land holdings were between 2.5 and

---

[3] Onkar Singh, "Shanta Kumar Calls for Modi's Resignation," *Rediff.com News*, April 11, 2002. Accessed July 2, 2014. http://www.rediff.com/news/2002/apr/11train.htm.

[4] Sukh Dev Singh Charak, *History and Culture of a Himalayan State, Himachal Pradesh*, Volume 1 (Minneapolis, MN: Light and Life Publishers, 1978), 90.

[5] Interview with Radha Raman Shastri, Shimla, June 3, 1991.

[6] TR Sharma, "Local Configurations and National Parties in Himachal Pradesh," *Economic and Political Weekly*, August 21–8, 1999, Vol. 34, nos. 34 and 35.

9.9 acres. Only 8 percent of the operational agricultural holdings exceeded 25 acres and only 9 percent were less than 1.2 acres.

The local population has always depended heavily on the forests and opposed the state and capitalists who have encroached on their traditional means of livelihood and way of life.[7] There is a long tradition of community forest management through clan and kinship arrangements that the state acknowledges in principle.

Until it became a full-fledged state in 1971, HP was unable to mobilize internal resources for growth. Since then, given low levels of industrialization and the slow development of private enterprise, the state has played a vital role in HP's development. As a result, human development indicators for HP compare favorably with the most successful states in India. HP ranks second nationally with respect to infrastructural facilities. Since 1987–1988, it has generated sufficient hydroelectric power to electrify all its villages and has provided every village with clean drinking water. Human development indicators are relatively high in education, health, sanitation, and nutrition. Nearly 11,000 primary schools employ more than 28,000 teachers in the state's 17,500 villages. The basic literacy rate increased from 42 percent to 77 percent from 1971 to 2003.[8] Ninety-seven percent of girls between the ages of six and seventeen are enrolled in school and 69 percent of women were literate in 2003.

There is strong popular commitment to development, civil liberties, and the protection of community assets in HP. Based on interviews he conducted, Javeed Alam found:

What people wanted mostly by development had to do with roads; piped water, if not to every house, then, at least, at a few places in the village; more buses and public transport at a cheaper rate; schools closer to the villages; public health centers; and other such things of common use.[9]

Third, Hindutva movements are not crucial to the BJP's electoral success. The one exception to this pattern was the movement around Ayodhya that galvanized cross-caste and cross-class support for the BJP. However, Hindutva activists' violence against Sikhs and Christians has not improved the BJP's electoral standing. The performance of both Congress and the BJP in Legislative

---

[7] The classics in this vast literature include Ramachandra Guha, *The Unquiet Woods: Ecological Change and Peasant Resistance in the Himalaya* (Berkeley, CA: University of California Press, 2000); Madhav Gadgil and Ramachandra Guha, *This Fissured Land: An Ecological History of India* (New Delhi: Oxford University Press, 1992); Nancy Lee Peluso, *Rich Forests, Poor People: Resource Control and Resistance in Java* (Berkeley, CA: University of California Press, 1992); and James C. Scott, *The Art of Not Being Governed: An Anarchist History of Upland Southeast Asia.* (New Haven, CT: Yale University Press, 2009).

[8] Government of Himachal Pradesh, *Himachal Pradesh Human Development Report* (Shimla: Himachal Pradesh Government Press, 2002).

[9] Javeed Alam, "Political Necessity Versus Lost Possibilities," *Economic and Political Weekly*, January 13–20, 1996, 107. Accessed July 9, 2014. http://www.epw.in/system/files/pdf/1996_31/2-3/himachal_political_necessity_vs_lost_possibilities.pdf.

Assembly elections rests primarily on anti-incumbent sentiment, the parties' record on development, and party factionalism.

The RSS has been more active in party politics than in civil society organizations. It began working in Shimla in 1943 and had forty-four branches in the state at its peak, from 1945 to 1949. However, as Mangat Dhuni, who directed twenty-two branches admitted, the RSS base was largely confined to Punjabi refugees.[10] Today, the RSS holds about eight *shakhas* in Shimla and 150 in the state and has had difficulties recruiting new members. The focus of RSS attention has been political rather than cultural. It has exercised enormous influence over the BJP's leaders and policies, for both pragmatic and ideological reasons.

The first section of this chapter describes the evolution of the state and political economy of HP. The second section describes the BJP's electoral performance. It shows that the BJP absorbed many of the leaders and ideas of the Janata Party and achieved its greatest success by upholding the Janata Party's commitment to rural development. The third section examines the impact of party factionalism on the BJP's moderation. The fourth section argues that, barring the Mandal-Mandir agitation, the BJP has been more successful when it has addressed the interests of rural constituencies than when it has embraced Hindutva. The fifth section examines the BJP's intermittent support for movements of rural cultivators and forest dwellers. It also describes movement activism against Christians.

The State and Political Economy

Some of the BJP's distinctive attributes in HP – its silence on Hindu-Muslim relations, uneven strength within the state, and base among the rural rich – are rooted in its history. HP became a federal state at a late stage after independence. Statehood brought about formal political unity, but the old and new regions had different political histories, class compositions, and political sympathies.

For much of HP's history, princely families exercised overwhelming power but had little contact with the people they ruled. The princely families governed in a highly autocratic manner. Their power was considered divine and their decisions constituted absolute law. The limited forms of political representation that the colonial state permitted elsewhere in the country were absent in HP. The segmented domains of princely power and later the reorganization of state boundaries brought about political fragmentation.

The nationalist movement was weak because the region was insulated from imperial rule. A small group of elites negotiated first with the princely families and later with the Congress Party to achieve independence and subsequently statehood. Praja Mandals, with links to the Congress Party, were formed between 1942 to 1945 to demand limited administrative reforms.

[10] Interview with Mangat Dhuni, Shimla, May 30, 1991.

A year after India gained independence, princely families joined the Indian union. HP became a centrally administered unit under a chief commissioner in April 1948. The province's leadership refused to comply with the national government's directive to merge with neighboring Punjab. As a compromise, HP became a union territory under a lieutenant governor and a territorial council. In the process, it lost the right to a democratically elected government. YS Parmar, who led the Praja Mandal movement and became the first chief minister of HP, described the state's history as follows:

[Himachal Pradesh] had a precarious childhood to be followed by a shaky adolescence. As being always a special ward of the Centre, its gains were outmatched by its lack of confidence and capacity to take decisions, and in the absence of peoples' associations, its resources, such as hydel potential, were taken by neighboring states for development and benefits. With its future insecure, its destiny was made dependent on doles, which were also used as a lever to suppress its legitimate aspirations.[11]

What is now HP comprised four districts, Chamba, Mahasu, Mandi, and Sirmur, in 1948. It expanded to include Bilaspur in 1954 and Kinnaur in 1960. In November 1966, the national government reorganized Punjab along linguistic lines and merged the mountainous areas of Punjab – Kangra, Kullu, Lahaul and Spiti, and parts of Shimla – with HP, almost doubling its area, to 21,495 square miles. The province, which comprised twelve districts, finally achieved full statehood on January 25, 1971.[12]

The major fault lines in HP are still between the Congress-dominated old or upper regions and the Jan Sangh/BJP-dominated new or lower regions of the state. Each party has sought to gain statewide influence and has accused the other of favoring the region which it dominates. As a result of pronounced regional divisions, social movements and parties have been unable to organize on a statewide basis. State parties – the Loktantrik Morcha, Himachal Kranti Party, Himachal Pradesh State Akali Dal, Lok Raj Party, and Himachal Vikas Congress (HVC) – have never been very strong.

The major political struggles historically were over landownership and tenancy rights. In 1953, the Congress government enacted the Himachal Pradesh Abolition of Big Landed Estates and Land Reforms Act, which transferred land rights to tenants upon compensation to landowners. However, large landholdings existed in the four districts comprising the new Himachal Pradesh (Una, Harimpur, Kangra, and Kullu), where the Land Reforms Act was not applicable. The Congress government faced two contending opponents. While the communists organized peasants to demand that Congress extend land reforms,

---

[11] YS Parmar, *Himachal Pradesh: Case for Statehood* (Shimla: Directorate of Public Relations, 1968), iii.

[12] They are Kangra, Harimpur, Mandi, Bilaspur, Una, Chamba, Lahul and Spiti, Sirmaur, Kinnaur, Kullu, Solan, and Shimla. Harimpur and Una became districts, and Mahasu was renamed Solan in 1972.

the Jan Sangh, under the leadership of Shanta Kumar and Kanwar Durga Chand, opposed tenancy reforms in the new HP.[13] The Jan Sangh organized mass protests against the land transfers.

The Communists played a major role in organizing tenant agitations, but credit for the reforms went to the Congress Party.[14] The Jan Sangh lost the battle against land reform but continued to back large landowners. It also gained the support of Punjabi Hindu refugees, particularly merchants and traders, many of whom were Punjabi Hindu refugees from what became Pakistan.[15] The BJP attracted the support of large landowners in the new HP but remained weaker in the old HP, where the small landowning population is larger. In the aftermath of land reforms, the BJP was a stronger advocate than Congress of privatization and of scaling back the state. However, the BJP has been compelled by electoral pressures to accommodate demands for state provision and protection of public resources.

BJP's Electoral Vicissitudes

The Congress Party was invincible in the early years of HP's history. It ushered in far-reaching land reforms and oversaw the state's administrative reorganization. However, Congress lost all four parliamentary seats in 1977.[16] There was significant rural opposition to Congress for its failure to adequately fund road construction, electricity installations, irrigation facilities, and drinking water supplies.[17] The abolition of tenancy from 1973–5 led to polarization between

---

[13] Shanta Kumar was the general secretary of the Jan Sangh, the leader of the Laghu Zamindar Sabha (Small Landowners' Organization), and the editor of its weekly publication, the *Himpradeep*.

[14] Interview with Mohan Singh Thakuria, Shimla, May 31, 1991.

[15] Pamela Kanwar, *Imperial Shimla: The Political Culture of the Raj* (New Delhi: Oxford University Press, 1990).

[16] It won 42 percent of the vote and almost 60 percent of the seats in the first Legislative Assembly elections in 1967. The Jan Sangh received only 13 percent of the vote. In 1971, Congress swept the parliamentary elections, increasing its share of votes in HP by 29 percent. In the 1972 state assembly elections, Congress won 79 percent of the vote. Javeed Alam, "Changing Equations," *Frontline*, November 19, 1993. "A Vision for India," *Frontline*, August 9–22, 1997. Accessed July 1, 2014. http://www.frontline.in/static/html/fl1416/14160150.htm. Steven Weisman, "Election results show weak spots in Gandhi party's armor," *New York Times*, March 9, 1985. Accessed July 1, 2014. http://www.nytimes.com/1985/03/09/world/election-results-show-weak-spots-in -gandhi-party-s-armor.html.

[17] The Congress Party's popularity declined in HP as in many other states because the national leadership undermined regional leaders. Furthermore, Virbhadra Singh, who served as chief minister four times (1983–90, 1993–8, 2003–7, 2012 to the present), reduced the power of the Council of Ministers. He was seen as authoritarian, elitist, and nepotistic. Corruption by state officials further undermined the Congress Party. The Congress high command removed Chief Minister Ram Lal Thakur (January–April 1977, 1980–3) from office after a High Court ruling found him guilty of corruption in a case involving timber export. Ashwini Chhatre, "Democracy on the

upper-caste landowners and tenants.[18] The Congress Party's twenty-point program included a provision to give one acre of land to anyone who owned less than that amount and whose primary occupation was agriculture. Class conflict emerged in the countryside as landlords sought to retain their land while the landless fought to acquire it. Landlords supported the BJP and initially the landless and land poor supported Congress. However, the program's flawed implementation resulted in prolonged litigation and many landless *dalits* turned against the Congress Party.

The Jan Sangh gained the support of rural cultivators by joining the socialists in opposing the Congress Party's declaration of a national emergency (1975–7). The Janata Party needed the Jan Sangh because it was well-organized, amply funded, and backed by students, teachers, small business people, and professionals. In the 1977 Legislative Assembly elections, the Janata Party won 49 percent of the vote and fifty-three seats. In 1972, the Jan Sangh had won only 8 percent of the votes and five seats.[19]

The Janata Dal disintegrated and the BJP acquired its constituency and some of its leading members, including DD Konaria, Prem Kumar Dhumal, Roop Dass Kashyap, and Maheshwar Singh, the Raja of Kullu, who became BJP president from 1990 to 1993. Members of other small regional parties joined the BJP. Thakur Sen Negi, formerly Speaker of the House, explained that the left-of-center Lok Raj (People's Rule) party, which he had led, had been hampered by a lack of resources and the absence of ties to national parties.[20] Joining the BJP enabled him to become a more effective advocate for the causes he supported. Absorbing members of the Janata Party and other regional parties moderated the BJP's stance and made it receptive to demands of environmental groups and agrarian cultivators.

The Janata government introduced popular rural development schemes. Shanta Kumar praised it for giving scholarships to children from uneducated families, providing drinking water to 3,000 villages, and introducing state-subsidized food rations for the poor.[21] Kishori Lal, Public Works Development (PWD) minister in the Janata government, echoed his views: "What Congress could not do in thirty years, the Janata government

Commons: Political Competition and Local Cooperation for Natural Resource Management in India" (PhD diss., Duke University, 2007), 92. Available at: http://dukespace.lib.duke.edu/dspace/bitstream/10161/211/1/D_Chhatre_Ashwini_a_052007.pdf. Accessed July 2, 2014.

[18] Alam, "Changing Equations."

[19] Jan Sangh members played leading roles in the Janata government. Shanta Kumar served as Public Works Department (PWD) minister and became chief minister of HP. Jan Sangh members became ministers for public works, tourism and public health, industry and agriculture, rural development, and animal husbandry and fisheries, and acquired legitimacy and experience during their tenure in office.

[20] Interview with Thakur Sen Negi, Shimla, May 31, 1991.

[21] Interview with Shanta Kumar, Shimla, June 3, 1991.

did in thirty months. We provided villages with drinking water, roads, and electricity. We also led a clean administration."[22]

The BJP's election manifesto in 1990 mirrored some of the Janata government's commitments. It promised to ration flour, food, and other staples at low prices. It promised a tap in every kitchen, jobs for all, wages for agricultural workers on par with Punjab, and higher prices for fruit and vegetable growers. Virbhadra Singh, the Congress Chief Minister whom the BJP's Shanta Kumar defeated in 1990, claimed:

[T]he BJP promised something for everybody. There was no sector of society which it ignored. Slogans like "hur hath ko calm, hur kheth ko pani" ["work for every pair of hands, water for every field"] sounded very nice but they were empty slogans. In fact the BJP's record has been poor. It could not meet these promises without a large subsidy which no state in India can afford.[23]

The BJP returned to office in 1990 with 42 percent of the vote (forty-six seats). Both Shanta Kumar and Prem Kumar Dhumal attributed its electoral success to its constructing roads, creating health care facilities, and building schools.[24] Shanta Kumar (chief minister from 1977–80 and 1990–2) described himself as *Paaniwala Mukhya Mantri* (Chief Minister of Water) and Prem Kumar Dhumal (chief minister from 1998–2003 and 2008–12) described himself as *Sarakwala, bijli wala, Malik Mantri* (Chief Minister of Roads and Electricity). Attar Singh, the election officer for the state, claimed that the BJP had benefited from the Janata government's fine performance, strong organization, and skilled campaigning.

Even before the BJP began its campaign, it visited various localities to find out what issues concerned people there. It decided on its candidates after seeing the interests of each region. It was the first party to begin its election campaign. It spent a minimum of fifteen to twenty lakhs ($31,739 – $42,319) on each candidate.... The Janata government's record on agrarian development also helped the BJP.[25]

Shimla was one of the few areas of BJP strength in the new HP. KN Lal, BJP president for Shimla, described the party's elaborate organizational structure, which included primary units at the polling booth level.[26] Each primary unit included between six and eleven active members. The municipal council elections of 1986 involved a heated contest between the BJP and Congress. The BJP organized *dharnas* and hunger strikes and registered a case in the High Court challenging the victory of Congress and its allies in the municipal council

---

[22] Interview with Kishori Lal, Shimla, June 3, 1991.
[23] Interview with Virbhadra Singh, Shimla, May 27, 1991.
[24] Interviews with Shanta Kumar, Shimla, June 3, 1991, and Prem Kumar Dhumal, Shimla, July 7, 2007.
[25] Interview with Attar Singh, Shimla, June 4, 1991.
[26] Interview with KN Lal, Shimla, May 29, 1991.

elections and the election of Shimla's mayor. However, by 1998, factional divisions eroded party strength.

Party Factionalism

Factionalism has undermined the BJP's programmatic commitments. Small politics concerning inner-party rivalries have displaced the big politics of Hindu nationalism. Furthermore, the large patronage networks that both Congress and the BJP have formed to dispense state subsidies have become mired in corruption and made corruption an important electoral issue.

Factional divisions are primarily rooted in ideological disputes. The RSS has exacerbated factional rivalries between the BJP's two major leaders in HP, Shanta Kumar and Prem Kumar Dhumal.[27] The RSS and top-ranking national BJP leaders supported Dhumal, enabling him to become chief minister and to form a government on a wholly expedient basis in 1998. The BJP made Ramesh Dhawal a minister despite the fact that it had expelled him for engaging in corruption. Similarly it included Sukh Ram, the head of the HVC, whom it had earlier lambasted for being corrupt.[28]

The BJP government sought to undermine its opponents within the party by appointing Dhumal loyalists and RSS functionaries to key positions. Sukhwinder Singh, president of the state youth Congress, alleged that the government had recruited 12,000 RSS and ABVP activists to government jobs.[29] Congress Chief Minister Virbhadra Singh alleged that the BJP government had ordered the transfer of 75,000 employees based solely on political considerations.[30] Khajan Singh Dhir claimed that the BJP government had recruited 9,000 teachers at salaries that exceeded official rates in order to avoid government regulations with respect to reservations.[31] According to Education Minister Asha Kumar and Chief Parliamentary Secretary Mukesh Agnihotri, the outgoing Dhumal government tried to destroy the records of the State Subordinate Services Selection Board that pertained to recruitment.[32] However, experts retrieved data that confirmed that the government had rejected qualified candidates.

---

[27] Archana Phull, "Baijnath More a Fight for Supremacy within BJP, Congress," *The Indian Express*, November 23, 1998. Accessed July 9, 2014. http://expressindia.indianexpress.com/ie/daily/19981123/32751194.html.

[28] The national Congress government had expelled Sukh Ram from his post as telecommunication minister because he faced corruption charges. The HVC headed by Sukh Ram won six Assembly seats in 1998.

[29] *The Tribune*, September 1, 1999.

[30] *The Tribune*, November 17, 1998.

[31] Interview with Khajan Singh Dhir, Shimla, June 3, 1991.

[32] "Dhumal's Hand Alleged in Job Scam, Incriminating Data Retrieved from Computers," *The Tribune online*, October 26, 2003. Accessed July 9. 2014. http://www.tribuneindia.com/2003/20031027/himachal.htm#1.

Public interest litigation resulted in the HP High Court issuing notices to the vice-chancellor of HP University and the University Grants Commission (UGC) to terminate twenty-one appointments that circumvented established procedures.[33]

Four rebel BJP ministers (Krishan Kapoor, Ramesh Dhawala, Hari Narain Singh, and Rajan Sushant) issued strongly worded corruption charges against Chief Minister Dhumal on February 28, 2001. These ministers and three BJP MLAs, who were Shanta Kumar loyalists, resigned from the government. Although Dhumal accepted the resignations, the RSS re-inducted the four ministers and LK Advani, then deputy prime minister, exonerated the Dhumal government, and dismissed the charges. The RSS supported Dhumal despite the fact that he was neither a *swayamsevak* nor a BJP old-timer. He had formerly been a Janata Party member and only joined the BJP in 1982, as state president of its Youth Organization; he became president of the Himachal Pradesh BJP in 1993. RSS support for Dhumal was both pragmatic and ideological. The Dhumal government provided patronage to the RSS. Shanta Kumar criticized the government for allowing the RSS to make key appointments to educational institutions, including HP University's vice-chancellor, pro-vice-chancellor, and thirty-five faculty members.[34]

The Dhumal government also lavishly funded RSS-affiliated charitable organizations like the Himgari Kalyan Ashram in Solan and Saraswati Vidya Mandir in Shimla. The RSS and VHP have been active in social and educational work through Sewa Bharatis, Vanvasi Kalyan Ashrams, and Vidya Bharatis. The Sewa Bharati claimed to have organized ninety-one centers in forty-six locations in the state in 2008 and 2009. Most of these are educational in nature; others include centers for cultural activities, social harmony, tailoring, and economic development.[35] There are 1,019 *ekal vidyalaya* schools in HP, most of them in Palampur, Chamba, Kullu, and Shimla districts.[36]

The RSS was angered that Shanta Kumar became outspoken against Hindutva violence. Earlier Kumar had demonstrated Hindu nationalist commitments by supporting the construction of a temple in Ayodhya. He said in an

---

[33] The notice focused on the appointment of RSS cadre Vir Singh Thakur (who did not have the necessary certification to teach at a high school), IC Kapoor, a consultant on the construction wing of the university, and Malika Nadda, wife of health minister JP Nadda, who was appointed lecturer without a PhD. "HP Notices to HPU VC, UGC," *The Tribune*, August 7, 2001. Accessed July 9, 2014. http://www.tribuneindia.com/2001/20010808/himachal .htm#10; and Tikender Singh, "BJP-Led Govt Proves a Dismal Failure," *People's Democracy*, April 8, 2001. Accessed July 9, 2014. http://archives.peoplesdemocracy.in/2001/april08/april8_ himachal.htm.

[34] "Virbhadra for Probing Regional Discrimination," *The Indian Express*, March 9, 1999. Accessed July 9, 2014. http://expressindia.indianexpress.com/ie/daily/19990309/ige09126.html.

[35] Official Web site of the Sewa Bharati Foundation, http://www.sevabharati.com/profile.aspx.

[36] Official Web site of the Ekal Vidyalaya Foundation, http://www.ekalindia.org/.

interview in 1991, "The *mandir* is not a burning issue here as it is in UP and Bihar. But there is general acceptance that the *mandir* should be constructed. This is a totally Hindu population so they have no opposition to *mandir* construction."[37] Kumar subsequently criticized the BJP's role in the 2002 Gujarat violence, called for Narendra Modi's resignation, and demanded that the BJP control elements who, in the name of Hindutva, were giving the Sangh a bad name. He stated:

What has happened in Gujarat after the Godhra incident is inhuman. The burning of the train must be condemned in the strongest possible terms. But what happened thereafter would shake the conscience of any right thinking and self-respecting man.[38]

A senior RSS leader claimed that Kumar was engaging in a personal vendetta against Modi because when "Modi was [BJP] general secretary in charge of Himachal Pradesh, he did not allow Kumar to fill the state party posts with his yes-men."[39] BJP national president Jana Krishnamurthy indicated that disciplinary action would be taken against Kumar "for speaking out of turn and out of line with the party view," leading to Kumar's apology for his comments about Modi.[40] Despite Kumar's attempts to demonstrate his support for the VHP and the RSS, Dhumal and Modi continued to pressure the national BJP to dismiss him.[41] After initially resisting the pressure, Prime Minister Vajpayee accused Kumar of "gross indiscipline" and asked him to resign from his post as union rural development minister in April 2003.[42]

A faction of the BJP turned against Dhumal. Kumar publicly blamed the BJP's defeat in 2003 on the poor performance of the Dhumal government and on infighting within the party. Ram Lal Thakur, forest minister, and Mukesh Agnihotri, chief parliamentary secretary for health, charged Dhumal with "misleading the people regarding the memorandum of understanding on fiscal reforms." They accused Dhumal of discriminating against Kangra and imposing a blanket ban on filling government posts in the state.[43]

[37] Script of 1992 discussion in Parliament, Official Web site of the Indian Parliament. Accessed July 9, 2014. http://parliamentofindia.nic.in/ls/lsdeb/ls10/sess5/1822129203.htm.
[38] Omkar Singh, "Shanta Kumar Calls for Modi's Resignation," *Rediff.com News*, April 11, 2002. Accessed July 9, 2014. http://www.rediff.com/news/2002/apr/11train.htm.
[39] Ibid.
[40] "Shanta Kumar apologizes," *The Hindu*, April 18, 2002. Accessed July 9, 2014. http://www.hinduonnet.com/thehindu/2002/04/18/stories/2002041802181100.htm.
[41] "Shanta Kumar Denies Criticizing VHP," *Rediff.com News*, April 22, 2002. Accessed July 9, 2014. http://www.rediff.com/news/2002/apr/22shanta.htm.
[42] Onkar Singh, "No, I Am Not Quitting BJP: Shanta Kumar," *Rediff India Abroad*, April 9, 2003. Accessed July 9, 2014. http://www.rediff.com/news/2003/apr/09shanta.htm. "Shanta Kumar Not to Leave Party," *The Tribune*, April 13, 2003. Accessed July 9, 2014. http://www.tribuneindia.com/2003/20030413/himachal.htm#2.
[43] "Himachal Pradesh," *The Tribune*, October 6, 2004. Accessed July 9, 2014. http://www.tribuneindia.com/2004/20041006/himachal.htm.

The BJP's strategy of building alliances with small regional parties was unsuccessful in 2003. Although both Congress and the BJP experienced a 3 percent decline in their share of the popular vote, Congress returned to power with 41 percent of the vote and forty-three seats; the BJP won 36 percent of the vote and sixteen seats. Six rebel candidates ran as independents and won.[44] The HVC won only one seat and 10 percent of the vote. In keeping with this general trend, Congress won three and the BJP one parliamentary seat in the 2004 general elections. Shanta Kumar lost his seat because OBCs voted for the rival candidate and because of factional disputes within the BJP.[45]

Corruption contributed to the BJP's electoral defeat in 2003. Fifty-nine percent of the people surveyed said they believed that the BJP government was corrupt or very corrupt.[46] BJP officials faced corruption charges both in HP and at the national level. In mid-March, *Tehelka* reported on massive fraud by MPs on defense contracts, leading to the resignation of BJP chief Bangaru Laxman for accepting a bribe of $2,174.[47] The Congress Party published photographs of Bangaru Laxman grasping rupee notes. It also publicized Dhumal's wealth from properties in the Punjab, a petrol pump for his son and nephews, and providing government jobs for fifty-eight relatives. Surprisingly, Congress neither pursued investigations nor pressed charges against BJP functionaries after attaining power in 2003. Ramesh Loumia speculated that Congress feared that the BJP would in turn investigate corruption in Congress.[48] As a result, each party brought corruption charges against the other but dropped the charges thereafter.

The RSS had Prem Kumar Dhumal and Shanta Kumar canvass together in the 2007 elections. It accorded important roles in ticket distribution and campaigning to Kumar in Kangra and Dhumal in Harimipur. This show of party unity helped the BJP attain power, especially because factional divisions within Congress were clearly evident.[49] The Congress Party's failure to announce its candidate for chief minister reinforced the view that it was highly centralized and lacking in transparency.[50]

---

[44] "Congress Leaders Attack BJP on MoU Issue," *Tribune India*, October 5, 2003. Accessed July 9, 2014. http://www.rediff.com/election/hoth03.htm.

[45] Ramesh K. Chauhan and SN Ghosh, "Himachal Pradesh: Bipolar Contest," *Economic and Political Weekly*, December 18–24, 2004, 5505. Accessed July 9, 2014. http://www.epw.in/system/files/pdf/2004_39/51/Himachal_Pradesh__Bipolar_Contest.pdf.

[46] Ibid., 2928.

[47] Devsagar Singh, "Tehelka Tailspin Continues," *Express India*, March 25, 2001. Accessed July 9, 2014. http://expressindia.indianexpress.com/fe/daily/20010325/fec25015.html.

[48] Interview with Ramesh Loumia, Shimla, July 7, 2007.

[49] Pratibha Chauhan, "BJP Manifesto Tries to Woo Every Section – Big Promises: Power, Jobs, Tourism," *The Tribune*, December 6, 2007. Accessed July 9, 2014. http://www.tribuneindia.com/2007/20071207/himachal.htm#1.

[50] The taint of corruption did not hurt the BJP in the 2007 elections. The HP Election Watch report on the criminal records of Legislative Assembly candidates found that there were criminal charges against twenty-eight (41 percent) of the sixty-eight MLAs whose records it reviewed. Of

The BJP contested the Legislative Assembly elections in both Gujarat and HP in 2012. However, whereas the BJP retained power in Gujarat, it lost in HP by a wide margin because of factionalism and anti-incumbency sentiment, mainly concerning corruption. Congress defeated the BJP and won thirty-six of sixty-eight seats (42.8 percent of the vote). Virbhadra Singh resumed office as chief minister for the sixth time. Independent candidates, some of whom were dissidents from the BJP, won five seats. Days before the 2012 Legislative Assembly elections, BJP dissidents who opposed the BJP high command's refusal to investigate charges of corruption against Dhumal left the BJP. Some of them, under the leadership of Maheshwar Singh, formed the Himachal Lokhit Party. The split cost the BJP dearly.

The Electoral Unpopularity of Hindutva

The Hindutva platform failed in HP, despite the BJP's best efforts. Hoping to learn from Gujarat, the BJP put Modi in charge of the 2003 election campaign in HP. Vajpayee attended the first election campaign in Mandi and promised to construct a temple in Ayodhya. He reissued a long-standing and highly provocative demand for a ban on cow slaughter: "There will be a complete ban on cow slaughter even covering those areas where it [cow slaughter] has not so far been forbidden."[51]

However, all the ministers who served in the BJP government (1990–2), with the exception of Jagdev Chand, were defeated. Six of the eight newly elected BJP MLAs were newcomers to the party.[52] A post-poll survey of the 2003 elections

---

them, twenty-four out of forty-one (59 percent) were from the BJP and three out of twenty-three (13 percent) were from the Congress Party. Five of the sixty-eight MLAs, four from the BJP and one from Congress, faced serious criminal charges. There were also criminal charges pending against eight out of eleven BJP ministers, one of whom was Chief Minister Dhumal. Association for Democratic Reform, *Analysis of Criminal, Financial and other Details of MLAs from Himachal Pradesh*. Himachal Pradesh Election Watch and Association for Democratic Reforms, 2007. Accessed July 9, 2014. http://adrindia.org/content/himachal-pradesh-mlas-report.

[51] "Vajpayee disapproves of indecent campaign," *Tribune online*, February 20, 2003, Accessed July 9, 2014. http://www.tribuneindia.com/2003/20030221/main2.htm

[52] After 1993, power alternated between Congress and the BJP. Congress assumed power in 1993 with 50 percent of vote; the BJP won 37 percent, and the CPM and independents the rest. Election Commission of India, *Statistical Report on the General Election, 1993 to the Legislative Assembly of Himachal Pradesh* (New Delhi: Election Commission of India, 1993). Accessed July 9, 2014. http://eci.nic.in/eci_main/StatisticalReports/SE_1993/Statistical%20 Report%201993 percent20Himachal%20Pradesh.pdf. The BJP returned to power in 1998 with the support of the HVC. The BJP won 39 percent of the vote, the HVC 10 percent, Congress 44 percent, and other parties won the remainder. Election Commission of India, *Statistical Report on the General Election, 1998 to the Legislative Assembly of Himachal Pradesh* (New Delhi: Election Commission of India, 1998). Accessed July 9, 2014. http://eci.nic .in/eci_main/StatisticalReports/SE_1998/StatisticalReport-HP98.pdf.

highlighted the importance people accorded to governance.[53] Only 2 percent of voters named Hindutva when asked which issue had decisively influenced their vote. By contrast, government performance was of critical importance to 43 percent and development to 31 percent; 67 percent believed that government jobs had drastically declined during the five years of BJP rule.[54] Under these circumstances, they especially resented the fact that the BJP government had recruited RSS members to government jobs.

The BJP's 2007 election manifesto focused on creating employment opportunities, quality education, diversification of agriculture and horticulture, women's empowerment, and better roads and drinking water.[55] The BJP sought to attract female voters by promising to reserve half the *panchayat* seats for women. It appealed to farmers and apple growers by promising higher support prices. The BJP vigorously opposed the Congress government's record on inflation, unemployment, and corruption. "The United Progressive Alliance government and the ministry of Shimla have betrayed the common man by failing to check spiraling prices of essential goods. They should be thrown out," Advani exhorted at a rally in Kullu.[56] The BJP also played on nationalist and regional sentiments by criticizing the UPA government for "surrendering national interests to the US" over the nuclear agreement and for the Congress Party's failure to get central government sanction for a special development project.

Ideological differences between Congress and the BJP around religious questions were muted. In fact, BJP president Rajnath Singh claimed that the Congress Party was seeking to divide the country along religious lines.[57] A Congress rather than a BJP government approved the HP Freedom of Religion Bill (passed in 2007) to curtail conversions out of Hinduism. Apart from promises like making education "Bharat centric" by replacing sex education with yoga education, and Advani's election promise to construct a temple in Ayodhya, Hindu nationalist themes did not figure prominently in the BJP's campaign.

The BJP returned to power in 2007 as a result of its unified stance, increased attention to development, and anti-incumbent sentiment. The BJP's share of the

[53] Sanjay Kumar and Ramesh K. Chauhan, "Elections 2003: Understanding Complex Choices," *Economic and Political Weekly*, July 12, 2003, 2930–1. Accessed July 9, 2014. http://www.epw.in/system/files/pdf/2003_38/28/Himachal_Pradesh_Elections_2003_Understanding_Complex_Choices.pdf.
[54] Yogendra Yadav, Sanjay Kumar, and Ramesh K. Chauhan, "The Missing BJP Wave," *Frontline*, March 15–28, 2003. Accessed July 8, 2014. http://www.hindu.com/thehindu/thscrip/print.pl?file=20030328006401200.htm&date=fl2006/&prd=fline&.
[55] Chauhan, "BJP Manifesto Tries to Woo Every Section."
[56] "BJP Top Brass Hits the Campaign Trail in Himachal," *Rediff India Abroad*, December 5, 2007, Accessed July 9, 2014. http://www.rediff.com/news/2007/dec/05hppoll.htm.
[57] *The Tribune*, Chandigarh edition, December 6, 2007.

vote increased by 12 percent from 2003 to 2007. In its best performance ever, it won 43 percent of the vote (forty-one of sixty-eight seats in the Assembly). The RSS newspaper *Organiser* boldly claimed, "The Bharatiya Janata Party has proved that now it could easily climb the Himalayas by taking over Himachal Pradesh with a thumping majority."[58]

Thus the BJP lost the 2003 elections when it emphasized Hindu nationalist themes and won the 2007 elections when it downplayed them. With the exception of the Mandal-Mandir agitation, the BJP has gained more electorally by supporting economic rather than religious demands.

Movements and Parties

Mandal, Mandir, and Violence

The politicization of caste and religious identity in HP resulted from national developments: first, VP Singh's implementation of the Mandal Commission recommendations and then the BJP's opposition to Mandal and support for the Ayodhya movement. The BJP inflected these struggles with its interests in winning over upper-caste apple orchardists and government employees, both of whom it had alienated in the past because of its support for economic liberalization and pro-privatization stance. A powerful federation of non-gazetted officers (the Himachal Pradesh State Non-Scheduled Caste, Non-Scheduled Tribe Welfare Association), went on strike for three months against implementation of the Mandal Commission. BD Sharma, one of its major leaders, reported that the BJP in HP supported the agitation.[59] The BJP took the audacious step of filing a writ petition in the Supreme Court opposing the Mandal recommendations.

The anti-Mandal agitation was violent and disruptive. Young men organized *bandhs*, blocking roads. Busloads of students traveled to Shimla to attend demonstrations where they shouted ugly slogans like, "gulli, gulli meh koorah heh; VP Singh choorah heh" ("The streets are filled with trash; VP Singh is dirt") that were blasted through loudspeakers. According to official estimates, the protests caused $2,115,950 worth of damage.

In response, a group of government employees formed a committee to support caste-based reservations in government institutions. It pressured the government to comply with official orders, recruit more OBCs to government positions, and improve the conditions of lower-caste groups. Khajan Singh Dhir, its chair, said:

---

[58] Ajay Srivastava, "Dhumal Takes BJP to Big Win in Himachal," *Organiser online*, January 6, 2008. Accessed July 9, 2014. http://organiser.org/archives/historic/dynamic/modules07c7
.html?name=Content&pa=showpage&pid=217&page=4.

[59] Interview with BD Sharma, Shimla, June 3, 1991.

We organized a few rallies in support of Mandal including one in Kangra on September 4th, and then another in Palampur on September 9th. Twelve thousand people attended this [September 9th] rally. Every time we organized a rally, the police put us through a strict security check and did everything it could to stop us. But the police did not take any action against the people who were protesting Mandal.

This is part of an on-going movement against reservations which began in Gujarat and Bihar in the 1970s and spread here. The Jan Sangh is the major force behind it. The people who oppose reservations for OBCs are also against reservations for SCs (Scheduled Castes) and STs (Scheduled Tribes). The upper castes have been agitating against reservations for SCs and STs for a long time. The BJP government has been recruiting teachers on an ad hoc basis so that it can ignore reservations.

OBCs, *dalits* and tribals are starting to distrust the BJP. Shanta Kumar won the elections in Kangra because of OBC support. He will lose it in the next elections.[60]

Vidya Sagar, minister of state for health and family welfare, and the only OBC minister in the BJP government, publicly supported the official position but was troubled by it.

I addressed 3,200 public meetings in Kangra district. I defended the government's stance and said that reservations should be designed in a proper way so they could help the poor. But I also spoke to the chief minister privately and persuaded him to take some steps to win back OBCs.[61]

In 2002, Sagar resigned from the BJP and formed the Janhit Morcha Party on grounds that the government had broken its promise to reserve 26 percent of seats for OBCs.[62]

The BJP government ordered the police to fire on the protesters and dismissed thirteen government employees who participated in two strikes. The first was a strike of non-gazetted employees, lower-level bureaucrats, and clerical workers and the second, a joint strike of teachers, students, and employees. The government implemented a no-work, no-pay policy and had strikers arrested. It expelled thirty-three students, although they were reinstated after a judicial inquiry ruled in their favor.

As OBCs and *dalits* turned against the BJP because of its opposition to the Mandal Commission recommendations, the Sangh tried to win them back through the Ayodhya campaign. Gyan Chand Sankotia, VHP president for HP, said that the organizers had been particularly eager to gain *dalit* support.[63] He said that the VHP had performed *Ram shila puja* in Balmiki temples throughout the state. VHP members VC Sood and Devraj Sood reported that a group

---

[60] Interview with Khajan Singh Dhir, Shimla, June 3, 1991.
[61] Interview with Vidya Sagar, Shimla, May 31, 1991.
[62] "State Agricultural Minister Quits," *Tribune India*, November 16, 2002. Accessed July 9, 2014. http://www.tribuneindia.com/2002/20021117/himachal.htm#1."MLA vows to fight for OBCs," *Tribune India*, December 6, 2002. Accessed July 9, 2014. http://www.tribuneindia.com/2002/20021207/himachal.htm#4.
[63] Interview with Gyan Chand Sankotia, Shimla, May 30, 1991.

of *sanyasis* began working intensively among tribals and had drawn them to the BJP.[64] The close ties between the VHP and BJP during this time led newspaper reporter Najibullah Hassan to characterize the organizations as "VHP by night and BJP by day."[65]

The VHP in HP organized a *jan jagran* (mass contact campaign), *ekta mata yatra*, and *Ram shila puja*. It claimed to have performed *Ram shila puja* in 2,386 out of 2,780 *panchayats* in the state. It took *shiladaans* to each of these *panchayats* – including one located 13,500 feet above sea level – and sent the bricks to Ayodhya. It alleged that 1.1 million out of a total population of 5 million people participated in the *pujas* and 325,000 people participated in *yajnas* in 4,251 places. It stated that 2,500 people went to Ayodhya from HP and 500 of them reached there in 1990. The VHP raised 613,937 rupees from HP for the construction of the temple in Ayodhya. During the 1990 elections, Sadhvis Rithambara and Saraswati campaigned for the BJP in HP and filled the air with slogans like, "joh Hindu hit kah baat kureh gah" ("We will not tolerate insults to our God").[66] The VHP also organized agitations demanding that the government cede control over thirteen temples and authorize the VHP to manage them and control the revenues they generated.

The Ayodhya movement did not overcome the opposition of OBCs and apple growers to the BJP. Kumar's announcement in 1991 that he would construct a temple in Manali dedicated to Manu the lawgiver met with a tepid response. Mangat Dhuni, BJP publicity officer and member of the state executive committee of the BJP for HP, reported that opposition to the BJP was so great in Kangra that it could not even put up posters there.[67]

Horticulturalist Movements

One of the BJP's major goals and challenges was to gain the support of apple orchardists, the backbone of the region's economy and Congress Party patrons. Championing struggles of horticulturalists enabled the BJP to rival Congress but contradicted its commitments to economic liberalization and antagonized its wealthier constituencies. It thus alternated between championing this group when it was in opposition and withdrawing support when it occupied power.

The state promoted horticulture because it was well-suited to the mountainous terrain and an important source of revenue for both farmers and the state. Fruit trees are grown on about 32 percent of the state's arable land. Apples, 90 percent of the fruit, are mainly cultivated in the temperate districts of Kullu

---

[64] Interview with Devraj Sood and VC Sood, Shimla, May 30, 1991.
[65] Interview with Najibullah Hassan, Shimla, May 28, 1991.
[66] This information was provided by Gyan Chand Sankotia, VC Sood, and Devraj Sood, Shimla, May 30, 1991.
[67] Interview with Mangat Dhuni, Shimla, May 30, 1991.

and Shimla.[68] Apple yields are highly sensitive to fluctuations in the weather and crop diseases and cultivation costs are high. Periodic gluts and crashes in the market drive down prices, sometimes below production costs. State support has been vital to apple producers, who are mostly small farmers.

Strengthened by the Janata government's commitment to farmers, associations of apple growers emerged throughout HP. In 1984, these associations successfully lobbied the HP government to provide horticulturalists hydroelectric power, irrigation, and support prices (which stipulate that the government would prevent apple prices from dropping below a certain price). Apples sold to government procurement agencies at the support price were processed into juices and jams, which increased the market for apples without lowering prices for good-quality apples.

Apple growers' agitations in 1987 and 1989 demanded that the government increase support prices to offset the uncertainty and expense of fruit production and the vagaries of the market.[69] They also demanded more transportation facilities and cartons for transporting supplies. The BJP joined the movement. Daulat Ram Chauhan, who had been elected BJP MLA from Kotgarh several times, led the Kotgarh apple growers' association. Raju Chauhan, professor of political science at HP University and an orchard owner, commented, "The BJP joined the movement because it didn't want leftists to take over leadership. Unlike Congress, it promised support prices to apple growers in its election manifesto."[70] The BJP's stance contributed to its electoral success in several regions in 1990, including Kumarsain, Shimla, and Kullu and Manali.

However, once the BJP was elected to power, it reversed its position, opposed support prices for apple growers, and reduced the price that traders had to pay for fruit from six to three rupees a pound. When orchardists organized protests in Shimla in response, the government ordered the police to open fire, killing several people. Shanta Kumar defended the government's actions and claimed that the BJP had reduced support prices because apple producers were forcing the state to buy apples at inflated prices. He also described the Congress government's decision to introduce support prices as politically motivated. Raju Chauhan disagreed:

When the BJP claims that the government incurred huge losses on apples, it doesn't recognize how much the government depends on revenue from apples. The economy could collapse if it withdrew support prices.

Chief Minister Virbhadra Singh also questioned the BJP's motivations.

[68] Neeraj Vedwan, "Apple Growers' Associations in Northwestern India: Emergence, Success, and Limitations in the Context of State-Society Interactions," *Human Organization*, Spring 2008, Vol. 67, no. 1.
[69] Alam, "Changing Equations."
[70] Interview with Raju Chauhan, Shimla, June 1, 1991.

Basically our philosophies are completely different. We believe in social welfare whereas the BJP believes in laissez faire. We introduced support prices for fruit growers for the first time in 1984, which was not an election year. We felt that if farmers got support prices for their crops, orchard owners should receive them too. Ninety-five percent of apple growers are small farmers and they are mostly at the mercy of middle men, who have reaped huge profits.[71]

Raju Chauhan explained:

Delhi is the prime market for apples in India; commission agents in Delhi sell apples to agents in Bombay, Calcutta, and Madras. The Delhi market falls in Kalka Das's [BJP MP] constituency in Delhi. Das is very close to commission agents in Delhi who are a powerful lobby. They helped finance the BJP's campaign. The BJP has tried to appease commission agents by reducing support prices.

The BJP's reversal on support prices angered members of its own constituency. Several BJP MLAs, Maheshwar Singh, BJP MP from Kullu, and Kishori Lal, horticultural minister, were orchard owners. The BJP spent many years trying to regain apple orchardists' support by promising them higher support prices. Class differences compounded ideological differences between longtime BJP members and new recruits from the Janata Party.

Struggles over the Forests

The BJP is keenly aware of the importance people place on access to forests.[72] Although it supports the commercialization of agriculture, it has conceded to demands of NGOs and social movements for environmental protection, devolution of power, and indigenous control over local resources, especially when it has been in opposition. After attaining power, the BJP has reneged on some of its commitments and pursued capital intensive, environmentally destructive policies. Divisions within the BJP have surfaced on this issue.

The state has long recognized that decentralized systems of governance are effective in administering dispersed rural communities and has relied on local governing bodies. It has created drinking water facilities, rural dispensaries, and health care facilities. It has accorded important roles to *panchayats*, particularly since the passage of the HP Panchayat Raj Act of 1994. This has been politically popular because, as Alam notes, the *panchayats* are "networks and repositories of traditional values and act as conscience keepers of the people."[73]

Social movements have opposed forestry policies that have replaced natural forests with monoculture plantations of pine and eucalyptus that furnish

---

[71] Interview with Virbhadra Singh, Shimla, May 27, 1991.
[72] Ashwini Chhatre and Vasant Saberwal, "Political Incentives for Biodiversity Conservation," *Conservation Biology*, April 2005, Vol. 19, no. 2, 214.
[73] Ibid., 109.

industrial raw materials. In 1984, in direct response to the demands of one such movement a few years earlier, HP became the first state in India to ban eucalyptus on public lands. In 1993, it adopted the Joint Forest Management system, which created village forest development committees to work with the Forest Department. These committees have created forums for deliberation among government officials and local activists.

In the early 1990s, the BJP government contracted with international funding agencies, including the World Bank, to create an eco-development project in the Great Himalayan National Park. It did not tell villagers that they were legally entitled to compensation for the loss of usufruct land.[74] In November 1994, a coalition of NGOs informed villagers that park authorities were withholding information about the eco-development project. In the spring of 1995, villagers blocked the road connecting the park and the district headquarters to prevent the entry of a bus carrying forest personnel. These villagers demanded information about how the project money was being spent. Local women roughed up a park director who held a public meeting to disseminate project information.

The BJP seized the opportunity to capitalize on opposition to the eco-development project, which the ruling Congress Party supported. The BJP performed extremely well in the 1998 *panchayat* and Legislative Assembly elections by allying with progressive social movements. However its position changed once it achieved power. In November 1998, the state government signed a memorandum of understanding with the National Hydro Power Corporation for the construction of a hydroelectric project inside the national park. In June 1999, it announced a ban on villagers entering the national park. As details of the settlement award spread, people mobilized against the compensation that the government was offering and opposed the closure of the park for summer grazing and medicinal plant collection. Departing from the government's position, BJP MP Maheshwar Singh supported villagers' demands, criticized the administration, and ordered the deputy commissioner to allow people back into the park. He was re-elected to Parliament in 1999.

The BJP government also faced a great deal of opposition from local *panchayats* when international donors and multilateral agencies created village committees that sought to bypass constitutionally mandated *panchayats*. The government agreed to channel all future projects through the *panchayats* and extended the *panchayats'* authority by amending the Panchayat Raj

[74] The Indian Wildlife Protection Act requires state governments to "settle" or "acquire" rights of local populations prior to designating an area as a national park. Such acquisition of rights, through a process legally known as a "settlement of rights," takes place either through the payment of monetary compensation or through the provision of alternative areas within which such rights can be exercised.

Act in 2001. It promulgated the Participatory Forest Management Rules to provide detailed guidelines for involving *panchayats* in decentralized forest management the following year.

Several years later, villagers protested the state government's decision to promote foreign investment in tourism. In 2006, it authorized Alfred Ford, the great-grandson of Henry Ford, to build a $300 million ski resort in the region. Activists contended that the resort would result in water pollution, deforestation, forest erosion, and the destruction of natural habitats. Maheshwar Singh opposed the construction of the ski resort, in part to rally opposition to the Congress government that had sanctioned the project.[75] He claimed religious justification for opposing foreign investment and organized a *jagati puch*, an open court of representatives of the local deities, on February 16, 2006. He concluded after this meeting, "The gods rarely differ. Since a couple of Kullu *devatas* have already expressed their opposition to the project, the trend is quite clear."[76] Villagers rejected the project on grounds that it would be environmentally destructive. The controversy continued. A group of NGOs supported Maheshwar Singh and filed public interest litigation opposing the project in the High Court in 2007. When the court rejected its demands, a network of twenty-four NGOs submitted a memorandum to a government-created expert advisory committee. The committee expressed serious concerns about the project in March 2008.

Poor people's movements in HP are strong and politically savvy. Many social movements have pressured parties to support their demands prior to elections. Take, for example, the Ekal Nari Shakti Sangathan (ENSS), which is dedicated to securing the rights and well-being of unmarried women.[77] The ENSS presented political parties with a charter of demands prior to the 2007 Legislative Assembly elections, including government provision of free medical care and subsidized land leases to poor, single women. The BJP promised, if elected, to reserve 50 percent of *panchayat* seats for women. After the BJP came to power, the ENSS organized 3,000 single women from eight districts

---

Reckong Peo, "Power Project: Devta 'Summons Virbhadra for Talks,'" *The Tribune*, October 13, 2006. Accessed July 9, 2014. http://www.tribuneindia.com/2006/20061014/himachal.htm#2.

76 Chander Suta Dogra, "Ford vs the Icons," *Outlook India Online*, February 6, 2006. Accessed July 9, 2014. http://www.outlookindia.com/article.aspx?230097.

77 Women in HP have been active in monitoring the forests, opposing the illegal confiscation of timber, and protesting district officials who have licensed liquor stores. Women's activism is a product of both the autonomy and freedom that women have exercised and the threats posed by commercialization of the forests. *Pahari* women have traditionally played vital roles in economic production. In 2000, the government, in collaboration with banks and NGOs, created self-help groups (SHGs) to provide approximately 70 percent of the rural poor who do not have access to credit with income generation assets through a mix of bank credit and government subsidies. Ninety-five percent of the SHGs are exclusively female. Loan recovery in Himachal is 100 percent. HP ranks at the top of almost all gender-related indicators across Indian states.

to march to the state legislature and present the government with a charter of demands. ENSS co-coordinator Nirmal Chandel complained that the ENSS's demands were not reflected in budgetary allocations and MLAs had failed to raise their concerns in the legislature.[78]

To take another example, the Himalayan Niti Abhiyan, a federation of grass-roots environmental movements, released a vision statement for HP prior to the 2009 Lok Sabha election. Guman Singh, the federation's national coordinator, said that the federation had asked all political parties to implement a pro-people and equitable agenda involving sustainable utilization of natural resources and called for a ban on environmentally destructive industries like cement, mining, hydropower dams, mega tourism, Special Economic Zones and unregulated development.[79] BJP spokesman Ashok Kapatia responded that his party fully supported the movement, although he went on to qualify his statement.[80]

Hindutva Activism

The Jan Sangh members who became active in the "new" HP that was once part of Punjab harbored lingering anti-Sikh prejudices. Following Indira Gandhi's assassination by her Sikh bodyguards in 1984, Hindutva activists attacked Sikh families and property, especially in Kullu and Manali. Many Sikh families fled HP and settled in Punjab during this time. From 1984 to 1990, whenever Hindus were killed in Punjab, Hindu nationalist organizations would organize *bandhs* and processions replete with derogatory and threatening slogans. The Sikh families I interviewed said that BJP municipal corporators Rohitash Chander and Ganesh Dutt organized these *bandhs* and the police tolerated them.

Increasingly over the past decade, Hindutva activists have vandalized churches, burned Bibles, and attacked priests. Anti-Christian activism has been spurred by rumors that Christians forcibly convert tribals and the lower castes. Articles like "The Misdeeds of Christians" in the Hindi newspaper *Dainik Jagran* allege that Christians eat beef and engage in forced conversions. The Sangh Parivar can easily bring charges of coercion against Christians because anti-conversion laws consider caring for the poor and the sick "allurement."[81]

[78] *The Hindu*, April 2, 2008 and Nirupuma Dutt, "Women of Substance," *The Tribune*, June 8, 2008. Accessed July 8, 2014. http://www.tribuneindia.com/2008/20080608/spectrum/society.htm.
[79] Kanwar Yogendra, "NGOs Seek Action on Environment," *The Hindu*, May 8, 2008. Accessed July 9, 2014. http://www.hindu.com/2009/05/09/stories/2009050955651200.htm.
[80] Ibid.
[81] "Anti Conversion Law Targets Christians," *Gospel for Asia*, January 11, 2007. Accessed July 9, 2014. http://www.gfa.org/news/articles/anti-conversion-law-targets-christians/. The National Commission for Minorities expressed "profound concern" over the Act's attempt "to interfere with the basic right of freedom of religion that is the birthright of every Indian" and appealed to the central and state governments to reverse it.

The RSS has engaged in extensive conversions (or what it deems reconversions) of Christians to Hinduism. It celebrated the birth centenary of its founding leader, MS Golwalkar, in January 2007, by organizing eighty-five rallies against Christian conversions in twelve districts. Ganesh Dutt said that RSS members regularly attended church services to identify recent converts to Christianity and persuade them to reconvert.[82] The RSS-affiliated HP Unit of the All India Scheduled Caste and Scheduled Tribe Federation claimed to have reconverted fifty Christian families to Hinduism at a ceremony in Solan four months after the Freedom of Religion law was passed in 2006.[83]

Hindu nationalist allegations that Christians are engaging in forced conversions have been a pretext for anti-Christian violence. However, there is no evidence for these charges. Naresh Scott, the general secretary of the Young Men's Christian Association and a member of the HP Christian Forum for Human Rights, pointed out that not a single court case has been filed against Christians for coercing conversions.[84] Neither the National Commission for Minorities nor the media have provided reliable information about coerced conversions.

There are several explanations for the Sangh Parivar's hostility to Sikhs and Christians. Both communities are relatively prosperous – Christians own expensive properties in Shimla – and are thus potential targets of class resentments by poorer Hindus. Furthermore, Hindu nationalists can depict both groups as anti-national. Sikhs were once committed to creating a linguistic state and some of them supported the creation of a Sikh state of Khalistan. Christians migrated to India centuries ago and often have strong ties to Western ecclesiastical organizations. Many international Christian organizations, including the All India Christian Council, the Indian Christian Forum, and HP Christians for Human Rights, have publicized and protested harassment of Christians. This has resulted in spiraling activism on both sides of the divide.

However, Hindu nationalists have engaged in greater and more sustained violence against Christians than Sikhs for several reasons. First, the BJP's anti-Sikh stance in HP contradicted its national stance. The national BJP defended Sikhs when members of the Congress Party organized attacks against them in 1985. Once Hindu-Sikh conflicts and Sikh support for Khalistan declined in Punjab, Hindutva activism against Sikhs waned in HP. Second, RSS opposition to the

[82] Interview with Ganesh Dutt, RSS, Shimla, July 9, 2007.
[83] Ashwani Sharma, "After Law, Himachal Sangh Parivar on Reconversion Drive," *The Indian Express*, April 16, 2007. Accessed July 9, 2014. http://archive.indianexpress.com/news/after-law-himachal-sangh-parivar-on-reconversion-drive/28567/.
[84] Interview with Naresh Scott, Shimla, July 9, 2007.

cultural consequences of globalization feeds its antagonism toward Christians. RSS *pracharak* Narendra Kumar explained that *shakha* meetings devoted extensive attention to the detrimental effects of globalization on moral values, opposed sex education in schools, and sought to foster more culturally appropriate understandings of women.[85]

Third, the Sangh has targeted Christians both to gain the support of *dalits* and to compete with Congress over opposition to conversion. Seventy percent of Christians are *dalits*. Ajay Srivastava, a writer and political analyst, said that the RSS had taken up reconversion activities to encourage *dalits* to claim Hindu identities.[86] Although Congress usurped the BJP's agenda when it passed the bill on religious conversions in HP, the RSS claimed that the Congress government had done nothing to stop conversions. Indeed, Dutt stated that Christians had converted 3,000 people while Congress was in power. He was convinced that Sonia Gandhi had missionary ties and was diverting foreign aid to missionaries.

Fourth, according to Naresh Scott, the BJP opposes the demand of many Christians, himself included, for reservations in educational institutions and public employment for Christian *dalits*. Many *dalits* converted to Christianity in the mistaken hope that they would escape caste discrimination. Official policy, as enunciated by a presidential order of 1950, does not consider converts from Islam and Christianity to be *dalits*. In 2005, two advocates, Prasant Bhushan and Franklin Caesar, filed public interest litigation in the Supreme Court challenging the constitutional validity of the 1950 presidential order, which deprived religious converts of reservation benefits. Since 2006, members of the National Council of Dalit Christians have organized protests demanding the inclusion of *dalit* Christians in the Scheduled Caste list. Various government commissions have identified discrimination against *dalit* Christians and proposed redress. The Mandal Commission recommended that Scheduled Caste and OBC converts to Christianity, Islam, and Buddhism should receive the same benefits as Hindu *dalits*. The Ranganath Mishra Commission made the same recommendations in 2007. The BJP vehemently opposed their views.

However, Hindutva activists' anti-minority violence has not strengthened the VHP and its affiliates. The VHP was strongest a decade after it was formed in HP in 1981 amid the Ayodhya movement, when it claimed a membership of twenty-seven life members and 13,000 annual members. The Bajrang Dal's organizing secretary, Surender Singh Rangta, lives in Tikkar, a remote village in Bilaspur district, and has kept a low profile. The most militant Hindutva organization is the Shiv Sena, which has the same name but a different ancestry than its Maharashtrian counterpart. Although the BJP and Shiv Sena share

---

[85] Interview with Narendra Kumar, Shimla, July 10, 2007.
[86] Interview with Ajay Srivastava, Shimla, July 10, 2007.

members – like Ganesh Dutt, the BJP's vice president – the BJP and the VHP generally distance themselves from the more militant Shiv Sena. The strongest mass organization affiliated with the RSS is the student organization, the ABVP, which is extremely powerful in public educational institutions. Sikander Kumar, professor of economics at HP University, said that the ABVP had been active in recruiting faculty and administrators.[87] Chaman Lal Gupta, state president of the ABVP, proudly claimed that, unlike the Student Federation of India, which took its orders from the Communist Party, the ABVP did not follow the BJP's orders.[88]

RSS strength has declined over time and its activists worry about its ability to attract new recruits. Srivastava described the RSS in HP as lacking direction and vision. The RSS privately criticizes the BJP for sacrificing ideology for political expediency. A *pracharak* who requested anonymity said:

The BJP has a larger membership than we do. But ours is a more uncompromising, committed membership. Our slogan is, "Bharat Hindu rashtra heh!" "Gareb seh koh meh Hindu hoon!" ("India is a Hindu nation. Say proudly, I am Hindu!").

Ganesh Dutt complained that the BJP's ideological commitment had declined because of its overriding desire to gain power. He criticized the BJP for marginalizing older, more dedicated activists and promoting more electable younger candidates.[89]

Kashi Ram Balinath, BJP general secretary for HP, commented that relations between the VHP and BJP were close during the Ayodhya movement, but had since become estranged.[90] The VHP explicitly distanced itself from the BJP prior to the 2003 Assembly elections. VHP leader Acharya Dharmendra stated, "We have nothing to do with the Assembly elections in HP and it is not our concern as to who wins or who loses in the polls."[91] After the BJP's defeat in the 2003 elections, an RSS activist said, "The BJP is in a trap. There is an entire generation of leaders who believe that the only route to power is by breaking other parties and buying MLAs. That's why they fail as a traditional party of governance."[92]

Thus, the BJP is not as dependent on Hindutva movements in HP as it is in many other states. The most dissatisfied Sangh members are not members of the party or state government. They feel they cannot organize around the issues that the Sangh has taken up elsewhere. Some correctly feel that their actions

---

[87] Interview with Sikander Kumar, Shimla, July 10, 2007.
[88] Interview with Chaman Lal Gupta, Shimla, June 4, 1991.
[89] Interview with Ganesh Dutt, Shimla, July 9, 2007.
[90] Interview with Kashi Ram Balinath, Shimla, July 7, 2007.
[91] "VHP Distances Itself from BJP Debacle," *Press Trust of India*, March 2, 2003. Accessed July 9, 2014. http://www.hindustantimes.com/News-Feed/NM2/VHP-distances-itself-from-BJP-debacle/Article1-5137.aspx.
[92] Saba Naqvi, "Exeunt, Followed by Modi," *Outlook India*, March 17, 2003. Accessed July 9, 2014. http://www.outlookindia.com/article/Exeunt-Followed-By-Modi/219413.

do not influence the overall orientation of the party, although they have sought to maintain a presence in the state through intermittent activism – against Christians, globalization, and "terrorism" in Kashmir.[93]

Conclusion

In some respects HP is an outlier among the states that the BJP has regularly governed, in that Hindutva is not a powerful force and has not consistently contributed to the BJP's electoral success. Hindutva movements are weak for a variety of reasons. HP achieved statehood relatively late and divisions between new and old regions have prevented political parties and social movements from attaining statewide strength. The unorthodox character of Hinduism has limited the appeal of Brahmanical Hinduism. Caste parties have not emerged and neither Congress nor the BJP has appealed much to identity groups. HP's low levels of industrialization, mountainous terrain, and the importance of horticulture, have made it reliant on central government support for economic development, environmental protection, and remunerative prices for orchard owners. These are the issues that parties, states, and movements have most actively addressed.

The BJP has subscribed to Hindu nationalist principles intermittently and pragmatically. For example, although it sought to achieve electoral advantage by supporting the Ayodhya movement, it relinquished its ties to the VHP once Ayodhya ceased to be electorally profitable. This is not to say that Hindu nationalists are simply driven by strategic considerations. Their attacks on Sikhs and Christians are not electorally driven but reflect their antipathy toward minorities and the local reverberations of the BJP's national preoccupations.

The BJP's approach to economic issues has been both pragmatic and ideological. The BJP and its predecessor, the Jan Sangh, have long been committed to defending dominant class interests and privatizing the economy. They have participated in movements and supported policies opposing land reform, tenancy legislation, and increased remunerative prices for horticulturalists. However, the BJP's positions have often been electorally unpopular. Apple growers turned against the BJP because of its opposition to support prices. NGOs and social movements have opposed government agreements with global financial institutions that have undermined local governing bodies

---

[93] Following a "terrorist" attack that killed thirty-five Hindus in Chamba, HP, which borders Jammu and Kashmir, an RSS-affiliated organization, the Rashtriya Raksha Samiti, began arming villagers in the border areas against Kashmir militants. RSS *pracharak* Narendra Kumar said that the RSS and the VHP had organized their members to identify and report "terrorist" infiltrators from Kashmir and to address the antinational sentiments of Sikh and particularly Christian minorities. Interview with Narendra Kumar, Shimla, July 10, 2007.

and supported capitalist encroachment on forests and communal land. The BJP has been sufficiently pragmatic to concede to some of its opponents' demands, especially when it has been in the opposition. It has affirmed the importance of environmental protection, reforestation schemes, and community-based development programs because of their importance to the electorate.

The RSS, VHP, and BJP collaborated for a relatively brief period (1990–2) at the height of the Ayodhya movement. After that the VHP receded from mainstream political life and the major Hindu nationalist players were the RSS and BJP. The RSS' role is complicated. On the one hand, it is deeply ideologically committed. Thus, it supported Dhumal over Kumar when Kumar spoke out against the Gujarat violence and it put Modi in charge of the BJP's electoral campaign. On the other hand, the RSS has also been sufficiently pragmatic to have supported Dhumal's concessions to the broad electorate and to progressive social movements. Both the RSS and the BJP have recognized that their success lies in party-state rather than in party-movement alliances.

There are some similarities between Hindu nationalism in HP and UP. The Jan Sangh and the BJP in its early years mainly relied on upper castes and classes. The BJP further consolidated this support by opposing the Mandal Commission recommendations but thereby encountered fierce OBC opposition. It partially and briefly counteracted this by joining the VHP in the Mandir agitation. The BJP was defeated in the 1993 elections in both states. Over the past decade, Hindu nationalists have engaged in anti-minority violence against Christians in HP and Muslims in UP.

However, differences in the BJP's trajectory in the two states are even more striking. Anti-minority violence was never as extensive in HP and the RSS and the VHP have been weaker there than in UP. The Ayodhya movement never became the kind of mass movement in HP that it did in UP. One important reason concerns differences in the character of opposition parties and movements in the two states. The Janata Dal disintegrated in HP and some of its leading members joined the BJP. As a result, the BJP did not have to contend with opposition from the Janata Dal and former Janata Dal leaders were receptive to demands of environmental groups and agrarian cultivators. By contrast, the Janata Dal metamorphosed into two lower-caste parties in UP. The BJP sought to meet the challenge by oscillating between moderation and militancy.

Militancy has not been electorally profitable to the BJP in HP in recent years and it has adjusted its strategy accordingly. After losing the 2003 elections by pursuing a militant stance, it won the 2007 elections by reverting to a moderate approach. The BJP's 2007 election manifesto focused on creating employment opportunities, quality education, diversification in agriculture and horticulture, women's empowerment, and better roads and drinking water.[94] By contrast, in UP the BJP adopted a militant stance in both the 2002 and 2007 Assembly elections and lost both times.

Differences in the character of the party, movement, and state government are crucial to explaining these differences. First, state governments are much more committed to development in HP than in UP and both Congress and the BJP have been most electorally successful when they have demonstrated success in achieving both growth and redistribution. In contrast to HP, UP's human development indicators are low because successive state governments have not adequately invested in human and physical infrastructure, such as health, education, and drinking water, and their projects have often failed as a result of weak local governance and corruption. Even governments headed by lower-caste parties have looked more to the market than to the state to address these problems.[95]

Second, there are important differences in the character of opposition movements and parties in the two states. The major opposition to the BJP in HP has come from farmers, horticulturalists, forest dwellers, and government employees, and their demands have been economic rather than identity-based. By contrast, the major opposition to the BJP in UP is from the lower castes. Unable to gain appreciable support of Muslims and lower castes, Hindu nationalists have resorted to violence. Third, although the BJP is factionalized in both states, it is more divided by caste in UP than in HP. The differences between Shanta Kumar and Prem Kumar Dhumal are not rooted in caste differences. The RSS has alternately both widened and helped mend these factional rifts. By contrast, even the most ideologically committed BJP leaders in UP are divided by caste.

The party rather than the movement has determined the trajectory of Hindu nationalism in HP. The movement has periodically played a critical role, around the Ayodhya campaign, in anti-Mandal protests, and in anti-Christian violence. But the movement has not pressured the party to take up its demands either when the BJP has been in opposition or when it has been in power. The party rules.

[94] Chauhan, "BJP Manifesto Tries to Woo Every Section."
[95] Atul Kohli, *Democracy and Development in India: From Socialism to Pro-Business* (New Delhi: Oxford University Press, 2009); and Zoya Hasan, *Politics of Inclusion: Castes, Minorities, and Affirmative Action* (New Delhi: Oxford University Press, 2009).

8

Rajasthan

Two Phases of Party-Movement Relations

Hindu nationalists are deeply embedded in Rajasthan's cultural and political life. They have identified with the socially conservative Rajput community as well as with the rural poor, especially tribals. The BJP, one of the two parties in the state, alternates in office with the Congress party. As in many other states, the movement is more militant than the party. However, unlike in UP, the movement has not subsided when the party has achieved office. Nor has the movement become weaker over time. To the contrary, the party was better able to control movement militancy until 1998 than it was thereafter.

The most obvious explanation for the difference between the two phases is the nature of BJP leadership, in particular between Chief Minister Bhairon Singh Shekhawat (1977–80, 1990–2, and 1993–8) during the first, and Chief Minister Vasundhara Raje (2003–8, 2013 to the present) during the second. Raje herself believed that the strength of the BJP in Rajasthan, unlike other states, rested on the character of its leaders.[1] Shekhawat earned the title of "the tallest leader" in Rajasthan, a reference to both his height and stature.[2] His governing style is often compared to that of his mentor, Congress Chief Minister Mohan Lal Sukhadia. Both leaders centralized power in the state government and cultivated patronage relations but were considered nonpartisan. Clearly Raje did not command as much respect as her mentor and predecessor, Shekhawat.[3] However,

---

[1] Interview with Vasundhara Raje, New Delhi, December 13, 1991.
[2] Shekhawat joined the Jan Sangh in 1952. On two of the occasions he was elected chief minister (1980 and 1992) he was reelected to power after the central government dismissed the governments he led. Shekhawat was a member of the Rajya Sabha from 1974 to 1977 and the eleventh vice president of India (2002–7).
[3] Raje had a long history of leadership within the Rajasthan BJP. She served as a member of its national executive (1984), vice president of the Rajasthan BJP's Yuva Morcha (1985–7), vice president of the Rajasthan BJP (1987), leader of the opposition in the Rajasthan Legislative Assembly (2008–9), and leader of the BJP parliamentary party in Rajasthan (2009). She was an MP from 1989 to 2003.

while Shekhawat and Raje had different leadership styles, their ideologies were similar. They both supported Hindu nationalist goals while personally rejecting Hindutva militancy. Nor do their different leadership styles adequately explain their responses to militant activists.

Relations among the party, movement, and state differed during these two phases. In the first, some party members and movement activists engaged in protests defending *sati*, the immolation of Hindu widows on their husbands' funeral pyres. The BJP as a whole supported the VHP's Ayodhya movement and some of its members participated in anti-minority violence. However, the party controlled the movement. During the second phase after 1998, Hindutva militancy and violence increased and the movement initially drove the BJP's electoral success. Beholden to the movement, the BJP government (2003–8) conceded to its demands but the movement turned against the party and the BJP lost the 2008 elections. What changed between these two periods?

First, the nature of party-state relations differed under the Shekhawat and Raje administrations. During the first phase, the BJP was cohesive and its state government was relatively nonpartisan.[4] The BJP initially allied with the Janata Party and later co-opted its leaders. Although the RSS sought to control the government, the party was sufficiently strong to withstand its pressure. After Shekhawat stepped down, hardline BJP leaders became increasingly powerful and sought to undermine Raje's leadership. The RSS ceased to support Raje when she proved incapable of controlling party factionalism. The national BJP leadership began to exert greater influence over the Rajasthan party's affairs and reduced Raje's authority.

Second, the BJP functioned more like a catch-all party during the first phase and a cleavage-based party during the second. In its earlier years, the BJP gradually broadened its social base, first by gaining the support of the powerful Rajput community and later Brahmins, and then incorporating Jats and tribals, without mobilizing lower-caste support. By contrast, in its later years the BJP functioned more like a cleavage-based party that mined social divisions and appealed to identity groups. Activists mobilized tribals through conversions and through anti-Christian and anti-Muslim violence. The BJP appealed to Jats and Gujjars, (historically classified as OBCs) by promising them reservations. The strategy backfired when Gujjars and Meena tribals turned against the BJP government on the issue of quotas.

Third, the Shekhawat government discouraged Hindutva activism by prioritizing rural development whereas the Raje government antagonized Hindutva activists and the rural poor by pursuing neoliberal policies. Shekhawat

---

[4] See, for example, Oliver Heath, "Anatomy of BJP's Rise to Power," *Economic and Political Weekly*, 1999, Vol. 34, no. 34–35, 2511–17; and Sanjay Lodha, "Rajasthan: BJP Knocks Out Congress in a Bipolar Contest," in Sandeep Shastri, KC Suri, and Yogendra Yadav, eds., *Electoral Politics in Indian States: Lok Sabha Elections in 2004 and Beyond* (New Delhi: Oxford University Press, 2009).

developed a strong reputation for addressing poverty when he served as chief
minister (1977–80). Given the weakness of movements of farmers and OBCs,
credit for these programs went to Shekhawat and the BJP. By contrast, Raje's
creation of Special Economic Zones in Rajasthan provoked antigovernment
protests.

The Foundations of Hindu Nationalism

Rajasthan is propitious terrain for Hindu nationalism. Political elites are drawn
from the upper castes and the lower castes have not formed political parties
or organized social movements opposing inequality and demanding political
representation. Both the Jan Sangh and the BJP have been able to identify with
the interests and traditions of upper-caste Rajputs while capturing the support
of nonelite groups.

Rajputana, as it was known before its integration into the Indian union in
1947, was insulated from colonialism and the mass nationalism it provoked.
With the exception of British-controlled Ajmer, twenty-one princely families
ruled Rajputana. Each of the princely states had its own courts and rulers
and was insulated from each other and from British colonizers. Congress only
became active in the region in the late 1930s through elite-dominated Praja
Mandals and Lok Parishads.[5]

All but two of the princely states were Jat; the rest were Rajput. Landlords
under the *jagirdari* system were primarily Rajputs and most of their tenants
were Jats who lacked formal occupancy rights. There were significant conflicts
between the Rajput aristocracy and Jat farmers. Jats created *Kisan Sabhas,*
(Peasant Associations) that organized uprisings against Rajput landlords.[6]
Rajputs resented the Congress Party's passage of the Jagirdar Resumption Act
in 1952, which sought to break up large landholdings, and its recruitment of
Brahmins, Mahajans, and Kayasths into its Praja Mandals. Rajputs were a
natural constituency for the Jan Sangh.

Rajasthan's caste and class structure have afforded greater opportunities for
the upper than the lower castes to organize on a statewide basis. According
to the 1931 census, and confirmed by subsequent accounts, upper castes constitute 21 percent of Rajasthan's population. Three upper castes, the Rajputs,
(6 percent) Brahmins (8 percent), and Mahajans (7 percent), are scattered
throughout the state; the other ten upper castes, including Jats (9 percent), are

[5] Richard Sisson, *The Congress Party in Rajasthan: Political Integration and Institution-Building
in an Indian State* (Berkeley, CA: University of California Press, 1972).
[6] Iqbal Narain and PC Mathur, "The Thousand Year Raj: Regional Isolation and Rajput Hinduism
in Rajasthan before and after 1947," in Francine Frankel and MSA Rao, eds., *Dominance and
State Power in Modern India: Decline of a Social Order*, Vol. 2 (New Delhi: Oxford University
Press, 1990), 20.

concentrated in particular regions. The Rajputs and Brahmins have regularly supported the BJP and Jats have done so intermittently.

The lower castes are stratified. OBCs, who oppose the BJP in some states, comprise only 8 percent of the population (Gujjars 5 percent and Malis 3 percent) and differ from one another with respect to their status, wealth, and political identifications. Scheduled Tribes constitute 13 percent of the population. The most numerous are the Meenas (5 percent) and Bhils (6 percent). Scheduled Castes, or *dalits*, who make up 17 percent of the population, include Chamars (6 percent), also known as Bairwas and Jatavs; the remainder are Valmikis, Regars, Kolis, and Balais. There are tensions between Chamars, who have benefited most from reserved quotas, and other *dalits*. Many Balais, who continue to engage in their caste occupations, feel demeaned by Chamars, who have given up their hereditary caste occupations. Some *dalits* believe that Chamars precipitate needless conflict by waging struggles for rights and justice.[7]

Rajasthan's class structure has discouraged class-based organizing by landless agricultural laborers and industrial workers. With the abolition of the *jagirdari* system, 4.2 million people, more than 90 percent of rural households, became owner – cultivators.[8] Two factors associated with agrarian unrest elsewhere in India – absentee landlordism and landlessness – were absent in Rajasthan. According to National Sample Survey data, the proportion of landless rural households declined from 25 percent to 3 percent from 1953–4 to 1970–1. As a result of low levels of industrial development, the working class is relatively small.[9]

The Jan Sangh patronized key upper-caste groups. It secured the support of Rajputs, whom the Congress Party had underrepresented.[10] As the major aristocratic class, the Rajputs commanded particular power and status, and their backing enabled the BJP to identify with Rajput cultural traditions and ancient lineage.[11]

---

[7] Bela Bhatia, "Dalit Rebellion against Untouchability in Chakwada, Rajasthan," *Contributions to Indian Sociology*, Vol. 40, no. 29, 2006, 29–61.

[8] Narain and Mathur, "The Thousand Year Raj," 8.

[9] Ibid., 15.

[10] The Jan Sangh fared poorly at the polls in its early years. It won 6 percent of the total vote and eight out of fifty seats in the 1952 Legislative Assembly elections. It won 5 percent of the vote and six out of forty-seven seats in 1957, 9 percent of the vote and fifteen out of ninety-four seats in 1962, and 12 percent of the vote and twenty-two out of sixty-three seats in 1967. Opposition parties tried but failed to keep Congress from forming a government. For a detailed account of the first general elections in Rajasthan, see Susanne Hoeber Rudolph and Lloyd I. Rudolph, "From Princes to Politicians in Rajasthan: The Political in Social Change," ch. 6., "The Old Regime Confronts the People" (unpublished manuscript).

[11] Rob Jenkins, "Rajput Hindutva, Caste Politics, Regional Identity and Hindu Nationalism in Contemporary Rajasthan," in Thomas Blom Hansen and Christophe Jaffrelot, eds., *The BJP and the Compulsions of Politics in India* (New Delhi: Oxford University Press, 1998), 104–5.

The Jan Sangh, in its early years, represented large absentee landlords. Six of its eight members who were elected to the Legislative Assembly in 1952 opposed the Jagirdari Abolition and Resumption Bill. Shekhawat, by contrast, supported *jagirdari* abolition. He was himself a Rajput from a *bhumia* (small landowner) family who worked as a farmer before joining the police as a sub-inspector.[12] Shekhawat supported farmers and championed their interests after he was elected MLA on a Jan Sangh ticket at the age of twenty-nine. He said in an interview that the Jan Sangh sanctioned him for his actions:

I supported the Bill because I believed that land should go to the tiller. My party [the Jan Sangh] expelled me. Syama Prasad Mukherjee [Jan Sangh leader] told the party to take me back and suspend those who had expelled me.[13]

In the long run, Shekhawat's decision was prescient, for he enabled the Jan Sangh to acquire a broader class base.[14]

Under Shekhawat's leadership, the Jan Sangh developed a close relationship with the Janata Party. As chief minister of the Janata government in Rajasthan, Shekhawat launched landmark poverty alleviation programs, such as Antyodhya (Food for Work) and Apna Gaon Apna Kaam (Our Village, Our Work), in 3,300 villages across the state. The Antyodhya scheme enabled the poorest rural groups to engage in animal husbandry, cultivation, village and cottage industries, and wage employment. The scheme in Rajasthan, the first state to introduce it, became a national model. The beneficiaries the Rajasthan government selected were poorer than the national government required. A Planning Commission survey found that the Antyodhya scheme had significantly improved people's standard of living and incomes.[15]

The BJP won 25 percent of the vote and eighty-five seats in the 1990 elections and participated in a coalition government with the Janata Dal from March 1990 to December 1992. When the national BJP withdrew support from the National Front government, Shekhawat saved the government in Rajasthan by precipitating a split in the Janata Dal. Twenty-six Janata Dal MLAs led by Digvijay Singh formed the Janata Dal-Digvijay (JD-D), which backed the BJP. When the Janata Dal-BJP coalition came to power in Rajasthan in March 1990, the JD-D had eleven ministers and the BJP nineteen, including

---

[12] For a fine analysis of class differentiation within the Rajput community, see Susanne Hoeber Rudolph and Lloyd I. Rudolph, "From Landed Class to Middle Class: Rajput Adaptation in Rajasthan," in Amita Baviskar and Raka Ray, eds., *Elite and Everyman: The Cultural Politics of the Indian Middle Classes* (New Delhi: Routledge, 2011).

[13] Interview with Bhairon Singh Shekhawat, Jaipur, June 26, 1991.

[14] KL Kamal, "Rightist Political Parties in Rajasthan," in Iqbal Narain, ed., *State Politics in India* (New Delhi: Meenakshi Press, 1968), 505.

[15] "Evaluation Report on Antyodaya Programme (1979–81), PEO Study No. 125," Official Web site of the Planning Commission of India. Accessed July 14, 2014. http://planningcommission .nic.in/reports/peoreport/cmpdmpeo/volume2/eroa.pdf.

Shekhawat. After the split the following year, the BJP had twenty ministers and the JD-D had fifteen ministers.

The BJP could divide the already fractured Janata Dal because its members lacked ideological and programmatic commitments. Furthermore, those members of the Janata Dal who joined the BJP did not believe they were compromising ideologically because they considered Congress more "communal" and less democratic than the BJP. Digvijay Singh, who became Minister for Home Affairs, said in an interview: "Congress has made many more compromises on the temple issue than we have. Our main commitment was to oppose the Congress Party and we have maintained that resolve."[16] Babu Lal Khanda, minister for labor and employment, who left the Janata Dal and joined the JD-D, stated:

The BJP in Rajasthan is not a communal party and cannot be considered communal unless a government commission investigates the riots and finds that the BJP was responsible for them. Besides, we're not concerned about Mandir or Masjid but about development.[17]

A strong administrator, Shekhawat enjoyed the confidence of state bureaucrats. Narpat Singh Razvi, BJP general secretary, contrasted the CPM in West Bengal with the BJP in Rajasthan.[18]

In West Bengal the senior most leaders put the government's interests first but lower ranking leaders are only concerned about the party. It's different here in Rajasthan. From the district level up to Jaipur, BJP members put the government's interests first.[19]

Shekhawat did not allow party interests to dominate state policy. Ratan Kumar Sharma, a member of the BJP's state executive committee for Rajasthan, stated that the government's views always prevailed; the party played an advisory role.[20]

The BJP returned to power in the 1993 elections with 38.6 percent of the vote (95 seats), despite having been dismissed from office in December 1992. Constructing a temple in Ayodhya did not figure significantly in its campaign. In contrast to 1990, BJP candidates contested most of the 199 seats independently in 1993. Its share of the vote increased by 13 percent and it gained ten additional seats from 1990 to 1993. Particularly noteworthy was its increased popularity among *dalits* and Jats. Of the thirty-one seats reserved for *dalits,* the BJP captured a remarkable twenty-three, compared to five for Congress

---

[16] Interview with Digvijay Singh, Jaipur, June 27, 1991.
[17] Interview with Babu Lal Khanda, Jaipur, June 27, 1991.
[18] Several of Bhairon Singh Shekhawat's family members were Hindu nationalists: Narpat Singh Razvi, general secretary of the BJP, was his son-in-law; Bahadur Singh Shekhawat, general secretary of the VHP in Rajasthan, was his cousin; and Pratap Singh Khachariya, president of the state's BJP youth organization and a major pro-sati activist, was his nephew.
[19] Interview with Narpat Singh Razvi, Jaipur, June 25, 1991.
[20] Interview with Ratan Kumar Sharma, Jaipur, June 24, 1991.

and three for independents. In 1992, it recruited six Jats, including Krishendra Kaur of the Bharatpur royal family, who had formerly been a Janata Dal MLA.[21] With each succeeding election, BJP MLAs came to represent a broader caste spectrum.

With the Janata Dal in shambles, 1993 marked the start of a two-party system in which Congress and the BJP regularly alternated in office.[22] Shekhawat cultivated the support of non-BJP leaders, ranging from Congress MLAs to senior bureaucrats. The BJP rewarded former Janata Dal members who joined it by appointing them to Cabinet positions. Only sixteen of thirty ministers were from the BJP. The party's national leadership fully supported Shekhawat.[23] By contrast, the national Congress Party undermined its Rajasthan branch by frequently replacing chief ministers and constantly intervening in its affairs.[24]

Movement Militancy

The BJP was more internally divided on cultural than on political issues. Certain conservative cultural nationalist groups associated Rajput identity with masculinity, valor, and martial acumen, and strenuously opposed Westernizing forces. These sentiments surfaced with particular virulence around the issue of *sati*. Hindutva activists organized pro-*sati* countermovements partly in reaction to feminists' anti-*sati* protests. Shekhawat opposed *sati* while many senior party members supported it.

The case that generated the most controversy concerned eighteen-year-old Roop Kanwar of Deorala, Sikar district who lost her husband, Maal Singh, on September 4, 1987. Within a few hours of his death, she was burned alive on her husband's funeral pyre. Women's organizations and civil liberties groups swung into action to stop the promotion and glorification of *sati*. Hemvata Prabhu, past president of the People's Union for Civil Liberties (PUCL) and one of the leading activists in anti-*sati* agitations, explained:

---

[21] Rob Jenkins, "Where the BJP Survived: Rajasthan Assembly Elections, 1993," *Economic and Political Weekly*, March 12, 1994, Vol. 29, no. 10, 635–41. Accessed July 11, 2014. http://www .epw.in/system/files/pdf/1994_29/11/special_articles_where_the_bjp_survived.pdf.

[22] The formation of the Janata Dal-D decimated the Janata Dal while strengthening the BJP. The Janata Dal plummeted from 23 percent of the vote and fifty-five seats in the Legislative Assembly in 1990 to only 7 percent of the vote and six Assembly seats in 1993. After 1992, the JD-D became even more fragmented. Fourteen of its MLAs joined the BJP and the rest joined Congress. The following year the JD-D split again; one faction, the Bharatiya Janata Dal, which consisted of three MLAs from the Janata Dal, joined the BJP in the state legislature.

[23] Milap Chand Dandia, "Shekhawat's Arthashastra," *Asian Age*, January 26, 1997.

[24] Harideo Joshi, who served as Congress chief minister in Rajasthan (1973–7, 1985–8, 1989–90), said, "The Congress high command wanted to have its own people in power in Rajasthan. I was a successful leader but Rajiv Gandhi transferred me to Assam and then brought me back to Rajasthan after Congress did badly in the elections. Congress leaders destroyed the party in Rajasthan. This was one reason that the BJP grew." Interview with Harideo Joshi, Jaipur, January 25, 1991.

We brought charges against Roop Kanwar's in-laws for aiding and abetting murder and against the state government for its inaction. We won. A court order banned the glorification of *sati* and stopped Rajputs from building a *sati* temple in Deorala.[25]

Women's groups were largely responsible for the passage of the Rajasthan Sati Prevention Ordinance, followed by the Sati Prevention Act, 1987. The law made punishable any activity that glorified *sati*.

In response, RSS, VHP, and BJP members organized pro-*sati* activists to march through the streets wielding swords and chanting slogans in Jaipur, Alwar, and Sikar. Powerful segments of the Rajput community defended *sati* as symbolizing honor and fidelity to tradition and depicted feminists as their major adversaries. BJP MP Kalyan Singh Kalvi described feminists who opposed *sati* as *bau katah* (eyebrow-plucking) *sheehri* (urban) women. He identified opposition to *sati* with a repudiation of Rajput cultural values.

Several prominent women Hindu nationalist leaders, including Gayatri Devi, former *maharani* of Jaipur, and Vijayraje Scindia, a member of the royal family of Gwalior and an important VHP leader, defended women's rights to commit *sati*. Scindia argued that Hindu scriptures regarded women's primary duties as wives and mothers. She described *sati* as "a noble ideal that very few women have the courage to undertake."[26] Referring to religious scriptures, she drew a distinction between voluntary *sati*, which she associated with a glorious tradition, and the coerced *sati* of recent times, which she considered immoral. She was evasive when asked how she would describe Roop Kanwar's *sati*, saying that it would have been wrong if it had been coerced but she could not be sure. She argued that crusaders against *sati* sought to undermine Hindu culture and traditions.

The BJP was internally divided on the question. Vidhya Pathak, a BJP minister, said in an interview that she defended the principle of *sati* but condemned coercion.

Sati is the realization of truth. It is a noble idea. The Rajputs consider many women who have not immolated themselves *satis*. A woman who enjoys good relations with her husband and contributes to society can be called a *sati*.[27]

Bhairon Singh Shekhawat distinguished himself by opposing *sati*. He recounted in an interview the conflict around Roop Kanwar's *sati*:

Huge numbers of people came to meet me. They asked me to pay my respects to Roop Kanwar's family in Deorala. When I went there, I told them that I could not defend this practice. I told them that my father had died when I was young and my mother had raised me. I would not be where I am today if she had committed *sati*. They were outraged. They organized processions where they hurled abuses at me.[28]

---

[25] Interview with Hemvata Prabhu, Jaipur, June 26, 1991.
[26] Interview with Vijayraje Scindia, New Delhi, December 13, 1991.
[27] Interview with Vidhya Pathak, Jaipur, June 27, 1991.
[28] Interview with Bhairon Singh Shekhawat, Jaipur, June 26, 1991.

Hemvata Prabhu acknowledged that Bhairon Singh Shekhawat had taken a courageous stance in openly opposing *sati* but she felt he could have taken a stronger stance against his party members who supported it. She and other feminists were also critical of Shekhawat for not addressing the growing incidence of sexual violence in Rajasthan. One of the most notorious cases concerned a *dalit* woman named Bhanwari Devi who worked for the government-run Women's Development Project. When she opposed child marriage, upper-caste men retaliated by severely beating her husband and gang raping her on September 22, 1992. The local judge acquitted the accused. Shekhawat was unsympathetic to Bhanwari Devi's claims (which a higher court later upheld). Nor did he stop a BJP MLA, Kanhaiya Lal Meena, from leading a rally in Jaipur where he denounced Bhanwari Devi and defended child marriage.

Hindu-Muslim Violence

The Ayodhya campaign was strong in Rajasthan, judged by the number of activists who traveled there, the amount of money the VHP raised, and the emergence of new Hindu nationalist organizations. Eighteen thousand Hindutva activists traveled to Ayodhya from Rajasthan in 1990. Five thousand people, including 700 to 800 women, went from Kota to Ayodhya for the *Ram shilas*. Bahadur Singh Shekhawat reported, "We collected 58 *lakhs* ($127,000) from Rajasthan for the Ram Janmabhoomi campaign. We sent ten trucks filled with 26,000 *ram shilas* inscribed with Shri Ram to Ayodhya."[29] Mani Bai Patel, the BJP district president for Kota, reported that he had collected $175,218 from the district during the *Ram shila puja*.[30]

Several militant Hindu nationalist organizations, including the Bajrang Dal, Hindu Jagran Manch, Kesari Vahini, and Shiv Sena, emerged. Acharya Dharmendra, a diehard Hindutva leader from Rajasthan, estimated that the Bajrang Dal had between 70,000 and 80,000 members in the state in 1991.[31] Among the most incendiary of Hindutva leaders, he expressed venomous hatred toward Muslims and spoke forcefully in an interview about the need for Hindus to rise up against them.

Chief Minister Bhairon Singh Shekhawat was deeply ambivalent about the Ayodhya movement. On the one hand, as Narpat Singh Razvi reported, Shekhawat prohibited ministers from visiting Ayodhya unless they left their official posts.[32] Lalit Kishore Chaturvedi resigned from the ministry and went to Ayodhya in December 1992. Shekhawat also sought to gain the confidence of Muslims. Ramzan Khan, a Muslim member of the BJP's state executive committee and minister for wool, sheep, fisheries, and ex-service men, said that

---

[29] Interview with Bahadur Singh Shekhawat, Jaipur, June 28, 1991.
[30] Interview with Mani Bai Patel, Kota, January 11, 1992.
[31] Interview with Acharya Dharmendra, Jaipur, June 26, 1991.
[32] Interview with Narpat Singh Razvi, Jaipur, June 25, 1991.

Muslims liked and trusted Shekhawat.[33] He had been open-minded enough to organize negotiations between the Babri Masjid Action Committee (BMAC) and the VHP.

On the other hand, the government allowed the VHP to hold a massive anti-Mandal demonstration in Jaipur. One observer commented, "It lasted fifteen or twenty days and one and a half lakh (150,000) people attended it. I think that anti-Mandal sentiment in Jaipur led many people to support the VHP's demands in Ayodhya."[34] Razvi acknowledged that although the BJP officially supported Mandal because it was in a coalition government with the Janata Dal in Rajasthan, it unofficially criticized reservations for OBCs and supported the VHP's demonstrations against them. Shekhawat also participated in the *shilanyas*, greeted LK Advani's *rath yatra* when it came to Jaipur, and allowed the VHP to construct a temple in southwest Rajasthan to transport to Ayodhya.

Hindu nationalists engaged in numerous episodes of anti-Muslim violence from 1989 to 1992, in Banswara, Udaipur, Kota, Jaipur, and Malpura.[35] Many of them coincided with the Ayodhya movement. Violence erupted amid the *Ram shila puja* in Jaipur in September 1989 and the *Ram jyoti* procession in Udaipur in October 1990. After Advani's arrest following his *rath yatra* to Ayodhya on October 24, 1990, the Sangh Parivar declared a *bharat bandh* (nationwide strike) that precipitated violence in Udaipur and Kota. Shekhawat did not condemn the violence.

If the BJP first came to power in 1977 as part of a left-of-center coalition headed by the Janata Party, it attained power for the second time in 1990 as a result of movement activism. The violence that Hindu nationalists organized in 1989-90 was designed to undermine the Congress government and polarize the electorate. The Congress government's failure to curtail the violence, despite clear warnings that it was likely, further reduced the Congress' credibility.

Kota became the site of serious violence in September 1989 when a Congress government was in power in Rajasthan. A former princely state, Kota was the base of the Ram Rajya Parishad (Forum of Ram's Kingdom), a Hindu nationalist party formed in 1948. After it collapsed, most of its members joined the Jan Sangh and later the BJP. In the months preceding the violence, several religious ceremonies became occasions for Hindu nationalist activism. Hindutva groups shouted provocative anti-Muslim slogans during a Pratab Jayanti procession in January 1989 and during the Hedgewar centenary procession in May 1989.

---

[33] Interview with Ramzan Khan, Jaipur, June 28, 1991.

[34] Interview with Mahesh Daga, Jaipur, June 26, 1991.

[35] Steven Wilkinson's data from *Times of India* reports provide the following estimates of deaths in Hindu-Muslim violence in Rajasthan: one person was killed in Banswara on September 2, 1989, one in Jaipur on June 1, 1989, five in Jaipur on November 27, 1989, twenty-four in Kota on September 14, 1989, twenty-three in Jaipur on December 7, 1992, and twenty-four in Malpura on December 8, 1992.

Bakarul Ahmed, an advocate and human rights activist, observed: "When I was a child, these festivals never passed through Muslim neighborhoods. And the festivals were never so well planned. These processions were meant to pick a fight."[36] Ahmed said that Hindutva activists recruited supporters from *akharas* (wrestling dens) and from a dalit colony.

The Congress government failed to curb the violence. Ahmed said that the chief minister had not responded to his letter stating that the RSS and its affiliates were using Hindu festivals to generate hatred and violence. Somnath Sharma, a Congress Party member, showed me a copy of a letter he had written to the DM warning him that violence was likely.[37] The DM ignored his advice to increase security in the city and posted only about a dozen police officers there. Violence raged for several hours before the administration declared a curfew and for several more hours before it called in the army. Nor did the administration bring charges against the people who organized the processions.[38]

Hindutva activists mobilized thousands of people to march to the heart of Kota on the Hindu festival of Anant Chaturdashi (September 14, 1989). The procession stopped in front of a mosque while Muslims were reciting *namaz*. When Muslim youths began shouting at the procession to move on, verbal dispute gave way to physical violence. Twenty-six people were killed, 100 people were injured, and property worth 10 million rupees was damaged. A Muslim business community, the Dawood Bohras, suffered the most significant property losses. Shops that sold hardware, paint, guns, and leather goods were destroyed. The owner of two shops that were demolished estimated that the damage amounted to $328,515 and refused the government's paltry offer of $44 compensation.[39] He said that the police had failed to bring charges against the four culprits responsible for the killings.

Many observers, including Congress Chief Minister SC Mathur, alleged that the VHP, Bajrang Dal, RSS, and their affiliates instigated and conducted the violence.[40] Several people reported seeing Deputy Mayor Ravindra Nirbhay and a number of former or current BJP MLAs, including Dau Dayal Joshi, Reghuveer Singh, Kaushal Harish Sharma, Mani Bai Patel, and Madan Dilawar, in the procession. The police filed an FIR against Madan Dilawar, a *swayamsevak* and Bajrang Dal leader in Kota, for inciting violence. Dilawar claimed that the Congress Party's Muslim supporters had planned the violence, probably with support from Pakistan. He charged that Muslims had been abducting and

---

[36] Interview with Bakarul Ahmed, Kota, January 12, 1992.
[37] Interview with Somnath Sharma, Kota, January 10, 1992.
[38] Interview with Jamal Ahmad, Kota, January 11, 1992.
[39] Interview with respondent who requested anonymity, Kota, January 13, 1992.
[40] Asghar Ali Engineer, "Kota: Another Case of Planned Violence?" *Economic and Political Weekly*, December 9, 1989, 2703–5. Accessed July 11, 2014. http://www.epw.in/system/files/pdf/1989_24/49/reports_kota_another_case_of_planned_violence.pdf.

killing Hindu girls for years and that if Hindus had engaged in any violence, it was wholly in self-defense.[41]

Dau Dayal Joshi, who had been elected three times to the Legislative Assembly and twice to Parliament, contended that Muslims had attacked the Anant Chaturdashi procession and killed a guard; his followers retaliated to defend themselves. He observed, "Muslims here are poor and ignorant. They keep having children. Congress is to blame for their miserable condition. They set off a bomb blast. We simply tried to protect ourselves."[42] Joshi reported that the police had detained 194 Muslims and several Hindus under provisions of the Terrorism and Detention Act (TADA). He said that the administration released most of the Hindus within twenty-four hours of his undertaking a hunger strike demanding this. Jamal Ahmad, a human rights activist, tried to assist Muslims detained under TADA through a Legal Aid committee, but Hindutva activists threatened to launch a protest whenever the committee sought information about the detainees.

Jaipur experienced violence when newly elected BJP MP Girdhari Lal Bhargav organized a victory procession on November 27, 1989. He was joined by Ujala Arora, who was elected to the Legislative Assembly in 1990, following the violence, as well as by BJP state president Bhanwar Lal Sharma and members of the Shiv Sena and Bajrang Dal. Bhargav's victory came on the heels of a rumor Hindutva activists spread that if elected, Congress candidate Bhawani Singh would allot land to Muslim religious authorities to build a mosque in the city.[43] They also circulated a false rumor that Muslims had kidnapped and molested Hindu girls from the Kamala Nehru School and taken them to the walled city. Although the administration advised Bhargav and Sharma against visiting the predominantly Muslim neighborhood of Ram Gunj Chowraka because of escalating tensions, they led a procession there shouting anti-Muslim slogans like "Hindusthan Hindu-oh kah hen" ("India belongs to Hindus"), and "Jo humarah Ram kah neigh, voh sub haram kah" ("Whoever does not belong to Ram is 'Haram,' " an Arabic word for prohibited or forbidden). Bhargav mobilized unemployed youth from *akharas* to attack Muslims in Purani Basti where he lived. Muslims threw stones at the procession and Hindutva activists retaliated by destroying Muslim shops. Bhargav said in an interview:

Muslim *goondas* [thugs] and Congress planned the riot because they were angry that Bhawani Singh had lost. I realized that violence had broken out but I refused to stop. I would have looked like a coward if I had turned back. The Shiv Sena and Bajrang Dal did nothing wrong. They simply shouted slogans to express pride and celebrate my victory.[44]

---

[41] Interview with Madan Dilawar, Kota, January 11, 1992. Dilawar boasted that under his leadership the Bajrang Dal had recruited 10,000 members in Kota.

[42] Interview with Dau Dayal Joshi, Kota, January 12, 1992.

[43] Interview with Bakrul Ahmad, Kota, January 12, 1992.

[44] Interview with Girdhari Lal Bhargav, Kota, January 13, 1992.

274 *Episodic Violence*

Lalit Kishore Chaturvedi echoed his sentiments, "A *goonda* is a *goonda*, not a Hindu or a Muslim. Congress describes *goondas* as Hindus and Muslims just to stir up trouble."[45]

The local press inflamed already tense relations. The *Rajasthan Patrika* newspaper reported, without providing corroboration, that busloads of Muslims had been brought to the city to participate in the violence. It did not report on the extensive damage Muslims suffered. When interviewed about the incident, *Rajasthan Patrika* editors Kochar and Kuleesh denied the BJP was responsible for the violence.[46] They claimed that whereas Hindus who had come to celebrate Bhargav's election were peaceful, Muslims were angry because a Congress candidate had lost the elections.

The Congress government was slow to respond, despite many warnings that violence was likely. A PUCL delegation met with the chief minister just before the 1989 elections and warned him that tensions were running high. Superintendent of Police AS Gill only arrived in Jaipur at 4 P.M. on November 27, after the worst damage had occurred.[47] The DM did not instruct the police to open fire. The 150 poorly armed police who were present could not control the 15,000 people who poured onto the streets. By 11 P.M., when the administration called in the army, five people were dead and 200 people were seriously injured.[48]

Violence recurred in Jaipur on October 25, 1990, a day after Advani's arrest in connection with his *rath yatra* to Ayodhya. The BJP had organized a meeting in Jaipur the previous day that Bhargav, Satish Chander Agarwal, Kali Charan Saraf, Bhanwar Lal Sharma, and Bhairon Singh Shekhawat addressed. Some of them made highly provocative speeches and called for a *bandh* the next day. They tried unsuccessfully to force Muslims to close their shops. The police prevented the procession from entering one Muslim neighborhood but could not keep them out of two others. Hindutva activists stoned a mosque and Muslims retaliated by attacking a temple. Shortly thereafter, the walled city was engulfed in burning, looting, and mayhem. According to many accounts, BJP MLA Kali Charan Saraf directed the police to open fire and enter peoples' homes. A false rumor that Muslims were holding Hindu children captive in a mosque in Ram Gung led to further bouts of anti-Muslim violence. The administration imposed a curfew at 11:15 A.M., after two hours of serious violence, but was unable to regain control over the city for five days. According to official estimates, fifty people were killed and property worth millions of rupees was destroyed.

[45] Interview with Lalit Kishore Chaturvedi, Kota, January 13, 1992.
[46] Interview with Kochar and Kuleesh, the editors of the *Rajasthan Patrika*, Jaipur, June 28, 1991.
[47] Interview with Mahesh Daga, Jaipur, June 26, 1991.
[48] "Investigation Report: A Summary, Jaipur Communal Riots," November 1989 (unpublished report issued by PUCL Rajasthan Unit, Bapu Nagar, Jaipur, 1989).

The worst-affected area was Rishi Galab Nagar, where seventeen people were killed. The government had created this housing colony for migrant slum dwellers in 1984. Many of the original *dalit* homeowners had sold their homes to better-off Hindus and Muslims and moved to Khaiton kah *mohalla* on the outskirts of the housing colony. Muslims reported that Hindutva activists had organized *dalits* to attack their homes. They said that Guptaji, a Shiv Sena activist, had put glow-in-the-dark "Jai Sri Ram" ("Victory to Lord Ram") stickers on Hindus' homes to ensure that they were not damaged. They said that *dalits* from the nearby Khaiton ka *mohalla* had destroyed twenty to thirty of their homes by lighting rags drenched in kerosene and throwing them into houses after taking the contents.[49]

A third episode of violence in Jaipur followed the destruction of the *babri masjid* in Ayodhya on December 6, 1992. Syed Shahabuddin called for a *bandh* the next day to protest the destruction of the mosque and many Muslims heeded his call. The police had prepared for the event by imposing Section 144 (proscribing public assemblies) and posting police pickets throughout the city. The Bajrang Dal and Shiv Sena provoked Muslim youth, who then attacked Hindu-owned shops. Hindutva activists retaliated. Although the conflict did not escalate into widespread interethnic violence, the police shot and killed thirty-one Muslims.

There are significant differences between the roles of Congress and the BJP in the violence that occurred in 1989, 1990, and 1992. Whereas the Congress government failed to prevent the violence, the BJP government actively precipitated it. Many more people were killed under the BJP than the Congress government, particularly in Jaipur, where five people were killed in 1989 compared to fifty in 1990 and thirty-one in 1992. In 1992, the police engaged in more violence against Muslims than it had in earlier years.

The material losses and fraying of community relations were much greater in 1990 and 1992 than in 1989. Muslims in Jaipur experienced lasting damage to their homes, communities, and livelihoods. Only 50 out of 200 Muslim families living in Rishi Galab Nagar remained there after the violence. Hindus repossessed many of the homes of Muslims who fled and ostracized those who returned. Manohar Arora, principal of the Bal Rashmi School, said that seventy-two Muslims were among the 472 students who attended the school before the violence; in its aftermath, only twelve Muslim students remained.[50] Muslims found it hard to regain their jobs. The tools of those who engaged in crafts like tie and die, leather, and brass work had been destroyed and families often lacked the means to replace them. Several women whose families worked

---

[49] Shail Mayaram concurs on the role of *dalits* from the neighboring *basti* in the violence. Shail Mayaram, "Communal Violence in Jaipur," *Economic and Political Weekly*, 28, no. 46–47 (1993): 2524–41. Accessed July 11, 2014. http://www.epw.in/special-articles/communal-violence-jaipur.html.

[50] Interview with Manohar Arora, Jaipur, June 24, 1991.

in the gemstone industry said that the Banias who had employed them in the past were reluctant to rehire them. Many of the gem merchants were BJP supporters who preferred to hire lower-caste Hindus over Muslims. Relief and compensation for victims of the violence was sparse. Most of the Hindu-dominated NGOs that provided relief after the violence favored Hindus. The Bal Rashmi society, which Alice and Krishna Garg directed, was one of the only NGOs that primarily worked with Muslim victims. A report by voluntary organizations to document conditions after the 1990 violence found that 1,120 victims received some government compensation, but 650 people had not received any two months after the violence. The compensation that families received was paltry.[51] The BJP government treated the victims and perpetrators of violence in a highly discriminatory fashion. It detained 111 Muslims and only one Hindu under TADA. It acquitted fifty-five people for want of evidence and reframed the charges against some of the other detainees. Even after TADA was repealed, the government detained thirteen Muslims under its provisions.[52] The Congress government finally withdrew all the cases registered under TADA in 2001.

Although Shekhawat did not personally condone the violence, he exonerated party leaders who provoked it. Shekhawat claimed in an interview that the violence had occurred spontaneously because the Ayodhya campaign had unleashed powerful passions among members of both communities. The only group he blamed was the Shiv Sena.[53] Hemvata Prabhu said that the PUCL pleaded with Shekhawat to condemn the perpetrators of violence and quoted him as having responded, "Little incidents always occur during elections. If I were to issue a statement I might be misunderstood." The BJP government's refusal to hold its party members responsible for violence in 1990 increased the likelihood of their repeating their actions two years later.

There are several possible explanations for the government's refusal to condemn Hindu nationalist violence. The Mandal-Mandir agitation broadened the BJP's caste base of support and even enabled the BJP to gain votes from the Jat community, which was excluded from reservations for OBCs. It is also possible that Shekhawat recognized and yielded to the movement's power because his opponents, including Satish Chandra Agarwal and Vijay Warga, claimed

---

[51] The committee recommended that the government provide all victims easier access to bank loans and 10,000 rupees (rather than the 2,000 rupees it had been providing) to families whose belongings had been destroyed, and 50,000 rupees (rather than 15,000 rupees) to people whose shops had been destroyed. It also called for arresting the guilty and stopping people from moving out of their homes and neighborhoods. "Coordination Committee, Communal Harmony, Relief and Rehabilitation, "Riot Affected Area Survey: Jaipur, 1991" (unpublished manuscript).

[52] "Row Brewing between Rajasthan Government, Muslims," *The Hindu*, January 9, 2001. Accessed July 11, 2014. http://www.hindu.com/2001/01/09/stories/1409221i.htm.

[53] Interview with Bhairon Singh Shekhawat, Jaipur, June 26, 1991.

that he was not doing enough to protect Hindus.[54] Shekhawat's task was made harder because his opponents achieved significant electoral gains as a result of the violence. The BJP captured one Parliamentary seat and eight Legislative Assembly seats in 1990. Lalit Kishore Chaturvedi and Madan Dilawar were among the MLAs elected from Kota. Shekhawat later appointed Dilawar social welfare minister and Chaturvedi PWD minister.

Shekhawat probably feared mounting opposition from the VHP. BJP Minister Ramzan Khan reported that when the VHP planned to take a procession through a sensitive Muslim area in Bhilwara in March 1991, Shekhawat instructed the local administration to stop it. When the VHP ignored official injunctions and proceeded with the procession, the police opened fire and killed two VHP members. The VHP was so angry with Shekhawat that it stopped him from holding an election meeting in the area. It contributed to the defeat of Ram Swaroop Gupta, the BJP parliamentary candidate in 1991, by refusing to campaign for him.

Shekhawat faced continuous pressure from the VHP. According to Bahadur Singh Shekhawat, its state president, the VHP lobbied the government to impose more stringent restrictions on cow slaughter and met with some success:

Cows are often smuggled from Rajasthan to slaughter houses in Mathura and Bandra. Mr. Bhandari, the director of animal husbandry, has been working closely with us to ban cow slaughter. He has dispatched notices to collectors and superintendents of police throughout the state telling them to look for cows that are transported across state borders.[55]

The RSS and its affiliates became increasingly critical of the BJP government. The BMS opposed the government's decision to close down certain public-sector corporations and the ABVP launched an agitation to reinstate RSS member Rameshwar Sharma as vice-chancellor of Rajasthan University. The RSS lambasted ministers for their lavish lifestyles and urged them to meet regularly with grassroots party workers.[56] The RSS monitored and influenced official appointments. It criticized Shekhawat for not selecting its members to chair various boards, corporations, and autonomous bodies, and for appointing ML Mehra, who did not have an RSS background, as chief secretary. It pressured the BJP government to appoint Lalit Kishore Chaturvedi, Gulab Chand Kataria, and Madan Dilawar, to the Council of Ministers.[57] While Shekhawat was out of the country, it persuaded the government to appoint RSS member Hari Shankar Bhabra deputy chief minister,

54 Interview with Satish Chandra Agarwal, Jaipur, June 27, 1991 and interview with Vijay Wargah, the district president of the Congress Party in Kota, January 10, 1991.
55 Interview with Bahadur Singh Shekhawat, Jaipur, June 28, 1991.
56 *Hindustan Times*, October 24, 1994.
57 *The Hindu*, April 3, 1994.

instead of Shekhawat's choice, Narpat Singh Razvi. A number of disaffected MLAs lodged a formal protest against the party high command.[58] Sunder Singh Bhandari, vice president of the party, Satish Agarwal, MP, and Lalit Kishore Chaturvedi, PWD minister, became increasingly powerful and hostile to Shekhawat. The RSS deputed Om Mathur, one of its senior leaders, to monitor the government's functioning.[59] The national BJP caved to the RSS by delaying announcing that Shekhawat would serve as chief minister if the BJP won the 1998 elections.[60]

The VHP revived its campaign to construct a temple in Ayodhya and organized several violent campaigns in Rajasthan from 2000 on. In July 2001, the VHP and its affiliates destroyed a shrine at a mosque in Jahazpur, southern Rajasthan. They also demolished a sixteenth-century mosque in Asind, Bhilwara and replaced it with a Hanuman statue to mark the place where they planned to construct a temple. They named the structure Mandir Peer Pachar Hanumanji, the god who defeated the Muslim peer. Amrit Lal Khemka, the VHP district president, stated that like the *babri masjid*, it was an illegal structure that had to be removed.[61]

The Bajrang Dal and the VHP launched a *trishul diksha* (trident distribution ceremony) starting in August 2001 in Raipur, Kota, Jaipur, and Asind. The *trishuls*, traditional Rajasthani tridents that are used for decorative purposes, can inflict serious wounds but are exempt from legal restrictions on arms because they are considered symbols of faith. In November 2001, Congress Chief Minister Ashok Gehlot estimated that the Sangh Parivar had distributed more than 4 million *trishuls* and called for a ban on the Bajrang Dal. He cited a Bajrang Dal pamphlet that stated, "Hathon mein talwaren, seene mein hai toofan; raksha kare desh ki, Bajrang Dal ke jawan." ("The Bajrang Dal volunteers are defending the nation with swords in their hands and a storm raging in their hearts.")[62] Gehlot wrote to Prime Minister Vajpayee that *trishuls* could be used as dangerous weapons against innocent people. He ordered the arrest of the powerful VHP leader Praveen Togadia, who had made a provocative speech wielding a *trishul* in Beawar on April 13, 2003.[63] The police confiscated 650 *trishuls*.

[58] *Hindustan Times*, December 15, 1993.
[59] *Hindustan Times*, August 19, 1994.
[60] The BJP lost the 1998 elections because of party factionalism and popular dissatisfaction with the BJP government's response to unemployment, poverty, and starvation, amid the crop failures caused by a serious drought. Jats, who influenced electoral outcomes in sixty Assembly constituencies, largely voted for Congress because it supported their demand to be classified as OBCs.
[61] "Demolition Dynamics," *The Indian Express*, August 3, 2001. http://insaf.net/pipermail/sacw_insaf.net/2001/001099.html.
[62] Teesta Setalvad, "Rajasthan: Attempting a Replication," *Communalism Combat*, November 2001. Accessed July 11, 2014. http://www.sabrang.com/cc/archive/2001/nov01/cover.htm.
[63] Chief Minister of Rajasthan Ashok Gehlot made this statement in Jaipur on November 19, 2001. Setalvad, "Rajasthan: Attempting a Replication."

Mobilization of Tribals and Gujjars

Under the broad umbrella of the RSS, a number of organizations, including the Vanvasi Kalyan Parishad (VKP), Hindu Jagran Manch, Vidya Bharati, Saraswati Sadar, and Adarsh Vidhya Bhavan, incited tribals to engage in violence against Christians and Muslims in southern Rajasthan. Reports of civil liberties groups are filled with accounts of Hindutva activists attacking minorities' homes, businesses, and places of worship in towns like Beawar, Jahazpur, Asind, and Sikar.[64]

The VKP intensified its work among tribals in southern Rajasthan, in part to bolster the BJP's electoral prospects in the 2003 Legislative Assembly elections. It pursued a two-pronged strategy; the first consisted of providing social services to six impoverished and largely illiterate tribal communities (Bhils, Meenas, Damors, Kathodis, Garasias, and Sahriyas) in 3,000 villages in eleven districts.[65] It received substantial foreign funding from the India Development and Relief Fund and Sewa International. The Sangh Parivar sought to win over lower-status, less affluent Bhil Meenas by calling on higher-status, more affluent Meenas to accept the Bhil Meenas as equals and establish *roti and beti rishta* (inter-dining and intermarrying relations). The BJP joined the VHP in encouraging lower castes to adopt upper-caste practices to achieve upward mobility.

The second prong entailed fostering tensions between tribals and Christian and Muslim minorities. Christian missionaries had engaged in conversion activities and provided medical services and education to tribals in the mid-nineteenth century. They remained active among the large Christian tribal population in southern Rajasthan. There is also a sizable community of Muslim traders and moneylenders in the region. The VHP appreciated that tribals could engage in anti-Muslim activity with relative impunity because the Scheduled Castes and Tribes (Prevention of Atrocities) Act protected them from prosecution.

The Sangh Parivar began organizing Meena tribals against Muslim traders and moneylenders in Jhalawar district in December 2002. From August

---

[64] The VKP became active in social reform work among tribals in Kota in 1978, but in the early years either ignored or opposed their struggles against exploitation. Consider the events in Hadmatiyar, southern Udaipur, after the police and money lenders' henchmen surrounded the village and opened fire on tribals on April 2nd 1990. They stripped and beat the women and killed thirty-five tribals. The local BJP MLA, Narayanbhai, said little about these incidents and the VKP claimed, without evidence, that a progressive social movement in the area was forcing religious conversions. However, once Hindu nationalists sought to gain tribals' support, they increasingly opposed exploitative moneylenders – so long as the latter were Muslim. "The Story of Hadmatiya: Adivasi Struggles in South Rajasthan" (New Delhi: People's Union of Democratic Rights, May 1991) and *Rajasthan Patrika*, March 19, 1991

[65] Sarbeswar Sahoo, "Ethno-Religious Identity and Sectarian Civil Society: A Case from India," *Studies in Ethnicity and Nationalism*, December 2008, Vol. 8, no. 3, 3. The districts are Banswara, Udaipur, Dungarpur, Pali, Baran, Kota, Sirohi, Jhalawar, Rajsamand, Chittor, and Pratapgarh.

to September 2003, the RSS, VHP, and Bajrang Dal led hundreds of armed Meena villagers to engage in attacks on Muslims.[66] Vasundhara Raje, the MP from Jhalawar at the time, visited Aklera and gave an inflammatory speech a day after particularly serious violence began. Local newspapers reported that her speech emboldened Hindutva activists to attack Muslim shops and homes in the neighboring villages shortly thereafter.[67] The Sangh also recruited the Gujjars to engage in violence against Muslims in Asind, Bhilwara, on July 28–9, 2001.[68] Leaders included Ramlal Gujjar, a BJP MLA, and two RSS members who headed the Temple Trust.[69] Although the BJP was the immediate beneficiary of the VHP's efforts, it later became a victim of the Gujjar and Meena communities' aspirations for power.

Party-Movement Collaboration

The RSS provided full support to the BJP in the 2003 elections. Its national leader, Pramod Mahajan, designed an elaborate campaign for chief minister nominee Vasundhara Raje. Senior BJP functionary Sunil Bhargava, the media director, said that the extent of RSS participation in the campaign was unprecedented.[70]

The BJP returned to power in 2003 with 39.2 percent of the vote and 120 seats, three times the number it received in the previous election, and for the first time secured a majority in the state assembly.[71] BJP leader Ghanshyam Tiwari credited the VHP, VKP, and other RSS affiliates with playing a major role in the BJP's electoral success.[72] Hindutva activism among tribals paid

---

[66] Kavita Srivastava, "Violence for Votes," *Communalism Combat*, October 2003. Accessed July 11, 2014. http://www.sabrang.com/cc/archive/2003/octo3/sreport.html.
[67] TK Rajalakshmi, "A Communal Plot," *Frontline*, September 11–24, 2004. Accessed July 11, 2014. http://www.hindu.com/thehindu/thscrip/print.pl?file=20040924002903400.htm&date=fl2119/&prd=fline&.The VKP, Hindu Jagran Manch, VHP, and Bajrang Dal also organized Meena tribals to attack Muslims in Sarada Tehsil, Udaipur, in July 2004.
[68] "Sonia Urged to Help Rebuild Asind Mosque," *The Hindu*, August 16, 2001. Accessed July 11, 2014. http://hindu.com/2001/08/16/stories/0216000b.htm.
[69] Soma Wadhwa, "Preying at a Mosque," *Outlook*, August 13, 2001. Accessed July 11, 2014. http://www.outlookindia.com/printarticle.aspx?212887. The Sangh organized Gujjars to engage in anti-Muslim violence in Bhilwara again in March 2005. TK Rajalakshmi, "Striking Terror," *Frontline*, May 7–20, 2000, Vol. 22, No. 10. Accessed July 11, 2014. http://www.hindu.com/thehindu/thscrip/print.pl?file=20050520002204100.htm&date=fl2210/&prd=fline&.
[70] TK Rajalakshmi, "A Shock in Rajasthan," *Frontline*, December 20 2003–January 2, 2004. Accessed July 11, 2014. http://www.hindu.com/thehindu/thscrip/print.pl?file=20040102006301300.htm&date=fl2026/&prd=fline&.
[71] Devi Singh Bhati, a Rajput leader expelled from the BJP, formed the Rajasthan Samajik Nyay Manch (RSNM, the Rajasthan Social Justice Front), which registered as a political party in 2003 and vowed to achieve reservations for poor members of the upper castes. It won only 2 percent of the vote and one of the sixty-three seats it contested, which Devi Singh Bhati won. The RSNM was virtually eliminated after the 2003 Legislative Assembly elections.
[72] Interview with Ghanshyam Tiwari, Jaipur, January 16, 2007.

off. The BJP's share of tribal votes increased from 32 percent to 38 percent between the 1998 and 2003 Legislative Assembly elections. In reserved seats for Scheduled Tribes, the BJP won fifteen out of twenty-four seats in 2003, compared to two out of twenty-four seats in 1998.[73] The BJP's Meena MLAs increased from 0.5 percent to 7 percent from 1952 to 2003. Jat support for the BJP also increased. The BJP won over half of all seats in Jat-dominated constituencies, a total of thirty-six out of sixty-three seats.[74] The BJP projected Raje as a Jat leader because she had been married briefly to the Jat Maharaja of Dholpur.[75] During the 1999 Lok Sabha election campaign, the BJP assured Jats that it would designate them OBCs if it was elected to power. The Jat Mahasabha endorsed the BJP in the 2003 elections.[76]

Thirty-nine BJP candidates elected in 2003 had criminal records.[77] Most notable among them was Madan Dilawar, who had been booked on seventeen criminal charges. He was re-elected, as were several other BJP MLAs who had been charged with "rioting" and other criminal activities.[78] Forty percent of those with criminal records were charged with "serious" crimes. The BJP had more candidates than any other party (nineteen of forty-three) who were charged with committing serious crimes.

The BJP actively defended and promoted the movement. It was elected by a wide margin, did not have to accommodate other parties in the government and was beholden to the movement. VHP activism had contributed to its

---

[73] Congress won nineteen of these seats in 1998 and only five in 2003, see Rajalakshmi "A Shock in Rajasthan."

[74] Jai Mrug, "Changing Patterns of Support," *Economic and Political Weekly*, January 3–9, 2004, 18. Accessed July 11, 2014. http://www.epw.in/system/files/pdf/2004_39/01/Elections_2003_Changing_Patterns_of_Support.pdf.

[75] In the parliamentary elections the following year, 65 percent of Jats voted for the BJP, which won sixteen out of twenty-five seats in the parliamentary elections. The BJP won two of the three seats reserved for Scheduled Tribes, one of which, in Banswara, the Janata Dal had traditionally held. From 1996 to 2004, tribal support for the BJP in the parliamentary elections grew from 15 percent to 39 percent. In the thirty-three reserved constituencies for Scheduled Castes, the BJP won twenty-six, Congress five, and other parties the remaining two. Congress had won thirty-one of these seats in the 1998 elections. In the 2004 parliamentary elections, the BJP won all four of the reserved constituencies for Scheduled Castes (Jalore, Tonk, Sri Ganganagar, and Bayana). From 1996 to 2004, dalit support for the BJP grew from 15 percent to 26 percent. Sanjay Lodh, "Rajasthan: India Shines as BJP Trounces Congress," *Economic and Political Weekly*, December 18, 2004. Accessed July 11, 2014. http://www.epw.in/system/files/pdf/2004_39/51/Rajasthan__India_Shines_as_BJP_Trounces_Congress.pdf.

[76] "Battle Intensifies for Jat Votes in Rajasthan," *Hindustan Times*, November 26, 2003. Accessed July 11, 2014. http://www.hindustantimes.com/News-Feed/NM1/Battle-intensifies-for-Jat-votes-in-Rajasthan/Article1-9565.aspx.

[77] The Rajasthan Election Watch, a nonpartisan NGO, analyzed affidavits of 950 of the 1,541 candidates who contested the 2003 elections. It found that 124 candidates had criminal records. The largest number were from the BJP.

[78] They included Banwari Lal Singhal, Kalyan Singh Chowdhury, Bhagwan Singh Rajawat (with two criminal cases against him), Gyan Dev, and Kali Charan Saraf.

electoral success and the RSS and affiliates had organized its election campaign. Conversely, the movement could undermine Raje's authority when it judged that she had failed to comply with its dictates and choice of political advisors. The RSS had a free hand in determining government policies and appointments. Three days after Raje was sworn in, RSS chief Sudarshan met with BJP legislators in Kota to instruct them on governance. It played a major role in the appointments of Ghanshyam Tiwari as minister of education and Lalit Kishore Chaturvedi as minister of social welfare. Tiwari announced that there was no question of the BJP forsaking Hindutva. He said that the party would promote all the issues in its election manifesto, especially a bill restricting conversions.

Soon after coming to power, the BJP government took steps to demonstrate its appreciation of the movement. It lifted the ban on the Bajrang Dal and allowed it to resume *trishul* distribution. The Bajrang Dal and VHP saw this as a major victory and established six camps that trained 400 young men and women to use arms.[79] The government allowed the Bajrang Dal to organize menacing rallies and some government officials participated in them. For example, in September 2004, the Bajrang Dal organized a massive rally in Kanwas, Kota district, in celebration of "Akhand Bharat Diwas (Undivided Indian Independence Day)." Although the administration negotiated an acceptable route, Bajrang Dal activists defied the agreement and took a procession through a minority neighborhood. GR Dhanwani, the BJP's deputy president, and Madan Dilawar, Rajasthan social welfare minister, participated in the rally.

The BJP government withdrew 122 cases that the previous Congress government had filed against the VHP and its affiliates for inciting Hindu-Muslim violence.[80] Civil liberty groups found that the government had withdrawn ten FIRs against Sangh members accused of violence against minorities in Kalinjara (Banswara district) in 2002 and in Aklera (Jhalawar district) in August and September 2003.[81] Most of the thirty-two cases it withdrew in Aklera were still under investigation. The government dropped charges against Acharya Dharmendra for inciting violence.

The government actively promoted Hindu nationalist education. It sanctioned an RSS proposal to produce an encyclopedia entitled *Apni Dharti, Apna Log* (Our Land, Our People), which provided a revisionist understanding of the state's history. Ghanshyam Tiwari authorized the recitation of *bhojan mantras,* (Hindu prayers before meals) at state-run hospitals. Under his orders, the government also revived a practice that the Congress government had

[79] *Asian Age,* May 23, 2006.
[80] Sowmya Kerbat Sivakumar, "Is Rajasthan the Next Hate Laboratory?" *Tehelka,* September 4, 2004. Accessed July 11, 2014. http://archive.tehelka.com/story_main6.asp?filename=Ne090404in_rajasthan.asp.
[81] DK Singh, "Rajasthan: Draw Adivasis into the Hindu Fold, Lost Tribes, Part II," *Communalism Combat,* October 2004. Accessed July 11, 2014. http://sabrang.com/cc/archive/2004/oct04/cover.html.

discontinued of reciting "Vande Mataram" every morning in government-run hostels. The administration suspended the superintendent of a hostel in Jalpura for failing to enforce this policy.[82] Tiwari directed his department to provide the RSS with resources to establish a private university named Keshav Vidyapeeth Vishwavidyalaya (KVV) on 2,300 acres of land in Jandoli, on the outskirts of Jaipur. The purpose of the university, Tiwari stated, was to promote Hindu nationalist philosophy and to offer postgraduate courses on Ayurvedic science and yoga. The BJP promoted the KVV as a model that it planned to replicate in other parts of the state. The KVV was supposed to open in 2005–6 but a Supreme Court verdict stalled its plans.[83]

The government actively supported the VHP's social work and conversion of tribals. It allotted $101,325 per annum to VKP-run hostels for tribals in 2003. VKP schoolteachers, especially in its *ekal vidyalayas*, were only hired if they supported and promoted RSS philosophy.[84] The VKP created 415 "faith awakening" centers that encouraged tribals to give up magic, witchcraft, theft, adultery, alcoholism, and meat consumption. It also constructed hundreds of temples to promote the worship of the Hindu god Ganesh. The Vanvasi Kalyan Ashram, another RSS affiliate, established 4,100 centers that organized weekly or fortnightly *bhajan mandals* (congregations to sing devotional songs.).

The VHP and Bajrang Dal intensified their conversions of Christian tribals to Hinduism. They presided over a *ghar vapsi* ceremony in which 650 Christian tribals participated in Richaawar village, Udaipur district, on February 29, 2004. The VHP warned of the dangers of Christian proselytization and gave them "OM" (a sacred mantra)-inscribed lockets and calendars. Certain BJP government members actively supported these initiatives. Barely a month after the BJP took office, Tribal Area Development Minister Kanak Lal Katara announced that the government would exclude Christian tribals from the list of Scheduled Tribes. Although Katara retracted his decision under pressure from civil liberties organizations, Hindutva activists spread rumors that

[82] "Vande Mataram Restored," *The Hindu*, December 13, 2003. Accessed July 11, 2014. http://www.hindu.com/2003/12/13/stories/2003121310940100.htm.

[83] Sandipan Sharma, "Rajasthan Opens Doors to First RSS University," *The Indian Express*, February 2, 2006. Accessed July 11, 2014. http://archive.indianexpress.com/oldStory/87113/. J. Venkatesan, "Supreme Court Declares 112 Private Universities in Chhattisgarh Illegal," February 12, 2005. Accessed July 11, 2014. http://www.hindu.com/2005/02/12/stories/2005021205600100.htm. SS Negi, "SC Orders Closure of 117 Varsities in Chhattisgarh," *The Tribune*, February 11, 2005. Accessed July 11, 2014. http://www.tribuneindia.com/2005/20050212/main6.htm.

[84] This, according to the VKP's own estimates, enabled the VKP to run sixty-three *ekal vidyalayas*, fourteen boarding schools, thirty-one primary schools, two middle schools, and one secondary school. The VKP created 128 sport centers and many women's centers. It established ten-member committees in each of these villages that organized health camps every fifteen days for nominal fees. It trained tribals in agricultural production, tailoring, and small-scale industries. "Saffronising the Tribal Heartland," *Frontline*, March 13–26, 2004. Accessed July 11, 2014. http://www.hindu.com/fline/fl2106/stories/20040326004601900.htm.

Christians would lose their Scheduled Tribe status unless they "reconverted" to Hinduism. The government did not assuage Christians' anxieties.

Human rights teams documented extensive assaults on Christians in 2005 and 2006.[85] The most common pattern was for Bajrang Dal and VHP members to attack Christians whom they accused of engaging in forced conversions, abducting children, and trafficking women. They sometimes reported these cases to the police, who would generally detain or arrest the accused. One of Hindutva activists' major targets was the Christian Emmanuel Mission (EM) in Kota. They raided one of the EM's orphanages on February 2, 2003, killing one child and injuring several staff members. Two years later, activists forced 250 youth who had traveled by train from Andhra Pradesh to visit the orphanage to accompany them to the police station, where activists filed charges against the EM for coerced conversions.[86] The attacks resumed in 2006.[87]

The government provided institutional support for Hindutva activists. It banned the book *Haqeeqat* (The Truth) for criticizing Hinduism and arrested its author, MG Mathew. It revoked the licenses of an EM Bible institute, orphanage, school, hospital, and church, and froze the EM's bank accounts. Authorities detained EM president Samuel Thomas for several months in 2006 and charged him with sedition because a map of India on an EM-affiliated Web site did not include Jammu and Kashmir.[88] Social Welfare Minister Madan Dilawar refused to prosecute Hindu activists who had injured Christians and damaged their property. The Jaipur High Court subsequently instructed the state government to show cause regarding the closing of the EM property and unfreeze its accounts.

The BJP government also sacrificed women's rights to the cause of Hindu nationalism. Unlike Bhairon Singh Shekhawat, Raje cultivated the support of the orthodox Rajput community by countenancing *sati*. During her campaign

---

[85] US Report on International Freedoms documented the frequency of Hindutva attacks on Christians. "Report on International Religious Freedom," Bureau of Human Rights, Democracy and Labor Releases, *U.S. Department of State*, http://www.state.gov/j/drl/rls/irf/2006/index .htm. Similar anti-Christian attacks occurred in 2006. "2007 Report on International Religious Freedom," Bureau of Human Rights, Democracy and Labor Releases, *U.S. Department of State*, http://www.state.gov/j/drl/rls/irf/2007/index.htm.

[86] *Asian Age*, February 20, 2005.

[87] On February 10, 2006, Hindutva activists set fire to an EM school and orphanage in Ramganjmandi, Rajasthan. They attacked the EM headquarters in Kota on February 14, 2006, an EM primary school in Sanganer on February 22, 2006, and the Jhowara Emmanuel Secondary School and church on February 24, 2006. "Police Harass Christian Leader's Family in Rajasthan, India," *Compass Direct News*, March 8, 2006, Accessed July 11, 2014. http:// www.worthynews.com/861-police-harass-christian-leader-s-family-in-rajasthan.

[88] Social Welfare Minister Madan Dilawar announced that he had directed his officers to conduct an inquiry into the mission's activities, but he cancelled the mission's registration before the inquiry took place to protect innocent Hindus from Christians, whom he said were kidnapping and mistreating children. Interview with Madan Dilawar, Jaipur, November 2006.

for the November 2003 Assembly elections, she paid respects at the Rani Sati temple in Jhunjhunu. After becoming chief minister, she did not appeal the verdict of a special sessions court in Jaipur that acquitted eleven people who had been charged with violating the Rajasthan Sati Prevention Ordinance in connection with Roop Kanwar's *sati*. Women's groups organized protests outside the State Assembly in 2004 and filed a public interest writ petition.[89] As feminist organizations anticipated, the acquittals strengthened pro-*sati* forces. On March 20, 2005, close to 20,000 people descended on Sumel village, Pali district, and goaded recently widowed Basanti Devi Vaishnav toward the funeral pyre, but, under pressure from women's organizations, the police prevented the murder and made arrests.

The identification of *sati* with Rajput cultural identity had deepened. Less than a month after the episode in Sumel, the government announced that Rajasthan's urban development minister, Pratap Singh Singhvi, would inaugurate a Rani Sati Nagar housing complex in Jaipur. The Rajasthan Tourism Development office published a guidebook in 2005 on Popular Deities of Rajasthan, which described Rajasthan as "best-known for various *Sati Matas*" and provided detailed information about them. Human rights groups protested the name of the housing complex and the publication and distribution of the book.

Through her concessions on *sati* to conservative Hindu nationalists, Raje may have hoped to demonstrate that she was not a Westernized woman, as her opponents often claimed. She may also have been afraid to confront senior party leaders. Appealing the High Court judgment on *sati* would have meant challenging such powerful figures as former PWD minister Rajendra Singh Rathore, Rajput Maha Sabha president and nephew of Vice President Bhairon Singh Shekhawat, Pratap Singh Khachariawas, and Education Minister Ghanshyam Tiwari.

With Assembly elections approaching, the RSS and its affiliates heightened fears of "terrorism." A bomb blast at the Ajmer *dargah* (also known as the Ajmer Sharif blast) on October 11, 2007 killed three people and injured seventeen. Authorities blamed the blast on the Pakistan-based Lashkar-e-Taiba and the media characterized it as the work of Islamic extremists. In fact, three years later (October 2010), Indian intelligence forces determined that Hindu nationalists had masterminded the attack. Swami Asemanand of an organization called the Abhinav Bharat, who was arrested, implicated the RSS in the plan. Bharat Rateshwar, who was also accused, revealed that BJP MP Yogi Adityanath had funded Hindutva activists to plan the attacks.[90]

[89] *The Indian Express*, Jaipur, August 7, 2004 and "Rajasthan High Court Accepts Sati Writ Petitions: Issues Notices," *South Asian Citizens Web*, August 6, 2004. Accessed July 11, 2014. http://www.sacw.net/Wmov/SatiRajasthanHC_Aug62004.html.

[90] See, for example, Leena Gita Reghunath, "The Believer: Swami Aseemanand's Radical Service to the Sangh," *The Caravan: Journal of Politics and Culture*, February 1, 2014. Accessed August 4, 2014. http://Www.Caravanmagazine.In/Reportage/Believer?Page=0,6; and Smruti Koppikar,

A second attack occurred in Jaipur on May 13, 2008. Official reports estimate that nine synchronized bomb blasts killed sixty-three people and caused
at least 216 injuries. Although the India-based Mujahideen or Guru-al-Hindi
claimed responsibility for the attacks, the BJP government alleged that the
Bangladeshi-based Islamist group Harkat-Ul-Jihad-i-Islami was responsible.[91]
The Rajasthan government then hounded Bangladeshi immigrants. It ordered
authorities to retrieve ration cards from those who had obtained them ille-
gally and to cancel their names from electoral lists.[92] Violating the Criminal
Procedure Code, the police denied the 116 people it arrested the opportunity
to provide proof of citizenship; some courts denied them the right to counsel.
The police seized land that Bangladeshi immigrants had occupied for fifty years
and deported them.

Raje commented, "Crime takes place on a small scale. This is not a crime;
we are in the middle of a war."[93] She criticized the Indian President for
not signing an antiterrorism bill that the Rajasthan Legislative Assembly
had passed in 2006 and vowed to pass antiterrorism legislation that resembled POTA and legislation that Gujarat had passed. She announced that
Rajasthan would create an antiterrorism force, possibly jointly with other
states.

Party-Movement Tensions

Raje's concessions to her Hindutva opponents only made them more vociferous and hostile both to her economic policies and her stance toward minorities.
They opposed her decision to create a Special Economic Zone at unfavorable
terms to farmers and to create accommodations for Muslim pilgrims on public
land. Both positions reflected RSS commitments and concerns – in the first case,
its opposition to economic liberalization, and in the second, its anti-Muslim
sentiments. The Raje government was more successful in placating opponents
of the Special Economic Zone than of the Muslim pilgrimage site.

Debarshi Dasgupta, and Srigdhar Hasan, "The Mirror Explodes: Hindu Terrorism Is a Reality
Yet India Refuses to Utter Its Name," *Outlook Magazine*, July 19, 2010. Accessed August 4,
2014. Http://Www.Outlookindia.Com/Article/The-Mirror-Explodes/266145.

[91] "Jaipur Blasts, BJP Lashes Out at Center," *Times of India*, May 15, 2008. Accessed July 11,
2014. http://timesofindia.indiatimes.com/india/Jaipur-blasts-BJP-lashes-out-at-Centre/article
show/3041352.cms?curpg=2.

[92] Palak Nandi, "We Won't Let Rajasthan Go Gujarat Way: Raje," *Times of India*, May 15, 2008.
Accessed July 11, 2014. http://timesofindia.indiatimes.com/city/jaipur/We-wont-let-Rajasthan-
go-Gujarat-way-Raje/articleshow/3041205.cms?curpg=2. "Rajasthan to Have Anti-terror
Force," *The Hindu*, May 15, 2008. Accessed July 11, 2014. http://www.hindu.com/thehindu/
holnus/000200805152069.htm.

[93] "We Are in the Middle of a War," *Indo-Asian News Service*, May 15, 2008. Accessed July 11,
2014. http://www.dnaindia.com/india/report-we-are-in-the-middle-of-war-1164588.

The Rajasthan government established a private-public partnership with Mahindra Lifespaces Developers to establish an export-oriented unit, the Mahindra World City (MWC) outside Jaipur.[94] The agreement stipulated that the government would acquire and sell Mahindra 3,000 acres of land at concessionary rates. The Jaipur Development Authority (JDA) already owned 1,000 acres of land, which it could transfer to the MWC without the approval of local *panchayats*. The contentious matter involved the government's acquisition of 2,000 acres of private farmland. The JDA started formal eminent domain proceedings, using the central Land Acquisition Act in 2005 to acquire the land. It did not consult with affected farmers, who first learned of the project from land acquisition notices in local newspapers.

The RSS and high-ranking BJP officials, including Narpat Singh Razvi and Ghanshyam Tiwari, opposed the scheme on grounds that it exploited poor farmers and deprived them of grazing land. They also claimed, inaccurately, that Raje had decided to pursue the scheme without adequately consulting government officials. Raje agreed to bring the plans before a full cabinet and consult MLAs who represented the communities that would be affected. She also made some concessions to farmers, for example, increasing their option of receiving 25 percent rather than 15 percent of their original land area, as she had initially proposed, as commercial and residential plots adjacent to the project. This ingenious model gave farmers a stake in the MWC project while compensating them at a fraction of the cost at which the MWC leased land to companies.

Hindutva activists accused Raje of "pampering" Muslims because she allocated land for the construction of a Haj house, that provided accommodations for Muslim pilgrims traveling to Mecca. They were far more critical of Raje than they had been of Shekhawat, although he was more attentive to Muslim sensitivities. Shekhawat had the Jama Masjid in Jaipur reopened and allocated considerable funds to its renovation. He also authorized about $1.5 million to renovate and restore the Ajmer *dargah* that Hindutva activists had damaged.

The previous Congress government had authorized land for a Haj house. The land Raje allotted, fifteen miles from Jaipur and two miles from the Sanganer airport, was in Education Minister Tiwari's predominantly Hindu constituency. Tiwari and Home Minister Gulab Chand Kataria, both RSS members, opposed Raje's decision to construct the Haj house in the proposed area on grounds

[94] The Mahindra World City (MWC), which became operational in August 2008, the largest public-private partnership in Rajasthan's history, is a joint venture between Mahindra Lifespaces Developers (the real estate subsidiary of the $7 billion Mahindra and Mahindra Co.) and the Rajasthan government. For detailed, thoughtful accounts of the MWC project, see Michael Levien, "Special Economic Zones and Accumulation by Dispossession in India," *Journal of Agrarian Change*, October 2011, Vol. 11, no. 4, 454–83, and "India's Double-Movement: Polanyi and the National Alliance of People's Movements," *Berkeley Journal of Sociology*, 2007, Vol. 51, 119–49.

that the government had underpaid villagers for their land. It misrepresented the conflict as discriminatory toward Hindus and favoring Muslims. The VHP demanded that the government create a special Pilgrim House for Hindus and also demanded a subsidy for Hindu pilgrims to Mansarovar. Kishore declared, "The state government may take care of its minorities but it also needs to pay attention towards the Hindus."[95] When Raje attempted to lay the Haj house foundation on September 20, she found that VHP, Shiv Sena, and Bajrang Dal members, joined by villagers, had blocked the route to the site and organized a violent protest. It took six hours before the protests subsided and Raje could lay the foundation stone.

Another quite different source of opposition to Raje came from Gujjars and Meenas around reservations. Gujjars and Meenas were politicized by the BJP's increased recognition of caste identities. The NDA government designated Jats OBCs and made them eligible for preferential admissions to public educational institutions and employment. Gujjar leaders realized that they would be competing with the powerful Jat community for reservations for OBCs and demanded that they should be designated Scheduled Tribes rather than OBCs.

Raje promised to support Gujjars' demand if she was elected, but wavered after coming to power. The Gujjar Arakshan Sangharsh Samiti (Association to Struggle for Reservations) organized a series of agitations over a two-year period demanding that the Rajasthan government recommend Gujjars' eligibility for Scheduled Tribe status. When Gujjars organized a procession on May 28, the police made large numbers of arrests, and violence soon followed. Gujjar protesters blocked the national highway, dismantled railway lines, and burned bridges, public buses, and railway property. Police firings killed thirty-seven Gujjar activists in 2007 and 2008.

After a year of protests and mixed signals from the government, the State Assembly passed a law in June 2008 providing for 5 percent reservation in government jobs to Gujjars and three other castes. However, this only fuelled discontent. While Gujjars considered this settlement inadequate, Meena tribals feared that Gujjar inclusion on the Scheduled Tribe list would reduce the benefits they received. Discontent among Gujjars and Meenas contributed to the BJP's electoral defeat in the 2008 Assembly elections. The RSS openly expressed its displeasure at Raje's handling of the Gujjar protest.

Meanwhile, the BJP's stance on reservations heightened caste conflicts. *Dalits*, who were often exploited by Gujjar employers, resented Hindu nationalists' cultivation of Gujjar support. Tensions between Gujjar and *dalit* communities erupted in Ajmer district during Navratri festivities on October 1, 2006. A Gujjar priest, Mewa Ram, accompanied by his community members, assaulted an eighty-year-old *dalit* priest and banned *dalits* from entering the

---

[95] "VHP Dares Raje on Haj House," *The Indian Express*, September 24, 2006. Accessed July 11, 2014. http://archive.indianexpress.com/news/vhp-dares-raje-on-haj-house-/13334/.

temple. The village was in the constituency of Kalu Lal Gurjar, a BJP MLA and rural development minister. In an attempt to regain *dalit* support, Gurjar brought members of the BJP's Scheduled Caste Morcha from other villages to enter the temple on November 26. However, *dalits* from the community hoisted black flags on their homes, boycotted the event, and complained that it was "stage-managed."[96] The incident demonstrated the reverberations of demands for reservations. It also demonstrated *dalit* anger at political parties for failing to address the atrocities they experienced.[97]

The RSS became increasingly displeased by Raje and sought to undermine her authority. Some of the BJP's national leaders became her staunch critics. The most prominent was Jaswant Singh, leader of the opposition in the Rajya Sabha.[98] In 2006, the national BJP, supported by the RSS, replaced LK Chaturvedi with Mahesh Sharma to head the party.[99] Two years later, despite Raje's opposition, the RSS replaced Sharma, who became Raje's aide, with Om Mathur as party president.[100] Mathur, unlike Sharma, was an RSS *pracharak* and closely allied with Raje's hardline opponents.

Vasundhara Raje claimed to be a victim of RSS and BJP sexism. She said that she hadn't believed this in the past, perhaps recalling my interview with her in 1991 when she blamed women for inviting sexism.[101] She explained in a lengthy interview in 2007:

[96] Mohammed Iqbal, "Dalits Enter Temple Amidst Tension," *Asian Age*, December 13, 2006. Accessed July 11, 2014. http://www.thehindu.com/todays-paper/tp-national/tp-otherstates/dalits-enter-temple-amid-tension/article3033476.ece.

[97] The Centre for Dalit Rights (CDR) disputed a claim made by Rajasthan Home Minister Gulab Chand Kataria that the state had registered a sharp decline in atrocities against Scheduled Castes and Tribes and a twofold increase in convictions under the Scheduled Castes and Tribes (Prevention of Atrocities) Act. The CDR claimed that the committee headed by Social Welfare Minister Madan Dilawar was defunct and ineffective. "Dalits Dispute Minister's Claim," *The Hindu*, December 17, 2006. Accessed July 11, 2014. http://www.thehindu.com/todays-paper/tp-national/tp-otherstates/dalits-dispute-ministers-claim/article3034611.ece. For additional information, see "Growing Atrocities on Rajasthan Dalits: Report," February 12, 2007. Accessed July 11, 2014. http://www.hindu.com/2007/02/12/stories/2007021208540300.htm.

[98] The rift widened when Jaswant Singh's wife, Sheetal Kanwar, filed a police complaint in May charging that posters depicting Raje as a goddess and other senior BJP leaders as part of the Hindu holy pantheon had hurt Hindus' religious sentiments. The Raje-led government subsequently charged Singh with violating the Narcotics Act and serving opium to his guests at a gathering at his village of Jasol in Jodhpur. Many BJP leaders who felt marginalized by Raje had attended the gathering to develop a strategy to curtail Raje's power.

[99] "Mahesh Sharma Appointed Rajasthan's BJP President," *The Economic Times*, February 8, 2006. Accessed July 11, 2014. http://articles.economictimes.indiatimes.com/2006-02-08/news/27426984_1_bjp-gears-rajasthan-unit-rajnath-singh.

[100] Varghese K. George, "Snubbing Advani, Raje, Rajnath Put RSS Man to Head Rajasthan BJP," *The Indian Express*, January 3, 2008. Accessed July 11, 2014. http://archive.indianexpress.com/news/snubbing-advani-raje-rajnath-put-rss-man-t/257185/.

[101] Interview with Vasundhara Raje, New Delhi, December 13, 1991.

People used to tell me that there was a lot of discrimination against women who went into politics but I didn't believe it till I experienced it myself. Men are so jealous and resentful towards women who have power. Men are good for one thing only so they should stick to that and let women do the rest.[102]

Raje described an incident that came to be known as the Liplock Scandal. A *Times of India* photographer published a picture in the newspaper in which Raje appeared to be passionately kissing another woman. The angle from which the picture was taken distorted the image and the photographer said he published the picture as a joke. But Raje said that some of her rivals within the party made posters using this picture to damage her reputation. Congress leaders also used the incident to condemn her. She said that while male political leaders could enjoy certain personal freedoms, she was constantly under scrutiny. She had given up a social life to avoid becoming the object of scandalous rumors.[103]

The national BJP and the RSS withdrew support for Raje prior to the 2008 Legislative Assembly elections. They accused her of corruption and mismanagement. They blamed her for ignoring grassroots workers in distributing seats. Factionalism within the BJP became so severe that fifty of its members who hoped to contest the elections were Raje's opponents. When she vetoed their nominations, several of them left the BJP and joined other political parties. Incensed that the BJP refused to accommodate his nominees and that Raje had supported Scheduled Tribe status for Gujjars, former state minister Kirori Lal Meena resigned from the BJP and contested the elections as an independent candidate. The RSS was angered by Raje's decision to accept his resignation and by the fact that Kirori Lal Meena, his wife, and two other candidates won the elections and influenced Meena voting patterns. Vishvendra Singh, ex-royalty of Bharatpur, to whom the BJP denied a ticket, joined Congress. Senior BJP leader, RSS member, and former deputy chief minister Hari Shankar Bhabra resigned as the Vice-Chairman of the Economic Policy and Reforms Council

[102] Interview with Vasundhara Raje, Jaipur, January 16, 2007.
[103] Vasundhara Raje's diminished popularity also resulted from her exercise of personalistic forms of power and her reliance on the advice of nonelected individuals. The most notorious among them was Lalit Kumar Modi, the president and managing director of Modi Enterprises, an industrial conglomerate that his family created and ran. Modi became Raje's trusted aide and powerful advisor. Critics described him as super chief minister and his suite in the Ram Bagh Palace hotel as the alternate chief minister's office. Modi influenced cabinet decisions and was said to have had complete control over the government's apex investment body, the Board of Infrastructure Development and Investment, which approved large infrastructure projects, Special Economic Zones, and the construction of luxury hotels. Modi was also executive director of Godfrey Phillips India, one of the largest national tobacco companies. Chief Minister Raje helped Modi become president of the Rajasthan Cricket Association by pushing through an act in the Rajasthan Assembly that changed the laws governing the association in 2004. His election was mired in controversy. After returning to office as chief minister in 2008, Congress Chief Minister Ashok Gehlot reported that a government-appointed committee had found that Raje had tacitly supported Modi's land scams and misuse of government machinery.

in December 2008. The RSS supported three of the sixty rebels officially and possibly more unofficially.[104] Raje was unable to overcome the opposition that she faced both from within and outside the BJP.

The BJP lost the 2008 Assembly elections to Congress. It received 34.3 percent of the vote and seventy-eight seats in the 200-member Assembly; Congress won 36.8 percent of the vote and ninety-six seats; eight independents joined Congress so that it was able to gain a majority. The BJP lost Gujjar, Jat, and particularly, Scheduled Caste, Scheduled Tribe, and Muslim votes to Congress.

Conclusion

Hindu nationalism in Rajasthan has become more militant. Party-movement relations that were distant until 1998 became closer thereafter and became fraught once again while the BJP was in office from 2003 to 2008. The party was able to establish dominance over the movement during the early years in part because of Bhairon Singh Shekhawat's stature and appearance of non-partisanship. Under Shekhawat's leadership, the BJP took up the Janata Dal's programmatic commitments and absorbed many of its leaders. The BJP's early commitment to rural development and poverty alleviation prevented identity issues from becoming the major axes of conflict. Shekhawat faced pressures from the RSS and conceded to some of its demands, particularly with respect to political appointments. The BJP lost the Assembly elections in 1998 in part because party activists backed by the RSS withdrew support from Shekhawat.

The movement may have challenged Vasundhara Raje because she was a female chief minister in a male-dominated party, state, and society. However, some of the same RSS leaders, including Hari Shankar Bhabra and Gulab Chand Kataria, opposed both Shekhawat and Raje. The RSS gained greater influence over the party and the party became more beholden to the movement. The Hindu nationalist movement grew during the period of Congress rule (1998–2003). The VHP gained the support of lower-caste Hindus and tribals by organizing them to engage in violence against Muslims and Christians. The BJP was re-elected on its own in 2003, in part because of significant movement support.

The Raje-led BJP government repaid its debt to the movement by conceding to many Hindu nationalist demands. It withdrew cases that the previous Congress government had filed against the VHP and its affiliates for inciting Hindu-Muslim violence. It actively promoted Hindu nationalist values in government-run schools and hospitals and provided the RSS with funding to establish a large private university to promote Hindu nationalist views. The BJP government sought to pass the 2006 Rajasthan Freedom of Religion Act that increased surveillance and penalties for those who sought to convert out of Hinduism. It promoted *sati* as a cultural tradition. When Rajasthan experienced

---

[104] *The Telegraph*, December 9, 2009.

a "terrorist" attack in May 2008, the government engaged in repression against Bangladeshi immigrants, seized their land, and deported them. The movement that brought the BJP to power turned against it and contributed to its electoral defeat in 2008. Far from being placated by Raje's concessions, Hindutva activists were emboldened to escalate their demands. The BJP's commitment to neoliberal reform, particularly to Special Economic Zones, antagonized the RSS. Furthermore, the BJP contributed to the growth of caste-based movements. It ignited identity-conflicts by first appealing to tribals and OBCs for support and promising to provide them reservations if it came to power but then conceding less than it had promised. It thereby antagonized some of its party members, the RSS, and Gujjar and Meena communities.

The BJP government's pursuit of Hindu nationalist goals also suffered a setback after the UPA government came to power at the center. The UPA blocked the passage of the freedom of religion bill. Its passage of the Right to Information (RTI) law and the National Rural Employment Guarantee Act in 2005 contributed to the growth of progressive social movements. The Mazdoor Kisan Shakti Sangathan (MKSS) and other groups organized large-scale campaigns to inform the rural poor of the RTI's provisions and promote poverty alleviation.[105] They formed the Rajasthan Election Watch to monitor elections and give the electorate information about candidates' assets and criminal records. They exposed high levels of corruption in the BJP and the government's failure to adequately address poverty and unemployment.

Some of the distinctive features of Hindu nationalism in Rajasthan are evident in comparative perspective. Compared to HP, militant Hindu nationalism is stronger in Rajasthan because it has gained a following among the lower-caste rural poor and upheld certain culturally conservative upper-caste practices. The antidote to militant Hindu nationalism in both states is social movements that have addressed economic inequality and gender discrimination.

However, the BJP was able to return to power in Rajasthan but not in UP in 1993. A major part of the explanation concerns differences in the nature of caste and party politics in the two states. Both *dalits* and OBCs are more numerous and more politically organized in UP than in Rajasthan. According to the 1931 Census, Scheduled Castes account for 21 percent of UP's and 17 percent of Rajasthan's population and OBCs for 42 percent of UP's and

[105] Rajasthan has been one of the most successful states in India in securing employment for men and women under NREGA. In the first year of NREGA (2006–7), the average rural household in Rajasthan worked for seventy-seven days under the program; the share of women's employment was 67 percent. NREGA has increased employment, raised wages, slowed migration, and created productive assets in poor, rural households. Reetika Khera, "'Group Measurement' of NREGA Work: The Jalore Experiment," Centre for Development Economics, Delhi School of Economics, Accessed July 11, 2014. http://www.cdedse.org/seminar/seminar34.pdf; and Reetika Khera, "Access to the Targeted Public Distribution System: A Case Study in Rajasthan," *Economic and Political Weekly*, November 1, 2008. Accessed July 11, 2014. http://www.indiaenvironmentportal.org.in/files/Access%20to%20the%20Targeted%20Public%20Distribution%20System.pdf.

8 percent of Rajasthan's population. The BJP could only attain power by allying with the BSP, securing defections from other political parties, and drawing
lower-caste members into the party. This, in turn, created serious strains among
upper- and lower-caste leaders of the BJP. The BJP's leadership in Rajasthan
was less divided along caste lines. Tensions within the Rajasthan BJP were
more ideological than caste-based.

Movement strength and militancy grew over time in Rajasthan as in Gujarat,
leading many observers to suggest that Rajasthan might be Hindutva's next
laboratory. But although minorities were subject to persecution, violence, and
harassment under BJP rule from 2003 to 2008, the violence was confined to
particular rural localities. The BJP did not achieve the kind of cross-caste support in Rajasthan that it did in Gujarat. As a result, the BJP's electoral success
in Rajasthan has been less consistent than in Gujarat. Furthermore, relations
among party, movement, and state were more fractured in Rajasthan than
in Gujarat. Although some members of the RSS and BJP resented what they
described as Modi's authoritarian leadership style and disagreed with many of
his policies, unlike Raje he maintained complete control over the party and the
movement.

The BJP's future in Rajasthan is relatively secure. A two-party system is well
established and the BJP is adept at pursuing social engineering and economic
growth. Congress, the BJP's major rival, is besieged by factionalism and corruption. The BJP returned to power in 2013 with a record 163 seats (46 percent of
the vote) and reinstalled Vasundhara Raje as chief minister. The BJP's victory
reflected anger at the Congress government, which was mired in corruption.
Narendra Modi played a major role in the election campaign. The national
BJP leadership that had earlier questioned Raje's leadership came to support it.
The RSS influenced key appointments to the Cabinet including Gulab Chand
Kataria in the influential post of home minister.

The challenge that still confronts the BJP is whether to align more closely
with the RSS. Doing so would enable it to benefit from powerful Hindu nationalist civil society organizations. In the absence of strong, nonpartisan leadership, and given the likelihood of continued factionalism within the party, this
may be the most attractive path. However, it will not protect the BJP from the
growing demands of lower castes and tribals nor from civil liberties groups
and poor people's movements. The phases of Hindu nationalism that I have
described are likely to be followed by others in which social movements figure
prominently.

9

Conclusion

Why did Hindu nationalists' destruction of the *babri masjid* in 1992 and the violence with which it was associated not mark a turning point in Hindu-Muslim relations and the BJP's fate? Contrary to Mulayam Singh Yadav's predictions, the BJP did not "pursue a path of fascism" and did not consistently foster anti-minority violence to attain power. Nor, as some scholars predicted, was the BJP compelled by the centripetal pressures of democracy to become a centrist party and repudiate Hindutva. Rather, the BJP's approach has varied across time and place and Hindu nationalist violence has been conjunctural. I have argued in this book that the extent and timing of Hindutva militancy and violence depend on relations among its own party, social movement organization, and state governments, and on the character and caste composition of opposition states, parties, and movements.

Anti-minority violence in India is neither random nor spontaneous but the outcome of a confluence of forces. The "perfect storm" occurs when a cohesive, ideologically-driven party has strong ties to a radical social movement, and is undeterred (or even supported) by state and national governments. In the case of Hindu nationalism, this has entailed the BJP, when it is unified, forging close ties to the VHP and the RSS and occupying state power, generally independently rather than in coalition governments. Governments' acts of omission and commission permit violence to escalate. Violent conjunctures also occur when strong social movements and movement-parties that represent the poor and the low castes are weak or absent.

This chapter revisits the question of why anti-minority violence has been intermittent in India. The first section compares the extent and timing of violence in UP, Gujarat, Rajasthan, and HP. The second section shifts focus from the regional to the national level and situates Hindu nationalism within the democratic context. The third section explores the comparative, cross-national significance of my findings.

The Four States

India affords fruitful opportunities for comparative analysis across scales of political life because of remarkable differences in the character of movements, parties, and movement-party relations across states. To explain variations in the incidence of Hindu nationalist militancy and violence across time and space, I compared the roles of parties, movements, and states in four regions in the early 1990s and a decade later. Of the four states, Gujarat experienced the most extensive violence, albeit less in the early 1990s than in 2002. UP followed Gujarat in the extent of violence, although the sequences differed: violence was greater in the early 1990s than thereafter. Rajasthan experienced some violence throughout, although more in later than in early years. HP experienced relatively little violence either in the early 1990s or a decade later. I discuss the respective roles of parties, movements, and states in the pages that follow.

The Party

In Gujarat, UP, and HP, the BJP was most militant when it was most unified. In Rajasthan, by contrast, the party was less militant when it was more unified, in the early 1990s. As it became more factionalized, it made more concessions to movement activists.

In Gujarat, the BJP was better able to translate its rhetoric into action after 2002, when Chief Minister Narendra Modi put an end to party factionalism and forged strong links among the party, civil society organizations, and state government. Although party members whom Modi displaced resented his power and leadership style, his tight control of the Gujarat BJP prevented the recurrence of factionalism.

In UP, the BJP was a relatively small and cohesive party in the 1990s but became increasingly fragmented as a result of its rapid growth and caste divisions among the party leadership. Kalyan Singh was an ideal leader in the early 1990s because he combined a commitment to the movement with an ability to attract OBC and *dalit* votes. However, the BJP's upper-caste leaders became threatened by increased lower-caste representation. Unable to find a leader who was as popular as Singh, the BJP periodically expelled and re-inducted him into the party. Although it reverted back to a more militant posture after 2002, intraparty rivalries prevented it from pursuing a coherent, radical agenda.

In HP, the BJP was more cohesive and more activist around Hindu nationalist goals in early than in later years. It engaged in protests against Mandal and pro Ayodhya in the early 1990s. It became less programmatically-oriented when it became divided between the supporters of Shanta Kumar and Prem Kumar Dhumal. In Rajasthan, unlike the other states, party cohesion and militancy were inversely correlated. In the early 1990s, Bhairon Singh Shekhawat endorsed Hindu nationalist ideals but curtailed the influence of militant party and movement leaders. The BJP's anti-minority policies and actions intensified when the party became more factionalized under Vasundhara Raje's leadership. The case of Rajasthan demonstrates that party factionalism need not deter the BJP from pursuing Hindutva goals when activists are influential, ideologically-driven party members.

The Movement
The role and character of Hindu nationalist social movements are key determinants of the extent of Hindu nationalist militancy and violence. Although the VHP mobilized around the Ayodhya campaign in all four states, the campaign's strength and activists' abilities to sustain movement activities after 1992 differed significantly. Among the explanations for these differences are the extent to which Hindu nationalists forged regional cultural roots and organized social movements before engaging in violent Hindutva movements.

In Gujarat, Hindu nationalists laid the foundations for their subsequent actions in 2002 by participating in social movements against corruption, rising prices, and caste reservations. They thereby gained the support of the upper and middle castes, rich peasants, and the middle classes. They recruited tribals and *dalits* by encouraging caste mobility and providing lower castes and classes relief and social services. Not surprisingly, Gujarat was at the forefront of the Ayodhya movement. In subsequent decades, the VHP and RSS continued to build a dense network of social service organizations and became leaders of cooperatives, business associations, and political bodies. They also gained extensive financial support from the Gujarati diasporic community. Hindu nationalism was exceptional in Gujarat in forging a regional, national, and transnational identity.

In UP, as in Gujarat, Hindu nationalists allied with other social movements before launching the Ayodhya campaign. However, the OBC movement became strong enough to sever its ties to Hindu nationalists. Although the BJP expanded to new regions of the state and incorporated lower castes through the Ayodhya campaign, the VHP did not make sustained efforts to organize the *dalit* community thereafter. Hindutva activism has persisted only in regions of the state in which lower-caste movements are weak. UP has always lacked cultural cohesion, and Hindu nationalists were unable to cultivate a regional identity.

In HP, as in other states, the BJP participated in protests against the Mandal Commission to win over the upper castes and championed the Ayodhya movement to gain *dalit* and OBC support. As in Gujarat and UP, it mobilized tribals by fomenting anti-Christian violence. Hindu nationalists were more active and effective in addressing economic than social issues. The Jan Sangh initially defended the landed elites and later, as part of the Janata Party, agrarian cultivators. The BJP periodically championed the causes of horticulturalists in the 1980s and forest dwellers thereafter. However, Hindu nationalist social movements have been weak because of the distinctive character of Hinduism, weakness of Brahmanical Hinduism, and regional divisions between the old and new HP.

Hindu nationalists do not have a history of movement organizing in Rajasthan. However, the Sangh Parivar generated significant support for the Ayodhya temple issue in the early 1990s and the following decade. Members of the BJP have sustained the movement by engaging in activism both within and outside institutions. As in Gujarat and unlike UP, lower-caste parties and movements are weak in Rajasthan. Thus the RSS, VHP, and their affiliates have been able to mobilize tribals, Meenas, and Gujjars to engage in violence against Muslims and Christians. Yet, OBCs, *dalits*, and tribals have not consistently supported the BJP and, in contrast to Gujarat, the upper castes have not organized movements to defend and advance their interests.

Parties and Movements

Relations between parties and movements within the Hindu nationalist nexus have been both complementary and conflictual at different points in time. Ties between the RSS, BJP, and VHP were closest during the Ayodhya movement in all four states and in 2002, particularly in Gujarat. However, activists within the party and the movement have sometimes been critical of what they see as the BJP's capitulation to electoral considerations. Activists within the BJP, VHP and RSS in Rajasthan contributed to the BJP's defeat in the 2008 Assembly elections. In UP, Yogi Adityanath, a party and movement leader, is a formidable critic of the BJP. In HP, RSS and VHP leaders criticize the BJP for what they consider its political expediency.

Party-movement relations are especially complicated in Gujarat. Many RSS and VHP members turned against Modi during his second term as chief minister when he razed temples, cultivated Muslim support, and sidelined movement allies. However, the loss of VHP support did not de-radicalize the BJP. Chief Minister Modi, with RSS support, strategically distanced himself from the VHP without renouncing Hindu nationalist principles.

State Governments

If BJP state governments have not planned violence, they have often created the conditions which make it likely, and sometimes allowed or encouraged it. They have supported RSS and VHP initiatives around education, religious conversion, and cow protection, and thereby encouraged Hindu nationalist civil society organizations to engage in militancy and violence. The VHP and its affiliates have mobilized tribals against Christians, whom they claim are engaging in forced conversion and Muslims, whom they claim are slaughtering cows. BJP governments have delayed imposing curfews, calling in armed forces, and having Sangh Parivar members arrested for inciting violence.

BJP governments have been most apt to condone militancy and violence when movement activists have contributed to their formation and they rule independently rather than in coalitions. In UP, the BJP government was most ideologically-driven when it came to power through movement support (1991–2) and the goals of party, movement, and state converged. Since then, BJP governments have been constrained by coalitional governing arrangements with the BSP (1995, 1997). In HP, the movement has not played an important role in the BJP's election campaigns or in shaping government policies. In Rajasthan, the BJP attained power from 1990 to 1992 and from 1993 to 1998 by relying on defections from other political parties and alliances with them. Conversely, the BJP government that was formed in 2003 with strong support from Hindutva activists, partially pursued their agenda in office.

Of the four states, the BJP government's responsibility for anti-minority violence was greatest in Gujarat. Numerous government and nongovernmental investigations report that state government officials helped plan the violence. BJP, VHP, and Bajrang Dal members have publicly admitted to their roles in violence and implicated high-ranking government officials. Former bureaucrats and police officers have testified that the government punished police officers who sought to stop the violence and rewarded those who perpetrated it. In the immediate aftermath of the violence, although Sangh Parivar members who were named in FIRs were not arrested, large numbers of Muslims were arrested under the draconian POTA. Years later, as a result of Supreme Court directives, several high-ranking BJP members and government officials were convicted for their roles in the 2002 violence. The Gujarati government has continued to discriminate against victims by failing to adequately rehabilitate them and falsely accusing them of engaging in "terrorist" acts.

The National Government

The national government has ample legal authority and executive capacity to act preemptively to deter violence. Once violence erupts, it can call in the national army, invoke Article 356 of the Constitution, and impose President's Rule. Although the Congress government did not stop the buildup of the Hindu nationalist campaign in Ayodhya in 1992, it removed BJP governments from office thereafter. The act of discrediting the BJP contributed to its subsequent electoral reversals. By contrast, the NDA government did not impose President's rule on Gujarat after the 2002 violence. A distinguished lawyer and member of the Upper House of Parliament pointed to the unlikelihood of the party in power imposing president's rule in a state where it is in office.[1] Paradoxically, avoiding President's rule has sometimes safeguarded

---

[1] Manoj Mitta, "If NHRC Indicts Modi, He Must Be Sacked," *Indian Express*, March 31, 2002. Accessed November 15, 2015. http://www.indianexpress.com/ie20020331/op1.html.

one important democratic principle – namely the autonomy of elected state governments – at the expense of another – the protection of minority rights and stability.

Countervailing Parties, Movements, and States
The most effective deterrents to militant Hindu nationalism have been opposing parties, movements, and civil society organizations. I accord more significance to the character than the number of such parties, movements, and organizations. Gujarat and HP both have two-party systems, but the former experienced extensive anti-minority violence while the latter has not. Rajasthan evolved from a multiparty system to a two-party system after 1993. The BJP did not engage in anti-minority violence under the two-party system but made anti-minority appeals intermittently (in the 2003 and 2008 but not in the 1993 and 1998 elections.)

The Congress Party in Gujarat failed to adequately represent low castes and Muslims. In the aftermath of Madhav Singh Solanki's defeat, Congress primarily sought upper and middle caste support, which created a vacuum that the BJP filled among the lowest castes and tribals. Congress not only failed to challenge the BJP's anti-minority policies and actions, but many of its members participated in the 2002 anti-Muslim violence. In UP, Congress contributed to the BJP's growth by courting the Hindu vote around the Ayodhya temple and other issues. In HP, both Congress and the BJP promoted Hindu interests. Rajasthan is a partial exception: Congress Chief Minister Ashok Gehlot arrested VHP leader Praveen Togadia, stopped the distribution of *trishuls*, and banned the Bajrang Dal. However, these were isolated measures; militant Hindu nationalism grew significantly during the period of Congress Party rule (1998–2003).

The Janata Party and its successors had a double-edged impact on Hindu nationalism. On the one hand, they strengthened the Jan Sangh and the BJP by drawing them into coalition governments. On the other hand, they challenged upper-caste domination by mobilizing OBCs and rural cultivators in some states. Hindu nationalism has been strongest and most ideologically committed in Gujarat, where the Janata Party collapsed after 1990, leaving no successor, and low castes have not organized movements challenging caste inequality. In UP, at the other end of the spectrum, the Janata Party played an important role in state politics until 1992; its successor, the SP, is one of the strongest parties in UP today. Both the SP and the BSP have not only politicized caste identities but have also encouraged greater Muslim political participation.

The Janata Party was also short-lived in HP and Rajasthan. The BJP grew in both states by co-opting some of its leaders and pursuing some of its goals. Furthermore, Hindu nationalists have been forced to contend with autonomous social movements that have challenged it socially and economically.

In Rajasthan, women's groups opposed the BJP's stance on *sati* and other forms of violence against women. Farmers protested the creation of Special Economic Zones that take over agricultural land. Gujjar protest sparked discontent among *dalit* and Meena tribals, who feared competition over entitlements if Gujjars were granted Scheduled Tribe status. Discontent among Gujjars and Meenas contributed to the BJP's electoral defeat in the 2008 Assembly elections. In HP, the strongest social movements have organized around economic rather than identity issues. They have demanded support prices for fruit growers, employment, environmental protection, and better implementation of government schemes. Some leading BJP members have supported their demands and the BJP has competed with Congress to demonstrate its commitment to economic development in the region.

Violence and Militancy in Democratic India

India, by most accounts, is a remarkably – and increasingly – vibrant and healthy democracy. The 1990s witnessed the emergence of a multiparty system comprised of ideologically and ethnically heterogeneous political parties. Yogendra Yadav describes the increased political participation of formerly marginalized groups as constituting a second democratic upsurge.[2] Christophe Jaffrelot depicts *dalits'* growing political power as a silent revolution.[3] The devolution of power to state parties and governments is another mark of democratic deepening.

Violence has not threatened political stability because it has not occurred on a national scale. Most violence in India is local, from CPI-ML directives to landless laborers to annihilate class enemies, to upper castes' rape and murder of *dalits* who demand their rights, to Hindu violence against Muslims. In towns and neighborhoods of cities, social distinctions map onto economic differences and determine residential location. The physical proximity between groups with overlapping class and ethnic identities and quotidian animosities often ignites conflict. The CPI-ML has been especially successful at organizing tribals, whose cultural traditions have fueled their opposition to class inequality. In the town of Khurja, conflicts between *dalits* and Muslims in adjacent neighborhoods broke out over a class-related conflict: *dalits* who worked as servants for Muslims were aggrieved by their low wages and poor working conditions. Political activists framed these conflicts as religious and exacerbated tensions to promote their larger political agendas. However, activists

---

[2] Yogendra Yadav, "Understanding the Second Democratic Upsurge: Trends of Bahujan Participation in Electoral Politics in the 1990s," in Francine Frankel et al. eds., *Transforming India: Social and Political Dynamics of Democracy* (New Delhi: Oxford University Press, 2000), 120–45.

[3] Christophe Jaffrelot, *India's Silent Revolution: The Rise of the Lower Castes in North India* (New York: Columbia University Press, 2003).

have been less able to polarize identities and interests on a national scale. Myron Weiner aptly noted, "India is thus like a huge lorry with a dozen or more tires; a puncture in one or two tires does not throw the lorry into the ditch."[4] This frustrates both left- and right-wing movements that have national aspirations.

Hindu nationalist social movements have precipitated violence locally but not nationally. The strengths of the VHP and its affiliates are local and transnational. The VHP raises funds from diasporic communities to engage in tangible local activities like buying bricks to build a temple in Ayodhya and paying the salaries of teachers at *ekal vidyalaya* schools. The VHP, through its local and global affiliations, and the BJP, through its national and regional networks, have different and complementary strengths. The BJP has enabled the VHP to gain national standing while the VHP has helped the BJP acquire local and transnational visibility. Unlike virtually any other social movement organization, the VHP, backed by the RSS, has close and enduring ties to a party.

Most social movements in India, including the women's, environmental, and anticorruption movements, do not employ violence, and most movements that do, use limited violence to obtain specific demands. Some, like caste struggles to demand entitlements, have employed violence until the state has conceded to their demands. Similarly, ethnic self-determination movements generally decline if the state agrees to the devolution of power and the reallocation of resources. Compared to these movements, Hindu nationalists have been less willing to renounce violence in response to state concessions. Hindutva activists provoked violence in the early 1990s and in 2002, despite the fact that both the national government and UP and Gujarat state governments conceded, at critical times, to many of their demands.

The BJP officially subscribes to democratic principles and eschews violence. However, its actions have varied too much over time and place to consider it a centrist or moderate party. The BJP is not only subject to the pressures and constraints of the electorate and the electoral system but also to the non-electoral RSS and VHP. The NDA government made political appointments and pursued policies that advanced Hindu nationalist goals without jeopardizing political stability. Examples include funding RSS schools, refashioning academic institutions, rewriting textbooks, proposing stringent restrictions on Muslim immigration, and seeking passage of a constitutional amendment protecting cows. The NDA government tacitly supported amendments to so-called freedom of religion bills that several BJP state governments proposed.

---

4 Myron Weiner, *The Indian Paradox: Essays in Indian Politics* (New Delhi: Sage Publications, 1989), 36.

The BJP's 2014 Victory

The BJP's dramatic electoral victory in 2014, enabling it to form a government without the need for coalition partners, represents a remarkable new conjuncture in Indian politics. The scale of its victory is explained by a variety of factors – anti-incumbency sentiment, the popularity of Modi's neoliberal agenda, the BJP's expensive, media-savvy campaign, the impact of the youth vote, and Modi's personal popularity. In response to a post-poll survey, one in four respondents said that he or she voted for the NDA because Modi was the prime ministerial candidate.[5] As in the 1999 general election but unlike many state elections, the BJP did not gain power as a result of a social movement.

However, Modi's personal qualities should not obscure his powerful ties to Hindu nationalist forces. Modi rose to power with the support of a movement to head the party and state in Gujarat. In the 2014 general elections, as in Gujarat, once he had established his supremacy, Modi sidelined VHP movement activists and BJP leaders while relying on continuous, steadfast RSS support. As in the past, Hindu nationalists spoke in many voices, combining demands for growth and transparency with caste-based appeals, sometimes interlaced with anti-Muslim sentiment. It is not surprising that the RSS made an exception to its principle of discouraging the emergence of powerful leaders within its ranks. Modi's much vaunted charisma has detracted attention from the extent of RSS influence over Modi and the BJP government.

The most striking difference between the BJP's election campaign in 2014 and earlier years is the extent to which it unabashedly promoted neoliberalism. The BJP made far-reaching claims about Gujarat's economic success under Modi's leadership. It appreciated the extent of public dissatisfaction with the UPA government's failure to implement economic reforms because of poor administration and corruption. The middle class, which has grown significantly since 1991, opposed the UPA government's subsidies of food and gas cylinders. Surveys reveal that the issues that mattered most to the electorate were inflation, corruption, employment, industrialization, and development; secularism and "communalism" ranked far lower.[6] Given the low public salience of religious issues, the BJP would probably not have benefited from mobilizing around core Hindu nationalist concerns. However the election campaign fostered Hindu-Muslim polarization and resulted in a significant decline in Muslim representation.[7]

---

[5] Pradeep Chhibber and Rahul Verma, "The BJP's 2014 'Modi Wave': An Ideological Consolidation of the Right," *Economic & Political Weekly*, September 27, 2014. Vol. 49, no. 39, 52.

[6] Centre for the Study of Developing Societies, and IBN. 2014. National election study 2014. "All India Postpoll 2014-Survey Findings," Accessed December 14, 2014. http://www.lokniti.org/pdf/All-India-Postpoll-2014-Survey-Findings.pdf.

[7] This is the first time that a ruling party with a simple majority does not have a single Muslim MP. There are fewer Muslim MPs today than in the past fifty years: just 4 percent of MPs (or twenty-two Muslim MPs), although Muslims constitute 13.4 percent of the population.

The BJP was also the beneficiary of popular opposition to corruption, which not only fueled disillusionment with the Congress Party but, more broadly, with state management of the economy. As in the early 1970s, when the Jan Sangh and the RSS supported the JP movement against corruption, prior to the 2014 elections the RSS and BJP supported Anna Hazare's anticorruption movement. Although anticorruption protests spawned a movement-party, the Aam Admi Party, it fared poorly in the 2014 national elections. The BJP was the beneficiary of the anticorruption movement. Modi's strong, uncompromising leadership and apparent commitment to transparency and growth assuaged many opponents of corruption.

Modi rendered a VHP-led movement unnecessary. The RSS played a decisive role in ensuring his candidacy over other BJP leaders. Aware of intraparty rivalries and jealousies, it coordinated with trusted party leaders to ensure that grassroots BJP workers did not engage in antiparty activities. Although the RSS was willing to compromise on *swadeshi*, it remained faithful to its core Hindu nationalist ideals. In endorsing Modi's candidacy, Mohan Bhagwat reiterated the RSS commitment to constructing a temple in Ayodhya. Senior RSS leader MG Vaidya promised that, if elected, the BJP government would seek to repeal Article 370, granting special autonomous status to Kashmir, build a Ram temple in Ayodhya, and introduce a uniform civil code within the parameters of the Constitution.[8]

Electoral results demonstrate extensive caste and Hindu-Muslim polarization. Nearly 60 percent of the upper castes voted for the BJP while 43 percent of Muslims voted for Congress.[9] The polarization of voters on caste and religious lines was greatest in UP and Bihar. The BJP was able to gain upper- and lower-caste votes in Bihar by allying with the Lok Janshakti Party, which has a strong *dalit* following. By contrast, in UP, as Chapter 6 described, the BJP engaged in anti-Muslim propaganda to regain upper-caste and OBC votes.

Modi's election campaign became a surrogate for a social movement. The RSS was partly responsible for the high electoral turnout, especially by young, new voters. The campaign was suffused with movement repertoires. Hundreds of young, full-time volunteers organized "Namorath" carriages, evoking Advani's *rath yatra* and Modi's *yatras* in Gujarat, which carried huge portraits of Narendra Modi to remote villages. The RSS created organizations like the Jagruk Matdata Manch (Voters' Awareness Association), which issued pamphlets urging voters to consider such issues as the threat of "terrorism" and Maoism, shrinking borders, and "vote bank appeasement." The VHP and other

---

[8] Pavan Dahat, "Modi Must Deliver on Ram Temple: RSS Leader," *The Hindu*, May 15, 2014. Accessed November 19, 2014. http://www.thehindu.com/news/national/modi-must-deliver-on -ram-temple-rss-leader/article6009618.ece.

[9] Sanjay Kumar, "Role of Polarization in BJP's Big Victory," *Live Mint*, May 17, 2014. Accessed November 19, 2014. http://www.livemint.com/Opinion/ngZRP3dgVnoPJHh256eDsI/Role-of-polarization-in-BJPs-big-victory.html?utm_source=copy.

organizations popularized their anti-Muslim campaigns by calling for "bahu bachao, beti bachao" ("protect daughters-in-law and daughters" – by implication Hindu women – from Muslim predators). A spin on this slogan was heard in violence-torn Muzaffarnagar: "desh, bahu aur gai ko bachana hai toh Narendra Modi ko lana hai" (To save the country, women, and cows, bring back Narendra Modi).[10]

If Narendra Modi rose to power because of his success in combining the roles of party, movement, and state leader, his future as a Hindu nationalist movement leader is uncertain. As head of state, Modi must seek to ensure economic growth and political stability. National governments have not directly supported group violence against minorities, and the BJP government is unlikely to be an exception. However, Hindutva activism is likely both on the streets and within institutions. The "love jihad" campaign has grown since the 2014 national election. RSS members who occupy influential roles in major institutions have pressured the BJP government to abide by its promise of reviving the core Hindutva agenda.[11] They have also exerted their influence over educational institutions and the media. The extent to which they are successful depends on many factors, including the strength and character of opposition movements and parties.

Retheorizing Parties and Movements

My study rejects essentialist, a priori distinctions between social movements and ethnic struggles, left- and right-wing movements, and violent and nonviolent movements. First, I suggest we rethink our characterizations and categorizations of social movements in order to better appreciate their complex political dispositions. Social movement scholarship has tended to ignore ethnic struggles in Asia, Africa, and the Middle East, perhaps on the mistaken assumption that they are defined and delimited by primordial identities. However, ethnicity should be viewed as a symbolic boundary marker rather than a set of rigidly defined ascriptive traits. Although social movements may mobilize

[10] Manish Chandra Pandey and Vikas Pathak, "Muzaffarnagar: 'Love Jihad,' Beef Bogey Sparked Riot Flames," *Hindustan Times*, September 12, 2013. Accessed November 19, 2014. http://www.hindustantimes.com/india-news/muzaffarnagar-love-jihad-beef-bogey-sparked-riot-flames/article1-1120889.aspx.

[11] The BJP's 2014 election manifesto advocated construction of a Ram temple in Ayodhya, Ram Setu, the passage of a uniform civil code, legislation to protect the cow and its progeny, and abrogation of Article 370. All these demands appear, albeit more provocatively framed, in the BJP's 2009 election manifesto, which is considered a staunch endorsement of Hindu nationalist goals. By contrast, the BJP's vision document in 2004 did not demand the abrogation of Article 370 and affirmed the party's commitment to the construction of a Ram temple in Ayodhya, "if necessary through a judicial verdict but preferably through a process of speeded-up dialogue between parties to the dispute." The BJP did not have a manifesto for the 1999 parliamentary elections; the National Democratic Alliance produced a National Agenda for Governance, which omitted the core Hindutva issues.

Conclusion

305

people who share a set of ethnic markers, prior ethnic solidarity is not a pre-requisite for ethnic movements.[12] Collective action can create and strengthen ethnic consciousness. The recent explosion of ethnic movements is not a prod-uct of ancient history but of the intensification of globalization and expansion of state intervention into social life.

Second, we should devote greater attention to interactions among social movements. Analyses of social movements have devoted more attention to their ability to obtain immediate demands than to their equally important goal of changing cultural and political discourses. These broader social change goals help explain shared repertoires of contention among disparate social move-ments. Recognizing the spillover effects, coevolution and adaptive learning of social movements illuminates why social movements both persist and change over time.[13] In the United States, the civil rights movement laid the foundations for women's, students', and antiwar movements.[14] Conversely, women's move-ments in the 1980s influenced peace movements' tactical innovations, orga-nizational structures, and representation of women in leadership positions.[15] The Polish Solidarity movement influenced the Arab Spring and the Occupy Wall Street movements. Struggles against structural adjustment policies in the global South inspired the 1999 anti-WTO protest in Seattle. The protests in Tahrir Square, Cairo had an impact on the Occupy Wall Street movement in New York in 2011.

Third, we should recognize the potentially undemocratic qualities of civil society. An influential body of literature suggests that strong civil societies can check the spread of violence in stable democracies by fostering democratic values and challenging the centralization and abuse of power within political society.[16] Cohen and Arato, for instance, praise "self-limiting, democratiz-ing movements seeking to expand and protect spaces for both negative lib-erty and positive freedom."[17] The existence of exclusionary, nondemocratic groups calls into question sanguine assumptions about the positive implica-tions of strong civil societies for democracy. Civil societies have neither con-sistently fostered democratic values nor always challenged the state's abuse of power and civil society organizations are not necessarily autonomous from

[12] Susan Qizak, "Contemporary Ethnic Mobilization," *Annual Review of Sociology*, 1983, Vol. 9, 355–74.
[13] David S. Meyer and Nancy Whittier, "Social Movement Spillover," *Social Problems*, May 1994, Vol. 41, no. 2, 277–98; and Pamela E. Oliver and Daniel J. Myers, "The Co-evolution of Social Movements," *Mobilization: An International Journal*, 2002, Vol. 8, no 1, 1–24.
[14] See, for example, Sara Evans, *Personal Politics: The Roots of the Women's Liberation Movement in the Civil Rights Movement and the New Left* (New York: Knopf, 1978).
[15] Meyer and Whittier, "Social Movement Spillover."
[16] Robert Putnam, *Bowling Alone: The Collapse and Revival of American Community* (New York: Simon & Schuster, 2000).
[17] Jean L. Cohen and Andrew Arato, *Civil Society and Political Theory*. (Cambridge, MA: MIT Press, 1992), 17.

the state.[18] The rich literature on democracy without democrats and distributive authoritarian states suggests the responsibilities of elites within the state and civil society for obstructing democratization in the Middle East.[19]

Fourth, we should question a common scholarly tendency to ignore social movements that employ violence. Airtight distinctions between violent and nonviolent movements are misleading. Social movements that engage in violence in some contexts repudiate it in others and accept some forms of violence while rejecting others. Earlier scholarship on violent revolutions neglected their affinities with social movements. More recently, security studies of "terrorism" have ignored social movements.[20] Both studies that pathologize "terrorists" and that treat them as rational actors ignore the conditions that cause violence.[21] A more fruitful approach is to explore the relationship between the character of regimes and citizen subjectivities.[22]

Finally, and most important for my argument, we should dismantle boundaries that have traditionally separated scholarship on political parties and social movements. In particular, we should appreciate social movements' roles in invigorating political parties, which many scholars believe are in decline.[23] Movement-parties have challenged both authoritarian and democratic states by expressing distrust in political institutions and discontent with established parties and politicians. They voice what Peter Mair describes as a growing chasm between constitutional and popular democracy, or a tension between principles of government *for* and *by* the people. Underlying these developments, he argues, are changes in the location of political parties, which were once deeply rooted in society but have increasingly become state actors.[24] Similarly,

---

[18] For a sampling of views on this subject, see Sudipta Kaviraj and Sunil Khilnani, eds., *Civil Society, History and Possibilities* (Cambridge, UK: Cambridge University Press, 2001).

[19] See, for example, Ghassan Salame, ed., *Democracy without Democrats: The Renewal of Politics in the Muslim World* (London: IB Taurus, 1994); and Lisa Blaydes, *Elections and Distributive Politics in Mubarak's Egypt* (New York: Cambridge University Press, 2013).

[20] Jeff Goodwin, "Review Essay: What Must We Explain to Explain Terrorism?" *Social Movement Studies*, 2004, Vol. 3, 259–65.

[21] Charles Tilly, "Terror, Terrorism, Terrorists," *Sociological Theory*, 2004, Vol. 22, 5–13; and *The Politics of Collective Violence* (Cambridge, UK: Cambridge University Press, 2003). Donatella della Porta, *Social Movements, Political Violence and the State* (Cambridge, UK: Cambridge University Press, 1995); "Research on Social Movements and Political Violence," *Qualitative Sociology*, 2008, Vol. 31, no. 3, 221–30; and *Clandestine Political Violence* (New York: Cambridge University Press, 2013). Charles Demetrious, "Political Violence and Legitimation: The Episode of Colonial Cyprus," *Qualitative Sociology*, 2007, Vol. 30, 171–93.

[22] Sayres Rudy, "Subjectivities, Political Evaluation and Islamist Trajectories," in Birgit Schabler and Leif Stenberg, eds., *Globalization and the Muslim World: Culture, Religion and Modernity* (Syracuse, NY: Syracuse University Press, 2004).

[23] See, for example, David H. Everson, "The Communications Revolution in Politics," *Proceedings of the Academy of Political Science*, 1982, Vol. 34, no. 4, 49–60; and Mark P. Wattenberg, *The Decline of American Political Parties, 1952–1996* (Cambridge, MA: Harvard University Press, 1998).

[24] Peter Mair, "Democracy beyond Parties," Center for the Study of Democracy Working Paper, University of California, Irvine, 2005, Paper 05.

Sudipta Kaviraj identifies a tension between principles of participation and proceduralism. He argues that political parties representing large communities with deep-seated grievances often regard liberal procedures as unwelcome obstacles to their pursuit of justice.[25] Dipesh Chakrabarty describes pressures on Indian parties to appreciate popular understandings of lived democracy.

Disorder in public and everyday life – a culture of disrespect for the law, in other words – has come to be a major ingredient of democracy. A successful political party in India has to be in a position that allows it to use – at least as a bargaining strategy and in addition to its connections to the bureaucracy and legislatures – the threat of unlawful and 'popular violence' on the streets.[26]

Given popular distrust of political institutions, parties have sought legitimacy by participating in both law-breaking and law-making activities.[27]

Movement-parties have diverse origins and trajectories. Many political parties have grown out of nationalist and democratic movements that challenged undemocratic states, among other places, in East Germany, Poland, Hungary, Slovakia, and South Africa. Other parties have filled the vacuum caused by the decline and exclusions of leftist parties. Green parties, which had roots in environmental movements, have participated in national governments in Germany, Finland, the Netherlands, France, Ireland, and the Czech Republic, and in many local and state governments. Several Latin American parties that have formed national and provincial governments emerged from movements of workers, peasants, and indigenous communities. The Movement Towards Socialism in Bolivia grew out of the cocoa workers' union; the Workers' Party (PT) in Brazil from a coalition of workers, students, and church progressives; and the Pachakutik from the indigenous people's movement in Ecuador.[28]

[25] Sudipta Kaviraj, "The Post-Colonial State: The Special Case of India." Posted in Aditya Nigam, Empire, History, Modernity, Nation-State, Postcolonial, State, Critical Encounters: A Forum of Critical Thought from the Global South. Accessed August 16, 2014. http://criticalencounters .net/2009/01/19/the-post-colonial-state-sudipta-kaviraj/.

[26] Dipesh Chakrabarty, "'In the Name of Politics': Democracy and the Power of the Multitude in India," *Public Culture*, Vol. 19, no. 1, no. 56, Winter 2002: 56.

[27] According to a survey by the Center for the Study of Developing Societies in New Delhi, people trust political parties less than Parliament, the courts, army, police, Election Commission, and civil service, and state, local, and national governments. The survey questions the assumption that parties are more developed and desirable than movements. Center for Studies in Developing Societies, *State of Democracy in South Asia* (New Delhi, 2006).

[28] David Samuels, "From Socialism to Social Democracy: Party Organization and the Transformation of the Workers' Party in Brazil," *Comparative Political Studies* 37, no. 9 (2004): 999–1024; Donna Lee Van Cott, *From Movements to Parties in Latin America: The Evolution of Ethnic Politics.* (Cambridge, UK: Cambridge University Press, 2005); Judith Hellman, "The Study of New Social Movements in Latin America and the Question of Autonomy," in Sonia Alvarez and Arturo Escobar, eds., *The Making of Social Movements in Latin America: Identity, Strategy and Democracy* (Boulder, CO: Westview Press, 1992).

However, not all movement-parties grow out of social movements. Some parties, often driven by charismatic leaders rather than by a grassroots base, act as surrogates for movements.[29] For example, right-wing populist parties in Europe, starting with the French National Front after the 1984 local elections, have challenged mainstream parties by engaging in movement activities. By 2014, right-wing populist parties scored unprecedented gains in European elections. The National Front in France and the UK Independence Party in Britain each won about a quarter of the vote and far-right parties did well in Austria, Denmark, Sweden, and Hungary. Cross-national diffusion processes enabled these parties to adopt and adapt anti-establishment, populist frames.[30] These movement-parties have grown by addressing economic grievances and anxieties around identity through their strident nativist, xenophobic, anti-immigrant stance.[31]

If some parties function as movements, others form coalitions with social movement organizations. At one end of the ideological spectrum, note the close ties between the Republican Party and the Tea Party in the United States. The Tea Party is not, in fact, a party but a loose coalition of libertarian, populist, antigovernment activists. Since 2009, it has pressured the Republican Party to support its candidates and platforms and in the process has silenced and marginalized Republican Party moderates. At the other end of the spectrum are the Sōka Gakkai movement in Japan, a religious organization committed to peace and human rights, and the New Kōmeitō Party, the third largest party in Parliament and a junior partner in the ruling coalition. The New Kōmeitō's leadership and commitments are deeply influenced by the Sōka Gakkai.

The BJP's astounding political success invites us to question commonly accepted scholarly distinctions and approaches. Its ability to grow from a small niche party into the governing party of the world's largest democracy invites comparative scholars of parties and movements to explore how the BJP has transcended party-movement divides and successfully challenged opposing parties and movements. The complex mechanisms and processes that have contributed to its growth call for dissolving conceptual divides between violent and nonviolent, and secular and religious movements, as well as between social movements, political parties, and states. The ostensibly moderate BJP surprised us in the past when it reverted to militancy. If history is any guide, its ability to combine disparate, seemingly antithetical goals and strategies is likely to surprise us again.

---

[29] Herbert Kitschelt, "Movement Parties," in Richard S. Katz and William Crotty, eds., *Handbook of Party Politics* (London: Sage Publications, 2006), 286.

[30] Jens Rydgren, "Is Extreme Right-Wing Populism Contagious? Explaining the Emergence of a New Party Family," *European Journal of Political Research*, 2005, Vol. 44, 413–37.

[31] Cas Mudde, "The Far Right in the 2014 European Elections: Of Earthquakes, Cartels and Designer Fascists," *The Washington Post*, May 30, 2014.

Selected Bibliography

Advani, L. K. *My Country, My Life.* New Delhi: Rupa & Co., 2008.

The People Betrayed. New Delhi: Vision Books, 1979.

Ahmad, Aijaz. *On Communalism and Globalization: Offensives of the Far Right.* New Delhi: Three Essays Collective, 2004.

Alter, Joseph S. "Celibacy, Sexuality, and the Transformation of Gender into Nationalism in North India." *The Journal of Asian Studies* 53, no. 1 (1994): 45–66.

Aminzade, Ronald. "Between Movement and Party: The Transformation of Mid-Nineteenth Century French Republicanism." In *The Politics of Social Protest: Comparative Perspectives on States and Social Movements,* edited by J. Craig Jenkins and Bert Klandermans, 39–62. Social Movements, Protest, and Contention: Vol. 3. Minneapolis, MN: University of Minnesota Press, 1995.

Andersen, Walter K. and Shridhar D. Damle. *The Brotherhood in Saffron: The Rashtriya Swayamsevak Sangh and Hindu Revivalism.* Westview Special Studies on South and Southeast Asia. Boulder, CO: Westview Press, 1987.

Appadurai, Arjun. *Fear of Small Numbers: An Essay on the Geography of Anger.* Durham, NC: Duke University Press, 2006.

Bacchetta, Paola. "Hindu Nationalist Women Imagine Spatialities/Imagine Themselves: Reflections on Gender-Supplemental Agency." In *Right-Wing Women: From Conservatives to Extremists around the World,* edited by Paola Bacchetta and Margaret Power, 43–56. London: Routledge, 2002.

Basu, Amrita. "The Changing Fortunes of the Bharatiya Janata Party." In *Routledge Handbook of Indian Politics,* edited by Atul Kohli and Prerna Singh, 81–90. Abingdon, UK: Routledge, 2013.

"The Dialectics of Hindu Nationalism." In *The Success of India's Democracy,* edited by Atul Kohli, 163–89. Cambridge, UK: Cambridge University Press, 2001.

"Engendering Communal Violence: Men as Victims, Women as Agents." In *Invented Identities: The Interplay of Gender, Religion and Politics in India,* edited by Julie Leslie and Mary McGee, 265–85. New Delhi: Oxford University Press, 2000.

"Feminism Inverted: The Gendered Imagery and Real Women of Hindu Nationalism." In *Women and the Hindu Right: A Collection of Essays,* edited by Urvashi Butalia and Tanika Sarkar, 159–80. New Delhi: Kali for Women, 1995.

"Hindu Women's Activism in India and the Questions It Raises." In *Appropriating Gender: Women's Activism and Politicized Religion in South Asia*, edited by Patricia Jeffery and Amrita Basu, 167–84. London: Routledge, 1998.

"Mass Movement or Elite Conspiracy? The Puzzle of Hindu Nationalism." In *Contesting the Nation: Religion, Community and the Politics of Democracy in India*, edited by David Ludden, 55–80. Philadelphia, PA: University of Pennsylvania Press, 1996.

"Reflections on Community Conflicts and the State in India." *Journal of Asian Studies*, 56, no.2, (May 1997): 391–7.

"Rethinking Social Movements/Rethinking Hindu Nationalism." In *Public Hinduisms*, edited by John Zavos, Pralay Kanungo, Deepa S. Reddy, Maya Warrier, and Raymond Williams, 248–53. London: Sage Publications, 2012.

"Why Local Riots Are Not Merely Local: Collective Violence and the State in Bijnor, India, 1988-1993," *Theory and Society* 24, no. 1 (1994): 35–78.

"Women, Political Parties and Social Movements in South Asia." In *Governing Women: Women's Political Effectiveness in Contexts of Democratization and Governance Reform*, edited by Anne Marie Goetz, 87–111. Abingdon, UK: Routledge, 2009.

"Women's Activism and the Vicissitudes of Hindu Nationalism," Special Issue on Women and Twentieth-Century Religious Politics: Beyond Fundamentalism, *Journal of Women's History* Vol. 10, no. 4 (Winter 1999): 104–24.

Basu, Amrita and Atul Kohli, eds. *Community Conflicts and the State in India*. New Delhi: Oxford University Press, 1998.

Basu, Amrita and Srirupa Roy. "Beyond Exceptionalism: Violence and Democracy in India." In *Violence and Democracy in India*, edited by Amrita Basu and Srirupa Roy, 1–35. Calcutta: Seagull Books, 2007.

"Prose after Gujarat: Violence, Secularism and Democracy in India." In *Will Secular India Survive?*, edited by Mushirul Hasan, 320–355. New Delhi: Imprint One, 2004.

Baxi, Upendra. "The Second Gujarat Catastrophe." *Economic and Political Weekly* 37, no. 34 (2002): 3519–31. Accessed June 26, 2014. http://www.epw.in/special-articles/second-gujarat-catastrophe.html.

Behar, Amitabh, John Samuel, Jagadananda, and Yogesh Kumar. *Social Watch India: Citizens Report on Governance and Development*. New Delhi: Pearson Education India, 2006.

Berenschot, Ward. *Riot Politics: Hindu-Muslim Violence and the Indian State*. New Delhi: Rupa Publications, 2013.

Bharatiya Jana Sangh, *Party Documents 1951–1972*, Vol. 1. New Delhi: Bharatiya Jana Sangh Publishers, 1973

Bharatiya Janata Party. *Political Resolutions*, Vol. 5. New Delhi: Bharatiya Janata Party, 2005.

Bharatiya Janata Party. *Policy Documents, 1980–2005*, Vol. 2. New Delhi: Bharatiya Janata Party, 2005.

BJP's White Paper on Ayodhya and the Rama Temple Movement. New Delhi: Bharatiya Janata Party, 1993.

Bobbio, Norberto. *Democracy and Dictatorship: The Nature and Limits of State Power*. Translated by Peter Kennealy. Cambridge, UK: Polity Press, 1989.

Brass, Paul, R. *The Production of Hindu-Muslim Violence in Contemporary India.* Jackson School Publications in International Studies. Seattle, WA: University of Washington Press, 2003.

Theft of an Idol: Text and Context in the Representation of Collective Violence. Princeton Studies in Culture/Power/History. Princeton, NJ: Princeton University Press, 1997.

Burger, Angela Sutherland. *Opposition in a Dominant-Party System: A Study of the Jan Sangh, the Praja Socialist Party, and the Socialist Party in Uttar Pradesh, India.* Berkeley, CA: University of California Press, 1969.

Chakrabarty, Dipesh. "'In the Name of Politics': Democracy and the Power of the Multitude in India." *Public Culture: Bulletin of the Project for Transnational Cultural Studies* 19, no. 1 (2007): 35–57.

Chakravarti, Uma, Prem Chowdhury, Pradip Datta, Zoya Hasan, Kumkum Sangari, and Tanika Sarkar. "Khurja Riots 1990–91: Understanding the Conjuncture." *Economic and Political Weekly* 27, no. 18 (1992): 951–65.

Chandhoke, Neera. *Beyond Secularism: The Rights of Religious Minorities.* New Delhi: Oxford University Press, 1999.

Chandra, Kanchan. *Why Ethnic Parties Succeed: Patronage and Ethnic Head Counts in India.* Cambridge Studies in Comparative Politics. New York: Cambridge University Press, 2004.

Chatterjee, Partha. *The Politics of the Governed: Reflections on Popular Politics in Most of the World.* New York: Columbia University Press, 2004.

Chenoy, Kamal Mitra, S. P. Shukla, K. S. Subramanian, and Achin Vanaik. *Gujarat Carnage 2002: A Report to the Nation by an Independent Fact Finding Mission.* Ahmedabad: Centre for the Study of Culture and Society, 2002. Accessed June 26, 2014. http://www.sacw.net/Gujarat2002/GujCarnage.html.

Chhibber, Pradeep K. *Democracy without Associations: Transformation of the Party System and Social Cleavages in India.* Ann Arbor, MI: University of Michigan Press, 1999.

and Ken Kollman. *The Formation of National Party Systems: Federalism and Party Competition in Canada, Great Britain, India, and the United States.* Princeton, NJ: Princeton University Press, 2004.

Cohen, Jean L. and Andrew Arato. *Civil Society and Political Theory.* Cambridge, MA: MIT Press, 1992.

Concerned Citizens Tribunal. "Crime against Humanity: An Inquiry into the Carnage in Gujarat." Vol. 2, 108. Gujarat, 2002. http://www.sabrang.com/tribunal/.

Das, Veena. *Life and Words: Violence and the Descent into the Ordinary.* Berkeley, CA: University of California Press, 2007.

Mirrors of Violence: Communities, Riots and Survivors in South Asia. New Delhi: Oxford University Press, 1990.

Della Porta, Donatella. *Clandestine Political Violence.* New York: Cambridge University Press, 2013.

Desai, Manali. "From Movement to Party to Government: Why Social Policies in Kerala and West Bengal are so Different." In *States, Parties and Social Movements*, edited by Jack A. Goldstone, 170–96. Cambridge, UK: Cambridge University Press, 2003.

Dhattiwala, Raheel and Michael Biggs. "The Political Logic of Ethnic Violence: The Anti-Muslim Pogrom in Gujarat, 2002." *Politics & Society* 40, no. 4 (2012): 483–516.

Diamond, Larry Jay and Leonardo Morlino, eds. *Assessing the Quality of Democracy.* A Journal of Democracy Book. Baltimore, MD: Johns Hopkins University Press, 2005.

Downs, Anthony. *An Economic Theory of Democracy.* New York: Harper & Row, 1957.

Duverger, Maurice. *Political Parties, Their Organization and Activity in the Modern State.* London: Methuen and Co., 1954.

Eck, Diana L. *Darśan: Seeing the Divine Image in India.* New York: Columbia University Press, 1998.

Engineer, Ashgar Ali, ed. *The Gujarat Carnage.* New Delhi: Orient Longman, 2003.

Feldman, Allen. *Formations of Violence: The Narrative of the Body and Political Terror in Northern Ireland.* Chicago, IL: University of Chicago Press, 1991.

Freitag, Sandria B. *Collective Action and Community: Public Arenas and the Emergence of Communalism in North India.* Berkeley, CA: University of California Press, 1989.

Gadgil, Madhav. *This Fissured Land: An Ecological History of India.* New Delhi: Oxford University Press, 1992.

Gadgil, Madhav and Ramachandra Guha. *Ecology and Equity: The Use and Abuse of Nature in Contemporary India.* Abingdon, UK: Routledge, 1995.

Gamson, William A. *The Strategy of Social Protest.* The Dorsey Series in Sociology. Homewood, IL: Dorsey Press, 1975.

Ghassem-Fachandi, Parvis. *Pogrom in Gujarat: Hindu Nationalism and Anti-Muslim Violence in India.* Princeton, NJ: Princeton University Press, 2012.

Ghosh, Partha Sarathy. *BJP and the Evolution of Hindu Nationalism: From Periphery to Centre.* New Delhi: Manohar Publishers & Distributors, 1999.

Goldstone, Jack A., ed. *States, Parties and Social Movements.* Cambridge, UK: Cambridge University Press, 2003.

Golwalkar, Madhav Sadashiv. *Bunch of Thoughts.* Bangalore: Vikrama Prakashan, 1966.

Graham, Bruce D. *Hindu Nationalism and Indian Politics: The Origins and Development of the Bharatiya Jana Sangh.* Cambridge South Asian Studies: 47. Cambridge, UK: Cambridge University Press, 1990.

"The Jana Sangh and Bloc Politics, 1967–80." *Journal of Commonwealth & Comparative Politics* 25, no. 3 (1987): 248–266.

Guha, Ramachandra. *The Unquiet Woods: Ecological Change and Peasant Resistance in the Himalaya.* Berkeley, CA: University of California Press, 2000.

Gunther, Richard and Larry Diamond. "Species of Political Parties: A New Typology." *Party Politics* 9, no. 2 (2003): 167–99.

Hameed, Syeda Saiyidain, Ruth Manorama, Malini Ghose, Sheba George, Mari Thekaekara, and Farah Naqvi. "How Has the Gujarat Massacre Affected Minority Women?: The Survivors Speak." Citizen's Initiative, Ahmedabad: 2002. Accessed June 4, 2012. http://www.geocities.com/shrawan_k_s/Communalism/Gujrat/TheSurvivorsSpeakX .html.htm, annexure 1.6.

Hansen, Thomas Blom. "Governance and Myths of State in Mumbai." In *The Everyday State and Society in Modern India,* edited by Christopher John Fuller and Veronique Beneii, London: Hurst, 2001.

The Saffron Wave: Democracy and Hindu Nationalism in Modern India. Princeton, NJ: Princeton University Press, 1999.

Wages of Violence: Naming and Identity in Postcolonial Bombay. Princeton, NJ: Princeton University Press, 2001.

Harff, Barbara. "No Lessons Learned from the Holocaust? Assessing Risks of Genocide and Political Mass Murder since 1955." *American Political Science Review* 97, no. 1 (2003): 57–73.

Hasan, Zoya. *Dominance and Mobilisation: Rural Politics in Western Uttar Pradesh, 1930–1980*. New Delhi: Sage Publications, 1989.

Politics of Inclusion: Castes, Minorities, and Affirmative Action. New Delhi: Oxford University Press, 2009.

Quest for Power: Oppositional Movements and Post-Congress Politics in Uttar Pradesh. New Delhi: Oxford University Press, 1998.

Heath, Oliver and Yogendra Yadav. "The Rise of Caste Politics: Party System Change and Voter Realignment, 1962–2004." In *Diversity and Change in Modern India: Economic, Social and Political Approaches*, edited by Anthony Heath and Roger Jeffery, 189–218. Oxford, UK: Oxford University Press, 2010.

Human Rights Watch. "Compounding Injustice: The Government's Failure to Redress Massacres in Gujarat." New York: *Human Rights Watch*, July 2003, Vol. 15, No. 3(C). Accessed June 26, 2014. http://www.coalitionagainstgenocide.org/reports/2003/hrw.jul2003.vol15.no3c.pdf, 43.

Human Rights Watch. "Discouraging Dissent: Intimidation and Harassment of Witnesses, Human Rights Activists, and Lawyers Pursuing Accountability for the 2002 Communal Violence in Gujarat." New York: Human Rights Watch, 2002.

Jaffrelot, Christophe. *The Hindu Nationalist Movement and Indian Politics: 1925 to the 1990s*. London: Hurst & Co., 1996.

India's Silent Revolution: The Rise of the Lower Castes in North India. New York: Columbia University Press, 2003.

Religion, Caste, and Politics in India. Delhi: Primus Books, 2010.

Jahangir, Asma. *Report of the Special Rapporteur on Freedom of Religion or Belief*. United Nations Human Rights Council, 2007. Accessed December 2, 2012. http://daccess-dds-ny.un.org/doc/UNDOC/GEN/G09/101/04/PDF/G0910104.pdf?OpenElement.

Jaoul, Nicholas. "Dalit Processions: Street Politics and Democratization in India." In *Staging Politics: Power and Performance in Asia and Africa*, edited by Julia C. Strauss and Donal Cruise O'Brien, 173–194, International Library of Political Studies: 18. London: I. B. Tauris, 2007.

"Political and 'Non-Political' Means in the Dalit Movement." In *Political Process in Uttar Pradesh: Identity, Economic Reforms, and Governance*, edited by Sudha Pai, 191–220. New Delhi: Pearson Longman, 2007.

Jeffery, Roger and Patricia M. Jeffery. "The Bijnor Riots, October 1990: Collapse of the Mythical Special Relationship." *Economic and Political Weekly* 29, no. 10 (1994): 551–8.

Jeffrey, Craig and Jens Lerche. "Stating the Difference: State, Discourse and Class Reproduction in Uttar Pradesh, India." *Development and Change* 31, no. 4 (2000):872.

Jenkins, J. Craig and Bert Klandermans, eds. *The Politics of Social Protest: Comparative Perspectives on States and Social Movements*. Social Movements, Protest, and Contention: Vol. 3. Minneapolis, MN: Taylor and Francis, 1995.

Jenkins, Rob. "Rajput Hindutva, Caste Politics, Regional Identity and Hindu Nationalism in Contemporary Rajasthan." In *The BJP and the Compulsions of*

Politics in India, edited by Thomas Blom Hansen and Christophe Jaffrelot. New Delhi: Oxford University Press, 1998.

Jhangiani, Motilal A. *Jana Sangh and Swatantra: A Profile of the Rightist Parties in India*. Bombay: Manaktalas, 1967.

Johnston, Hank. "A Methodology for Frame Analysis: From Discourse to Cognitive Schemata." In *Social Movements and Culture*, edited by Bert Klandermans and Hank Johnston, 217–247. Minneapolis, MN: University of Minnesota Press, 1995.

Juergensmeyer, Mark. *Terror in the Mind of God: The Global Rise of Religious Violence.* Comparative Studies in Religion and Society: 13. Berkeley, CA: University of California Press, 2003.

Kalyvas, Stathis N. *The Rise of Christian Democracy in Europe.* The Wilder House Series in Politics, History, and Culture. Ithaca, NY: Cornell University Press, 1996.

Kamat, Sangeeta. *Development Hegemony: NGOs and the State in India.* New Delhi: Oxford University Press, 2002.

Kanungo, Pralay. *RSS's Tryst with Politics: From Hedgewar to Sudarshan.* New Delhi: Manohar, 2004.

Kanwar, Pamela. *Imperial Simla: The Political Culture of the Raj.* New Delhi: Oxford University Press, 2003.

Kapur, Ratna. "Normalizing Violence: Transitional Justice and the Gujarat Riots." *Columbia Journal of Gender and Law* 15, no. 3 (2006): 885–927.

Katju, Manjari. *Vishva Hindu Parishad and Indian Politics.* Hyderbad: Orient Longman Private Limited, 2003.

Katzenstein, Mary Fainsod. *Faithful and Fearless: Moving Feminist Protest Inside the Church and Military.* Princeton Studies in American Politics. Princeton, NJ: Princeton University Press, 1998.

Kaviraj, Sudipta and Sunil Khilnani, eds. *Civil Society: History and Possibilities.* Cambridge, UK: Cambridge University Press, 2001.

Kirchheimer, Otto. "The Transformation of the Western European Party Systems." In *Political Parties and Political Development*, edited by Joseph La Palombara and Myron Weiner, 177–200. Studies in Political Development: 6. Princeton, NJ: Princeton University Press, 1966.

Kitschelt, Herbert P. "Political Opportunity Structures and Political Protest: Anti-Nuclear Movements in Four Democracies." *British Journal of Political Science* 16, no. 1 (1986): 57–85.

Kohli, Atul. "Can Democracies Accommodate Ethnic Nationalism? The Rise and Decline of Ethnic Self-Determination Movements in India." In *Community Conflicts and the State in India*, edited by Amrita Basu and Atul Kohli, 17–32. New Delhi: Oxford University Press, 1995.

——— *Democracy and Discontent: India's Growing Crisis of Governability.* Cambridge, UK: Cambridge University Press, 1990.

——— *Poverty Amid Plenty in the New India.* Cambridge, UK: Cambridge University Press, 2012.

Kothari, Rajni. "The Congress System in India." *Asian Survey* 4, no. 12 (1964): 1161–73.

Kothari, Smitu, Uday Mehta, and Mary Katzenstein. "Social Movement Politics in India: Institutions, Interests and Identities." In *The Success of India's Democracy*, edited by Atul Kohli, 242–69. Contemporary South Asia: 6. Cambridge, UK: Cambridge University Press, 2001.

Kriesi, Hanspeter. "The Political Opportunity Structure of New Social Movements: Its Impact on Their Mobilization." In *The Politics of Protest: Comparative Perspectives on States and Social Movements*, edited by J. C. Jenkins and B. Klandermans, 152–84. Minneapolis, MN: University of Minnesota Press, 1995.

Lipset, Seymour Martin and Stein Rokkan. *Party Systems and Voter Alignments: Cross-National Perspectives.* International Yearbook of Political Behavior Research: Vol. 7. New York: Free Press, 1967.

Lodha, Sanjay. "Rajasthan: BJP Knocks Out Congress in a Bipolar Contest." In *Electoral Politics in Indian States: Lok Sabha Elections in 2004 and Beyond,* edited by Sandeep Shastri, K. C. Suri, and Yogendra Yadav, 176–201. New Delhi: Oxford University Press, 2009.

Madhok, Balraj. *RSS and Politics.* New Delhi: Hindu World Publications, 1986.

Mainwaring, Scott and Mariano Torcal. "Party System Institutionalization and Party System Theory after the Third Wave of Democratization." In *Handbook of Party Politics,* edited by Richard S. Katz and William J. Crotty, 204–27. London: Sage Publications, 2006.

Mair, Peter and Stefano Bartolini. "Challenges to Contemporary Political Parties." In *Political Parties and Democracy,* edited by Larry Jay Diamond and Richard Gunther, 327–43. Baltimore, MD: Johns Hopkins University Press, 2001.

Malik, Yogendra K. and Vijay B. Singh. *Hindu Nationalists in India: The Rise of the Bharatiya Janata Party.* New Delhi: Vistaar Publications, 1995.

Mayaram, Shail. "Communal Violence in Jaipur." *Economic and Political Weekly* 28, no. 46–47 (1993): 2524–41.

McAdam, Doug. "To Map Contentious Politics." *Mobilization: An International Quarterly* 1, no. 1 (1996): 17–34.

McAdam, Doug, John D. McCarthy, and Mayer N. Zald. *Comparative Perspectives on Social Movements: Political Opportunities, Mobilizing Structures, and Cultural Framings.* Cambridge Studies in Comparative Politics. Cambridge, UK: Cambridge University Press, 1996.

McAdam, Doug and Sidney Tarrow. "Ballots and Barricades: On the Reciprocal Relationship between Elections and Social Movements." *Perspectives on Politics* 8, no. 2 (2010): 529–42.

McAdam, Doug, Sidney Tarrow, and Charles Tilly. *Dynamics of Contention.* Cambridge Series in Contentious Politics. Cambridge, UK: Cambridge University Press, 2001.

McBride Stetson, Dorothy and Amy Mazur. *Comparative State Feminism.* London: Sage Publications, 1995.

McGuire, John and Ian Copland. *Hindu Nationalism and Governance.* New Delhi: Oxford University Press, 2007.

Meguid, Bonnie M. *Party Competition between Unequals: Strategies and Electoral Fortunes in Western Europe.* Cambridge Studies in Comparative Politics. Cambridge, UK: Cambridge University Press, 2010.

Menon, Kalyani Devaki. *Everyday Nationalism: Women of the Hindu Right in India.* Philadelphia, PA: University of Pennsylvania Press, 2010.

Meyer, David S. "Opportunities and Identities: Bridge Building in the Study of Social Movements." In *Social Movements: Identity, Culture, and the State,* edited by Nancy Whittier, Belinda Robnett, and David S. Meyer, 3–21. Oxford, UK: Oxford University Press, 2002.

Meyer, David S. and Suzanne Staggenborg. "Movements, Countermovements, and the Structure of Political Opportunity." *American Journal of Sociology* 101, no. 6 (1996): 1628–60.

Meyer, David S. and Sidney Tarrow. *The Social Movement Society: Contentious Politics for a New Century.* Lanham, MD: Rowman & Littlefield, 1998.

Miller, William Ian. *Humiliation and Other Essays on Honor, Social Discomfort, and Violence.* Ithaca, NY: Cornell University Press, 1993.

Mitta, Manoj. *The Fiction of Fact Finding: Modi and Godhra.* New Delhi: Harper Collins India, 2015.

Narain, Iqbal and P. C. Mathur. "The Thousand Year Raj: Regional Isolation and Rajput Hinduism in Rajasthan before and after 1947." In *Dominance and State Power in Modern India: Decline of a Social Order,* edited by Francine R. Frankel and M. S. A. Rao, Vol. 2, 1–58. New Delhi: Oxford University Press, 1990.

Narayan, Badri. "Inventing Caste History: Dalit Mobilisation and Nationalist Past." *Contributions to Indian Sociology* 38, no. 1–2 (2004): 193–220.

The Making of the Dalit Public in North India: Uttar Pradesh, 1950-Present. New Delhi: Oxford University Press, 2011.

Narayan, Jayaprakash. *Towards Total Revolution: Search for an Ideology.* Bombay: Popular Prakashan, 1978.

Narula, Smita. *We Have No Orders to Save You: State Participation and Complicity in Communal Violence in Gujarat.* New York: Human Rights Watch, 2002.

National Social Watch Coalition: Citizens' Report on Governance and Development, 2008-2009. New Delhi: Sage Publications, 2010.

Nayar, Baldev Raj. "The Limits of Economic Nationalism in India: Economic Reforms under the BJP-led Government, 1998–1999." *Asian Survey* 40, no. 5 (2000): 792–815.

Nikolenyi, Csaba. "Recognition Rules, Party Labels and the Number of Parties in India: A Research Note." *Party Politics* 14, no. 2 (2008): 211–22.

Noorani, Abdul Gafoor Abdul Majeed. *The RSS and the BJP: A Division of Labour.* Issues That Matter, Vol. 3. New Delhi: LeftWord Books, 2000.

Nussbaum, Martha C. *The Clash Within: Democracy, Religious Violence, and India's Future.* Cambridge, MA: Harvard University Press, 2007.

O'Donnell, Guillermo A., Jorge Vargas Cullel, and Osvaldo Miguel Iazzetta. *The Quality of Democracy: Theory and Applications.* Notre Dame, IN: University of Notre Dame Press, 2004.

Offe, Claus. "New Social Movements: Challenging the Boundaries of Institutional Politics." *Social Research* 52, no. 4 (1985): 817–68.

Omvedt, Gail. *Reinventing Revolution: New Social Movements and the Socialist Tradition in India.* Armonk, NY: M.E. Sharpe, 1993.

Pai, Sudha. *Agrarian Relations in Uttar Pradesh: A Study of the Eastern Districts.* New Delhi: Inter India Publications, 1986.

Dalit Assertion and the Unfinished Democratic Revolution: The BSP in Uttar Pradesh. New Delhi: Sage Publications, 2002.

"From Dalit To Savarna: The Search for a New Social Constituency by the Bahujan Samaj Party in Uttar Pradesh." In *Political Process in Uttar Pradesh: Identity, Economic Reforms, and Governance,* edited by Sudha Pai, 221–40. New Delhi: Pearson Longman, 2007.

Uttar Pradesh: Agrarian Change and Electoral Politics. New Delhi: Shipra Publications, 1993.

Pandey, Gyanendra. *Routine Violence: Nations, Fragments, Histories.* Stanford, CA: Stanford University Press, 2006.

Panikkar, K. N. "Religious Symbols and Political Mobilization: The Agitation for a Mandir at Ayodhya." *Social Scientist* 21, no. 242–43 (1993): 63–78.

Parmar, Y. S. *Himachal Pradesh: Case for Statehood*. Shimla: Directorate of Public Relations, 1968.

People's Union for Democratic Rights. *Cry the Beloved Country: Ayodhya*, December 6, 1992. Faizabad: People's Union for Democratic Rights, 1993.

Pocock, David Francis. *Kanbi and Patidar: A Study of the Patidar Community of Gujarat*. Oxford: Clarendon Press, 1972.

PUCL Investigation Report: A Summary, Jaipur Communal Riots. Bapu Nagar, Jaipur: PUCL Rajasthan Unit, November 1989.

Putnam, Robert D. *Bowling Alone: The Collapse and Revival of American Community*. New York: Simon & Schuster, 2000.

Rao, Hayagreeva, Calvin Morrill, and Mayer N. Zald. "Power Plays: How Social Movements and Collective Action Create New Organizational Forms." In *Research in Organizational Behavior: An Annual Series of Analytical Essays and Critical Reviews*. Volume 22, edited by Barry M. Staw and Robert I. Sutton, 237–81. New York: JAI-Elsevier Science, 2000.

Ray, Raka and Mary Fainsod Katzenstein, eds. *Social Movements in India: Poverty, Power, and Politics*. Lanham, MD: Rowman & Littlefield, 2005.

Roberts, Kenneth M. "From the Barricades to the Ballot Box: Redemocratization and Political Realignment in the Chilean Left." *Politics & Society* 23, no. 4 (1995): 495–519.

Roy, Beth. *Some Trouble with Cows: Making Sense of Social Conflict*. Berkeley, CA: University of California Press, 1994.

Rucht, Dieter and Friedhelm Neidhardt. "Towards a 'Movement Society'? On the Possibilities of Institutionalizing Social Movements." *Social Movement Studies* 1, no. 1 (2002): 7–30.

Rudolph, Lloyd and Susanne Hoeber Rudolph. "From Landed Class to Middle Class: Rajput Adaptation in Rajasthan." In *Elite and Everyman: The Cultural Politics of the Indian Middle Classes*, edited by Amita Baviskar and Raka Ray, 108–139. New Delhi: Routledge, 2011.

"Living with Multiculturalism: Universalism and Particularism in an Indian Historical Context." In *Engaging Cultural Differences: The Multicultural Challenge in Liberal Democracies*, edited by Richard A. Shweder, Martha Minow, and Hazel Rose Markus, 43–62. New York: Russell Sage Foundation, 2002.

Rudolph, Susanne Hoeber and Lloyd I. Rudolph. "New Dimensions in Indian Democracy." *Journal of Democracy* 13, no. 1 (2002): 52–66.

Rydgren, Jens, ed. *Movements of Exclusion: Radical Right-Wing Populism in the Western World*. New York: Nova Science Publishers, 2005.

Sachar, Rajinder, Saiyad Hamid, T. K. Oommen, M. A. Basith, Rakesh Basant, and Akhtar Majeed. *Social, Economic and Educational Status of the Muslim Community in India: A Report*. New Delhi: Prime Minister's High Level Committee, Cabinet, Government of India, 2006.

Samuels, David. "From Socialism to Social Democracy: Party Organization and the Transformation of the Workers' Party in Brazil." *Comparative Political Studies* 37, no. 9 (2004): 999–1024.

Sarkar, Tanika. *Hindu Wife, Hindu Nation: Religion, Community, and Cultural Nationalism.* Bloomington, IN: Indiana University Press, 2001.

Sartori, Giovanni. *Parties and Party Systems: A Framework for Analysis.* Vol. 1. Cambridge, UK: Cambridge University Press, 1976.

Schattschneider, E. E. *The Semisovereign People: A Realist's View of Democracy in America.* New York: Holt, Rinehart and Winston, 1960.

Schlesinger, Joseph A. "On the Theory of Party Organization." *The Journal of Politics* 46, no. 2 (1984): 369–400.

Schofield, Norman and Itai Sened. *Multiparty Democracy: Elections and Legislative Politics.* Cambridge, UK: Cambridge University Press, 2006.

Schwartz, Mildred A. "Interactions between Social Movements and US Political Parties." *Party Politics* 16, no. 5 (September 2010): 587–607.

Scott, James C. *The Art of Not Being Governed: An Anarchist History of Upland Southeast Asia.* New Haven, CT: Yale University Press, 2009.

Shah, Ghanshyam. "The 1975 Gujarat Assembly Elections in India." *Asian Survey* 16, no. 3 (1976): 271.

"The BJP and Backward Castes in Gujarat." *South Asia Bulletin* 14, no. 4 (1994): 57–65.

Shani, Ornit. *Communalism, Caste and Hindu Nationalism: The Violence in Gujarat.* Cambridge, UK: Cambridge University Press, 2007.

Sinha, Aseema. *The Regional Roots of Developmental Politics in India: A Divided Leviathan.* Bloomington, IN: Indiana University Press, 2005.

Sisson, Richard. *The Congress Party in Rajasthan; Political Integration and Institution-Building in an Indian State.* Berkeley, CA: University of California Press, 1972.

Snow, David A. "Framing Processes, Ideology, and Discursive Fields." In *The Blackwell Companion to Social Movements*, edited by Sarah Anne Soule, Hanspeter Kriesi, and David A. Snow, 380–412. Blackwell Companions to Sociology. Oxford, UK: Blackwell Publishing, 2004.

Snow, David, E. Burke, A. Rochford, Steven K. Worden, and Robert D. Benford. "Frame Alignment Processes, Micromobilization and Movement Participation." *American Sociological Review* 51, no. 4 (1986): 464–81.

Snow, David A., Sarah Anne Soule, and Hanspeter Kriesi, eds. *The Blackwell Companion to Social Movements.* Blackwell Companions to Sociology. Oxford, UK: Blackwell Publishing, 2004.

Snyder, Jack L. *From Voting to Violence: Democratization and Nationalist Conflict.* New York: Norton, 2000.

Spodek, Howard. "From Gandhi to Violence: Ahmedabad's 1985 Riots in Historical Perspective." *Modern Asian Studies* 23, no. 4 (1987): 765–95.

Sridharan, E. and Peter Ronald de Souza. *India's Political Parties.* New Delhi: Sage Publications, 2006.

Sud, Nikita. *Liberalization, Hindu Nationalism and the State: A Biography of Gujarat.* New Delhi: Oxford University Press, 2012.

Tambiah, Stanley Jeyaraja. *Leveling Crowds: Ethnonationalist Conflicts and Collective Violence in South Asia.* Berkeley, CA: University of California Press, 1996.

Thachil, Tariq. "Embedded Mobilization: Nonstate Service Provision as Electoral Strategy in India." *World Politics* 63, no. 3 (2011): 434–69.

"The Foreign Exchange of Hate." *Sabrang Communications and Publishing and the South Asian Citizens Web*, 2002. Accessed June 29, 2012. http://www.sabrang .com/hnfund/sacw/.

Tillin, Louise. "Questioning Borders: Social Movements, Political Parties and the Creation of New States in India." *Pacific Affairs* 84, no. 1 (2011): 67–87.

Tilly, Charles. "Afterword: Agendas for Students of Social Movements." In *States, Parties & Social Movements*, edited by Jack Goldstone, 246–56. Cambridge, UK: Cambridge University Press, 2003.

———. *The Contentious French*. Cambridge, MA: Belknap Press, 1986.

———. *The Politics of Collective Violence*. New York: Cambridge University Press, 2003.

———. "Social Movements and National Politics." In *Statemaking and Social Movements: Essays in History and Theory*, edited by Charles Bright and Susan Friend Harding. Ann Arbor, MI: University of Michigan Press, 1984.

U.S. Department of State Annual Report on International Religious Freedom for 2005 – India. United States Department of State, 2005. Accessed June 26, 2010. http://www.refworld.org/docid/437c9cf111.html.

Valiani, Arafaat A. *Militant Publics in India: Physical Culture and Violence in the Making of a Modern Polity*. New York: Palgrave Macmillan, 2011.

Van Cott, Donna Lee. *From Movements to Parties in Latin America: The Evolution of Ethnic Politics*. Cambridge, UK: Cambridge University Press, 2005.

Varadarajan, Siddharth, ed. *Gujarat: The Making of a Tragedy*. New Delhi: Penguin Books India, 2002.

Varshney, Ashutosh. *Ethnic Conflict and Civic Life: Hindus and Muslims in India*. New Haven, CT: Yale University Press, 2002.

Verkaaik, Oskar. *Migrants and Militants: Fun and Urban Violence in Pakistan*. Princeton, NJ: Princeton University Press, 2004.

Weiner, Myron. *The Indian Paradox: Essays in Indian Politics*. New Delhi: Sage Publications, 1989.

———. *Party Politics in India: The Development of a Multi-Party System*. Princeton, NJ: Princeton University Press, 1957.

Whittier, Nancy. "Meaning and Structure in Social Movements." In *Social Movements: Identity, Culture, and the State*, edited by David S. Meyer, Nancy Whittier, and Belinda Robnett, 289–307. New York: Oxford University Press, 2002.

Wilkinson, Steven I., ed. *Religious Politics and Communal Violence*. Critical Issues in Indian Politics Series. New Delhi: Oxford University Press, 2007.

Wilkinson, Steven I. *Votes and Violence: Electoral Competition and Ethnic Riots in India*. New York: Cambridge University Press, 2004.

Williams, Rhys. "From the 'Beloved Community' to 'Family Values': Religious Language, Symbolic Repertoires, and Democratic Culture." In *Social Movements: Identity, Culture, and the State*, edited by David S. Meyer, Nancy Whittier, and Belinda Robnett, 247–65. Oxford, UK: Oxford University Press, 2002.

Witsoe, Jeffrey. *Democracy against Development: Lower-Caste Politics and Political Modernity in Postcolonial India*. Chicago, IL: University of Chicago Press, 2013.

Wolpert, Stanley A. and Richard Sisson, eds. *Congress and Indian Nationalism: The Pre-Independence Phase*. Berkeley, CA: University of California Press, 1988.

Wood, Elisabeth, *Collective Action and Civil War in El Salvador*. New York: Cambridge University Press, 2003.
Wood, Richard L. *Faith in Action: Religion, Race, and Democratic Organizing in America*. Morality and Society Series. Chicago: University of Chicago Press, 2002.
Yadav, Yogendra. "Understanding the Second Democratic Upsurge: Trends of Bahujan Participation in Electoral Politics in the 1990s." In *Transforming India: Social and Political Dynamics of Democracy*, edited by Francine R. Frankel et al., 120–45. New Delhi: Oxford University Press, 2000.
Yagnik, Achyut   and Suchitra Sheth. *The Shaping of Modern Gujarat: Plurality, Hindutva and Beyond*. New Delhi: Penguin, 2005.
Zald, Mayer N. and Michael A. Berger. "Social Movements in Organizations: Coup d'Etat, Insurgency, and Mass Movements." *American Journal of Sociology* 83 (1978): 823–61.
Zald, Mayer N. and John D. McCarthy. *The Dynamics of Social Movements: Resource Mobilization, Social Control, and Tactics*. Cambridge, MA: Winthrop Publishers, 1979.
"Religious Groups as Crucibles of Social Movements." In *Social Movements in an Organizational Society: Collected Essays*, edited by Mayer N. Zald and John D. McCarthy, 67–96. New Brunswick, NJ: Transaction Books, 1987.

Index

feminist activism, 30, 56, 60, 107, 108, 132, 195
against domestic violence, 33, 193
against "dowry deaths," 33
against rape, 33, 270
against *sati*, 268–270, 285
First Information Reports (FIRs), 122, 169,
    171, 175, 197, 228, 272, 282, 298

Gandhi, Mohandas Karamchand (MK), 58,
    59, 102
gender, 85, 86, 107–108, 149, 175, 192–193,
    247, 291
and globalization, 105, 107, 111, 257
and sexuality, 15, 106, 108, 168, 290
gendered images, 86, 90, 98–100, 110, 150,
    167, 231
roles, 90, 105
globalization, 8, 20, 86, 100, 106, 110, 187,
    258–259, 305
and Western influences, 100, 105–107, 111,
    112, 268, 285
RSS opposition to, 100–104, 107, 256–257
government
Central Bureau of Investigation, 156, 197
Coalitions
    National Democratic Alliance (NDA), 1, 38
    National Front, 30, 35, 49, 50, 59–60, 63,
        81, 111, 122, 152, 208, 266
    Samyukta Vidhayak Dal (SVD), 208
    United Progressive Alliance (UPA), 28,
        40, 247
Commissions and Committees
    Election Commission, 42, 166, 168, 225,
        227–229
    Liberhan Commission, 91
    Mandal Commission, 36, 43, 145, 208,
        209, 248, 249, 257, 260, 296
    National Commission for Minorities
        (NCM), 48, 197, 256
    National Human Rights Commission,
        197–198
    Ranganath Mishra Commission, 257
    Reddy Commission, 165, 167, 171, 174
    Sachar Committee, 7, 43, 50,
        158–160, 220
    Legislative Assembly, 128, 145, 152, 158,
        181, 182, 206, 224, 286
    local, 10, 188
    panchayats, 253, 287
    national, 3, 12, 13, 15, 16, 18–21, 28, 29,
        36, 37, 41, 46, 49, 51, 159, 164,
        174–175, 180, 187, 188, 198,

212, 238, 266, 294, 298, 301,
    304, 307
Parliament, 29, 32, 34, 65, 74, 80, 108,
    121–122, 166, 203, 205, 231, 233,
    253, 273, 298, 308
lower house (Lok Sabha), 182, 203, 230,
    255, 281
upper house (Rajya Sabha), 173, 203,
    289, 298
Prime Ministers
Desai, Morarji, 69, 171
Gandhi, Indira, 1, 30, 32–35, 49, 50, 74,
    92, 171, 255
Gandhi, Rajiv, 30, 34, 35, 49, 126
Modi, Narendra. *See* BJP, leaders
Nehru, Jawaharlal, 30–32, 35, 50, 57, 58
Rao, Pamulaparti Venkata (PV)
    Narsimha. *See* Congress Party
Singh, Charan, 69, 207–209
Singh, Manmohan, 43
Singh, Vishwanath Pratap (VP), 30,
    36, 49, 50, 59, 60, 126, 152,
    208–209, 248
Vajpayee, Atal Bihari, 32, 33, 37–39, 67,
    74, 78–81, 103, 173, 227, 244,
    246, 278
state, 9, 12, 18, 20, 22, 28, 44, 45, 51, 58,
    94, 95, 102, 124, 125, 130, 134,
    143, 154, 161, 173, 174, 176, 185,
    187, 188, 195, 198, 200, 221, 253,
    254, 258, 261, 262, 269, 284, 288,
    295, 297, 298
Gujarat
1969 violence, 2, 162–168, 171, 174, 176
2002 violence, 1–3, 16, 19–21, 50, 80, 110,
    162–171, 173–176, 182, 185, 187,
    188, 194, 196–200, 204, 223, 244,
    295, 298, 299, 301
asmita, 192
bandh, 165–166, 171, 173
cities and towns
    Ahmedabad, 1, 104, 108, 164–166, 168,
        172, 173, 175, 176, 179, 184, 186,
        188–190, 193–194, 196, 198, 200
    Gandhinagar (capital), 170–171
    Godhra, 80, 163, 165, 167, 168,
        170–171, 173, 174, 185, 223,
        225, 244
    Rajkot, 165, 166, 168, 179
    Surat, 99, 163, 168, 180, 184
cooperatives, 181, 189, 190, 296
Gujarati language, 168, 192, 200

Books in the Series (*continued from page iii*)